D0107591

GIVE
ME
LIBERTY

GIVE ME LIBERTY

SPEAKERS AND SPEECHES THAT HAVE SHAPED AMERICA

CHRISTOPHER L. WEBBER

PEGASUS BOOKS
NEW YORK LONDON

GIVE ME LIBERTY

Pegasus Books LLC
80 Broad Street, 5th Floor
New York, NY 10004

First Pegasus Books cloth edition October 2014

Interior design by Maria Fernandez

ISBN: 978-1-60598-633-3

10 9 8 7 6 5 4 3 2 1

Printed in the United States of America
Distributed by W. W. Norton & Company, Inc.

This book is dedicated with love and thankfulness to Peg
for giving me the freedom to write, indeed the ability to live in freedom.

CONTENTS

FOREWORD
DEFINING FREEDOM

Give me liberty," demanded Patrick Henry as he held up his right arm and flourished an ivory letter opener, "or give me death!" Bringing the point of the letter opener down to his chest, he collapsed dramatically into his chair.

"Visual aids" can sometimes help get our attention, and they may have done so on that day, just over two years before July 4, 1776. Today, however, Patrick Henry's letter opener has been largely forgotten—one witness apparently failed to notice it in the first place and remembered only a gesture with his hands—while his words continue to echo in American history and the speech remains one of the two or three known to almost every American.

There are only a few speeches that most Americans remember, and all of them have to do with liberty. They seem to trace a rising arc of understanding, of broadening and clarifying the definition of liberty, a word that remains a central value in American life and is stamped on every United States coin in circulation.

But what exactly is liberty? There seems to be a wide range of opinion, and seldom have the ends of that range spread further apart than today. In Patrick Henry's day it was simple enough to think in terms of freedom from a foreign government's control of one's life; but now a variety of forces impact our lives in various ways, and freeing ourselves from one may make us more vulnerable to another. Sometimes we are eager to work for measures that seem to increase our own freedom without thinking or caring that they may limit the freedom of others who are seeking other goals, goals that may seem to us wrong-headed or even immoral—as ours may seem to them.

Questions about the meaning of freedom seem to rise up daily to challenge us. What limits, if any, should government place on our freedom to marry whom we choose or to purchase whatever weapons we want or smoke cigarettes or marijuana or cut down a tree or drain a swamp? Should American freedom include immigrants who arrive without documentation? Should American resources be used in an attempt to expand the freedom of those living elsewhere under oppressive regimes? The questions are endless, and no two people are likely to give the same answers to all of them. It is, however, questions like these that Americans have worked to resolve, sometimes peacefully and sometimes with great violence, over the span of our history.

Perhaps uniquely among the nations of the world, the United States traces its origins to groups and individuals who came specifically to create something new. For some of those who came, that "something new" was simply an escape from economic or political or religious oppression. For some, it was as simple as better farmland or economic opportunity for themselves. For still others, however, it was a society organized around specific, clearly stated principles. For all of them, the land that would become the United States of America represented freedom, freedom from the economic or political or religious or social systems they had known and freedom to live in a new way, however they might define it. Canadians and Australians and others might claim a similar history; but at one dramatic point in their past, Americans fought a war demanding freedom and created a Constitution to define and protect the freedom they envisioned. Freedom, then, became a unifying principle in a unique way, but still it was defined so differently by various individuals and groups that Americans have been arguing ever since as to what freedom truly means and what it should look like.

Among the most important groups who came were the Puritans and Pilgrims who began the settlement of the New England states. They came to be free of a church that was deeply offensive to them, and to be able to create a new society based on their own principles. As their ships neared the New England coast, their leader, John Winthrop, preached a sermon in which he highlighted a further dimension of the American experiment in freedom. "We must consider," he said, "that we shall be as a city upon a hill, the eyes of all people are upon us." Not only were the colonists creating a new society for themselves, but they were embarking on an experiment that would be watched, for better or worse, by others, some who would hope to see it fail and some who would hope to see it succeed and so establish a model for themselves as well. Winthrop's words would be remembered and cited by two American presidents, John F. Kennedy and Ronald Reagan, more than three centuries later. Reagan would cite it often and add the word "shining," to make it "a shining city on a hill." Winthrop's words would also take flesh as American presidents spoke in Berlin and Cairo and Beijing and Moscow and Capetown and were listened to as bearing witness to an ideal which, however poorly it may be realized in some respects in the United States, remains a hope that inspires millions living under tyranny.

In the time since John Winthrop spoke, ordinary Americans have been at work building the imagined city. Some have shared his vision very specifically while others have had different dreams—or none that they could articulate. Together they have created a working society in which freedom, variously defined and understood, has remained a central value. Along the way, there have been many who have expressed the vision in their own words, drawing on their own experience, and responding as well to new challenges in changing times and circumstances. Some of these have used words that seemed so appropriate that they have been remembered and quoted and held up to inspire others.

The effort to define freedom continues today and is reported almost daily in the media. John Winthrop is cited still, and so are Abraham Lincoln and Ronald Reagan and Martin Luther King, Jr. and others. Their words do remain relevant, yet our circumstances continue to change and the definition of freedom, if it is to be useful, must continue to be expressed in new ways. As we struggle to find ways to define freedom in our own day, it is useful to remember how it has been defined in the past by the particular men and women whose words have been most often remembered. What were the challenges they faced? What circumstances shaped their own vision and their ability to express it in memorable ways? What lessons can be learned from their various successes and failures?

Words, of course, are used eloquently on paper as well. The words of the Declaration of Independence echo through American history—but, although they were primarily the work of Thomas Jefferson, they were given final form by a committee. Other words, those of Walt Whitman or William Lloyd Garrison or those of "America the Beautiful," for example, have made an enormous impact. But limits must be set, and this book deals only with the spoken word and with some of those who spoke with particular eloquence. This book also is a collection of stories, not an essay about freedom, because freedom may be defined in human lives as well as words. Patrick Henry, Daniel Webster, and the others whose stories are told here believed passionately in the ideal of freedom and used words eloquently to express their understanding of that ideal and to inspire others with their vision.

But their words were less eloquent than their lives; indeed, it was the lives they lived that shaped the words they spoke. It is by understanding their lives that we will understand better what they sought to accomplish with their words, how they succeeded in some ways and failed in others, and how we should not be surprised at the need to continue to redefine freedom in our own new times and circumstances and in our own lives. Patrick Henry, Daniel

Webster, and the others whose stories this book tells were remarkably different people and were shaped by vastly different circumstances. What circumstances and ambitions led them to speak and act as they did? What different challenges do we now face, and how might their words and actions be relevant still? How do their ideas agree with our own—or differ from them?

The various visions of freedom given us by these speakers were distinctively shaped by their individual histories and by the circumstances in which they found themselves. The idea of freedom may begin as something experienced by children of the frontier like Henry, Lincoln, and Bryan, children of economic security like Roosevelt and Stevenson, children of psychological insecurity like Reagan, or children born into deprivation of freedom like Martin Luther King, Jr. One way or another, freedom is first envisioned in individual terms and then in terms of a political system that enables that freedom to exist for others also. And that vision needs constantly to respond to new realities, political, economic, and international, with a continuing reinterpretation and expansion of the ideal of freedom.

This book is not intended to discuss the particulars of present issues, but rather to provide a background for discussion of those issues and to focus attention on particular individuals who summed up the issues of their own day in phrases that have never been forgotten. It may be that in turning away for the moment from our own issues, we can gain perspective on them and, as a result, listen to each other with a greater depth of understanding and deal with our own problems more constructively.

ONE

Patrick Henry
1736–1799

GIVE ME LIBERTY OR GIVE ME DEATH

I

When he brandished the ivory letter opener and uttered the words for which he will always be remembered, Patrick Henry was no newcomer on the political stage and it was not the first time he had laid out choices for his audience in dramatic terms. It was eleven years before that, in early December 1763, that a gangling, red-headed twenty-seven-year-old lawyer had come to the Hanover Courthouse in Hanover, Virginia, to try his first important case. Older and wiser lawyers had turned the case down because they thought the cause was hopeless and they would be embarrassed to be on the losing side. But Patrick Henry saw something more involved than a local issue and was willing to challenge his community to see what he saw.

Life in eighteenth-century Virginia was dominated by tobacco. The first colonists had come seeking gold; instead, they found a strange weed with leaves that could be dried, placed in a pipe, and burned to produce smoke that was pleasantly soothing when inhaled. As the years went by, more and more

Europeans became addicted to this smoke, and the leaf of the tobacco became a kind of substitute for gold. In fact, when the colony issued paper money, it pictured not the king, as English money did, but crossed leaves of tobacco. No wonder, then, that tobacco itself was actually used as money and that even the clergy were paid in tobacco.

That payment system was the problem that confronted the court on that late autumn day and drew a larger than usual crowd to the Hanover Courthouse. Paying the clergy in tobacco was an old and well-established custom, fixed into law in the previous century. Since the Church of England was the established church in the colony, salaries were set by the government; the basic annual payment for each member of the clergy was sixteen thousand pounds of tobacco. The average price for tobacco was a few cents a pound, so clergy might expect to receive the equivalent of four or five hundred dollars a year when they sold their allotment. It was hardly a generous stipend, but it was sufficient to bring an adequate supply of clergy to the New World and sustain them. They would grumble, of course, when the price was low, but sometimes the price would rise and clerical spirits would rise as well.

All went smoothly enough until a severe drought struck the colony in the summer of 1755 and the tobacco crop suffered. A smaller crop, however, meant a higher price for tobacco and a pleasant windfall for the clergy. But the growers were less well pleased. A higher price for a smaller crop left them no better off and, indeed, worse off since they had to pay more to the clergy. The Assembly therefore passed a law allowing the clergy to be paid in money rather than tobacco at the rate of about two cents a pound. Normally acts of the colonial legislature had to be approved by the king, but this time the law was to be put in place without any such delay. The clergy, not surprisingly, were alarmed at this direct attack on their purses and began to send complaints and appeals and petitions to friends and representatives in England. It was, they said, "contrary to the liberty of the subject" that they should be treated in this way. Already, then, liberty had become an issue—and, as so often happens, the same act that brought greater freedom to some took it away from others. The planters' efforts to be free of debt meant a loss of economic freedom for the clergy.

With a long sea voyage separating the colony from the king, disputes such as this were not quickly settled. The law expired in any event after ten months, and the colony might have moved on to other matters—except that one of the leading clergy pushed back against the legislators a little too hard by suggesting that some of them should be hanged and by letting it be known that he would refuse them communion if they came to his church. That made it easier for the legislators to pass another "two-penny act" in 1758 when, again, the crop was small and the price high. This time, also, there was no provision for the royal approval, and this time the act was in effect for twelve months instead of ten.

If one side raised the stakes, the other side could do so as well. The clergy held a protest meeting in Williamsburg early in 1759 and sent one of their number, John Camm, to England to present their case to the Privy Council and Lords of Trade. Such an appeal, over the heads of the colonial governor and Assembly, was an extreme procedure and not likely to win points at home for the clergy. The planters enjoyed their comfortable lives at a distance from royal authority and were outraged that the clergy should appeal to royal authority against them. For all their faults, the clergy had not been unpopular in the colony, but now voices began to be raised against them; and when the Privy Council overruled the House of Burgesses, the colony's own legislature, and decreed an end to the tax, there were many who felt that the issue was no longer justice for the clergy but one of home rule versus a distant authority. Now the question was whether laws should be made and taxes imposed by people who had no knowledge of local American affairs and no need to answer to those they ruled.

Nevertheless, the law was the law, and it seemed that the clergy had the law on their side. When a local pastor named James Maury sued for back pay, the justices agreed that he was entitled to be paid at the full value of the tobacco crop and upheld his plea for the money due him under the law. So clear was the legal situation that the lawyer hired by the planters to defend their cause and their pocketbooks withdrew from what seemed a hopeless case. In desperation, the planters turned to the young and untested Patrick Henry, who had been admitted to the bar only three years earlier after a few brief months of training. Henry, who needed the money and welcomed the chance to become better known, agreed to take the case.

Virginia was the largest of the American colonies but still a small community by modern standards. It was a place where most people knew each other and family ties went back many generations. The Henry family, on the other hand, were relatively recent arrivals: Patrick's father, John Henry, had come from Scotland as a young man only thirty-three years earlier, but the family had quickly put down roots and become leading members of the community. Indeed, John Henry was chief justice of the court before which Patrick would make his case, and the uncle, for whom Patrick was named, was one of the clergy offended by the two-penny law. Thus, all eyes were on the young lawyer who would offend a substantial part of the community including his uncle if he won—and would embarrass himself before his father and friends if he lost.

There are no transcripts of the speech Patrick Henry made on that critical day in his career, but those who were there testified later that he began slowly and hesitantly, as if unsure of himself, but moved on with increasing confidence until his words rang out with authority and passion. The legal facts could hardly be argued, but there was room for a broad emotional appeal.

"Argument weak, shout louder," is an ancient oratorical technique. What was legal was one thing; what seemed fair, especially to the planters, was another. What right had an English court to rule for Virginians? What right had the clergy to the sympathies of those they had failed to serve?

The existing laws were clear, so the young lawyer spent little time discussing them but instead broadened the case to examine the very fundamentals on which government is based. Thomas Jefferson, who had just finished college and begun to study law, may well have been in the audience as Patrick Henry, only a few years older than he, moved away from the specifics of the case to discuss the natural rights of subjects and the compact theory of government. These rights, Jefferson would later assert in writing the Declaration of Independence, are "self-evident," and on that same basis the young Patrick Henry proclaimed to the courtroom that "a king, by annulling or disallowing laws of this salutary nature, from being the father of his people degenerates into a tyrant and forfeits all right to his subjects' obedience."

That was too much for the king's attorney, Peter Lyons, who interrupted angrily, "The gentleman hath spoken treason. I am astonished that your worships could hear it without emotion, or any mark of dissatisfaction." From the other clergy sitting behind Maury came mumbled agreement "Treason, treason, treason." It was the first time, but not the last, that Henry would hear that accusation. But Maury and his colleagues also were now the targets of Henry's oration:

> We have heard a good deal about the benevolence and holy zeal of our reverend clergy, but how is this manifested? Do they manifest their zeal in the cause of humanity by practicing the mild and benevolent precepts of the gospel of Jesus? Do they feed the hungry and clothe the naked? Oh, no, no, gentlemen! Instead of feeding the hungry and clothing the naked, these rapacious harpies would, were their powers equal to their will, snatch from the hearth of their honest parishioner his last hoe-cake, from the widow and her orphan children, their last milch cow! The last bed, nay, nay, the last blanket from the lying-in woman![1]

What sort of pagan, you might ask, would attack the clergy like that! Today there is a legitimate debate over the Christian faith of men like Washington, Jefferson, Franklin, and others: were they orthodox Christians, or were they Deists, rejecting the traditional claims of the Gospel? That can fairly be debated for some of them, but there can be little debate about Patrick Henry's orthodox faith and commitment. In his will, drafted at the end of his life, he wrote that his specific bequests were "all the inheritance I can give to my dear family. But the religion of Christ can give them one which will make them rich indeed."[2] Of Deism he once wrote that "with me [it] is but another name for vice and depravity." He told his daughter Betsy that when he was called a Deist:

> . . . it gives me much more pain than the appellation of Tory . . . and I find much cause to reproach myself that I have lived so long and have given no decided and public proofs of my being a Christian. But indeed my dear child this is a character which I prize above all this world has or can boast.[3]

Another daughter recorded that, in his later years at least, she would come downstairs in the morning to find her father sitting at the table reading his Bible. Nevertheless—or, perhaps, as a result—Henry was quite capable of being objective about the claims of churches and clergy and of valuing strong faith wherever he found it. Brought up though he was in the Anglican Church (later the Episcopal Church) and a member of it all his life, he was exposed in childhood to the preaching of the Great Awakening, an evangelical revival that swept through the colonies in the 1740s. While his uncle agonized over whether to expose his parishioners to these disruptive preachers who "screw up the people to the greatest heights of religious Phrenzy" [*sic*] and then leave the settled pastors to deal with the result, his mother, a Presbyterian, took him off to hear Samuel Davies, one of the best known of the new evangelists, and quizzed him on the text and message as they drove home.[4] In later life, Henry would be a staunch defender of the rights of frontier Baptists and other "non-conformists." Anglican though he was, he favored disestablishment but advocated a general assessment to provide public funding for religion.[5] Faithful Christian though he was, he hated to see power entrenched and freedom diminished. So, although he came to the Parsons' Cause with a reputation to establish and the eyes of the leadership on him, he spoke what was treason to the state and heresy to the church because it was consistent with his lifelong concern for freedom as he understood it.

Where did that lifelong concern for freedom begin? It might have had roots in his father's background, since John Henry was Scottish and could have been expected to question the authority of the English crown. But John Henry was also a member of the Episcopal Church of Scotland, which was a sister church to the Church of England. In Virginia, then, he would have been quite at home in the local congregations of the Church of England, and certainly he quickly found a place in the local establishment. Less than ten years after first setting foot on Virginian soil, John Henry had become a member of the local Vestry, the lay leaders of the parish church, and chief justice of the Hanover County court and a colonel in the local militia. Of course, Hanover County was primarily rural and lacked the prestige of Richmond or Williamsburg, but John Henry had no reason to question authority or raise his son to do so.

Patrick Henry, however, grew up in a very different world from that of his father or the Virginia establishment. Tidewater Virginia with its great plantations and established families extended from the coast to the head of navigation on the rivers. Beyond that was the Piedmont, an area of newer settlement where more recent Scottish settlers of Presbyterian and Baptist persuasion were more common and the taxes imposed to support the established church were resented. Life in the Piedmont was freer in many ways. Patrick had only a few years of formal schooling, but always he had the freedom to fish in the streams and hunt small game with a musket. Children in the Piedmont seldom wore shoes; even as a young man, Patrick Henry often went barefoot. Freedom, for him, was a way of life, not simply politics.

The early biographers of Washington and Lincoln exaggerate their heroic qualities. Washington, they said, chopped down a cherry tree but could not tell a lie. Lincoln, they said, walked miles at the end of the day to return a penny he had overcharged a customer. But William Wirt, Patrick Henry's first biographer, seems to exaggerate the young Patrick Henry's defects rather than his virtues. He tells us that:

> I cannot learn that he gave, in his youth, any evidence of that precocity which sometimes distinguishes uncommon genius. His companions recollect no instance of premature wit, no striking sentiment, no flash of fancy, no remarkable beauty or strength of expression; find no indication, however slight, either of that impassioned love of liberty, or of that adventurous daring and intrepidity, which marked, so strongly, his future character. So far was he, indeed, from exhibiting any one prognostic of his greatness, that every omen foretold a life, at best of mediocrity, if not of insignificance. His person is represented as having been coarse, his manners uncommonly awkward, his dress slovenly, his conversation very plain, his aversion to study invincible, and his faculties almost entirely benumbed by indolence. No persuasion could bring him either to read or to work. On the contrary, he ran wild in the forest, like one of the aborigines of the country, and divided his life between the dissipation and uproar of the chase, and the languor of inaction.[6]

Certainly Henry imbibed something of the frontiersman's passionate commitment to freedom, but where Wirt tells us that Henry had an "invincible" aversion to study and "faculties benumbed by indolence," a contemporary author reports that Patrick Henry had learned Latin, Greek, and French from his father, a graduate of the ancient and distinguished King's College in Aberdeen, and had read the *Odyssey* in Greek and Horace, Virgil, and Livy in Latin by the age of fifteen.[7] Oddly, both biographers knew the same source, a contemporary of Henry's, Samuel Meredith, who was four years older, lived four miles away for some time, and married Patrick Henry's sister Jane. Meredith testifies that Henry "had a knowledge of the Latin language and a smattering of Greek," while John Adams reported that Patrick Henry told him he had read Virgil and Livy in the original at the age of fifteen.[8] Another contemporary, Judge Spencer Roane, who served with him in the legislature, thought Henry had "some knowledge of Latin" but might never have been able to read Livy easily.[9] That may be the reason why he told a certain Judge Hugh Nelson that in his later years he read a translation of Livy every year.[10] So if Wirt magnifies Henry's deficiencies, the modern biographer seems to exaggerate his accomplishments. In fact, Henry lacked the formal education that Thomas Jefferson acquired, but he did have an education beyond many of his comrades and certainly a knowledge of the classics beyond almost all modern politicians. And if his formal education was incomplete, he did have the invaluable experience of a firsthand exposure to the harder lives of the frontiersmen and an ability to speak their language as well as that of the classics.

Wirt also tells us—and other biographers follow his lead—that Patrick Henry had failed as a businessman and farmer before becoming a lawyer. Still playing down his subject, Wirt speaks of Henry's "indolence" and "wretched" management skills and tells us that he hated the "drudgery of retailing and of bookkeeping."

What we know is that when Patrick was fifteen, he and his brother had been given a shipment of goods by their father and told to go and be merchants. It was, however, a poor time to go into business: a drought had left the local farmers without cash resources and, like the Tidewater planters who lived on credit from English merchants, the Piedmont farmers depended on the goodwill of the local merchants. The goodwill of the Henry brothers left them at the end of the year with £10 in hand and an accumulation of IOUs that might have been converted to cash in another year or two when the drought ended, but there were no reserves to tide them over. The second year of storekeeping brought them a total of twenty-six customers, so they closed the store and went out of business. You could call it "failure" or chalk it up as invaluable "experience." We cannot tell whether Henry "hated" the drudgery of bookkeeping or tolerated it, but we know he did it. We have the careful records he kept as evidence that he had not failed to do what he could to make the business succeed.

As for his "failure" at farming, Patrick moved on to that after his brief experience in business. Married at the age of eighteen, he was given a 300-acre farm and six slaves by his father-in-law. But the slaves were children of recently imported Africans who had less experience of farming than Henry and were more of a burden than an asset. Still, Patrick worked hard and might have made a go of it had not his house burned down. Fortunately his wife Sarah's parents owned the tavern across the road from the Hanover Courthouse, so the young couple, with a first child and a second on the way, moved into the tavern and Patrick became a bartender, hiring an overseer to do the best he could with the slaves and the farmland.[11]

If success or failure is to be measured in monetary terms, Henry had not succeeded in his first years of adult life; but how many recently married teenagers with two small children could have done better? As a storekeeper, farmer, and bartender, he had gained a firsthand knowledge of the lives of his neighbors and an ability to speak their language. When Thomas Jefferson met him at Christmas-time in 1759, he wrote that "his manners had something of coarseness in them" but "his passion was music, dancing, and pleasantry. He excelled in the latter and it attached everyone to him. . . . His misfortunes were not traced, either in his countenance or conduct."[12]

In the midst of misfortune, Patrick Henry had gained a working knowledge of his fellow citizens that would stand him in good stead the next spring, when he journeyed to Williamsburg to apply for admission to the bar. His coarse clothing and country accent did nothing to commend him to the examiners, but he had learned some legal phrases in visiting his father's courthouse and some knowledge of the theory of natural law from his reading in the classics. He spoke of the hard-working farmers of the frontier and their need for legal defenders, and "the music of his voice" and "natural elegance of his style and manner" convinced the examiners that there was sufficient potential beneath the rough surface. With his promise that he would continue to study the law, the examiners signed his license, and he returned to his rural home to begin still another career at the age of twenty-four.

Certainly, Patrick Henry had an educational background adequate to begin the work of a lawyer, and he had also been exposed to public speakers who could provide role models for a young orator. He had heard Samuel Davies, the evangelical preacher who was generally considered one of the great orators of his day, and he might also have heard the even better-known George Whitefield, a colleague of John and Charles Wesley, who had preached to vast audiences from New England to Georgia. Phrases that might have been heard from the lips of Samuel Davies can be picked out in some of Henry's later speeches. In a time when newspapers were few and even literacy was limited, people depended on oral communication to provide information and shape opinion. So Patrick Henry would have been exposed to the voices of preachers like his uncle and lawyers like those who came to the Hanover Courthouse across the way from the tavern, yet he seems from the beginning of his career to have known instinctively how to use voice, language, and gesture to command an audience as none of his colleagues could. Thus, to return to the story of the Parsons' Cause, he was far better prepared than his community realized to challenge their basic institutions. Not only was he prepared to challenge them, he was willing to risk condemning them:

> The only use of an established church and clergy in society is to enforce obedience to civil sanction, and the observance of those which are called dutics of imperfect obligation. . . . [By] refusing to acquiesce to the law in question, [the clergy] have been so far from answering, that they have most notoriously counteracted those great ends of their institution. Instead of useful members of the state, they ought to be considered as enemies of the community. In the case now before them, Mr. Maury, instead of countenance and protection and recovery of damages, very justly deserved to be punished with signal severity.[13]

Freedom, as always in Patrick Henry's speeches, was the central issue: by supporting the clergy in their appeal to English law, he told the jurors that they would "rivet the chains of bondage on their own necks." He told them that he knew they were bound to support the law, but that they had no need to award the damages requested beyond a symbolic penny. The jury needed only five minutes to act as Henry had suggested. Cheers rang out, and Henry was carried around the courtyard on the shoulders of the crowd.[14] A new force had arrived in Virginia's society.

II

The Parsons' Cause might have been nothing more than a minor incident in both a small community and an unimportant life, except that a variety of larger forces were at work to draw the American colonies together and separate them from the colonizing power. Patrick Henry would play a leading role in that process.

The thirteen colonies that came together in opposition to British rule had little in common except a growing resentment of British authority. Virginia had been settled primarily as a commercial enterprise and had built its life on the raising of tobacco, while the New England colonies were settled first by religious communities intent on finding freedom to worship in their own way and supporting themselves as farmers and fishermen. In between were settlements of varying character, Quakers and Roman Catholics and various kinds of Protestants, as well as Swedes and Dutch and various other ethnic groups, with little to unite them. The colonies lacked even a common language—Dutch was common in New York and German in Pennsylvania—and those who spoke English did so with such different accents that New Englanders and Virginians found it difficult sometimes to understand each other. Nevertheless, British economic policy offended them all and succeeded in uniting these various colonies in a common cause.

The British point of view was that the colonies existed to serve the mother country, and therefore their trade should flow within the empire. The colonists might see opportunities for trade with the Spanish or French, but this was contrary to the policies of the British government, which believed in controlling trade for its own economic and military advantage. The French and Indian War, called the Seven Years' War in Europe, brought matters to a climax because the British government, not unreasonably, tried to find ways to pay for the war by levying taxes on the colonies that they had successfully defended in this war, at great cost to themselves. But the policies they adopted seemed carefully designed to annoy the Americans and remind them that they had no voice in the decisions that were being made. The Stamp Act was the spark that ignited the long-burning fuse that led at last to the explosion of revolution.

To pay for the Seven Years' War, the British Parliament had enacted a law that required a stamp on all legal documents, newspapers and periodicals, playing cards, and a variety of consumer goods. The stamps ranged in price from a few pennies to a few shillings. They had been required in England for some years but were unfamiliar to Americans. Now Americans were to be reminded of this new tax every time they bought a newspaper or other minor items. Lawyers especially found the tax a constant annoyance, since it was required for all manner of legal documents. Nevertheless, most Americans were willing to accept this minor irritant, and it was not at the top of the agenda when the House of Burgesses assembled in the spring of 1765. Patrick Henry, not yet thirty years old, had just been elected to the legislature and, as a newcomer, would have been expected to sit quietly and learn how things were done. Slowly the House moved through a variety of bills: one to prevent hogs from running loose in Richmond, others dealing with the proper punishment for conspiracies and rebellions among the slave population. Not until the fifth day did they come to a matter that drew an active response from Patrick Henry.

The great Tidewater planters seemed chronically unable to balance their accounts. Trustingly, they sent off their shipments of tobacco to the same merchants year after year, assuming that their English colleagues were friends who would obtain the best price, pay their bills for them, and willingly wait through lean years for the better years when the accounts would balance.

Unfortunately, the value of the crop seemed less and less equal to the value of the planters' purchases; and their agents, who believed that economics trumped friendship, were less and less willing to wait patiently for better days. In the face of growing pressure to pay their bills, the planters proposed to the legislators that they create a loan office to provide help to the planters in their times of need, effectively transferring their debt to the general public. It was too much for Patrick Henry, representing farmers who had no such grand tastes or overwhelming debts. "What," he exclaimed, "is it proposed then to reclaim the spendthrift from his dissipation and extravagance by filling his pockets with money?"

In spite of Henry's dramatic protest, the measure was passed by the House and only defeated in committee when the upper house of the legislature, or Council, weighed in on the matter.[15] But the legislators had been put on notice that the new member from the country had an independent mind and a willingness to raise hard questions. They might, therefore, have been less surprised when they came to the last day of the session, May 29, Patrick Henry's twenty-ninth birthday, and found themselves confronted with a set of resolutions that left little room for moderation. Seeing that no one else was willing to confront the issue of the Stamp Act, Henry, without consultation, had drafted resolutions that asserted in the clearest terms that the power to tax Virginians must rest with Virginians: "The General Assembly of this Colony have the *only and sole exclusive* Right and Power to lay Taxes and Impositions upon the Inhabitants of this Colony. . . ." That was strong language enough, but it was the fifth and final resolution that most startled the comfortable members of the House: "That any person who shall, by speaking or writing, assert or maintain that any person or persons other than the general assembly of this colony, have any right or power to impose or lay any taxation on the people here, shall be deemed an enemy to his majesty's colony."[16] Obviously, that included Parliament and the king. Two further resolutions, not introduced, would have gone still further and called, in effect, for separation and even rebellion.

The first four resolutions passed by narrow margins, but the fifth elicited strong emotions. Thomas Jefferson, who was there, wrote that the debate on the fifth resolution was "most bloody."[17] Here, for the first time, Patrick Henry was given the opportunity to display his abilities to the established leadership of the whole colony. One member said of Henry's arguments that "they were beyond my powers of description," and Jefferson spoke of "the splendid display of Mr. Henry's talents as a popular orator." That display reached its climax in the often quoted words "Tarquin and Caesar had each his Brutus, Charles the First his Cromwell, and George the Third—" Henry paused dramatically while the air was filled, as at the Parsons' Cause trial, with cries of "Treason" from the Speaker of the House and "Treason, treason" from other members; Henry, who seems likely to have known exactly what he would say next, waited for silence before finishing his sentence: "—may profit by their example." Some accounts tell us that he went on to say "If this be treason, make the most of it," but not all witnesses agree.[18]

Whatever the exact words said, Patrick Henry had used his oratorical powers to raise the temperature of the debate between colonists and king. He had gained attention in the Parsons' Cause, but now he had placed himself squarely in the leadership of a growing chorus of opposition to British rule that was not confined to Virginia. The last resolution passed by a single vote—but that was enough to send a message to the other colonies. Copies of the Stamp Act resolutions were carried rapidly up the coast, and just ten days later, on June 8, the Massachusetts legislature responded by calling for a convention to meet in New York in October to discuss what they should do. Other colonial legislatures followed suit, and in due course the meeting brought together representatives of nine colonies—not including Virginia—meeting together for the first time. The Stamp Act, with Patrick Henry's resolutions, had taken divided colonies and started them on the road to becoming united states.

In Britain, the response was ten years of dithering that took a bad situation and made it worse, step by miscalculated step. The Stamp Act was repealed in February 1766, but only to be replaced by other irritants. The government could safely ignore the colonists' petitions, but not those of British merchants who found their goods no longer in demand and those of shipping companies that found their ships sailing half empty. There was also a new prime minister who agreed that the Stamp Act was bad policy. But the principle that Parliament had a right to tax its citizens wherever they were located could not easily be abandoned. One sensible remedy might have been to bring American representatives into Parliament, but Parliament was not being sensible. Instead, Parliament passed a Declaratory Act asserting their right to tax the colonies, and followed that a year later with a series of new taxes, the Townshend Acts, named for the Chancellor of the Exchequer. These, predictably, resulted in rioting in Boston, which was put down with armed force in the so-called Boston Massacre, when five civilians were killed and six others injured by British soldiers.

Seeing the difficulty of enforcing the Townshend Acts, these also were repealed in 1770—but not entirely. The duty on tea was left in place, as if to say "But we can still tax you if we want!" The colonies were briefly quiet but then, in 1773, the East India Company was given the right to ship tea directly to the colonies and a monopoly on the trade that excluded American merchants and retained the duty on tea. The result was the Boston Tea Party in December of that year. From that beginning, the chain of events then developed gradually into open warfare.

Parliament took the next step by closing the Port of Boston to commerce. When the Virginia Legislature responded mildly by calling for a day of prayer, the governor dissolved the assembly. In the summer of 1774, Parliament reduced the power of elected colonial officials and authorized the taking over of buildings, even homes, to provide quarters for British soldiers. The American-born governor of Massachusetts was then replaced by a British general, who declared martial law and marched into Boston with four divisions of soldiers.

The Virginia assembly, which had continued to meet in a tavern, voted to ban British imports and appointed delegates to a new colonial congress to meet in Philadelphia that fall. Patrick Henry, now thirty-eight years old and a familiar figure in Virginia politics, was one of the Virginia delegates and made his mark on the gathering as soon as the organization was complete. In his usual way, he began slowly and hesitantly, reciting the reasons for the meeting and deploring his inability to do justice to the issue confronting them. But then, as William Wirt tells the story,

> he launched gradually, into a recital of the colonial wrongs. Rising, as he advanced, with the grandeur of his subject, and glowing at length, with all the majesty and excitation of the occasion, his speech seemed more than that of mortal man. Even those who had heard him in all his glory, in the house of burgesses of Virginia, were astonished at the manner in which his talents seemed to swell and expand themselves, to fill the vaster theatre in which he was now placed. There was no rant—no rhapsody—no labour of the understanding—no straining of the voice—no confusion of the utterance. His countenance was erect—his eye steady—his action, noble—his enunciation clear and firm—his mind poised on its centre—his views of his subject comprehensive and great—and his imagination, corruscating with a magnificence and a variety, which struck even that assembly with amazement and awe. He sat down amidst murmurs of astonishment and applause; and as he had been before proclaimed the greatest orator of Virginia, he was now on every hand, admitted to be the first orator of America.[19]

Patrick Henry was there to represent Virginia, and representatives of other colonies heard him declaim: "The distinctions between Virginians, Pennsylvanians, New Yorkers, and New Englanders, are no more. I am not a Virginian, but an American." Non-Virginians had not heard Henry before; one of the other delegates said that he sounded more like a Presbyterian pastor than a politician.[20]

Henry came back from Philadelphia to take part in the last act of a slowly developing personal tragedy. Sarah, his wife, had developed some sort of psychiatric condition. The records are unclear but hint at extreme depression, attempted suicide, and possible violence toward her children. The first hospital for psychiatric patients had recently been opened in Richmond, but the treatment of patients was crude and included such "remedies" as bleeding and induced vomiting. She would have been locked into a windowless brick cell containing only a filthy mattress on the floor and a chamber pot and chained to the wall with a leg iron. Appalled by that, Henry instead created a private two-room apartment for her in the basement of their Scotchtown home in which each room had a window, providing light and air and a view of the grounds outside. The apartment also had a fireplace and a comfortable bed. Either servants or Henry himself cared for her, but her condition worsened rapidly during the winter of 1774–1775 and she died in early 1775.[21]

In the midst of Henry's personal tragedy, a second session of the Virginia convention met at St. John's Church in Richmond. The delegates had begun to think of themselves as an independent government and came prepared to levy taxes to support a state militia. Others, however, among them many of the leaders of the colony, had no desire at all to break the ties with England and could not imagine themselves taking on the armed might of Great Britain. Peyton Randolph, one of the most distinguished members of the assembly, therefore moved a resolution appealing simply for "a speedy return to those halcyon days when we lived a free and happy people." The established leadership expected to adjourn after a brief discussion and pro forma approval.

What happened instead proved to be a turning point in the events leading up to the Revolution. Patrick Henry moved for an amendment in three parts to Randolph's resolution, calling for the immediate "arming and disciplining" of a militia "to secure our inestimable rights and liberties from those further violations with which they are threatened." It wasn't quite a declaration of war, but it felt very much like it to the conservative members, and several of them spoke against this frightening increase in the tensions that already existed. Patrick Henry spoke last. What he said was not written down in advance or carefully recorded by those who were present, but the words were so striking that they were not easily forgotten—and the final passages are remembered as perhaps the most dramatic speech ever made in America.

Henry began by referring respectfully to the members who had spoken before him; he had no doubt, he said, of their patriotism and abilities. But "different men often see the same subject in different lights," and he hoped he would not be thought disrespectful if he were to express himself "without reserve." "It is natural," he told the delegates, "to indulge in the illusions of hope," but he could see nothing in the experience of the last ten years to justify any optimism. On the contrary, he told them,

> It is now too late to retire from the contest. There is no retreat, but in submission and slavery! Our chains are forged. Their clanking may be heard on the plains of Boston! The war is inevitable—and let it come! I repeat it, sir, let it come!
>
> It is in vain, sir, to extenuate the matter. Gentlemen may cry peace, peace—but there is no peace. The war is actually begun! The next gale that sweeps from the north, will bring to our ears the clash of resounding arms! Our brethren are already in the field! Why stand we here idle? What is it that gentlemen wish? What would they have? Is life so dear or peace so sweet, as to be purchased at the price of chains and slavery? Forbid it, Almighty God! I know not what course others may take; but as for me [here he extended both his arms aloft, his brows were furrowed and all his features "marked with the resolute purpose of his soul" while his voice swelled to the final, unforgettable crescendo], give me liberty or give me death!

An elderly Baptist pastor, years later, reported that "Henry rose with an unearthly fire burning in his eye" and that "his voice rose louder and louder, until the walls of the building, and all within them, seemed to shake and rock in its tremendous vibrations. Finally, his pale face and glaring eye became terrible to look upon. . . . His last exclamation—'Give me liberty or give me death'—was like the shout of the leader which turns back the rout of battle. Every eye yet gazed entranced on Henry. It seemed as if a word from him would have led to any wild explosion of violence."[22]

Thomas Marshall, father of the future Chief Justice of the Supreme Court, called the speech "one of the most bold, vehement, and animated pieces of eloquence that had ever been delivered." But Henry had been drawing such responses since his speech some twelve years earlier in the Parsons' Cause. Clearly there was something far beyond the ordinary in the spell cast by Patrick Henry's rhetoric. Some spoke of the melodious quality of his voice, but others said his voice was unremarkable. In spite of the testimony of the Baptist minister to a voice that seemed to shake the walls of the building, another witness said that he was "emphatic, without vehemence or declamation; animated, but never boisterous."[23] Still another witness, George Mason, a colleague and supporter, testified that "Every word he says not only engages but commands the attention; and your passions are no longer your own when he addresses them."[24] Thomas Jefferson, not always an admirer, confessed that Henry's speeches in opposition to him "always seemed directly to the point . . . [and] produced a great effect, and I myself had been highly delighted and moved," but afterwards "asked myself what the d—l has he said?"[25]

What he said was obviously important and how he said it as well; but beyond that, there was clearly something about the quality of his voice that commanded attention under any circumstances. The story is told that on one occasion he had gone to visit friends, and he drew no special notice until he said "I tell you, friends, it is a bitter, cold night," and immediately everyone stopped what they were doing to listen. That clear, resonant voice overcame his back-country accent and his total lack of sophisticated rhetorical devices.[26] There must have been something irresistibly captivating in his way of speaking, even on the most trivial subjects. A judge who practiced law with him remarked that he was not easily distracted from his work, but "when Patrick rose to speak . . . although it might be on so trifling a subject as a summons and petition, for twenty shillings, he was obliged to lay down his pen, and could not write another word, until the speech was finished. Such was the charm of his voice and manner, and the interesting originality of his conceptions!"[27] Obviously it was not simply his commitment to the cause of American freedom that made his speeches memorable. When the war was over and Henry could spend more time earning a living as a lawyer, the spell of his voice was said to have gained freedom also for horse thieves and murderers. One neighbor was heard to say that he would have no fear of being caught stealing a horse since Colonel Henry would clear his name for £50.[28]

Wirt sums up the genius of Henry's oratory by emphasizing his perception of his audience and the rapport he could establish with them even more than his vocal gifts:

> It was on questions before a jury, that he was in his natural element. . . . The jury might be composed of entire strangers, yet he rarely failed to know them, man by man, before the evidence was closed. There was no studied fixture of features, that could long hide the character from his piercing and experienced view. The slightest unguarded turn of countenance, or motion of the eye, let him at once into the soul of the man whom he was observing. Or, if he doubted whether his conclusions were correct, from the exhibitions of countenance during the narration of the evidence, he had a mode of playing a prelude as it were, upon the jury, in his exordium, which never failed to "wake into life each silent string," and show him the whole compass as well as pitch of the instruments and, indeed (if we may believe all the concurrent accounts of his exhibitions in the general court), the most exquisite performer

> that ever "swept the sounding lyre," had not a more sovereign mastery over its powers, than Mr. Henry had over the springs of feeling and thought that belong to a jury. There was a delicacy, a taste, a felicity, in his touch, that was perfectly original, and without a rival. . . . He sounded no alarm; he made no parade, to put the jury on their guard. It was all so natural, so humble, so unassuming, that they were carried imperceptibly along, and attuned to his purpose, until some master touch dissolved them into tears. His language of passion was perfect. There was no word "of learned length or thundering sound," to break the charm. It had almost all the stillness of solitary thinking. It was a sweet reverie, a delicious trance. His voice, too, had a wonderful effect. He had a singular power of infusing it into a jury, and mixing its notes with their nerves, in a manner which it is impossible to describe justly; but which produced a thrilling excitement, in the happiest concordance with his designs. No man knew so well as he did what kind of topics to urge to their understandings; nor what kind of simple imagery to present to their hearts. His eye, which he kept rivetted upon them, assisted the process of fascination, and at the same time informed him what theme to press, or at what instant to retreat, if by rare accident he touched an unpropitious string. And then he had such an exuberance of appropriate thoughts, of apt illustrations, of apposite images, such a melodious and varied roll of the happiest words, that the hearer was never wearied by repetition, and never winced from an apprehension that the intellectual treasures of the speaker would be exhausted.[29]

The spell of his voice did, however, have one drawback: in a day when modern shorthand had not been developed and scribes were often unable to keep up with the flow of oratory, Patrick Henry's voice often so charmed the stenographers that they stopped writing in order to listen.[30] There is, as a result, room for debate about every phrase ever attributed to Patrick Henry; but his earliest biographer was at pains to interview and gather testimony from those who had been there, and there is remarkable agreement about not only the substance but the words and even the gestures.[31]

Certainly no one ever doubted that he had ended his most memorable and important speech with the words "Give me liberty or give me death." The words "Liberty or Death" were soon on the shirts of Virginia volunteers heading off to fight.[32] More important, they persuaded the Virginia convention to adopt his resolutions in spite of strenuous opposition from some influential members. A final vote of 65–60 is evidence that not all were swept away by the force of Henry's rhetoric; but without it, it seems likely that Virginia would have stayed on the sidelines in the developing conflict.

The personal choice between life and death meant a choice for the delegates between war and peace. A conservative delegate grumbled that he had never heard anything "more famously insolent," but Edmund Randolph felt that the speech had "blazed so as to warm the coldest heart."[33] A committee was appointed, with Patrick Henry as chairman, to set about the task of raising and arming a militia. Significantly, a stronger resolution, for the raising of a regular army, was rejected. In September, Henry was commissioned as a colonel and put in charge of Virginia's armed forces, charged to "resist and repel all hostile invasions, and quell and suppress any insurrections." But Henry was no military leader; and when the Continental Congress merged regiments of the Virginia military into the Continental Army and took away Henry's position as Commander in Chief, he resigned and went back to a more useful place as a leader in the legislature and then as governor of the state. In that capacity, he was an invaluable support to George Washington, doing his best to provide the troops and weapons and funds without which Washington would have been unable to carry on.

"Liberty" was Patrick Henry's watchword, but a difficult word to apply in a time of war. As a wartime governor, Henry quickly experienced the conflict between popular freedom and effective government. Ironically, it was at this point that the possibility of making Patrick Henry a dictator was apparently discussed. There is no evidence that Henry himself was even aware of such a suggestion, but it seems to have been seriously considered by some of the members of the legislature. Before the war was over, a second attempt was made to make Henry a dictator—though, again, it seems to have been without his knowledge or consent.[34] Wars are not well suited to democracy; a general can hardly ask his troops to vote on which way to march, nor can an executive always resist the temptation to act promptly and decisively when he sees the need to act. Lincoln suspended the right of habeas corpus, which had been enshrined by then in the Constitution, and the government during World War II set wages and prices, controlled the supply of gasoline and other essentials, and, of course, conscripted men for the armed forces. Indeed, it went so far as to intern perfectly loyal citizens of Japanese ancestry without allowing any legal protest. As the war went on, Patrick Henry did at last find it necessary to put aside his principles to some degree. Without victory, freedom would be lost, so it could be sacrificed in the short term to reach the long-term goal. Virginians, however, were clearly satisfied with Henry's performance, since they elected him governor three times during the war (1776–1779) and twice more afterwards (1785–1786).

III

British attempts to put down the revolt of their American colonies concentrated primarily on the urban centers of New York and Philadelphia, rather than the more rural colony of Virginia; but the final, critical victory took place on Virginian soil when General Charles Cornwallis surrendered to General George Washington at Yorktown, Virginia, in September 1783. So the war was over, but the definition of a free country remained to be decided and Virginia became the setting for a battle of words that helped to determine what sort of government the new nation would have. Thirteen loosely affiliated states seemed unable to resolve the pressing issues that faced them: how to carry on relationships with other countries, how to protect American shipping, and how to satisfy debts acquired in the war. Finally, a convention was called for the announced purpose of improving that loose federation, but instead the convention drew up a completely new Constitution and asked the states to ratify it. Once again, Patrick Henry unleashed his oratorical gifts, but now to oppose the proposed new form of government as a potential destroyer of freedom.

How much government is too much? Americans are as deeply divided today on that issue as they have ever been, and Patrick Henry's fear of a strong centralized government still resonates for many. By the time the Virginia state convention met on the second day of June, 1788, eight other states had already ratified the Constitution. Approval of nine states was required to implement it, so the vote in Virginia, critical in any event since Virginia was the largest state in terms of territory and by far the most important of the Southern states, took on added importance. But Virginians would not be hurried. When the delegates gathered in Richmond, the first two days were spent appointing a doorkeeper and a "serjeant at arms" and deciding what rules of order to adopt; and then for nearly three weeks the delegates set forth their views until, finally, the scheduled meeting of the state legislature forced them to vote: for or against.

When first the floor was opened for debate, Patrick Henry was on his feet at once to ask that the papers be read concerning the convention that had produced the Constitution. The delegates to that gathering had been sent, he believed, to revise the existing Articles of Confederation,* not to create a new Constitution. Henry wondered whether they should even be there. Edmund Pendleton, however, an older and more conservative man, quickly pointed

* Formally "Articles of Confederation and Perpetual Union," an agreement among the thirteen founding states that established the United States of America as a confederation of sovereign states and served as its first constitution. (There was to be no president, by the way, just a legislature.) Its drafting by the Continental Congress began on June 12, 1776, and an approved version was sent to the states for ratification in late 1777. The formal ratification by all thirteen states was completed in early 1781.

out that whatever the instructions of the delegates to the Constitutional Convention, the delegates to the Virginia Convention had been appointed specifically to adopt or reject the Constitution before them. How it had come to them was irrelevant. So Henry withdrew his motion and waited through an opening speech by Wilson Nicholas, who was speaking for the Federalists, the supporters of the new document. It had been suggested that the Convention consider the Constitution section by section; so the clerk read the preamble and first articles concerning the House of Representatives, and Nicholas spoke to that subject for over an hour.

Patrick Henry led off for the opposition but saw no need to stick to the subject. He and his colleagues protested that their opposition was not to particulars but to the whole concept of a strong federal government. "Mr. Chairman," he said, "the public mind, as well as my own, is extremely uneasy at the proposed change of government." Five times in his first few sentences the word "uneasy" was repeated. For the best part of the next three weeks, Henry would be on his feet again and again for hours at a time, belaboring that theme. There were other important voices in opposition, but none so persistent as Henry's. In the twenty-three days of debate, Henry spoke on eighteen. On one day he spoke eight times, another five times, and once he spoke for seven hours before yielding the floor. Again and again that great voice rang out, holding the attention of his hearers as no other speaker could do; but somehow the subject at hand was never truly confronted. He had no specific proposals to improve the document before them, nor any specific criticisms of it, only one "what if" after another. What if the president were ambitious? What if the senators were corrupt? The advocates of the Constitution pointed to checks and balances and the ability of the citizens to remove corrupt officials from office. Patrick Henry was still "uneasy" and wanted to know "what if." But simple uneasiness lacked the compelling drama of "liberty or death."

What was his uneasiness? Henry himself found it hard to clarify the issue. He had no inherent objection to a union of the states: "the dissolution of the Union," he said, "is most abhorrent to my mind. The first thing I have at heart is liberty; the second thing is American union." With that priority in mind, he told the delegates they needed to be on their guard: "you ought to be extremely cautious, watchful, jealous of your liberty; for, instead of securing your rights, you may lose them forever. If a wrong step be now made, the republic may be lost forever. If this new government will not come up to the expectation of the people, and they shall be disappointed, their liberty will be lost, and tyranny must and will arise. I repeat it again, and I beg gentlemen to consider, that a wrong step, made now, will plunge us into misery, and our republic will be lost."

The debate went on for weeks, but Edmund Pendleton provided all the response that was needed the next morning. "Can society be formed without government?" he asked.

> There is no quarrel between government and liberty; the former is the shield and protector of the latter. The war is between government and licentiousness, faction, turbulence, and other violations of the rules of society, to preserve liberty. Where is the cause of alarm? We, the people, possessing all power, form a government, such as we think will secure happiness: and suppose, in adopting this plan, we should be mistaken in the end; where is the cause of alarm on that quarter? In the same plan we point out an easy and quiet method of reforming what may be found amiss. . . . No, we will assemble in Convention; wholly recall our delegated powers, or reform them so as to prevent such abuse; and punish those servants who have perverted powers, designed for our happiness, to their own emolument. We ought to be extremely cautious not to be drawn into dispute with regular government, by faction and turbulence, its natural enemies. Here, then, sir, there is no cause of alarm on this side; but on the other side, rejecting of government, and dissolving of the Union, produce confusion and despotism.

Henry, of course, was not convinced and conjured up again and again a vision of unscrupulous, power-hungry representatives and presidents. The checks and balances carefully enumerated by the Federalists counted for nothing in Henry's vision. To him, it was axiomatic that power corrupts and no checks and balances would prevent it. It was a dim view of his fellow citizens that led him to assume a quick transition to imperial splendors and corruption.

> Besides the expenses of maintaining the Senate and other house in as much splendor as they please, there is to be a great and mighty President, with very extensive powers—the powers of a king. He is to be supported in extravagant magnificence; so that the whole of our property may be taken by this American government, by laying what taxes they please, giving themselves what salaries they please, and suspending our laws at their pleasure.[35]
>
> Your President may easily become king. Your Senate is so imperfectly constructed that your dearest rights may be sacrificed by what may be a small minority; and a very small minority may continue forever unchangeably this government, although horridly defective. Where are your checks in this government? Your strongholds will

> be in the hands of your enemies. It is on a supposition that your American governors shall be honest, that all the good qualities of this government are founded; but its defective and imperfect construction puts it in their power to perpetrate the worst of mischiefs, should they be bad men; and, sir, would not all the world, from the eastern to the western hemisphere, blame our distracted folly in resting our rights upon the contingency of our rulers being good or bad? Show me that age and country where the rights and liberties of the people were placed on the sole chance of their rulers being good men, without a consequent loss of liberty! I say that the loss of that dearest privilege has ever followed, with absolute certainty, every such mad attempt.[36]
>
> If your American chief be a man of ambition and abilities, how easy is it for him to render himself absolute! The army is in his hands, and if he be a man of address, it will be attached to him, and it will be the subject of long meditation with him to seize the first auspicious moment to accomplish his design; and, sir, will the American spirit solely relieve you when this happens? I would rather infinitely—and I am sure most of this Convention are of the same opinion—have a king, lords, and commons, than a government so replete with such insupportable evils. If we make a king, we may prescribe the rules by which he shall rule his people, and interpose such checks as shall prevent him from infringing them; but the President, in the field, at the head of his army, can prescribe the terms on which he shall reign master, so far that it will puzzle any American ever to get his neck from under the galling yoke. . . . Can he not, at the head of his army, beat down every opposition? Away with your President! we shall have a king: the army will salute him monarch: your militia will leave you, and assist in making him king, and fight against you: and what have you to oppose this force? What will then become of you and your rights? Will not absolute despotism ensue?[37]

It was a nightmare scenario that Henry conjured up to frighten the delegates. They were supposed to be considering the first articles of the Constitution, but Henry had no time for that. He wanted only to raise doubts and fears, and that destroyed any possibility of an orderly and reasonable debate. After a week in which the debate had consisted of long tirades by Patrick Henry and *ad hoc* responses by those supporting the Constitution, an obviously irritated Governor Randolph rose to say: "I am astonished that the rule of the house to debate regularly has not been observed by gentlemen. Shall we never have order?" But there could be no order when the issue was nothing more specific than "uneasiness."

One strange side issue showed how hard it is to define freedom for oneself without limiting freedom for others. Patrick Henry railed against the proposed Constitution for its failure to specify a bill of rights—as the Constitution of the State of Virginia did. But one fundamental right specified in that Virginia Constitution had been violated a few years earlier by Patrick Henry himself, with the cooperation of Thomas Jefferson. It was forbidden to enact a "bill of attainder"—a bill convicting someone by legislative act rather than a jury trial. But Henry as governor and Jefferson as legislative leader had passed just such a bill and used it to execute a famous criminal without any judicial procedure. It was illegal under Virginia's Constitution, but they had done it anyway. Peyton Randolph cited it as evidence that freedoms could not be secured by any one state but must be guaranteed by the whole country. What Henry and Jefferson had done, he said, was an action

> of a most striking and shocking nature—an example so horrid, that, if I conceived my country would passively permit a repetition of it, dear as it is to me, I would seek means of expatriating myself from it. A man, who was then a citizen, was deprived of his life thus: from a mere reliance on general reports, a gentleman in the House of Delegates informed the house, that a certain man (Josiah Philips) had committed several crimes, and was running at large, perpetrating other crimes. He therefore moved for leave to attaint him; he obtained that leave instantly; no sooner did he obtain it, than he drew from his pocket a bill ready written for that effect; it was read three times in one day, and carried to effect. . . . Without being confronted with his accusers and witnesses, without the privilege of calling for evidence in his behalf, he was sentenced to death, and was afterwards actually executed. Was this arbitrary deprivation of life, the dearest gift of God to man, consistent with the genius of a republican government? Is this compatible with the spirit of freedom? This, sir, has made the deepest impression on my heart, and I cannot contemplate it without horror.[38]

Henry, however, saw no problem. The man, after all, had been a dangerous criminal and needed to be removed from the community, the sooner the better:

> He was a fugitive murderer and an outlaw—a man who commanded an infamous banditti, and at a time when the war was at the most perilous stage. He committed the most cruel and shocking

> barbarities. He was an enemy to the human name. Those who declare war against the human race may be struck out of existence as soon as they are apprehended. He was not executed according to those beautiful legal ceremonies which are pointed out by the laws in criminal cases. The enormity of his crimes did not entitle him to it. I am truly a friend to legal forms and methods; but, sir, the occasion warranted the measure. A pirate, an outlaw, or a common enemy to all mankind, may be put to death at any time. It is justified by the laws of nature and nations.[39]

But how can you sneer at "beautiful legal ceremonies" and remain secure in your own freedom? In one form or another, this fundamental conflict remains unresolved over two hundred years later: we may fear big government but still expect it to be there for us when our own lives or principles are at stake, or we may value big government when it is there to support us but want to limit its power when it sets out to regulate our own lives.

There was one other blind spot in Patrick Henry's understanding of freedom, and that was slavery. Southern whites had not yet dug their heels in on this issue as deeply as they would by the middle of the next century. Patrick Henry, like many others at the time, deplored slavery's existence but saw no way to eliminate it. In debating the Constitution, he pondered whether a federal government might at some future date use its power to eliminate slavery, and he was torn between feeling that it would be a good thing and his recognition that it would create practical difficulties. "Slavery is detested," he said; "we feel its fatal effects—we deplore it with all the pity of humanity." But "As much as I deplore slavery, I see that prudence forbids its abolition. . . . In this situation, I see a great deal of the property of the people of Virginia in jeopardy, and their peace and tranquility gone. I repeat it again, that it would rejoice my very soul that every one of my fellow-beings was emancipated. . . . But is it practicable, by any human means, to liberate them without producing the most dreadful and ruinous consequences?"[40] He would accept death rather than be enslaved himself but could not imagine giving others their freedom when it involved economic loss.

Striking in all of Henry's speeches is his frequent use of that standard orator's device, the rhetorical question. Human beings dislike being told; we prefer to find out for ourselves, and the rhetorical question gives the listener the illusion of providing his own answers: "Isn't it true that our goal is freedom?" Of course the listener nods in agreement and feels united with the speaker in a common cause. In the debate over the Constitution, Henry needed more than ever to draw others to his side, and rhetorical questions were a fundamental tool for that purpose. Again and again, Henry invites his listeners to agree with him, sometimes using as many as six rhetorical questions in a row. One example will suffice:

> When I call this the most mighty state in the Union, do I not speak the truth? Does not Virginia surpass every state in the Union, in number of inhabitants, extent of territory, felicity of position, and affluence and wealth? Some infatuation hangs over men's minds, that they will inconsiderately precipitate into measures the most important, and give not a moment's deliberation to others, nor pay any respect to their opinions. Is this federalism? Are these the beloved effects of the federal spirit, that its votaries will never accede to the just propositions of others?[41]

How could anyone fail to agree that Virginia is wonderful? How could anyone fail to see that federalists are unthinking in their positions? The first proposition is obvious (at least to Virginians!), the second less so. But it is typical of Henry to ask questions first whose answers are obvious to all so that the hearers find themselves nodding agreement, and then to continue with a more dubious proposition, hoping that the audience will continue to nod in agreement.

One modern biographer became so entranced with Henry's rhetorical questions that he painted a fictional scene in which the gallery responded to the questions with roars of agreement and made the clerk gavel for order.[42] In fact, however, those who were present told of an audience that listened in raptured silence. In that raptured silence, however, the hearers sometimes realized that they were not persuaded. A distinguished general, Thomas Posey, who supported the Constitution, reported afterwards that when Henry ended, he was certain that he would vote against ratification, only to realize a few minutes later that he still saw things exactly as he had before.[43]

Indeed, at the end as at the beginning, Henry's position remained more a matter of feelings than any specific language or provision of the new Constitution. He had been "uneasy" but without specifics; those who had thought the matter through needed more than rhetoric to change their minds. Henry's final speech relied entirely on feelings and had little to say about issues. He invoked unseen powers in a nearly mystical burst of oratory:

> I see the awful immensity of the dangers with which it is pregnant. I see it. I feel it. I see beings of a higher order anxious concerning our decision. When I see beyond the horizon that bounds human eyes, and look at the final consummation of all human things, and see those intelligent beings which inhabit the ethereal mansions reviewing the political decisions and revolutions which, in

> the progress of time, will happen in America, and the consequent happiness or misery of mankind, I am led to believe that much of the account, on one side or the other, will depend on what we now decide. Our own happiness alone is not affected by the event. All nations are interested in the determination.[44]

Henry was not alone in his uneasiness and fears; indeed, the celestial powers he invoked seemed to share his uneasiness. As he summoned them, a thunderstorm broke over the meeting place with so much violence that the stenographer noted that it "put the house in such disorder, that Mr. Henry was obliged to conclude."[45] The members rushed out without waiting for formal adjournment. Even so, when the vote was taken the next day, a bare majority (89–79) of the delegates were willing to make the experiment of a federal government. Patrick Henry had seen it coming and made clear how he would respond:

> If I shall be in the minority, I shall have those painful sensations which arise from a conviction of being overpowered in a good cause. Yet I will be a peaceable citizen. My head, my hand, and my heart, shall be at liberty to retrieve the loss of liberty, and remove the defects of that system in a constitutional way. I wish not to go to violence, but will wait with hopes that the spirit which predominated in the revolution is not yet gone, nor the cause of those who are attached to the revolution yet lost. I shall therefore patiently wait in expectation of seeing that government changed, so as to be compatible with the safety, liberty, and happiness, of the people.[46]

He would be "a peaceable citizen" and wait to see whether the guarantees of rights he asked for would be adopted and whether the federal power would impinge on his liberties. Meanwhile, he would take advantage of the personal liberties he was familiar with as a man who was happiest on the frontiers and distant from the constraints of a more settled community. He had invested in land to the west and even toyed with the idea of helping to create a new republic beyond the reach of the federal power; but when the constitutional debate was over, he put aside the political issues to become again a local lawyer and a fond father and grandfather.

The community would continue to seek Patrick Henry's presence and leadership. One after another, he turned down opportunities to be a Senator, Ambassador to Spain, Secretary of State, Chief Justice of the Supreme Court, Governor of Virginia (again), and Ambassador to France. He was not yet sixty, but he was not well; he suffered from recurring bouts of malaria; but most important to him was the feeling that he had given his best years to his country and that he deserved time to enjoy his family and read his Bible and experience the gift of freedom. In 1794 he bought an estate called Red Hill over a hundred miles west of Richmond and settled down there to enjoy the nine surviving children of his second wife, the six children of his first wife, and the grandchildren who had begun to appear. One biographer wonders how he could have lived quietly in a house filled with so many children,[47] but he seems to have wanted his children and grandchildren to enjoy the same freedom he had had as a child. Visitors told of finding him lying on the floor with children climbing over him in every direction and competing to see who could make the most noise. Freedom for Patrick Henry was a very personal matter; it was that sense of peaceful security that he had while playing with his children on the floor of his home that Henry so much valued for himself and so much desired for his country. For five years, he enjoyed that freedom as his health continued to decline. He died in 1799, just one week after his sixty-third birthday.

Finally, however, Patrick Henry's very personal vision of freedom was judged inadequate to the realities of a complex society. His colleagues listened patiently to his doubts and fears and then voted to put in place the structure they believed was necessary to preserve the freedom for which he had spoken so eloquently and worked so hard. Henry was undoubtedly right to hold up a vision of freedom and, indeed, to fear the potential of any government to grow out of control; but he was wrong in his unwillingness to trust his fellow citizens to work together to preserve their freedom. Any government composed of human beings can be destructive of freedom, but no freedom without government both to support and to rein in those same human beings could be maintained for long. The story of America is the story of the constant struggle to preserve and expand the freedom of its citizens while maintaining the delicate balance between too much government and too little. The story of Patrick Henry is a critical chapter in that story.

TWO

Daniel Webster
1782–1852

LIBERTY AND UNION, NOW AND FOREVER, ONE AND INSEPARABLE

> They said, when he stood up to speak, stars and stripes came right out in the sky . . . and, when he argued a case, he could turn on the harps of the blessed.

So Stephen Vincent Benét spoke of Daniel Webster's oratorical skills in a short story in which Webster argues a case against the devil and wins. Still, a century after his death, stories like that could be told about him.[1] Such was Webster's reputation that the term "godlike" was often applied to him, both before and after his death. His political career, from 1812 to 1852, spanned most of the years in which Americans fought most bitterly over the institution of slavery, and his best-known speech, a speech memorized by generations of schoolboys, summed up the central issue of that time: Could America survive as one nation, or not? Patrick Henry had grappled with the same issue, but the question remained: Could there be freedom and unity? In fact, a further question might be asked: In what sense did freedom exist where millions were still in chains, and in what sense did unity exist when the economic interests of the various sections of the country were increasingly different?

Daniel Webster was two years old when the Constitution was adopted and seventeen years old when Patrick Henry died. He was a leader in that next generation whose task it was both to build on the foundation their forebears had laid and to deal with the issues left unresolved by those who had gone before them. Chief of those unresolved questions was the very nature of the union that had been created and the ability of the federal government to deal with national issues for the general welfare. On that question, Webster was absolutely clear and deeply committed to the strong central government that Henry so instinctively feared. Had he not been so committed, Daniel Webster might have been president and the union might have come slowly apart; but then Webster would have been president of a very different kind of country and possibly a much smaller one.

I

The fact that Patrick Henry was shaped by growing up on the frontier made him somewhat of an exception in the first generation of leaders. Washington, Jefferson, Madison, Monroe, and the Adamses were planters or lawyers; for the most part, they were members of the colonial establishment. Henry also was a lawyer, but one who came from and represented the farmers and settlers at the growing edge of the country. He was a first example of what would become a common style in American politics. Andrew Jackson would make it fashionable to be born in a log cabin, and that fashion would persist for nearly a century. Candidates after Jackson learned to stress their humble origins and, if possible, birth in a log cabin.

Daniel Webster barely escaped being born in a log cabin because his father had built a frame house near his cabin two years before Daniel was born. His father was a powerful figure in the community, but he was an uneducated farmer who had rebelled against the master to whom he was apprenticed and run away to fight with Rogers' Rangers in the French and Indian War. Ebenezer Webster came back from the war to marry and take up a tract of land at the northern edge of settlement in New Hampshire. When his first wife died after giving him three children, he married a second wife who gave him five more. Daniel was the next to youngest of the five children of Ebenezer's second wife. He was frail as a child and given to reading. He took his turn with the work of the farm and would learn to boast of it later for political purposes, but his father always saw him as one who would get an education and make his living with his mind—as he wished he had done himself. Webster was thus technically a child of the frontier, but his experience of it was very different from that of Patrick Henry.

There were no slaves in New Hampshire to relieve the Websters of any burdens, nor did young Daniel have the freedom Patrick Henry did to wander in the woods and daydream beside a trout stream. He did, of course, swim and fish in the streams when there was time, and he showed how much energy and determination he possessed when he froze his feet one day by sledding downhill too long in the cold. The same intensity was displayed when a gamecock he kept was finally defeated and he walked twenty miles to get a replacement.[2] He did his share of the farmwork, but it held no interest for him. Child of the frontier or not, his instincts were those of a new generation of leaders who saw their future in commerce and industry. Webster would be their voice, and they could not have asked for a voice more eloquent.

But where did that voice come from? How did Webster become one of the greatest orators of American history? Certainly his reading, especially in the Bible, would have given him a feel for the cadences of the English language, but millions of others read the Bible without being able to form such sentences themselves. He memorized Isaac Watts's metrical version of the psalms and recited them to the teamsters as he took care of their horses, so he must have valued instinctively the sound of words, but others have memorized as much or more.[3] Physically, he grew from the thin and delicate child he had been to become an imposing, even "awe-inspiring" figure. "There was a grandeur in his form, an intelligence in his deep dark eye, a loftiness of his expansive brow . . . altogether beyond those of any other human being I ever saw," wrote Thomas Carlyle to a friend.[4] Some thought him too theatrical, but he could be rhetorical or conversational as the occasion required.[5] "No one ever looked the orator as he did," wrote one contemporary, "in form and feature how like a god . . . he appeared amid the smoke, the fire, the thunder of his eloquence, like Vulcan in his armory forging thoughts for the Gods."[6]

His first school was in a log cabin, but after that he went to the best schools his father could find for him.[7] He recalled later how on one hot July day in 1795 when he was working in the field with his father, another man came by and engaged his father in conversation. When the man moved on, Ebenezer sat him down and told him that the visitor was a member of Congress who journeyed to Philadelphia to represent them and was paid six dollars a day. "If I had had his early education," said Ebenezer Webster, "I should have been in Philadelphia in his place. I came near as it was. But I missed it, and I must work here. . . . I could not give your elder brothers the advantages of knowledge, but I can do something for you. Exert yourself, improve your opportunities, learn, learn, learn, and when I am gone, you will not need to go through the hardships I have undergone. . . ."[8] The next May, the boy rode with his father to what would become one of the greatest of the New England prep schools, Phillips Exeter Academy, then actually a year younger than the fourteen-year-old Daniel.

Then, perhaps, even more than now, most of the boys at the school had come from privileged backgrounds and Webster was painfully aware of the way his homespun clothes and unpolished manners made him stand out. Painfully embarrassed though he was, he worked hard and, in his own words, "made tolerable progress," but:

> . . . there was one thing I could not do. I could not make a declamation. I could not speak before the school. Many a piece did I commit to memory, and recite and rehearse, in my own room, over and over again; yet when the day came, when the school collected to hear declamations, when my name was called, and I saw all eyes turned to my seat, I could not raise myself from it. . . . When the occasion was over I went home and wept bitter tears of mortification."[9]

Perhaps it was that painful awareness of his lack of polish that held him back, but the man who would later make orations before thousands would have to overcome that initial overwhelming fear of standing before others.

Ebenezer Webster must have thought that an education could be acquired rather quickly, because only seven months after sending Daniel to Exeter, he brought him back to become a schoolteacher in Salisbury, New Hampshire. And, indeed, he must have learned enough to make an impression, because he was barely home again before a neighboring pastor convinced Ebenezer that the boy was meant for college and offered to provide the necessary preparation himself. So in February 1797, young Daniel climbed aboard a sleigh with his father and set off for nearby Boscawen, where he would study with Dr. Samuel Wood as one of over a hundred young men he had prepared for college, often at his own expense.

Immersed in the Greek and Latin classics, Webster again made rapid progress and within six months took his place at Dartmouth College in Hanover, New Hampshire. With 140 students, Dartmouth was one of the biggest colleges in the country, but set so deep in the forest that Daniel would have felt very much at home. Indeed, the local cows were so much a part of campus life that the students tired of scraping cow dung off their shoes and took occasion one night to chase the cows across the river into Vermont.[10]

Oddly parallel to the tales told about Patrick Henry's shiftless youth were tales told about Daniel Webster, that he had been a lazy and careless student. Perhaps they were told to magnify his later accomplishments by contrast, but Webster heard the stories and they enraged him. "I studied and read more than all the rest of my class," he said. It was true, however, that he did not need to spend the hours that others did because of his remarkable memory; he had the ability to read a twenty-page paper once and repeat it almost word for word. Nonetheless, his record in college was mixed: he was a leader in his fraternity, greatly respected by some, considered a bit pompous by others. He was changing rapidly from the awkward, tongue-tied country boy he had been. The records of the Hanover general store show that he purchased silk gloves and velvet trousers and went in debt to buy gin, brandy, and port. He had overcome his shyness enough to deliver a Fourth of July oration in Hanover. Nevertheless, even if he studied and read "more than all the rest of his class," he did not graduate at the top of his class. He was not chosen for the valedictory or salutatory addresses and indignantly turned down the offer of a third-place oration. He would be first or not participate.[11]

Graduating from Dartmouth, he went home again without a clear sense of direction. He taught school briefly, read law in a local office, lived for a while with his brother in Boston where, again, he read law, and finally, after his father's death in 1807, he set himself up as a lawyer in Portsmouth, New Hampshire, took a wife, and settled down. Perhaps of equal importance with these life-shaping events was his experience in the courts, where he was bested more than once by an older and wiser lawyer, Jeremiah Mason.

Mason seems to have been the quintessential small-town lawyer with a well-honed ability to convince the ordinary juror. He was the deadly enemy of pomposity and oratorical flourishes; it was said of him that "he relentlessly pricked all rhetorical bubbles, reducing them at once to . . . ignominious suds." He talked to the jurors, Webster wrote later, "in a plain conversational way, in short sentences, and using no word that was not level to the comprehension of the least educated man on the panel. This led me," he added, "to examine my own style, and I set about reforming it altogether."[12]

Reformed or not, Webster was building a reputation as an orator available on demand for the Fourth of July and similar occasions. Within five years, in 1813, he was elected to Congress, where his maiden speech drew spectators. Congressmen left their desks and moved forward so they could see his gestures as well as hear his words.[13] The War of 1812 was testing allegiances and political philosophies in new ways, as commercial concerns dominated the New England states and led to a Hartford Convention that objected to the war so strenuously that even secession was spoken of in some places. Webster was not at the Convention and never spoke of secession, but he did represent his region's interests and opposed the war at every turn. When state governors resisted sending their militias into the war, Webster protested that the federal government had no authority to order them under the Constitution. It was in December of his first year in Congress that he spoke on the subject in his first significant oration on a national stage. The great themes of liberty and union, grounded in the Constitution, were already present:

> Is this, Sir, consistent with the character of a free Government? Is this civil liberty? Is this the real character of our Constitution? No,

> Sir, indeed it is not. The Constitution is libeled, foully libeled. The people of this country have not established for themselves such a fabric of despotism. They have not purchased at a vast expense of their own treasure and their own blood a Magna Carta to be slaves. Where is it written in the Constitution, in what article or section is it contained, that you may take children from their parents, and parents from their children, and compel them to fight the battles of any war, in which the folly or the wickedness of Government may engage it? Under what concealment has this power lain hidden, which now for the first time comes forth, with a tremendous and baleful aspect, to trample down and destroy the dearest rights of personal liberty? Sir, I almost disdain to go to quotations and references to prove that such an abominable doctrine has no foundation in the Constitution of the country. It is enough to know that that instrument was intended as the basis of a free Government, and that the power contended for is incompatible with any notion of personal liberty. An attempt to maintain this doctrine upon the provisions of the Constitution is an exercise of perverse ingenuity to extract slavery from the substance of a free Government. It is an attempt to show, by proof and argument, that we ourselves are subjects of despotism, and that we have a right to chains and bondage, firmly secured to us and our children, by the provisions of our Government.[14]

As so often throughout his career, the Constitution and personal freedom were the issues that concerned him as they had concerned Patrick Henry, and here Webster shared Henry's concern that federal power might reduce the freedom of the individual. Henry had feared that the Constitution would be used to constrict such freedom, but Webster saw the Constitution as the guardian of freedom and suggested that the solution was for the states to interpose their authority between the federal power and their citizens.

> It will be the solemn duty of the State governments to protect their own authority over their own militia, and to interpose between their citizens and arbitrary power. These are among the objects for which the State governments exist, and their highest obligations bind them to the preservation of their own rights and the liberties of their people.[15]

Webster had no intention, he said, of dissolving the Union; it was the President and his party who threatened the Union by proposing measures destructive of everything that upheld it. Nearly forty years later, the shoe would be on the other foot when South Carolina believed the party in power was destroying the Union by adopting measures contrary to the interests of the South and moved to declare those measures null and void. That event would call forth Webster's most famous speech. In the meantime, he would complete two terms in the House before returning home to concentrate on his family and finances. Moving next to Boston, he immediately became involved in famous (and remunerative) cases, arguing often before the Supreme Court—where his work for Dartmouth College produced another long-remembered oration.

The issue in the Dartmouth College case was the right of the New Hampshire legislature to take control of the college, a private corporation. Webster argued that no such right existed under the Constitution. Perhaps as important as the legal arguments was Webster's emotional appeal, ending his argument with tears on his face as he told the justices,

> This, Sir, is my case! It is the case not merely of that humble institution, it is the case of every college in our Land! It is more! It is the case of every eleemosynary institution throughout our country—of all those great charities founded by the piety of our ancestors to alleviate human misery, and scatter blessings along the pathway of life! It is more! It is, in some sense, the case of every man among us who has property of which he may be stripped, for the question is simply this, "Shall our State Legislatures be allowed to take that which is not their own, to turn it from its original use, and apply it to such ends and purposes as they in their discretion shall see fit?"
>
> Sir, you may destroy this little institution; it is weak, it is in your hands! I know it is one of the lesser lights in the literary horizon of our country. You may put it out! But if you do so, you must carry through your work! You must extinguish, one after another, all those great lights of science which for more than a century have thrown their radiance over our land! It is, Sir, as I have said, a small college. And yet there are those who love it![16]

Choking back his tears (some say the Chief Justice brushed away a tear himself), Webster ended by comparing the college surrounded by enemies to Caesar surrounded by those who stabbed him to death and saying he would not want to be numbered with the assassins. The legal case had been made with arguments from English common law and other ancient precedents, as well as a careful analysis of the Constitution, but Webster's fame rested on his ability to add the emotional element to the dry logic of the law.[17] It was for those moments that the crowds waited when they gathered to hear him;

but the balance between law and liberty, the Constitution as bulwark of freedom or threat to individual liberty—that was the issue Webster addressed again and again in those critical early years in the development of the new country. And in the Dartmouth case, Webster would also find in the Constitution grounds to defend corporations against state regulation. The Supreme Court would much later find that corporations are "persons," and it was Webster who laid some of the foundation for that in his concern to give corporations the freedom they needed to thrive and prosper.[18] All this would require further thought and definition as the years passed and new issues arose. Webster himself would continue to work at that balance, and it would shape his destiny as well as his country's. Even as a private citizen, Webster was handling these critical issues. Inevitably he would be sent back to Washington, where the final decisions would have to be made.

Meanwhile, however, he kept his name before the public by speaking at a number of civic events. He had spoken at Independence Day celebrations while still at Dartmouth. In 1820 he was the featured speaker at the two hundredth anniversary of the arrival of the Puritans at Plymouth Rock; in 1825 he was the speaker at the fiftieth anniversary of Bunker Hill; and in 1826 he was chosen to be the chief speaker at a memorial event following the simultaneous deaths of John Adams and Thomas Jefferson. These were opportunities to burnish his reputation and to hold forth on some of the critical issues of the day. Here Webster moved clearly ahead of the first generation of leadership in his understanding of the economic dimension of freedom: freedom is not only a matter of restraint on government, but also of economic restraint. "Liberty," he said in later years,

> consists in restraint; that is to say, the liberty of each individual is in proportion to the restraint imposed on other individuals & public bodies who might otherwise have the power as well as the disposition to do him wrong.[19]

Webster is often thought of as a "conservative," and biographers write of his intimate relationship with the new generation of business leaders. Webster was constantly in debt, and business leaders raised thousands of dollars for him, seeing him as one who would protect their interests. But when Webster at Plymouth Rock laid out an understanding of democracy as based on property, he went far beyond a mere concern to protect the property of the wealthy: people, he said, will take an interest in the government only if it establishes and protects their property; but then property cannot all fall into a few hands, or those without property will have no stake in the government and will revolt. Government must find ways to maintain some balance and the broadest possible distribution of property, so that the largest number of citizens will have an interest in what the government does.

Here Webster was prophetic and speaking of issues that would become acute only toward the end of the century. When the distribution of wealth became grossly unfair in the 1890s, voters would, as Webster had foreseen, turn to candidates calling for a fairer social structure. The issue has risen again at the start of the twenty-first century: can a democracy survive if wealth flows more and more to the top one or two percent? Can there be freedom without equality? Webster thought there could not:

> In the nature of things, those who have not property, and see their neighbors possess much more than they think them to need, cannot be favorable to laws made for the protection of property. When this class becomes numerous, it grows clamorous. It looks on property as its prey and plunder, and is naturally ready, at all times, for violence and revolution.
>
> It would seem, then, to be the part of political wisdom to found government on property; and to establish such distribution of property, by the laws which regulate its transmission and alienation, as to interest the great majority of society in the support of the government. This is, I imagine, the true theory and the actual practice of our republican institutions. . . .[20]

The idea that we should "found government on property" may seem strange at first, a sort of Marxist or communist notion. But the point Webster is making deserves careful thought; in his analysis, the redistribution of property becomes a way to protect property and a conservative position. The problem will appear again as we read on and the American economy changes.

If it is remarkable to find a politician raising a matter like that on a ceremonial occasion, it is more remarkable to find that Webster pressed on to raise the issue of slavery. The Constitution (Article I, Section 9) prevented any legislation on the slave trade for twenty years; but as soon as that time expired, Congress did make the trade illegal. Nevertheless, ships for the slave trade continued to be built in most American ports and the trade continued. The southern economy was based on the slave trade, and New England mills increasingly depended on cotton from the South. Thus, for Webster to take a stand against the trade was not risk-free even in Boston, and to take that stand on a ceremonial occasion was evidence that Webster was acting out of a deep conviction. His statement was embellished as well with all the emotional language at his command:

> I deem it my duty on this occasion to suggest, that the land is not yet wholly free from the contamination of a traffic, at which every

> feeling of humanity must for ever revolt,—I mean the African slave-trade. . . . If there be, within the extent of our knowledge or influence, any participation in this traffic, let us pledge ourselves here, upon the rock of Plymouth, to extirpate and destroy it. It is not fit that the land of the Pilgrims should bear the shame longer. I hear the sound of the hammer, I see the smoke of the furnaces where manacles and fetters are still forged for human limbs. I see the visages of those who by stealth and at midnight labor in this work of hell, foul and dark, as may become the artificers of such instruments of misery and torture. Let that spot be purified, or let it cease to be of New England. Let it be purified, or let it be set aside from the Christian world; let it be put out of the circle of human sympathies and human regards, and let civilized man henceforth have no communion with it. . . .[21]

If the speech at Plymouth Rock was bold and prophetic, Webster was in another mood five years later when he was again the chief speaker at a patriotic event, the dedication of the monument commemorating the fiftieth anniversary of the Battle of Bunker Hill. This was purely an emotional occasion, and the language Webster used was designed purely to amplify emotions:

> We wish that this column, rising towards heaven among the pointed spires of so many temples dedicated to God, may contribute also to produce, in all minds, a pious feeling of dependence and gratitude. We wish, finally, that the last object to the sight of him who leaves his native shore, and the first to gladden his who revisits it, may be something which shall remind him of the liberty and the glory of his country. Let it rise! let it rise, till it meet the sun in his coming; let the earliest light of the morning gild it, and parting day linger and play on its summit.

But it was also an occasion to promote the "civic religion" that, in Webster's speeches, seemed sometimes to identify patriotism and Christianity:

> In the American Revolution, no man sought or wished for more than to defend and enjoy his own. None hoped for plunder or for spoil. Rapacity was unknown to it; the axe was not among the instruments of its accomplishment; and we all know that it could not have lived a single day under any well-founded imputation of possessing a tendency adverse to the Christian religion.

But that emphasis on patriotism and emotion were, of course, turned finally to the purpose of promoting Webster's vision of national unity:

> Let us cultivate a true spirit of union and harmony. In pursuing the great objects which our condition points out to us, let us act under a settled conviction, and an habitual feeling, that these twenty-four States are one country.[22]

Scarcely a year had gone by when Webster was called on once more to sum up the nation's feelings. John Adams and Thomas Jefferson, two chief architects of American independence, had died on the same day, July 4, 1826, exactly fifty years after the completion of the Declaration of Independence. That speech is interesting less for its content and impact than for the record we have of the care and work that Webster used in preparing the speech, first for delivery and afterwards for printing and distribution. He did not simply speak off the cuff and wait to see whether anyone would ask for copies; with this, as with most of his speeches, there was a careful plan designed to gain further influence for the speaker. Indeed, Webster went so far as to persuade Edward Everett, a younger politician-orator who would one day speak at Gettysburg and be eclipsed again, to put aside his own plans for a commemorative speech a few weeks earlier so that Webster would have the spotlight for himself. Then Webster consulted with a number of friends and sat down to review his own notes on Jefferson's writing of the Declaration of Independence and to study the letters Adams had written in the months before the Declaration of Independence was written. Friends like Thomas Pickering, Adams's Secretary of State, provided other materials that Webster was able to use. Businesses in Boston had closed for the day and Faneuil Hall was filled to overflowing. The governor was there and the President of Harvard, as well as John Quincy Adams, now President of the United States as his father had been before him.

Because there were two men being commemorated, the speech was constructed in such a way as to give "equal time" to both presidents. Adams was spoken of first in the introduction to the speech and then Jefferson; this was to be delivered in Boston, after all. In the body of the oration, there are four blocks of material alternately for each, and two for each in the closing peroration. The most remarkable feature of the speech was the so-called "ghost speech" in which Webster set out to let the founders speak for themselves. "Let us hear the firm-toned voices, of this band of patriots," he said, and then he quoted first John Hancock (another New Englander) and then Adams himself, beginning with the famous sentence spoken by Adams before he voted for independence: "Sink or swim, live or die, survive or perish, I give my hand and my heart to this vote." Webster went on to construct the speech he imagined Adams making, using blunt, bold statements more typical of Adams than Webster, and ending with the words "Independence now, and independence forever."

Webster told others later that when he finished that section of his speech, the paper under his pen was wet with tears. It was meant to awaken emotions, and, to do it, Webster had metaphorically brought back to life the great statesmen he had mourned at the beginning of his speech as "dead," "no more," and "lost." Suddenly that same lost founder was there in Boston again and speaking to his fellow citizens through the mouth of Daniel Webster.[23]

II

Webster was forty years old when he spoke at Bunker Hill, and he was recognized as the supreme orator in a country where John C. Calhoun of South Carolina and Henry Clay of Kentucky were renowned as well, but he was out of office and could not expect to play a part in shaping policy except in the Congress. It took only three years of residence in Massachusetts, however, before he was back in the House of Representatives to represent the people of his newly adopted state. The Massachusetts establishment, knowing that no one could represent them more effectively, arranged for his election to the Senate just four years later, in June 1827.* He had been there only two and a half years when he was provoked to make the speech that defined him for all time as the champion of American unity.

It was an economic issue that forced the political crisis. Jefferson, in particular, but many of the other founders also had envisioned America as a nation of farmers and hoped, in vain, that America would not build the teeming, smoke-filled cities they had seen in England and continental Europe. It seemed unlikely to them that the laboring poor of the growing European cities could play a role in a functioning democracy; but by his second term, even Jefferson had begun to see that the future lay with industry. Webster also had once believed that agriculture was more conducive to "individual respectability and happiness."[24] But New England with its abundant water power, to say nothing of its iron ore and forested hills for charcoal, was becoming America's industrial center, and the War of 1812 showed New England industrialists the value of freedom from English competition. The communities that had fought for free trade when England attempted to co-opt their commerce now began to see the value of some control.

---

* Under the Constitution, senators were to be elected by state legislatures so they would not be subject to popular pressures. Direct election to the Senate was created by the adoption of the Seventeenth Amendment to the Constitution in 1913.

Webster followed the concerns of his electors by shifting from support for free trade to support for tariffs. By 1814 he was arguing that "in the commerce of the country the Constitution had its growth, in the extinction of that commerce it will find its grave."[25] The tariff, he maintained, was justified not only by the need to protect America's young industries but also by the need to raise money for internal improvements such as harbors, canals, and roads. Help in maintaining American harbors would gain support from northern and eastern states, while roads and canals would help develop the West. Henry Clay called it "The American System." But Southern planters were hurt by the higher cost of manufactured goods and saw the tariffs as a benefit to the North and a loss to the South. When Congress passed a new tariff act in 1828 tailored to the interests of the northeastern and western states, South Carolina's spokesman in Congress, John C. Calhoun, argued that the state had the right to declare null and void an act which it judged contrary to its interests.

Here the power of the federal government was to be tested as never before. If South Carolina could be successful in its claim, the United States would be reduced to what it had been before the Constitution was adopted: a mere league of allied states, not a single country. Calhoun had been elected Vice-President in 1828 and so would preside at the Senate debates but would have no voice except through South Carolina's senior senator, Robert Hayne. When Hayne spoke to the Senate on the subject in January 1830, Webster responded briefly in a way that drew Hayne into a further defense, not only of the Southern position on the tariff but also on slavery. Webster then responded with a full-throated attack on every aspect of the South Carolina position in an oration that was memorized by generations of schoolboys. At issue was the very nature of the Constitution, which Hayne, like Patrick Henry, understood as an agreement among the states. Webster, on the other hand, argued that it was the creation of the people. Its first words were "We the people of the United States . . . do ordain and establish this Constitution." It was, Webster argued, as Lincoln would do at Gettysburg, "the people's government, the people's Constitution, made for the people, made by the people, and answerable to the people."* His closing paragraph remains memorable today:

> When my eyes shall be turned to behold for the last time the sun in heaven, may I not see him shining on the broken and dishonored fragments of a once glorious Union; on States dissevered, discordant, belligerent; on a land rent with civil feuds, or drenched, it may be, in fraternal blood! Let their last feeble and lingering glance rather behold the gorgeous ensign of the republic . . . not a stripe

* Lincoln certainly knew Webster's speech and may well have memorized it.

> erased or polluted, nor a single star obscured, bearing for its motto, no such miserable interrogatory as "What is all this worth?" nor those other words of delusion and folly, "Liberty first and Union afterwards"; but everywhere, spread all over in characters of living light, blazing on all its ample folds, as they float over the sea and over the land, and in every wind under the whole heavens, that other sentiment, dear to every true American heart. . . .

Taking his Adams-Jefferson peroration one step further, he ended with the cry of "—Liberty and Union, now and for ever, one and inseparable!"[26]

The speech, made from twelve pages of notes, took several hours to deliver over the course of two days. A stenographer took it down in shorthand and transcribed it, after which Webster edited it carefully, revising and polishing the text as he did with most of his published speeches. The final phrase, for example, had been delivered as "Union and Liberty"; but in published form, and as it was recited by generations of schoolboys, it was "Liberty and Union." Union, of course, was the point of the speech and therefore first in Webster's mind as he delivered the speech; but with time to consider, he undoubtedly realized that "Liberty" carried more emotional weight and must be given priority. It was well over a month before the published form was available. It was published in three installments in a national magazine and in pamphlet form sold over sixty thousand copies in the next few months. Thousands more were sold in unauthorized versions. Webster was deluged with honors and requests for speeches. Even Hayne said later that Webster had proven himself to be the greatest orator of all time.[27]

"Liberty and Union"; yes, but the issue could hardly be resolved by a slogan. Patrick Henry approved of union (with certain limits) and would defend liberty to his death, but he and Daniel Webster meant different things by union and would not have defined liberty in the same way. Both were conservative by instinct, but the circumstances facing Webster's age were radically different from those confronting Henry's. As a result, they took radically different stands in relation to the Constitution, the power of the federal government, and the very nature of freedom. For Henry, freedom was a very personal matter threatened by the Constitution and the federal government, while Webster saw it in terms of the personal security provided by an orderly and limited government. As the nation continued to change, the definition of freedom would change and expand with it.

Almost simultaneously, a second debate was raging concerning another aspect of the Constitution: the role of the executive. Alexander Hamilton had created a national banking system, with the United States Bank chartered by the Congress. That bank governed the money supply. Nicholas Biddle, the director of the U.S. Bank, was a skillful politician and had built a solid foundation of support in Congress. He had called on Webster to defend the Bank before the Supreme Court in 1819 and sent him regular "retainer" fees. Later, he made him a director of the Bank.

Andrew Jackson had come to the presidency in 1828 with a deep-seated distrust of the banking system and a determination to break it up and allow states to charter their own banks; but every time he asked Congress to act, he was defeated by substantial majorities. The economic aspect of this debate is too complex to discuss here; what matters is that, although the Congress defeated him at every turn, Jackson managed to win the fight by simply ordering the Secretary of the Treasury to withdraw the government's money from the Bank. When the Secretary of the Treasury refused, Jackson replaced him. When the Congress attempted to re-charter the Bank, Jackson vetoed the bill. Webster was outraged and told the Senate why:

> If these opinions of the President be maintained, there is an end of all law and all judicial authority. Statutes are but recommendations, judgments no more than opinions. Both are equally destitute of binding force. Such a universal power as is now claimed for him, a power of judging over the laws and over the decisions of the judiciary, is nothing else but pure despotism. If conceded to him, it makes him at once what Louis the Fourteenth proclaimed himself to be when he said, "I am the State."[28]

In effect, Webster was claiming that Patrick Henry's worst fears about the power of an over-reaching executive had come to pass.

III

No one could make such speeches as Webster had made without being considered for—and considering himself for—nomination for the presidency. The difficulty was that Webster's greatest speeches were speeches on great patriotic occasions when his goal was to urge Americans to rise above partisanship, to remember the common heritage that unites us so that, although he was cheered by all, it was hard for any to be sure he would support their particular issues. Although Webster grew up as a member of the Federalist Party, the first American political party and the party of Alexander Hamilton and John Adams, that party had been weakened by the election of Thomas Jefferson and had faded into irrelevance after the War of 1812. So Webster became a man without a party.

The Whig Party that eventually replaced the Federalists was torn between its northern and southern wings in factions that came to be called the "conscience Whigs" and the "cotton Whigs." Webster opposed slavery but believed the South had a right under the Constitution to its "peculiar institution"; as a result, the southern wing of the party was never comfortable with Webster and the more radical abolitionists of the North never supported him. As a man whose guiding star was the Constitution and national unity, Webster found himself admired by all but trusted by none. He thought often of organizing a new party that would stand for the Constitution and unity but somehow it never quite happened.

In every election after his Bunker Hill speech and election to the Senate, from 1836 until 1852, Webster was a potential candidate, but only in 1836 did he win votes in the electoral college. Martin Van Buren, the Democrat, won a clear majority in the Electoral College in that election, while the Whigs managed to divide the remainder of the electoral vote among four candidates. Webster won only the votes of Massachusetts and finished fourth in a field of five.

Webster was a great orator, but he was not a natural campaigner. He had grown up on a farm, but he had left it as soon as he could for the world of lawyers and bankers. As a result, although he bought a farm himself and loved to visit it, he sounded somehow artificial when he tried to speak to farmers. "You far surpass in fertility of soil and in the widespread and highly cultivated fields, the smiling villages and busy towns," he told an audience of farmers in Wisconsin; "you will reap a rich reward for your investment and industry."[29] One biographer writes that Webster was "almost embarrassing in insisting on his own rusticity."[30] He did improve as a campaigner over the years, but his natural environment was the ceremonial occasion where he could hold up the flag and Constitution, or the courtroom and Senate Chamber where his encyclopedic memory and ability to argue specific, concrete issues with other experts was most effective. His rebuttal of Hayne is remembered for the eloquent conclusion; but before that, he had dealt with the specifics of constitutional law and legal precedent for hours. He had demolished his opponent's case first, and only then appealed for unity.

Ironically, Webster would have become President on two occasions if he had been willing to accept his party's nomination for Vice-President. In the sectional rivalries that increasingly divided the country North and South, the Whigs quite naturally looked for a candidate not strongly identified with either side. The two candidates who won for them were both generals who had won fame as soldiers and had no strong identification with a political party. William Henry Harrison, the Whig candidate elected in 1836, had won fame for a victory over Indian tribes in the Battle of Tippecanoe in 1812. He then served briefly in the House and Senate before retiring to his farm in Ohio. He was sixty-eight years old when he was elected President. Webster would have made an excellent vice-presidential candidate but declined the offer. Less than a month after his inauguration, Harrison was dead and John Tyler of Virginia was President. Tyler had been nominated to balance the ticket with a representative of the South but, although he had resigned from the Democratic Party in protest against the policies of Andrew Jackson and Martin Van Buren, his actions quickly alienated the authentic Whigs in his cabinet and most of them resigned. Had Webster been willing to accept second place on the ticket, he would have been President.

Twelve years later, in 1848, the Whigs turned again to a retired general, Zachary Taylor, who, like Harrison, had won fame first in the War of 1812 and later in actions against Native American tribes. His chief claim to fame, however, was his victory over Mexican troops in the battles of Palo Alto and Monterrey. Reluctant though he was to run for political office, the Whigs persuaded him to do so[31] and turned to Daniel Webster as, again, the obvious man to balance the ticket. Webster, however, saw the vice-presidency—as many others have done—as a dead end and is said to have responded that "I do not propose to be buried until I am really dead and in my coffin."[32] So, when Taylor died after sixteen months in office, it was a disciple of Webster's, Millard Fillmore of New York, who became President instead.

Although he was still working to be nominated one more time only months before his death in 1852, Webster never became President, but perhaps he accomplished more in the last twenty-five years of his life as a Senator and Secretary of State than he could have done in one or two terms as President. Senators have often served also as Secretary of State, but only Webster went twice from the Senate to the State Department. His familiarity with both arms of government undoubtedly made him more effective in both places. The State Department was also an appropriate position for someone of Webster's fundamentally cautious and moderate disposition.

Webster first served as Secretary of State under President Harrison, whose Vice-President he could have been. As one of the two most prominent leaders of the Whig party, Webster was an obvious choice and, in spite of their radically different backgrounds, he got along well with the old Indian-fighter. They met together almost every day and spent long hours in consultation. Ironically, it was in the area of Webster's greatest expertise that Harrison failed to take his advice—and may have died as a result. Webster advised him to shorten his inaugural address significantly but Harrison delivered it uncut. On a cold and rainy March day, he took an hour and a quarter to give the longest inaugural address ever made and then participated in the inaugural parade. The next day he had a cold that developed into pneumonia and he died a month later.[33]

Senator Henry Clay of Kentucky was the other prominent Whig leader, and it had been assumed that he and Webster would be the powers behind the throne of the elderly general. Webster's supporters assumed that Webster, in the President's Cabinet, would, in fact, be the real leader, but Clay's admirers saw it differently. If Clay and Webster were to go duck hunting together, said Judge Rowan of Kentucky, "Mr. Clay would expect Mr. Webster to assume the office of spaniel, to bring out the birds, and the latter would not perceive that there was any degradation in his assumption of such an office."[34]

All these calculations were changed, however, when John Tyler, whose expected function had been simply to balance the ticket, suddenly became president. Although he asked Harrison's Cabinet choices to stay on, almost all quickly found themselves unable to do so and resigned. Webster hung on the longest, hoping to save something from the first Whig administration, but after two years even he was unable to support the President. He resigned on May 8, 1843.[35]

During his two years in office, however, Webster was able to record major accomplishments, not least to avoid still another war with the British. Such a war was a serious possibility for a number of reasons. The most prominent issue was the American border with Canada. The negotiations at the end of the Revolution had left the location of a long stretch of that border unresolved. As a result, there were thousands of square miles of territory that the British believed were part of the colony of New Brunswick but Americans thought were part of the State of Maine. The area has never been thickly populated, but some population growth and competing lumber interests in the upper Saint John River valley created the need for a definite boundary. During the winter of 1838–1839, the situation deteriorated to the point that both Maine and New Brunswick had called out their militias. The "Aroostook War" (sometimes called the "Pork and Beans War") never came to the shedding of blood, but the tension was very real, and sensible heads were needed to resolve the matter.

Unfortunately, the situation was complicated by a festering incident involving Canadian rebels who had been attempting to create a Canadian republic and who were being supplied by the *Caroline*, an American steamboat. A loyalist Canadian force seized the steamboat, killed at least one member of its crew, and sent it ablaze over Niagara Falls. One of the loyalists, a man named McLeod, was foolish enough to brag about his exploits while on the American side of the border and was therefore arrested, charged with murder, and jailed. Webster had been in England as the matter was unfolding and had been assured on good authority that the British were prepared to go to war over the matter. President Van Buren was prepared to accommodate the British; but the new Whig governor of New York, William Seward, insisted on a trial for McLeod. Webster sent a United States attorney to work for McLeod and dispatched General Winfield Scott and a small force of soldiers to prevent mob action of any sort. Fortunately, it was proven that McLeod had lied, and he was therefore acquitted and returned to Canada under armed guard; but American feelings were still bruised, and they insisted that the British owed them at least an apology and the cost of the *Caroline*.[36]

Webster saw his primary task as the resolution of the border dispute, and he had the necessary skills for the task. He might have been at his best in front of a large audience, but he was a lawyer who often argued cases before the Supreme Court and he had spent a good deal of his political life trying to find mutually acceptable positions between hostile factions and individuals. He also had no innate hostility toward the British; he had just secured appointment to the Court of St. James for one of his closest supporters. The British, willing to seek a peaceful solution, dispatched Lord Ashburton, who, though he was the Foreign Secretary, was not a professional diplomat. He was, however, a man of independent wealth, married to an American, and an acquaintance of Webster's. He rented a mansion near Webster's home in Washington, and the two men spent considerable time in the spring and summer of 1842 enjoying dinners and receptions at which personal diplomacy could lay the groundwork for a settlement.

All of that seemed hopeful, but there were still further complications. Not only did the Americans feel that apologies were in order for the *Caroline* incident, but there was also the matter of an American-owned slave ship, the *Creole*. The slaves on the ship had mutinied, taken over the ship, and sailed it into Nassau in the Bahamas. Since the British had outlawed slavery, they released the 128 slaves, outraging American slave owners who wanted their "property" returned. Beyond that, the British wanted American help in suppressing the slave trade off the coast of Africa.

All this was still further complicated by the fact that Ashburton had to satisfy a home office that tended to see things in terms of the letter of the law and that Webster had to satisfy a deputation of commissioners from New Hampshire and Maine who had not forgotten the War of 1812. When his home office pressed for more than he thought could be done, Ashburton reminded his Prime Minister that a negotiation required two parties and that "our other party in this case is a jealous, arrogant, democratic body." Webster, for his part, made good use of two old maps that had been discovered in various archives, one supportive of the American claims which he showed the British, and one supportive of British claims which he showed the Senate.[37]

When the British learned what had happened and charged Webster with being less than honest, Ashburton consulted experts as to whether Webster "was bound in honour to damage his own case by telling all" and found no clear consensus. He himself thought that Webster could not be reproached in the matter. In any event, the negotiators were able to agree on a line that gave the Americans some two-thirds of the disputed area, sufficient to make Americans feel they had won and to allow the British to feel they had made a necessary concession in the cause of peace. In the case of the *Caroline*, the British apologized "for the necessity of the act."[38] As for the *Creole*, Ashburton had to make the home office understand how sensitive the Southern states were on the subject and how important some conciliatory language was. Grudgingly, the British agreed that they would not in the future receive an American slave ship taken over by mutineers, though they would keep the captives from the *Creole*.

It was further agreed that the Americans would work with the British in patrolling the coasts of Africa—though succeeding administrations did nothing to carry out that provision. For his part, Webster hired a journalist to draw on a secret fund to persuade the Maine press that the treaty was beneficial to that State. He knew when to rely on oratory and when to use other methods of persuasion. Having worked all this out, the successful negotiators signed what is known as the Webster-Ashburton Treaty, and the Senate ratified it by a substantial majority. President Tyler, happy to have a significant accomplishment to point to, blessed the "peacemakers," and newspapers throughout the country hailed Webster as not only "Defender of the Union" but also "Defender of the Peace."[39]

Treaties, however, are seldom a matter of concern in local politics, and Webster was pressed again by his New England supporters to leave the administration. He held off until the spring of 1843 before recognizing that Tyler's interest in annexing Texas was incompatible with his principles, and so resigned and accepted President Tyler's thanks for his accomplishments.

Even out of office, Webster might have been a logical candidate for vice-president the next year when the Whigs nominated Henry Clay for president. Clay, however, preferred Theodore Freylinghuysen of New Jersey, a man who had served one term in the Senate nine years earlier and was best known for a speech he had made in 1830 opposing Jackson's relocation of the Seminole Indians. Webster dutifully campaigned for the ticket, though he had more to say against James K. Polk, the Democratic candidate, than in support of Clay: "Did any of you ever know that there was such a man as James K. Polk?" he asked one audience.[40]

But Polk won the election, and it was clear where he wanted to take the country. One important campaign slogan was "Fifty-four forty or fight!" Polk was an expansionist and wanted to claim not only Texas but also the Oregon territory in the northwest up to parallel 54°40'. Webster saw only trouble in a policy which would, among other things, threaten the improved relationship with England that he and Ashburton had worked to create. He and Ashburton had talked about Oregon and decided there was no need to worry about it; now it was a campaign issue. As it turned out, Polk had no real interest in the northern border and easily agreed to the present border at the 49th parallel, hundreds of miles south of the 54th.

Webster went back to his farm in Massachusetts, contemplated his cattle, sailed on Cape Cod Bay, and gave an occasional speech. He also built up his legal practice so that when deputations came to ask him about returning to the Senate, he asked them whether they would replace his $15,000 annual income. So funds were raised and Webster returned to Washington for five more years.

There were, of course, many issues to be dealt with in those years, and Webster, inevitably, was in the midst of them. Most significantly for Webster and his supporters there were battles over tariffs, but looming ominously on the horizon was the issue that had separated Webster from John Tyler's Cabinet: the status of Texas and the possibility of war with Mexico. As one of the nation's most prominent men, Webster could never avoid such subjects, as he had acknowledged in a speech in New York City in 1837: "I should feel myself wanting in candor," he said, "if I did not express my opinion; since all must suppose that, on such a question, it is impossible that I should be without some opinion." Indeed, Webster did have an opinion and it was, in brief, that the United States had no need for additional territory and especially no need for a policy that would extend slavery. He had spoken out on that topic in that same New York speech at a gathering of the Whig Party:

> Gentlemen, we all see that, by whomsoever possessed, Texas is likely to be a slave-holding country; and I frankly avow my entire unwillingness to do anything that shall extend the slavery of the African race on this continent, or add other slave-holding States to the Union. When I say that I regard slavery in itself as a great moral, social, and political evil, I only use language which has been adopted by distinguished men, themselves citizens of slave-holding States. I shall do nothing, therefore, to favor or encourage its further extension. We have slavery already amongst us. The Constitution found it in the Union; it recognized it, and gave it solemn guaranties. To the full extent of these guaranties we are all bound, in honor, in justice, and by the Constitution. All the stipulations contained in the Constitution in favor of the slave-holding States which are already in the Union ought to be fulfilled, and, so far as depends on me, shall be fulfilled, in the fulness of their spirit and to the exactness of their letter. Slavery, as it exists in the States, is beyond the reach of Congress. It is a concern of the

> States themselves; they have never submitted it to Congress, and Congress has no rightful power over it. I shall concur, therefore, in no act, no measure, no menace, no indication of purpose, which shall interfere or threaten to interfere with the exclusive authority of the several States over the subject of slavery as it exists within their respective limits. All this appears to me to be matter of plain and imperative duty.[41]

So there it was: allegiance to the Constitution was the rock on which Webster would always stand, for better or worse. It irritated more and more of his New England constituents, but Webster's commitment was to Union above all. Abolitionists like William Lloyd Garrison would rather divide the country than be part of a nation in which slavery existed. But Webster stood for Union, the Union and the Constitution as the foundations of American liberty. Increasingly, it cost him support, but he would not change his principles.

Webster was concerned also that the acquisition of new territory was not envisioned in the Constitution. The Louisiana Purchase, he felt, might have been justified as necessary to allow free access to the Mississippi and Gulf, but there was no excuse for adding the useless territories of Texas and, especially, of New Mexico and California which, he was sure, could never support any significant population. He quoted travelers who reported that New Mexico (which then included Arizona) "is poor, sterile, sandy, and barren, with not a single tree of any size or value on our whole route. . . . For any useful or agricultural purpose, the country is not worth a 'sous.'"

And as for the population:

> Liars by nature, they are treacherous and faithless to their friends, cowardly and cringing to their enemies; cruel, as all cowards are, they unite savage ferocity with their want of animal courage. . . . These, Sir, are soon to be our beloved countrymen! . . . Have they any notion of our institutions, or of any free institutions? Have they any notion of popular government? Not the slightest! Not the slightest on earth!

But quite apart from that, Webster saw no basis in the Constitution for incorporating new territory:

> I thought there must be some limit to the extent of our territories, and that I wished this country should exhibit to the world the example of a powerful republic, without greediness and hunger of empire. And I added, that while I held, with as much faithfulness

> as any citizen of the country, to all the original arrangements and compromises of the Constitution under which we live, I never could, and I never should, bring myself to be in favor of the admission of any States into the Union as slave-holding States; and I might have added, any States at all, to be formed out of territories not now belonging to us.

These new states, Webster thought, would have two Senators but only one representative, and that would be a massive distortion of the shape of the government:

> Can any thing occur to disfigure and derange the form of government under which we live more signally than that? . . . The Senate, augmented by these new Senators coming from States where there are few people, becomes an odious oligarchy. It holds power without any adequate constituency. Sir, it is but "borough-mongering" upon a large scale. I hold it to be enormous, flagrant, an outrage upon all the principles of popular republican government, and on the elementary provisions of the Constitution under which we live, and which we have sworn to support.[42]

Webster would lose that fight. The country, inevitably, united behind its troops as they fought their way across Mexico, and the story of heroic defenders of the Alamo also aroused patriotic feelings. In a contest between the flag and the Constitution, the flag would always win. But the Senate was the place where these decisions were made, and Webster needed to be a part of it.

In 1848 he saw his party turn again to a soldier rather than a politician and nominate Zachary Taylor, a hero of the Mexican War. Webster had traveled in the South to look for support for another presidential bid and attempted to find language inoffensive to slave owners but, as one biographer puts it: "to attempt to walk with equanimity through the cotton fields in South Carolina while still claiming the united loyalty of Massachusetts Whigs had become impossible. He might as well have attempted to walk on water."[43]

With a president of his own party whom he could not support, Webster turned again to his law practice as a source of income and a useful adjunct to his work in the Senate. The Mexican War had resulted in a spate of claims against the government for war damages. The Supreme Court was the place where these claims needed to be adjudicated, and the Court held its sessions in those days in a room underneath the Senate chamber so Webster could combine the two roles without undue hardship. "I am overwhelmed with labor," he wrote in early 1849, "obliged to study from 5 to eleven AM, to be in court from eleven to three; and all the rest of the day in the senate till ten o'clock."[44]

Perhaps because he was "overwhelmed," he took no leadership in the primary work the Senate was engaged in that year: one further attempt to find a compromise between North and South that would preserve the Union. The proposal was brought forward instead by Henry Clay, of course, "the Great Compromiser," representing the border state of Kentucky, and Stephen A. Douglas, the young Senator from Illinois known as the "Little Giant," who hoped such an achievement would open a door for him to the presidency. The need for compromise was greater than ever. Southern politicians had called for a convention to meet in Knoxville, to unite themselves to demand their rights or to secede. Henry Clay said the "feeling for disunion was stronger than I supposed it could be." Webster at first dismissed it as "agitation that would eventually subside," saying "The Union is not in danger. . . . No bones will be broken."[45] He thought slavery would "dissolve" in the course of time. His constituents, however, were not willing to wait for the millennium; the pressure from the abolitionists was stronger every year and the Southern leaders were tired of hearing them. Clay, with a better sense of the national mood, was working on a set of proposals, which he spread out for Webster to look at in January 1850. Webster thought they made good sense and agreed to support them.[46] One of the provisions of the 1850 Compromise was that ordinary citizens were required to assist in the arrest of fugitive slaves or be fined. Even free Northern blacks would be susceptible to arrest and enslavement, since there were few legal procedures to protect them.

As discussion of Clay's proposals began and tensions rose, it became obvious to Webster that the South was very serious about leaving and that he needed to use whatever influence and powers of persuasion he had to preserve the Union. Remembering the impact of his reply to Hayne twenty years earlier, the Senate and the public waited nervously for Webster to speak. When it was announced that he would speak on March 7, crowds gathered to hear him and filled the Senate chamber to the point that many of the Senators, who had offered their seats to the ladies, were unable to find a place to sit themselves. "Mr. President," Webster began,

> I wish to speak to-day, not as a Massachusetts man, nor as a Northern man, but as an American, and a member of the Senate of the United States. . . . It is not to be denied that we live in the midst of strong agitations, and are surrounded by very considerable dangers to our institutions and government. The imprisoned winds are let loose. The East, the North, and the stormy South combine to throw the whole sea into commotion, to toss its billows

> to the skies, and disclose its profoundest depths. I do not affect to regard myself, Mr. President, as holding, or as fit to hold, the helm in this combat with the political elements; but I have a duty to perform, and I mean to perform it with fidelity, not without a sense of existing dangers, but not without hope. I have a part to act, not for my own security or safety, for I am looking out for no fragment upon which to float away from the wreck, if wreck there must be, but for the good of the whole, and the preservation of all; and there is that which will keep me to my duty during this struggle, whether the sun and the stars shall appear, or shall not appear, for many days. I speak to-day for the preservation of the Union. Hear me for my cause.

They listened with care, and with hope that Webster would offer a way through the crisis. His own party, the Northern Whigs, found themselves, however, not only startled but "angered and revolted" by what he said. On the issue of fugitive slaves, Webster told them, "the South, in my judgment, is right, and the North is wrong." The Constitution, he told them, was clear and must be obeyed. He went on to say that the South was also wrong in some respects: they had gone from disliking slavery to cherishing it and seeking to extend it, they had compared the lot of slaves favorably to that of the free working men of the North, and they had imprisoned free blacks on the crews of ships that came into Southern ports. Most of all, he was troubled by talk of secession:

> I hear with distress and anguish the word "secession," especially when it falls from the lips of those who are patriotic, and known to the country, and known all over the world, for their political services. Secession! Peaceable secession! Sir, your eyes and mine are never destined to see that miracle. The dismemberment of this vast country without convulsion! The breaking up of the fountains of the great deep without ruffling the surface! Who is so foolish, I beg everybody's pardon, as to expect to see any such thing? Sir, he who sees these States, now revolving in harmony around a common centre, and expects to see them quit their places and fly off without convulsion, may look the next hour to see the heavenly bodies rush from their spheres, and jostle against each other in the realms of space, without causing the wreck of the universe. There can be no such thing as a peaceable secession. Peaceable secession is an utter impossibility. Is the great Constitution under which we live, covering this whole country,—is it to be thawed and melted away by secession, as the snows on the mountain melt under the influence

> of a vernal sun, disappear almost unobserved, and run off? No, Sir! No, Sir! I will not state what might produce the disruption of the Union; but, Sir, I see as plainly as I see the sun in heaven what that disruption itself must produce; I see that it must produce war, and such a war as I will not describe. . . .

He had more to say on that subject, and he had never been more eloquent:

> Peaceable secession! Peaceable secession! The concurrent agreement of all the members of this great republic to separate! A voluntary separation, with alimony on one side and on the other. Why, what would be the result? Where is the line to be drawn? What States are to secede? What is to remain American? What am I to be? An American no longer? Am I to become a sectional man, a local man, a separatist, with no country in common with the gentlemen who sit around me here, or who fill the other house of Congress? Heaven forbid! Where is the flag of the republic to remain? Where is the eagle still to tower? or is he to cower, and shrink, and fall to the ground? Why, Sir, our ancestors, our fathers and our grandfathers, those of them that are yet living amongst us with prolonged lives, would rebuke and reproach us; and our children and our grandchildren would cry out shame upon us, if we of this generation should dishonor these ensigns of the power of the government and the harmony of that Union which is every day felt among us with so much joy and gratitude.

He tried to end on a positive note:

> . . . instead of dwelling in those caverns of darkness, instead of groping with those ideas so full of all that is horrid and horrible, let us come out into the light of day; let us enjoy the fresh air of Liberty and Union; let us cherish those hopes which belong to us; let us devote ourselves to those great objects that are fit for our consideration and our action; let us raise our conceptions to the magnitude and the importance of the duties that devolve upon us; let our comprehension be as broad as the country for which we act, our aspirations as high as its certain destiny; let us not be pygmies in a case that calls for men.[47]

It was all very logical to Webster: the Constitution must be preserved because the freedom and prosperity of the nation depended on it. He had been in the

South and he knew their representatives well. He saw the bloodshed that would flow from a failure to find and enforce a compromise. He spoke for over three hours from his notes. The edited version ran to forty-two pages. But his hearers were no longer much moved by rhetoric. The struggle had been going on too long, and there were not many who were still really listening. Webster did his part by speaking wherever he could on the subject.

At Buffalo on the twenty-second of May, 1851, he told them how deeply committed he was to the words he had spoken:

> I felt that I had a duty to perform to my country, to my own reputation; for I flattered myself that a service of forty years had given me some character, on which I had a right to repose for my justification in the performance of a duty attended with some degree of local unpopularity. I thought it was my duty to pursue this course, and I did not care what was to be the consequence. And, Gentlemen, allow me to say here to-day, that if the fate of John Rogers had stared me in the face,* if I had seen the stake, if I had heard the fagots already crackling, by the blessing of Almighty God I would have gone on and discharged the duty which I thought my country called upon me to perform.[48]

It might have seemed an opportunity to step away from the battle when the old soldier, Zachary Taylor, died and Millard Fillmore became President and asked Webster to leave the Senate and become Secretary of State, but the Secretary of State in those days was responsible for domestic affairs as well as foreign. His last words to the Senate were "If we mean to live together, common prudence should teach us to treat each other with respect."[49]

But there were many on both sides who no longer did mean to live together, and Webster saw that there were all too many even in Massachusetts who would no longer follow his lead. As Secretary of State, however, he had other ways to arouse patriotic fervor. A revolution in Hungary had failed, but its hero, Lajos Kossuth, had won widespread support in England and America. An American emissary who was dispatched to study the situation advised that America should not become involved, but Webster saw an opportunity to burnish his credentials as an advocate for freedom and sent an American naval vessel to bring Kossuth to America, where he was saluted by cannons in New York Harbor and toasted at dinners attended by the leaders of the New York community. Professionals in the State Department were appalled by

---

* John Rogers was the first martyr in Queen Mary's reign and was burned at Smithfield on February 14, 1554.

this involvement in the internal affairs of the Austrian Empire, but Webster toasted Kossuth in person when he came to Washington: "Let it be everywhere proclaimed what we of this great republic think of the principle of human liberty, and of that oppression which we abhor." It was easier, as it often is, to be clear about that at a distance when no direct involvement is possible. It was also at Webster's initiative that Commodore Perry was sent to open Japan to Western trade and other agents were sent to explore the possibility of creating a canal across Central America. For all his concern for domestic politics, he was deeply involved in enhancing America's status abroad. He negotiated a trade agreement with Costa Rica and ended a hostile relationship with Venezuela.[50]

But the rising tide of abolitionist sentiment in the North was only strengthened whenever Webster attempted in his new role not only to advocate the return of fugitive slaves but also to enforce the law. He was scorned in Boston, and John Greenleaf Whittier, once an admirer, spoke for many in writing:

> . . . from those great eyes
> The soul has fled:
> When faith is lost, when honor dies
> The man is dead.[51]

Webster was always a politician. Perhaps he had calculated the cost in a deliberate attempt to build the coalition he had often dreamed of, one that would rise above party and section to unite Americans in support of the Constitution. One biographer writes of Webster's "lack of moral vision,"[52] but perhaps it would be fairer to try to understand a *different* moral vision, one that balanced the horrors of slavery with the horrors of civil war and believed that slavery could not last forever and that the war could be avoided. Another biographer sees the issue as one of politics, that Webster had become a captive of the legislative process with its constant need for compromise: "Webster became convinced that successful legislation was more important than ideological posturing or moralizing."[53] That is a viewpoint that has sometimes been tested in Congress to the breaking point.

For well over a year, Webster did his best to move the country toward his vision of a constitutional democracy founded in compromise. In 1851, while campaigning with Millard Fillmore in upstate New York, he spoke about the dangers of a "house divided." Through the winter of 1851–1852, as the nominating conventions of 1852 neared, he was still attending rallies in Boston and New York and elsewhere to keep his name before the party while still attending to his work as Secretary of State. Then in May, a carriage he was riding in fell apart and he was thrown to the ground, striking his head on the road. He never fully recovered. When he attempted to speak to a rally at Boston's

Faneuil Hall, he was rambling and often incoherent. That summer, he spent more time than usual at his farm near Boston; and when he returned there in early September, it was to stay. He refused to support General Winfield Scott, the Whig candidate, or to let his own name be placed on an independent ticket. He died at his farm in the early morning hours of October 24, 1852.

Ralph Waldo Emerson said of him: "He was a statesman and not the semblance of one, but Alas! He was the victim of his ambition."[54] No politician can be free of personal ambition, but Webster was ambitious also to help build a country firmly grounded on the Constitution. Two years before he died, he told the Senate:

> I shall stand by the Union . . . with absolute disregard of personal consequences. What are personal consequences . . . in comparison with the good or evil which may befall a great country in a crisis like this? . . . Let the consequences be what they will. . . . No man can suffer too much, and no man can fall too soon, if he suffer or if he fall in defense of the liberties and constitution of his country.[55]

No American has done more toward reaching that goal.

THREE
THE ABOLITIONISTS

James W. C. Pennington
c. 1807–1870

GOD OF LIBERTY, SAVE US FROM THIS CLAUSE

I

On Thursday, October 28, 1828, the Hagerstown, Maryland *Torch Light & Public Advertiser* ran an ad offering a $200 reward for James Pembroke, a fugitive slave who had disappeared from a plantation belonging to Frisby Tilghman. As Tilghman described the fugitive, he was "very black and clumsily made . . . has a down look and mumbles. . . ."[1]

Two hundred dollars was a lot more than was offered in any other ad in the paper that year. Tilghman obviously thought well of his slave and wanted him back—even if he mumbled. But Pembroke, after a series of misadventures, had finally made his way to Pennsylvania and been taken in by a Quaker named William Wright. Wright learned quickly that Pembroke was illiterate, and offered to pay him and teach him to read and write in exchange for his help around the farm. He also suggested a new name, since "Pembroke" was being advertised as a fugitive, so Pembroke took a name famous in Quaker history and became James Pennington. He added two middle names: "William" in honor of William Wright and "Charles" for reasons unknown.

The arrangement went well for some months, but Pennington became increasingly uncomfortable with the frequent appearance of slave hunters coming past a house so near the border. Reluctantly, Wright sent him on to another Quaker family near Philadelphia. There Pennington was often left in charge when his hosts went off on missions. After the farmwork was done, he would sometimes go into the barn and try to make a speech. It frustrated him that he had learned so little and had so little to say.[2] But why was he trying to make a speech in the first place? A traveling evangelist had come by the plantation once but had been threatened with jail if he came back again, so Pennington had not heard much preaching. He had never even heard of Jesus when he fled the plantation, and Quakers are not preachers. But Pennington wanted to become a speaker, and eventually he would become one of the most eloquent black voices demanding freedom for his people.

Many years later, a friend wrote an appreciation of Pennington as a speaker:

> . . . as he proceeded, his voice deepened and mellowed into indescribable sublimity, till at last theme and speaker alone retained place in our thoughts; and like the setting summer's sun, they ended, shedding a golden hue over all.[3]

But it would require a long journey to reach that point.

From that second Quaker home, Pennington moved on after another six months to Brooklyn, where he found work as a coachman for a wealthy merchant. There he could take advantage of far more educational opportunities. He paid tutors out of the money he earned as a coachman and made such progress that five years after his escape from slavery, he was hired to be a schoolteacher in Newtown, Queens, Long Island. Some years later, he told how he had refashioned himself as a free man: "It cost me two years' hard labour, after I fled, to unshackle my mind; it was three years before I had purged my language of slavery's idioms; it was four years before I had thrown off the crouching aspect of slavery."[4] Years later, when he was on a speaking tour in England, the *Gloucester Journal* told its readers in self-satisfied tones that "Dr. Pennington's address was characterized by moderation and good sense, and, but for his features and colour, no person would have supposed him to be anything other than a very well educated and sensible Englishman."[5] He had set out to make himself the equal of those around him, white or black, and he had succeeded.

Pennington had been in Brooklyn scarcely a year when the first Negro National Convention was held in Philadelphia. Well-intentioned citizens including Daniel Webster, Francis Scott Key, and the presidents of Princeton, Harvard, Columbia, and Yale had formed the American Colonization Society to solve America's racial problem by sending black Americans to Africa. In response, African Americans gathered for the first time to assert their views, and James Pennington went to represent Brooklyn. On his return, he met with associates in Brooklyn and issued a statement grounded in the Constitution and printed in local newspapers. They insisted that under the Constitution, "we are already American citizens; our fathers were among the first that peopled this country; their sweat and their tears have been the means, in a measure, of raising our country to its present standing. Many of them fought and bled and died for the gaining of her liberties; and shall we forsake their tombs, and flee to an unknown land?"[6] "I am," Pennington later insisted, "an American to the backbone."[7]

While working as a coachman, Pennington had become a member of his employer's church and then moved on to a black Presbyterian congregation where he was not assigned separate seating in the balcony. He became so valuable a member of the congregation that arrangements were made to send him to seminary at Yale to prepare for ordination. Yale had never had a black student before, but Pennington by that time had taught himself Latin and Greek and was clearly qualified. Yale finally agreed to accept him but stipulated that he must sit in the back row and not ask questions. He would not be allowed to borrow books from the library and he would not be listed in the catalog.[8] Nonetheless, after three years of work Pennington was examined by a committee of clergy and pronounced well qualified for ordination.

He returned to Long Island to create a congregation where he had been a schoolteacher; but before long a congregation in Hartford called him, and he became pastor of the Talcott Street Congregational Church from 1840 to 1848.

II

Pennington had been in Hartford less than a year when he published the first black history, *A Text Book of the Origin and History, &c. &c. of the Colored People.*[9] It was just under a hundred pages in length and obviously not fully developed; but nothing like it had been done before, and it laid the groundwork for the more scholarly studies that would follow many years later.

Six months after that, Pennington took the opportunity provided by Thanksgiving Day, November 17, 1842, to preach a sermon that had little to do with the traditional Thanksgiving Day themes and everything to do with the legal basis of slavery. On moral and Biblical grounds, Pennington proclaimed the constitutional clauses dealing with slavery to be a "covenant with hell" and told his audience (and readers, since the sermon was immediately published) that "covenants involving moral wrong are not obligatory on man."

The "sermon" was, in fact, not a sermon in the usual sense at all but instead a rather dry and didactic analysis of the argument, often made in the North, that fugitive slave laws were based on the Constitution and must therefore be obeyed even in states where slavery was no longer legal. Pennington had learned at Yale to see God as the "moral governor of the universe," and he would now bring that theology to bear directly on the case at hand.

"Covenant agreements," said Pennington at the outset of his sermon, "do not necessarily make a thing right." If a thing is right, he reasoned, it is so because of "our duty as subjects of God's moral government" and would be right and our duty whether there were a covenant or not and whether we were even willing to do it or not. On the other hand, if a thing is morally wrong, no solemn covenant can make it right: "God neither wills or commands any thing that is wrong" and "No law, Covenant, or agreement, can legalize wrong." All this is laid out in the opening sentences in a clear and logical sequence with no rhetorical flourishes. Quoting the specific language of the Constitution, Pennington sets out, like any good preacher, to demonstrate three points: 1) what is involved, 2) that it is a moral wrong, and 3) that it has no obligation in the sight of God.

Against the authority of the Constitution, Pennington, as Lincoln would do almost exactly twenty-one years later at Gettysburg, sets the authority of the Declaration of Independence and the Bible. The Declaration of Independence had asserted "that all men are created equal, that they are endowed by their Creator with certain unalienable Rights, that among these are Life, Liberty and the pursuit of Happiness." That, in turn, Pennington told his congregation, is rooted in a universal truth: it "has its foundation in the nature of God, of man, and also of things." Here it is worth noting that Pennington uses as an illustration the example of "a man from the state of Maryland," who we would assume to be free since we see that he is a man and since we have agreed that all men are born free. But now comes another man from Maryland to claim the first man as property. None of Pennington's listeners knew that the first man was their preacher and that the second man was still looking for him. Preachers often use stories from their own lives as illustrations, and the fact that it is a firsthand account adds interest. Pennington, however, was not yet free under the law and, therefore, not free to give his story the added interest of stating it as his personal experience.

So the issue is the right of one man to claim another as property; this, said Pennington, "cannot be done! A thief may successfully carry off another man's property, but that does not ESTABLISH his right." But that is what the Northern states have covenanted to do, "and it is *wrong*, morally wrong." It is wrong and therefore it is not binding. This clause of the Constitution is a dead letter. The framers of the Constitution had no right to require an immoral action.

Pennington points out that the Declaration of Independence is, in effect, a statement that actions of the British king and legislature could not compel American obedience and that it appealed, as he is doing, to a universal moral law and "the Supreme Judge of the world."

Pennington used language from the prophet Isaiah to call this section of the Constitution "a covenant with death and an arrangement with hell" and cited as evidence of its immorality "the bleeding hearts and the manacled limbs; the nakedness, the starvation, the darkness of mind, the premature death, and all the LOSS OF THE IMMORTAL SOUL."

"God of Liberty, save us from this clause," he concluded, " and thanks shall be thine forever! Amen."[10]

It wasn't really a sermon and it wasn't at all about Thanksgiving. It was a careful, reasoned statement of a basis for passive resistance to the evil of slavery, the same argument that Rosa Parks and Martin Luther King, Jr. would make more than a century later. Something may be legal, Pennington argued, but nevertheless not moral, and moral is what matters. There had been denunciations of slavery before but nothing quite like what this speech provides. It was printed and widely distributed. William Lloyd Garrison almost immediately added Pennington's basic text to his masthead: "A covenant with death and an agreement with hell." But unlike Garrison's diatribes, Pennington's speech was a reasoned appeal to reasonable people. He did not denounce the Constitution as such; on the contrary, he called himself a constitutionalist who was only concerned to point out a defect in it. There is no suggestion of a path forward; but if a law has no power to bind, there must be consequences. It would still be a dozen years before Pennington himself would act on the basis of his reasoning; but when the crisis came, he had already left himself no alternative except to resist an immoral law.

Six months later, Pennington was on his way to England, chosen to serve as a delegate from Connecticut to the Second International Convention on the Slave Trade in 1843. Given opportunity to address the Convention, Pennington made an analogy between the human race and a human body, suggesting that the world was in crisis because not all members of the body had been given opportunity to develop equally. African members of the body, for example, had been dismembered, causing "mutual disease, mutual agony, mutual trouble throughout the body." "What is the remedy?" he asked. "It is direct, it is close, it is reasonable. Restore the dismembered limb. [Cheers.]" As for the "great crisis," he suggested that "the hand of Providence" had been placed on the car of human progress so that it could proceed no further until all passengers were in. Or it is like a ship, he went on to say, with a hundred passengers who are registered and have paid their fare. If only fifty are on board, "shall the ship sail without the rest?"

Remarkable in this speech is the ease with which James Pennington, who fifteen years earlier had been stumbling through the dark woods and swamps of Maryland with a price on his head, had made himself completely comfortable in addressing an English audience presided over by such a member of the nobility as George William Frederick Howard, 7th Earl of Carlisle KG PC and member of the Privy Councils of the United Kingdom and Ireland. This was different from speaking to a hypothetical audience in a Pennsylvania barn, but James Pennington continued as if it were the most natural thing in the world for him to be speaking to English nobility and to say "I am persuaded that if the noble lord were commander of the ship, he would not weigh anchor till all were aboard. [Cheers.]"[11]

In England, Pennington found himself free for the first time to travel on public transportation without restriction and to preach and minister communion in white congregations. He came back to the United States with a new and larger sense of what it meant to be free. He challenged his white colleagues to invite him into their pulpits as they invited each other and as he had been invited in England. It hadn't occurred to them before, but they began to do so.

III

In 1848, Pennington was invited to become pastor of the Shiloh Presbyterian Church in Manhattan, where he had begun his journey into ordained ministry. He came back to Manhattan not long before the Congress enacted the Compromise of 1850, one last attempt to find a balance between North and South that both sides could live with. California was admitted as a free state; the New Mexico and Utah Territories were allowed to decide for themselves to be slave or free; but, most significantly, the fugitive slave law was greatly strengthened. Now a suspected slave could not ask for a jury trial or testify on his or her own behalf. In addition, any person aiding a runaway slave by providing food or shelter was to be subject to six months' imprisonment and a $1,000 fine. Now, the ordinary citizens of free states could be summoned to join a posse and be required to assist in the capture and custody and transportation of the alleged escaped slave, or be fined. The testimony of a person accused of being an escaped slave could no longer be used as evidence at the judicial hearing; so a freedman, claimed to be an escaped slave under the Fugitive Slave Law, could not resist his or her return to slavery by truthfully telling his or her own actual history.

Northern citizens were outraged by the law; but for Pennington himself, still technically a fugitive slave, it meant a greatly increased danger that he could be taken back into slavery. Friends advised him to return to England until they could arrange to buy his freedom. Since Frisby Tilghman had recently died, the estate was not settled, and it was some time before legal arrangements could be made by Pennington's friends to purchase his freedom. Meanwhile, he traveled in Scotland and England and France and Germany, raising money for the abolition cause. The University of Heidelberg conferred an honorary doctorate on him. It was the first time anyone of African descent had been so honored by any European university.

Returning at last to New York after over two years of freedom in Europe, Pennington was more aware than ever of his lack of freedom in his own community. Streetcars were segregated, and only a few of the horse-drawn cars on rails that ran up and down Manhattan avenues were available to black residents. Not long after Pennington's return, a young black woman, Elizabeth Jennings, on her way to church on Sunday morning, insisted on her right to ride in the first car that came along and so strongly resisted attempts to remove her that she was battered and bruised and unable to get to church at all. The next morning, Pennington met with Elizabeth Jennings's father and others to form the Legal Rights Association and take her case to court. A young lawyer named Chester Alan Arthur was hired, and he won damages for Jennings and an order that the streetcar company must open its cars to all.[12]

When the other streetcar companies persisted in segregating their cars, Pennington called on his congregation to resist and was himself shortly arrested for entering a car not designated for black riders. When the jury ruled against Pennington, the Legal Rights Association decided not to appeal his case but instead chose one involving a couple who had been thrown off another car. In the struggle, the woman, who was pregnant, had been so badly injured that she lost her baby. That more dramatic case was lost at the city level but won on appeal to the state court, which ordered all streetcars in the city to be open to all. "Liberty" for black Americans involved an ongoing struggle to obtain the freedoms that white citizens took for granted.[13]

Years later, Pennington returned to Hartford to speak at a celebration of West Indian freedom. Slavery had been abolished in the West Indies in 1833, and African Americans had taken to celebrating the event annually as a foreshadowing of what they longed for in the United States. Pennington told them that no legal process could make a human being less than he or she was by creation:

> And here is an eternal truth that is destined to beat away every refuge of lies that can be brought by the ingenuity of critics, tyrants and cavilers, to support slavery. When you have made of man a

> slave by a seven-fold process of selling, bartering and chaining, and garnishing him with that rough and bloody brush, the cart-whip, and set him to the full by blowing into the eyes of his mind cloud after cloud of moral darkness, his own immortality still remains. Subtract from it what you *can*, immortality still remains; and this is a weapon in the bosom of the slave which is more terrible and terrifying to the slaveholder than the thunder of triumphal artillery in the ears of a retreating army. . . . Oh, what moral sublimity is here, when the law spoke with such stirring eloquence to the tyrant, in regard to the personal liberty and rights of the slave, and the mandate was, *"give them, give them back!"* and when the man of chains and stripes came forth and reached out his hand to receive the precious trust!

Webster had argued that the Constitution set the bounds for discussion and that any solution must be found within its terms. Pennington saw it differently:

> They tell us that slavery is here, and that it must remain; and that it is useless to discuss it. They say that however desirable it may be that slavery should be abolished, it cannot be done. It is impossible. So said the British slaveholder. We lay down as a general truth, that what is desirable is possible with God; is possible unto us, with his aid. *Upon this basis, what have we to do in order to success?* Why, to concentrate our energies upon this desirable object. Let our means harmonize with the moral government of God. Let our plans harmonize with His wisdom. Let our plans harmonize with the perceptible economy of Providence. And what becomes of the impossibility? It is annihilated.

The speech summed up the paradox of Pennington's life and ministry: he appealed to reason to combat an institution founded not on reason but on economics and emotion, but he advanced his reasons in rhetoric that appealed as much to the heart as to the mind.

The Declaration of Independence spoke of life and liberty as "unalienable rights," and Pennington insisted that black Americans must have the same rights under the Constitution as everyone else. He spelled it out in a speech in Scotland during his years of exile:

> The colored population of the United States have no destiny separate from that of the nation in which they form an integral part.

> Our destiny is bound up with that of America. Her ship is ours; her pilot is ours; her storms are ours; her calms are ours; if she breaks upon any rock, we break with her. If we, born in America, cannot live upon the same soil upon terms of equality with the descendants of Scotchmen, Englishmen, Irishmen, Frenchmen, Germans, Hungarians, Greeks, and Poles, then the fundamental theory of America fails and falls to the ground. . . . We do not expect to remain in slavery. . . . We expect to overcome the spirit of caste and enjoy the full American liberty.[14]

IV

In pursuit of that goal, James Pennington worked primarily as a pastor and teacher. When he and the congregation in Manhattan could not work together, he became an itinerant speaker for a while in the abolition cause. When war came, he did what he could to recruit black soldiers for the Union army. When the war was over, he went south to serve a congregation in Natchez, Mississippi. He saw the desperate need of the Southern black population for education and hoped to play some part in that work. Unfortunately, his wife's health brought him back to New York in less than a year. He then took a congregation in Portland, Maine, for almost three years. When his wife died and the Presbyterian Church finally made mission work in the South possible, he went to Jacksonville, Florida, and established a congregation there.

It was while he was in Mississippi that Pennington had read a *New York Herald* editorial that looked forward to a new era in which the black population would settle in "the rice and cotton lands of the Atlantic coast and south Georgia . . . [in] regions adapted to his constitution . . . [where he can] luxuriate under a tropical sun in canebrakes and rice swamps, where the white man cannot."[15] Unfortunately, James Pennington, "American to the backbone," was no better adapted to the climate than anyone else and died less than a year after arriving in Florida.

Slavery, he once wrote, is "a malignant cancer that leaves its roots after apparently being cured." But he knew the ultimate cure to be "the gospel and education."[16] Liberty without education was of little use. He had gained freedom for himself first by getting north of the Mason and Dixon line and second by doing all in his power to get an education. That education had freed him to travel widely and help organize the black population so that they, too, could experience more fully the gift of liberty.

James W. C. Pennington was a pioneer, one of those who believed what the Declaration of Independence proclaimed and worked to make it a reality for all.

Wendell Phillips

1811–1884

I AM A FANATIC

I

Wendell Phillips met Ann Greene* on the nineteenth-century equivalent of a "blind date." His story and hers were somewhat different (as often happens), but they both reported that they had met in a group of several young people who were traveling from Boston to Greenfield, Massachusetts, by stagecoach, a journey of over a hundred miles. Phillips, at that point in November or December 1835, was a young lawyer without much practice and without much knowledge of the abolition movement. Ann, on the other hand, had some very strong convictions and made use of the stagecoach time to share those convictions with Wendell. "I talked abolition to him all the way up," she said, and "all the time there. He listened, came again, and it sealed his fate."[17] Ann's parents were dead, so she lived in Greenfield with an uncle and aunt, Henry and Maria Chapman, both committed abolitionists and friends of William Lloyd Garrison. Before long, Phillips met Garrison in their home. Soon, Ann and Wendell were engaged, and in October 1837 they were married.[18] Many young people marry and settle down; Wendell Phillips's marriage to Ann Greene not only unsettled him but led him to a life dedicated to unsettling his world.

Wendell Phillips's father was a wealthy merchant who had been mayor of Boston. The Phillips family traced their ancestry to George Phillips, who came to Massachusetts with John Winthrop in 1630 on the *Arabella*. Wendell Phillips grew up within the comfort and security of the Boston establishment. At the opposite end of the social scale were the black families on "Nigger Hill." Wendell and other little boys threw stones at the black children when their paths crossed. At Harvard, Phillips helped defeat an attempt to establish a temperance society, and his first speech was a defense of the status quo against the "untried theories" and "mad schemes" of those who set out to put the "wisdom of yesterday in competition with the wisdom of the ages."[19] That was, of course, exactly what his Puritan ancestors had done, but two centuries

---

* George Lowell Austin, in *The Life and Times of Wendell Phillips*, spells Ann with an "e," but no other source does so.

had left many New Englanders with changed perspectives. Ann Greene also changed Wendell Phillips's perspective.

Wendell Phillips had graduated from Harvard in 1833, had graduated from law school two years later, and was admitted to the bar in 1836. He hung out a sign and waited for clients, but few turned to him for help. He was sitting in his office one day in 1835 when a tumult outside got his attention. Looking out, he saw a mob surging past, drawing a man with a rope. "Kill him!" they shouted, "Lynch him! Kill the abolitionist!" The man was William Lloyd Garrison, and the mob had formed when they heard that the Boston Female Anti-Slavery Society would meet to listen to a noted British abolitionist named George Thompson. Handbills had been circulated offering one hundred dollars to the first person to assault George Thompson who, in fact, had already left town rather than suffer from such attention. As Phillips watched, the twenty young women who had come to their Society's meeting were escorted out while the mayor pleaded with the mob to disperse. The mob, however, was in no mood to disperse and hauled Garrison out of his hiding place in a nearby carpenter's shop. Eventually the mayor managed to rush Garrison away in a carriage and stow him in the jail overnight for his own safety.[20]

The early part of the nineteenth century was a tumultuous era in American life. Cities were growing rapidly, poverty and injustice were endemic, and organized police forces were as yet unknown. The mobs were formed not only from the lower end of the social scale but also from among the people of "property and standing," since they too were unaccustomed to democratic procedures and felt their security threatened by advocates of reform. Garrison's attacks on slavery brought howls of protest from Southern planters to Northern merchants, and Northern merchants expressed their anger through the newspapers that were constantly vying for readers. Abolitionists were denounced as fanatics, traitors, incendiaries, and infidels in both press and pulpit. A report on activities in an abolition newspaper at the end of 1835 spoke of agents being mobbed in Worcester County, Massachusetts, in the western part of New York State, and in New Hampshire. In November 1837, Elijah Lovejoy, an abolitionist writer and publisher, was shot and killed by a mob in Alton, Illinois.

Wendell Phillips had been trained to speak in public in college and law school. At the age of thirteen, he had won a prize for his recitation of a section of Patrick Henry's most famous speech. Phillips had also heard the great Daniel Webster. It was not surprising, therefore, that he would make a speech at an abolition meeting only a few months after meeting Ann. The meeting was held in Lynn, Massachusetts, in March 1837, and had to do with a struggle in the Congress between Northern and Southern representatives over abolitionist activity. Former President John Quincy Adams, once again a member of Congress, had been irritating Southern members by presenting petitions from anti-slavery societies for the abolition of slavery in Washington, D.C. Thousands of such petitions were flooding Congress, and Southern members finally adopted a rule that all such petitions would be automatically tabled. Adams used every means at his command to get around the so-called "gag rule," and abolition societies came to his support.

Wendell Phillips's first speech was therefore not about abolition itself, but was simply the right guaranteed by the First Amendment to the Constitution "to petition the Government for a redress of grievances." The point Phillips wanted to make was that the institution of slavery was not simply a violation of the slave's freedom but that of every American. "Our fate," he said, "is bound up with that of the South, so that they cannot be corrupt and we sound, they cannot fall and we stand. Disunion is coming unless we address this subject; for the spirit of freedom and the spirit of slavery are contending for mastery. They cannot live together. . . ."[21] The point is remarkably like the one made by Lincoln in his "house divided" speech, and the phrasing already has the polished and balanced cadences of an experienced orator.

The murder of Elijah Lovejoy not only brought Wendell Phillips to Faneuil Hall, Boston, to a rally mourning Lovejoy's death, but it also prompted him to make a speech which, Frederick Douglass wrote, "changed the whole current of his life, and made him pre-eminently the leader of anti-slavery thought in New England."[22] It was hardly surprising that the first speech that day, after some resolutions were proposed, would be made by Attorney General James Austin of the Commonwealth of Massachusetts; but Phillips was not alone in his surprise that the speech was a fierce denunciation of people like Elijah Lovejoy who outrage their fellow citizens by stirring up trouble. The mob in Alton, Austin argued, had had a right to protect itself against the dangerous ideas Lovejoy was spreading. Just as the patriots in Boston had had a right to throw the tea into the harbor, so the people of Illinois had had a right to throw Lovejoy's printing press into the river and kill him to prevent him from causing further trouble.

A good many of those present had come specifically to express their anger at the abolitionists, so Austin's tirade was greeted with cheers as well as hisses and boos. Phillips had come prepared to speak only if he felt he should, and Austin's speech seemed to him to require a response. There was no seating in Faneuil Hall in those days, so Phillips had to make his way through the crowd to get to the platform. Not many of those present would have recognized the young man who now stood in front of them, or known what he was likely to say, so they grew quiet to listen. Once again, as in his first speech, the issue was a basic American freedom guaranteed by the First Amendment to the Constitution. In Lynn, it had been the right to petition; in Faneuil Hall, it was freedom of the press. Phillips was very clear in his refutation of the attorney general:

> Sir, when I heard the gentleman lay down principles which place the murderers of Alton side by side with Otis and Hancock, with Quincy and Adams, I thought those pictured lips [pointing to the portraits in the Hall] would have broken into voice to rebuke the recreant American,—the slanderer of the dead. [Great applause and counter-applause.] The gentleman said that he should sink into insignificance if he dared to gainsay the principles of these resolutions. Sir, for the sentiments he has uttered, on soil consecrated by the prayers of Puritans and the blood of patriots, the earth should have yawned and swallowed him up.

There was applause and hissing, and the uproar became so great that for a long time no one could be heard. Finally, the chairman of the meeting managed to calm the uproar and let Phillips proceed:

> The gentleman says Lovejoy was presumptuous and imprudent . . . and a reverend clergyman of the city tells us that no citizen has a right to publish opinions disagreeable to the community! If any mob follows such publication, on him rests its guilt! He must wait, forsooth, till the people come up to it and agree with him! . . . This clerical absurdity chooses as a check for the abuses of the press, not the law, but the dread of a mob. By so doing, it deprives not only the individual and the minority of their rights, but the majority also, since the expression of their opinion may sometimes provoke disturbance from the minority. A few men may make a mob as well as many. The majority, then, have no right, as Christian men, to utter their sentiments, if by any possibility it may lead to a mob! . . . Imprudent to defend the liberty of the press! Why? Because the defence was unsuccessful? Does success gild crime into patriotism, and the want of it change heroic self-devotion to imprudence? . . . Imagine yourself present when the first news of Bunker Hill battle reached a New England town. The tale would have run thus: "The patriots are routed,—the red-coats victorious,—Warren lies dead upon the field." With what scorn would that Tory have been received, who should have charged Warren with imprudence! who should have said that . . . he was "out of place" in that battle. . . . [Great applause.] How would the intimation have been received, that Warren and his associates should have waited a better time? . . . Presumptuous to assert the freedom of the press on American ground! . . . Who invents this libel on his country? It is this very thing which entitles Lovejoy to greater praise.[23]

It was Frederick Douglass who said "Liberty is meaningless where the right to utter one's thoughts and opinions has ceased to exist."[24] After Faneuil Hall, Phillips would face down other mobs and dedicate his life to protecting that freedom. His graceful bearing, rich voice, and gift for dramatic language gave him the title "abolition's golden trumpet." Henry Ward Beecher said of him, "He was not a man of tempests; he was not an orchestra of a hundred instruments; he was not an organ, mighty and complex. The Nation slept, and God wanted a trumpet, sharp, far-sounding, narrow and intense; and that was Mr. Phillips."[25]

II

Wendell Phillips and Ann Greene were married in October 1837. In 1838, he organized the Boston Anti-Slavery Society and was chosen its first president. In 1839, he became the General Agent of the Massachusetts Anti-Slavery Society. But Ann's health, which had been frail since childhood, had declined, and it was agreed that they should spend time in Europe to see whether that would be helpful. They sailed in June 1839 and spent the better part of a year traveling in England, France, Germany, and Italy. While in Europe, they learned that a world conference on slavery had been called to meet in London in June and that they had been appointed to serve as delegates.

Arriving in London in June 1840, they made their way to Exeter Hall along with some five hundred others and stood to honor Thomas Clarkson, the grand old man of the English anti-slavery movement. When the meeting was called to order, Phillips was asked to present the credentials of the American delegation, which included Ann Phillips, Lucretia Mott, Elizabeth Cady Stanton, and others. He was immediately informed by the British Executive Committee that women would not be admitted to membership. English customs would be outraged. "Wendell, don't shilly-shally," his wife told him as he went forward to argue for the American delegation. He was very blunt and clear:

> It is the custom there in America not to admit colored men into respectable society; and we have been told again and again that we are outraging the decencies of humanity when we permit colored men to sit by our side . . . shall we yield to parallel custom and prejudice here in Old England? We cannot yield this question if we would. It is a matter of conscience, and British virtue ought not to ask us to yield.[26]

The debate raged on for the better part of the day, but the Americans were outvoted and the American women were forced to withdraw to the gallery. It was an unfortunate way to end an otherwise enjoyable and useful journey. Ann's health did not improve; but she was able to see something of the great monuments of Europe, and Wendell valued the opportunity both to reflect on his first experiences in the abolition movement and to see something of a European poverty that was very different from anything he had seen in America. Writing to Garrison, he said:

> Europe is the treasure house of rich memories, with every city a shrine. But all the fascinations of art and the luxuries of modern civilization are no balance to the misery which bad laws and bad religion alike entail on the bulk of the people. . . . I hope the discussion of the question of property will not cease until the Church is convinced that from Christian lips *ownership means responsibility for the right use* of what God has given. . . .[27]

Once home in Boston, he was immediately embroiled in the storm that seemed constantly to swirl around Garrison. There were some who wanted more moderate language, but Garrison had made it clear in the first issue of the *Liberator* almost ten years earlier that he had no time to be moderate:

> I am aware, that many object to the severity of my language; but is there not cause for severity? I will be as harsh as truth, and as uncompromising as justice. On this subject, I do not wish to think, or speak, or write, with moderation. No! no! Tell a man whose house is on fire, to give a moderate alarm; tell him to moderately rescue his wife from the hand of the ravisher; tell the mother to gradually extricate her babe from the fire into which it has fallen;—but urge me not to use moderation in a cause like the present.[28]

The latest efforts to moderate him would fail. While the Phillipses were in Europe, Garrison and his supporters had further outraged their opponents by outvoting conservatives to seat women at meetings of the national abolition society, and so to create a permanent division between his followers and the more conservative abolitionists centered in New York.

In 1842, a fugitive-slave incident helped to clarify the issue for Phillips. A man named George Latimer had made his way from Virginia to Boston, where he was arrested on a charge of theft and jailed. When it was learned that he was a fugitive, a judge ruled that under the Constitution he must be returned to his owner without a trial. Now the city that had mobbed Garrison was ready for violence again. Friends of Latimer distributed a flyer calling for a protest meeting in Faneuil Hall. A turbulent crowd came together and shouted down one speaker after another. Wendell Phillips angered them still more when he told them it was the Constitution that "binds you to the car of slavery." "This old hall," he added, "cannot rock as it used to with the spirit of liberty. It is chained down by the iron links of the United States Constitution."[29] When people "trample on their consciences and the rights of their fellow men," he said, "at the bidding of a piece of parchment, I say, my CURSE be on the Constitution of the United States." There were hisses and shouts, but Phillips saw the Constitution as responsible for dragging a human being back into slavery and could not tolerate it. John Quincy Adams was another powerful voice condemning the Constitution for the "saturation of the parchment" with the "infection of slavery, which no fumigation could purify."[30]

Latimer was saved when an offer was made and accepted for his freedom, but abolitionists petitioned the legislature for a bill to prohibit anyone holding office in the State from contributing to the capture and return of fugitive slaves. A Personal Liberty Act to accomplish that purpose was enacted in March 1843. But while Daniel Webster was working to maintain the Union at almost any cost, Phillips began to make speeches pronouncing Union the enemy of Freedom. "If I must choose between Union and Liberty, then I choose Liberty first," he said, "and Union afterwards. . . . Has not idolatry of the Union been the chief bulwark of slavery?"[31]

Underlying the stand taken by Phillips and Garrison were both an unwillingness to have any involvement in a government hostile to human freedom, and an advocacy for a separation between the Northern states and those where slavery ruled. Wendell and Ann Phillips supported Garrison in seeing abolition as a moral crusade, aimed at changing people's minds, not government and laws. Phillips summed it up in an essay in 1845:

> The experience of the fifty years . . . shows us the slaves trebling in numbers—slaveholders monopolizing the offices and dictating the policy of the Government—prostituting the strength and influence of the Nation to the support of slavery here and elsewhere—trampling on the rights of the free States, and making the courts of the country their tools. To continue this disastrous alliance longer is madness. The trial of fifty years only proves that it is impossible for free and slave States to unite on any terms, without all becoming partners in the guilt and responsible for the sin of slavery. Why prolong the experiment? Let every honest man join in the outcry of the American Anti-Slavery Society.[32]

All of this was strong language and as offensive to many now as it was to many then, but Phillips had memorized Patrick Henry's speech when he was still very young and had taken it seriously. "What have we to dread in the word Revolution—we the children of rebels! We were born to be rebels—it runs in the blood."[33] He denounced the churches, too, for their unwillingness to take a principled stand. "No Christian now can be *respectable*," he said.[34] Phillips had never worried about being respectable!

Even when Lincoln was elected, even when gunfire was said to have started at Fort Sumter, Phillips stood by his belief that Lincoln was too moderate to destroy slavery and reshape the South, that restoring the Union would simply preserve slavery. "If the Administration provokes bloodshed, it is a trick—nothing else. It is the masterly cunning of the devil of compromise, the Secretary of State. . . . In twelve months you will see this Union reconstructed with a constitution like that of Montgomery. . . . But when the battles of Abraham Lincoln are ended . . . New England may claim the right to secede. . . . The only hope of liberty is fidelity to principle, fidelity to peace, fidelity to the slave."[35]

That was on April 9, 1861. Six days later, the Governor of Massachusetts received a telegram from Washington asking him to send fifteen hundred troops. By the next day, three regiments were ready to start and volunteers were pouring in from around the state. Suddenly political divisions disappeared. On Sunday, April 15, rallies were held in Boston, and Phillips was scheduled to speak. There was some fear that he would repeat his opposition to the administration and provoke a riot. But for Phillips, as for Garrison and many others, the objective was freedom for the slave; and if now it seemed that that freedom might come by means of war, he would accept that possibility with good grace:

> MANY times this winter, here and elsewhere, I have counseled peace,—urged, as well as I knew how, the expediency of acknowledging a Southern Confederacy, and the peaceful separation of these thirty-four States. One of the journals announces to you that I come here this morning to retract those opinions. No, not one of them! I need them all,—every word I have spoken this winter,—every act of twenty-five years of my life, to make the welcome I give this war hearty and hot. Civil war is a momentous evil. It needs the soundest, most solemn justification. I rejoice before God to-day for every word that I have spoken counseling peace; but I rejoice also with an especially profound gratitude, that now, the first time in my antislavery life, I speak under the stars and stripes, and welcome the tread of Massachusetts men marshalled for war. [Enthusiastic cheering.] No matter what the past has been or said; to-day the slave asks God for a sight of this banner, and counts it the pledge of his redemption. [Applause.][36]

III

Phillips was a reluctant convert, but he understood the words of James Russell Lowell's abolitionist hymn "The Present Crisis," which said "New occasions teach new duties."[37] When the election of 1864 came, Phillips did what he could to prevent Lincoln from being renominated, clashing with Garrison at conventions of the Boston and Massachusetts anti-slavery societies. He even forsook his non-political position to become a delegate to the Massachusetts Republican convention and vote against endorsing Lincoln. Only after the assassination could he say at last:

> With all his shortcomings, we point proudly to him as the natural growth of democratic institutions. [Applause.] Coming time will put him in that galaxy of Americans which makes our history the day-star of the nations,—Washington, Hamilton, Franklin, Jefferson, and Jay. History will add his name to the bright list, with a more loving claim on our gratitude than either of them. No one of those was called to die for his cause. For him, when the nation needed to be raised to its last dread duty, we were prepared for it by the baptism of his blood.[38]

But he could not follow Garrison when the Thirteenth Amendment to the Constitution was adopted by the Congress and Garrison moved to dissolve the Abolition Society, claiming that its work was done. Phillips disagreed.

> We stand with the black race on the heights of Canaan, it is true, but by no means in it. Prejudice is very rife. All over the country the colored man is a Pariah. Now friends, my abolitionism . . . was "Absolute equality before the law; absolute civil equality;" and I shall never leave the Negro until, so far as God gives me the power, we achieve it.[39]

At the end of December 1865, Garrison published the last issue of *The Liberator*. He had set out to bring an end to slavery, and slavery was abolished. Phillips had set out to reform the world, and his work continued. He never held an elective office, but his speeches set the tone for the policies adopted by Thaddeus Stevens in the House and Charles Sumner in the Senate and their radical colleagues. "For the first time," Phillips said, "Congress proposes action to which it does not ask Southern assent. Like a conqueror it dictates terms—terms to which it orders submission."[40] Whether any government action could have accomplished a peaceful rebuilding of the South is doubtful, but the intransigence of Southern whites was matched by the single-mindedness of Northerners like Phillips, who said "The whites of the South are our enemies. If the Union is ever reconstructed, it must be reconstructed from the blacks."[41]

Ten years earlier, at a dinner honoring the Pilgrim founders of Massachusetts, Phillips had spoken abut the single-minded idealism of the Pilgrims and told a story of how a farmer had seen an owl on his neighbor's barn and taken a rifle to shoot it. The bullet ricocheted into dry straw and started a fire that destroyed the barn. When the story came to a group of farmers at the local store, they lamented the loss, but one quiet man sitting in a corner asked, "Did he get the owl?"

> No matter what the name of the thing be; no matter what the sounding phrase is, . . . always ask the politician and the divine, "Did he hit that owl?" Is liberty safe? Is man sacred? They say, Sir, I am a fanatic, and so I am. But, Sir, none of us have yet risen high enough. Afar off, I see Carver and Bradford, and I mean to get up to them. [Loud cheers.][42]

While the abolition of slavery was always the primary owl Phillips aimed at and he would accept the destruction of the barn to kill that owl, he was not single-minded in his radicalism. He knew there was always more to do. "Never expect heaven in Boston," he said. Nor did he expect heaven to be brought about by legislatures. "The city government and the legislature are an organized hypocrisy," he said on one occasion.[43] On another occasion, he said of the city government: "They are mere puppets, fluttering before us for a little while; they are only victims of a great system, which they did not originate and cannot control."[44] Phillips was a co-founder of the Boston Radical Cub in 1867[45] and embraced a number of causes along the way: the death penalty, women's suffrage, temperance, the eight-hour day, the Boston school system, municipal reform, and independence for Ireland and Crete, among others. A letter to a Boston newspaper said of him, "It is well known that Mr. Phillips deliberately throws his weight into the scale of the weakest side, provided it be deserving, without much care for himself."[46] On every issue he was blunt, clear, logical, and not without a sense of humor.

When he spoke against the death penalty to the Massachusetts legislature, he pointed out that those who carry it out have always been tarnished by their association with it, and that "To call a man a hangman is the greatest insult you can cast upon him." He was immediately interrupted by one of the clergymen who had testified in favor of the penalty who said, "I suppose that is because he has touched sin and been polluted." Phillips responded immediately, "But the mob does not pelt the clergyman who takes the man's hand only the moment before he is executed!" The retort "excited great merriment, the audience loudly applauding."[47] But Phillips was never more eloquent than on the subject of capital punishment:

> Who are the men that are hung? Are they the rich, the educated, the men that are cared for by society? No, that is not the class that

> supplies the harvest for the gallows. The harvest of the gallows is reaped from the poor, the ignorant, the friendless,—the men who, in the touching language of Charles Lamb, "are never brought up, but dragged up"; who never knew what it was to have a mother, to have education, moral restraint. They have been left on the highways, vicious, drunken, neglected. Society cast them off. She never extended over them a single gentle care; but the first time this crop of human passion, the growth of which she never checked, manifests itself,—the first time that ill-regulated being puts forth his hand to do an act of violence, society puts forth her hand to his throat, and strangles him! Has society done her duty? Could the intelligence, the moral sense, and the religion of Massachusetts go up and stand by the side of that poor unfortunate negro who was the last man executed in this Commonwealth, and say that they had done their duty by him? He had passed his life in scenes of vice; he had never known what it was to have a human being speak to him in a tone of sympathy. Had society done her duty?[48]

Phillips may have enlisted in many causes, but he did have a single aim for his bullets, and that was human equality. The cause of the slave was the most egregious example of inequality in the country, but there were children in Boston whose freedom was limited by lack of education. Child labor and twelve-hour days left them no opportunity to learn, and Phillips was their advocate as well. As early as 1846, he fought to end the segregation of the Boston school system.[49] In a speech in Faneuil Hall in 1865, he spoke again for the children:

> To-day one of your sons is born. He lies in his cradle as the child of a man without means, with a little education, and with less leisure. The favored child of the capitalist is borne up by every circumstance, as on the eagle's wings. The problem of to-day is how to make the chances of the two as equal as possible; and before this movement stops, every child born in America must have an equal chance in life.[50]

Yet his primary cause after abolition was women's suffrage. Phillips was a member of the National Woman's Rights Central Committee, which organized annual conventions throughout the 1850s, a close adviser of Lucy Stone, and a major presence at most of the conventions for which he wrote resolutions defining the movement's principles and goals. His address to the 1851 convention, later called "Freedom for Woman," was used as a woman's-rights tract into the twentieth century. In his opinion, women's rights were a matter of human rights and very similar to abolition. In both cases, he saw enormous numbers of people being kept from a free and equal place in society, and it offended him. The suffrage movement had come to birth out of the abolition movement but was set aside during the war. "It is not the woman's but the Negro's hour," said Phillips; "after the slave then the woman."[51] When the Civil War was over, Phillips was able to direct his eloquence—and sense of humor—to that issue:

> I do not think woman is identical with man. I think if she was, marriage would be a very stupid state. God made the races and sexes the complement one of the other, and not the identical copy. I think the world, and literature itself, would be barren and insipid, if it was not for this exquisite variety of capacities and endowments with which God has variegated the human race. I think woman is different from man, and by reason of that very difference, she should be in legislative halls, and everywhere else, in order to protect herself.
>
> But men say it would be very indelicate for woman to go to the ballot-box or sit in the legislature. Well, what would she see there? Why, she would see men. [Laughter.] She sees men now. In "Cranford village," that sweet little sketch by Mrs. Gaskell, one of the characters says, "I know these men,—my father was a man." [Laughter.] I think every woman can say the same. She meets men now, she could meet nothing but men at the ballot-box; or, if she meets brutes, they ought not to be there. [Applause.] Indelicate for her to go to the ballot-box!—but you may walk up and down Broadway any time from nine o'clock in the morning until nine at night, and you will find about equal numbers of men and women crowding that thoroughfare, which is never still. You may get into an omnibus,—women are there, crowding us out sometimes. [Laughter.] You cannot go into a theatre without being crowded to death by two women to one man. If you go to the Lyceum, woman is there. I have stood on this very platform, and seen as many women as men before me, and one time, at least, when they could not have met any worse men at the ballot-box than they met in this hall. [Laughter and applause.]
>
> My dear, religiously, scrupulously fashionable, exquisitely anxious hearer, fearful lest your wife or daughter or sister shall be sullied by looking into your neighbors' faces at the ballot-box, you do not belong to the century that has ballot-boxes. You belong to the century of Tamerlane and Timour the Tartar; you belong to China, where the women have no feet, because it is not meant that they shall walk. You belong anywhere but in America.[52]

IV

With the passage of years, Phillips was more and more limited in his activities, more by his wife's increasing disability than by his own. The city took their home in 1882 for a street-widening project, and neither he nor his wife ever felt quite comfortable in the house to which they were forced to move. Phillips spoke in public for the last time at the unveiling of a plaque honoring Harriet Martineau* on December 26, 1882. He had a heart attack a few weeks later and died on February 2, 1883. Ann Phillips died three years later.

Frederick Douglass said of him:

> Of all the multitudes now doing honor to the memory of Wendell Phillips, none have a better right to engage in such manifestations than the colored people of the United States. . . . He was primarily and pre-eminently the colored man's friend, not because the colored man was colored, not because he was of a different variety of the human family from himself, but because he was a man, and fully entitled to enjoy all the rights and immunities of manhood. The cause of the slave was his first love, and from it he never wavered . . .

Frederick Douglass
1818–1895

FREEDOM . . . IS THE RIGHT TO CHOOSE

I

Wendell Phillips was present at an abolition meeting in Nantucket in August 1841, when Frederick Douglass first spoke in public:

> He came forward to the platform with a hesitancy and embarrassment, necessarily the attendants of a sensitive mind in such a novel

* Harriet Martineau (June 22, 1802–June 27, 1876) was an English social theorist and Whig writer, often cited as the first female sociologist. She visited the United States in 1834, supported the abolition movement, and wrote an important study of American society.

> position. After apologizing for his ignorance, and reminding the audience that slavery was a poor school for the human intellect and heart, he proceeded to narrate some of the facts in his own history as a slave, and in the course of his speech gave utterance to many noble thoughts and thrilling reflections. As soon as he had taken his seat, filled with hope and admiration, I rose, and declared that PATRICK HENRY, of revolutionary fame, never made a speech more eloquent in the cause of liberty, than the one we had just listened to from the lips of that hunted fugitive. So I believed at that time—such is my belief now.[53]

Frederick Douglass had come to New Bedford in September 1838 after escaping from slavery in Maryland. He had found work and begun to attend church services and abolition meetings. At one of the latter, at which Wendell Phillips was present, he was unexpectedly asked to speak.

Eloquence is, of course, much more than words and voice. We will frequently say of people at a meeting "Their silence was eloquent," and it is often true that an immigrant, using English as a heavily accented second language, can speak more eloquently of the problems of the immigrant than someone with a polished command of the language. Douglass's eloquence on that first occasion came in some part surely from the fact that he had escaped from slavery less than three years earlier and could speak with an authority on that subject that Wendell Phillips, a renowned orator, could never match. Phillips and others quickly took advantage of that eloquence to put Douglass to work as a regular speaker at abolitionist events, and he soon made a career of writing and speaking about slavery. He spoke not only of the experience of slavery in the South, but before long of exclusion from equality in the life of the North:

> You degrade us, and then ask why we are degraded—you shut our mouths, and then ask why we don't speak—you close our colleges and seminaries against us, and then ask why we don't know more.[54]

In Douglass's case, his eloquence came from something more than the simple fact of his experience. Phillips says that he "gave utterance to many noble thoughts and thrilling reflections," and the implication is of something more than the stammering of an uneducated slave. In fact, Douglass *was* something more: he had been preparing himself for the opportunity of that night for a number of years. Two years later, he told the story of his journey from slavery to freedom in his autobiography, *Narrative of the Life of Frederick Douglass, an American Slave*, a book that became an immediate best seller and was published in Europe in French and German.

As Douglass told his story, he had been given one enormous gift that James Pennington was not given: he was taught to read. While still a small child, he came to belong to the new wife of a slave owner, a woman who, at first, had a warm response to the small boy put in her care. She taught him the alphabet and had begun to teach him to read three- and four-letter words when her husband realized what she was doing and forbade it. He told his wife, "If you give a nigger an inch, he will take an ell. He should know nothing but the will of his master and learn to obey it. Learning would spoil the best nigger in the world; if you teach that nigger how to read the bible, there will be no keeping him. It would forever unfit him for the duties of a slave; learning would do him no good, but probably a great deal of harm, making him disconsolate and unhappy."[55]

Douglass overheard all that. As he thought about it, he saw that he had been given the key to the difference between a white man and a black man and he resolved to make use of that knowledge. He asked white children he met how to read or pronounce a word or two, sometimes giving them a piece of bread in exchange since some of them were hungrier than he was.[56] His master had been quite right: the ability to read had put a desire for freedom in Douglass' heart. As he continued to read, he began also to find more and more words with which to express that desire.

When Douglass was about twelve years old, he came upon a book titled *The Columbian Orator* and began to read it at every opportunity. He found a dialogue in it between a master and his slave that gave the whole argument against slavery, as well as speeches made by the Irish playwright, Richard Sheridan, on behalf of freedom for Roman Catholics from the English penal laws.[57] All this he soaked up. It gave him arguments against slavery and gave him language in which to clothe those arguments. All that and more lay behind that first public speech in Nantucket.

After a few years in the house in Baltimore, Douglass was sent back to a plantation to work as a field hand, but the dream of freedom went with him. For a while, he lived a short distance from Chesapeake Bay, where the white-sailed ships spoke to him of his dream:

> [W]ith saddened heart and tearful eye, [I watched] the countless number of sails moving off to the mighty ocean. The sight of these always affected me powerfully. My thoughts would compel utterance; and there, with no audience but the Almighty, I would pour out my soul's complaint, in my rude way, with an apostrophe to the moving multitude of ships:—
>
> "You are loosed from your moorings, and are free; I am fast in my chains, and am a slave! You move merrily before the gentle

> gale, and I sadly before the bloody whip! You are freedom's swift-winged angels, that fly round the world; I am confined in bands of iron! O, that I were free! O, that I were on one of your gallant decks, and under your protecting wing! Alas! betwixt me and you, the turbid waters roll. Go on, go on. O that I could also go! Could I but swim! If I could fly! O, why was I born a man, of whom to make a brute! The glad ship is gone; she hides in the dim distance. I am left in the hottest hell of unending slavery. O God, save me! God, deliver me! Let me be free! Is there any God? Why am I a slave? I will run away. I will not stand it. Get caught, or get clear, I'll try it. I had as well die with ague as the fever. I have only one life to lose. I had as well be killed running as die standing. Only think of it; one hundred miles straight north, and I am free! Try it? Yes! God helping me, I will. It cannot be that I shall live and die a slave. I will take to the water. This very bay shall yet bear me into freedom.[58]

Douglass's first speech on abolition, like James Pennington's, was made without an audience. He expanded his skills by creating a class for his fellow slaves and teaching them to read. In 1834, when he was about seventeen years old, he began teaching two friends, but others heard of it and came from other nearby plantations until he had a class of forty of his fellow slaves meeting in the home of a free African American on Sundays. It had to be done in secrecy, because their masters would have beaten them had they learned what was going on.

Almost inevitably, the thoughts of the small group of friends turned to freedom and they explored a variety of plans, all beset with the very real possibility of far greater suffering and even death if they were discovered. At last they set a date but, on the day they were to leave, their plan was discovered. They were put in jail and Douglass was lucky to escape with his life. He was, however, simply released from jail after a few days and sent back to Baltimore, where he was put to work in the shipyards. This was, of course, a totally different kind of work, but he learned how to caulk and earned a wage, which he had to give at first to his owner. Eventually he negotiated to keep some part of the wages himself, and he began to dream again about a world in which he could not only earn wages but keep them.

II

When Douglass finally escaped, he went alone with clothes and money provided by his fiancée, Anna Murray, a free woman. Making his way to New York with passes and tickets she was able to provide, he found himself free and alone in the big city with no idea what to do next and a fear of asking.

> There I was in the midst of thousands, and yet a perfect stranger; without home and without friends, in the midst of thousands of my own brethren—children of a common Father, and yet I dared not to unfold to any one of them my sad condition. I was afraid to speak to any one for fear of speaking to the wrong one, and thereby falling into the hands of money-loving kidnappers, whose business it was to lie in wait for the panting fugitive, as the ferocious beasts of the forest lie in wait for their prey. The motto which I adopted when I started from slavery was this—"Trust no man!" I saw in every white man an enemy, and in almost every colored man cause for distrust.[59]

Somehow, in spite of those fears, he found David Ruggles, a New York grocer and one-man welcoming committee for fugitives, who helped him find his way in his new world. Anna Murray followed quickly, and they asked Ruggles for help in finding a pastor to marry them. Ruggles sent word to James Pennington, who was happy to perform the ceremony and give them a certificate of the event. Douglass noted later that they had no money for a marriage fee but that Pennington "seemed well pleased with our thanks."[60]

Ruggles often sent fugitives on to Canada but, learning that Douglass had worked in shipyards and knew how to caulk, he sent him to New Bedford where his skills could be used. In the event, the white caulkers refused to work with him, but there was plenty of other work to do and Douglass was happy to do whatever work was available. He could keep all that he earned for the first time in his life, and that was all he asked.

It was some three years later that Wendell Phillips heard Douglass speak, and the abolition society immediately signed him up as a speaker. His reading and experience as a teacher in Maryland, combined with a deep and resonant voice, made him an instant star of the abolition circuit. There were communities that had no desire to hear a black speaker—in some, in states like Vermont and New York, he was physically threatened—but others were willing to listen and were deeply moved by the stories Douglass could tell of what he had seen himself of the reality of slavery. He told them about his master:

> . . . a cruel man, hardened by a long life of slaveholding. He would at times seem to take great pleasure in whipping a slave. I have often been awakened at the dawn of day by the most heart-rending shrieks of an aunt of mine, whom he used to tie up to a

> joist, and whip upon her naked back till she was literally covered with blood. No words, no tears, no prayers, from his gory victim, seemed to move his iron heart from its bloody purpose. The louder she screamed, the harder he whipped; and where the blood ran fastest, there he whipped longest. He would whip her to make her scream, and whip her to make her hush; and not until overcome by fatigue, would he cease to swing the blood-clotted cowskin. I remember the first time I ever witnessed this horrible exhibition. I was quite a child, but I well remember it. I never shall forget it whilst I remember any thing. It was the first of a long series of such outrages, of which I was doomed to be a witness and a participant. It struck me with awful force. It was the blood-stained gate, the entrance to the hell of slavery, through which I was about to pass. It was a most terrible spectacle.[61]

He told about the conditions under which they lived:

> The men and women slaves on Col. Lloyd's farm, received, as their monthly allowance of food, eight pounds of pickled pork, or their equivalent in fish. . . . With their pork or fish, they had one bushel of Indian meal . . . of which quite fifteen per cent was fit only for pigs. . . . The yearly allowance of clothing for the slaves on the plantation consisted of two tow-linen shirts . . . one pair of trousers of the same material for summer, and a pair of trousers and a jacket of woolen . . . for winter, one pair of yarn stockings, and one pair of shoes of the coarsest description. The slaves' entire apparel could not have cost more than eight dollars per year. . . . Children who were unable to work in the field, had neither shoes, stockings, jackets, nor trousers given them. Their clothing consisted of two coarse tow-linen shirts—already described—per year, and when these failed them, as they often did, they went naked until the next allowance-day.[62]
>
> Our food was coarse corn meal boiled. This was called MUSH. It was put into a large wooden tray or trough, and set down upon the ground. The children were then called, like so many pigs, and like so many pigs they would come and devour the mush; some with oyster-shells, others with pieces of shingle, some with naked hands, and none with spoons. He that ate fastest got most; he that was strongest secured the best place; and few left the trough satisfied.[63]

"As a public speaker," Wendell Phillips wrote of him, "he excels in pathos, wit, comparison, imitation, strength of reasoning, and fluency of language.

There is in him that union of head and heart, which is indispensable to an enlightenment of the heads and a winning of the hearts of others."[64] The difficulty was that Douglass was too eloquent and thus encountered frequent doubters who would not believe he had ever been a slave. Even the abolition committee sponsoring him urged him to keep his story simple and not sound quite so educated. They wanted him to keep telling his story, but Douglass got bored saying the same thing over and over again and wanted to explain the evils of the slavery system.

But educated or not, Douglass could not tell his story without publicizing the fact that he was still a fugitive. When he was urged to write his story down so even more could hear it, he finally did so—but then was told that it was unsafe for him to remain in America now that his owner could find him. He should go to England, they told him, while arrangements were made to purchase his freedom. For almost two years, then, Douglass traveled in England and Ireland, raising money for the abolition cause and experiencing, as James Pennington had done, the new sensation of being free of all restrictions based on race:

> I gaze around in vain for one who will question my equal humanity, claim me as his slave, or offer me an insult. I employ a cab—I am seated beside white people—I reach the hotel—I enter the same door—I am shown into the same parlor—I dine at the same table and no one is offended. No delicate nose grows deformed in my presence. I find no difficulty here in obtaining admission into any place of worship, instruction, or amusement, on equal terms with people as white as any I ever saw in the United States.[65]

Douglass came back from his time abroad with money raised in the British Isles to help him purchase a printing press so that he could establish a newspaper to spread his message further. To his surprise, friends of the abolition movement advised him against the project, telling him that he could be of more value to the organization as a speaker and that another paper was not needed.

Douglass nevertheless established the abolitionist paper *The North Star* on December 3, 1847, in Rochester, New York, and it became the most influential black anti-slavery paper published during the antebellum era. Douglass used his publication not only to denounce slavery, but also to fight for the emancipation of women. Its motto was "Right is of no Sex—Truth is of no Color—God is the Father of us all, and we are all brethren." It reached over four thousand readers in the United States, Europe, and the West Indies. In June 1851, the paper merged with the *Liberty Party Paper* of Syracuse, New York, and was renamed *Frederick Douglass' Paper*. It circulated under that name until 1860, when it was succeeded by a magazine named *Douglass' Monthly*. In 1870, Douglass took over the *New Era*, a weekly established in Washington, D.C. to serve former slaves. He renamed it *The New National Era* and published that until 1874.

The move to Rochester was made to avoid direct competition between the journal Douglass was planning and the *Liberator*, the paper published by William Lloyd Garrison in Boston. The move also freed Douglass to think out for himself some of the positions he had adopted simply because Garrison and the Boston abolitionists held them. Was the Constitution really a slavery document, for example, as Garrison maintained? Did it really make sense for abolitionists not to vote? Was it a good idea to call for a division between North and South so that Northerners would have no part in slavery? Douglass studied the issues for himself and decided that these positions did not commend themselves to him.

> I became convinced that there was no necessity for dissolving "the union between the northern and southern states"; . . . that to abstain from voting, was to refuse to exercise a legitimate and powerful means for abolishing slavery; and that the constitution of the United States not only contained no guarantees in favor of slavery, but, on the contrary, it is, in its letter and spirit, an anti-slavery instrument, demanding the abolition of slavery as a condition of its own existence, as the supreme law of the land.[66]

Over the next ten years after the move to Rochester, Douglass continued to publish his newspaper and to travel extensively for some six months every year, giving lectures. During the winter of 1855–1856, for example, he gave about seventy lectures on a tour that covered four to five thousand miles. While at home in Rochester, he was also asked to take part in local abolition events such as a Fourth of July celebration in 1852 in which he spoke plainly to his new neighbors:

> This Fourth of July is yours, not mine. You may rejoice, I must mourn. To drag a man in fetters into the grand illuminated temple of liberty, and call upon him to join you in joyous anthems, were inhuman mockery and sacrilegious irony. Do you mean, citizens, to mock me, by asking me to speak today?
>
> Standing with God and the crushed and bleeding slave on this occasion, I will, in the name of humanity, which is outraged, in the name of liberty, which is fettered, in the name of the Constitution and the Bible, which are disregarded and trampled upon, dare to call in question and to denounce, with all the emphasis I

> can command, everything that serves to perpetuate slavery—the great sin and shame of America!

His neighbors may have been made uneasy, but they could only admire the rhetoric that Douglass deployed in his cause:

> Oh! had I the ability, and could I reach the nation's ear, I would today pour out a fiery stream of biting ridicule, blasting reproach, withering sarcasm, and stern rebuke. For it is not light that is needed, but fire; it is not the gentle shower, but thunder. We need the storm, the whirlwind, and the earthquake. The feeling of the nation must be quickened; the conscience of the nation must be roused; the propriety of the nation must be startled; the hypocrisy of the nation must be exposed; and its crimes against God and man must be denounced.[67]

In October 1859, Douglass had to abandon a speaking tour when John Brown challenged the status quo at Harper's Ferry, Virginia. Douglass, who had met secretly with John Brown shortly beforehand, was deeply implicated and quickly made his way back to Rochester and then to Canada. He was well aware of Brown's plan and, although he had advised against it, he had every reason to fear that the government would extradite him to Virginia, where there would be little likelihood of a fair trial. He therefore moved ahead with an already planned trip to England and stayed abroad for six months. He came back to find that the congressional investigating committee dealing with Harper's Ferry had abandoned its work and that Brown was now being hailed in the North as a martyr.

III

When war came, Douglass went to work to raise black troops and finally went to Washington to present President Lincoln with his concerns about the unequal treatment black soldiers were given.

> Mr. Lincoln listened with patience and silence to all I had to say. He was serious and even troubled by what I had said and by what he himself had evidently before thought upon the same points. He, by his silent listening not less than by his earnest reply to my words, impressed me with the solid gravity of his character.

Douglass went back to his work as a recruiter, and gradually conditions for black soldiers did improve. But not until the Emancipation Proclamation was issued could Douglass give his whole heart to the war effort. Like other abolitionists, he felt that:

> We fought the rebellion, but not its cause. The key to the situation was the four millions of slaves; yet the slave who loved us, was hated, and the slaveholder who hated us, was loved. We kissed the hand that smote us, and spurned the hand that helped us.

But victory came at last; and when the celebration was over, Douglass had the strange feeling

> that I had reached the end of the noblest and best part of my life; my school was broken up, my church disbanded, and the beloved congregation dispersed, never to come together again. The anti-slavery platform had performed its work, and my voice was no longer needed. "Othello's occupation was gone." The great happiness of meeting with my fellow-workers was now to be among the things of memory.[68]

In fact, however, Douglass quickly found that the battle for equal rights had barely begun. Garrison dissolved the abolition society, thinking its work was done; but amendments to the Constitution were necessary to assure black citizens of the right to vote—a right even Garrison was not ready to push for at first. Some held that the freedmen were not educated enough to vote, others that giving them the vote would only increase resentment against them in the South. But Douglass responded that "the ballot in the hands of the negro was necessary to open the door of the school-house and to unlock to him the treasures of its knowledge." It was an issue Douglass was called on to speak to frequently:

> It is said that we are ignorant; I admit it. But if we know enough to be hung, we know enough to vote. If the Negro knows enough to pay taxes to support the government, he knows enough to vote; taxation and representation should go together. If he knows enough to shoulder a musket and fight for the flag, fight for the government, he knows enough to vote. If he knows as much when he is sober as an Irishman knows when drunk, he knows enough to vote, on good American principles. [Laughter and applause.][69]

His career as a public speaker was, in fact, expanded. He developed a speech called "The Self-Made Man," and that also was in demand. He argued that he had risen from the shackles of slavery to become an author, newspaper publisher, and respected abolitionist. What was possible for him, he maintained, was possible for any man who was willing to work hard. Less "political" in nature than his abolition speeches, it became his most popular lecture. A Philadelphia newspaper called it "noble and eloquent," full of "richness of thought and manly sentiment."

> [W]e may explain success mainly by one word and that word is WORK! WORK!! WORK!!! WORK!!!! Not transient and fitful effort, but patient, enduring, honest, unremitting and indefatigable work into which the whole heart is put, and which, in both temporal and spiritual affairs, is the true miracle worker. Everyone may avail himself of this marvelous power, if he will.[70]

Friends urged him to go south and let himself be elected to Congress, but Douglass felt he could serve freedmen better by speaking for them in the North and representing all of them rather than those of a particular district.

In 1872, Douglass's house in Rochester burned down (arson was suspected but not proved), and Douglass moved to Washington, where he was given a series of positions by Republican administrations eager to use his influence to secure the support of black voters. From 1877 to 1881, he served as U.S. Marshal for the District of Columbia under the administration of President Hayes. President Garfield made him Recorder of Deeds for the District of Columbia, and he served in that post from 1881 to 1886. He was the U.S. Minister to Haiti under President Harrison and served in that post from 1889 to 1891. He continued to speak for the rights of African Americans and for women's rights and died just after attending a meeting of the National Council of Women in Washington, D.C. on February 20, 1895, where he was brought to the platform and given a standing ovation. He died of a massive heart attack or stroke shortly after he returned home.

In 1880, Douglass, writing the third and final version of his autobiography, looked back and saw progress, but not enough to make him happy. The Constitution had been revised to deal with his concerns, but the Constitution without the will to enforce it was meaningless.

> How stands the case with the recently-emancipated millions of colored people in our own country? What is their condition to-day? What is their relation to the people who formerly held them as slaves? These are important questions, and they are such as trouble the minds of thoughtful men of all colors, at home and abroad. . . . By the law and the constitution, the negro is a man and a citizen.

> . . . To this end, several amendments to the constitution were proposed, recommended, and adopted. They are now a part of the supreme law of the land, binding alike upon every State and Territory of the United States, North and South. . . . But to-day, in most of the Southern States, the fourteenth and fifteenth amendments are virtually nullified. The rights which they were intended to guarantee are denied and held in contempt. The citizenship granted in the fourteenth amendment is practically a mockery, and the right to vote, provided for in the fifteenth amendment, is literally stamped out in face of government. The old master class is to-day triumphant, and the newly-enfranchised class in a condition but little above that in which they were found before the rebellion.[71]

Because he was asking for freedom from a greater condition of slavery than Patrick Henry or Daniel Webster had ever experienced, Douglass was required to seek more fundamental answers to the question "What is freedom?"

> What is freedom? It is the right to choose one's own employment. Certainly it means that, if it means anything; and when any individual or combination of individuals undertakes to decide for any man when he shall work, where he shall work, at what he shall work, and for what he shall work, he or they practically reduce him to slavery.

"To be free," he had told his Rochester neighbors, "is to be able to choose and that necessarily involves the right to choose those who will serve in the various offices of the government."

> It may be asked, "Why do you want it? Some men have got along very well without it. Women have not this right." Shall we justify one wrong by another? This is the sufficient answer. Shall we at this moment justify the deprivation of the Negro of the right to vote, because some one else is deprived of that privilege? I hold that women, as well as men, have the right to vote [applause], and my heart and voice go with the movement to extend suffrage to woman; but that question rests upon another basis than which our right rests. We may be asked, I say, why we want it. I will tell you why we want it. We want it because it is our right, first of all. No class of men can, without insulting their own nature, be content with any deprivation of their rights.[72]

Douglass would continue to advocate but also to serve in several government positions, perhaps as a reward from the Republican Party for his support and as evidence of the party's commitment to civil rights for African Americans.

Frederick Douglass had been born in slavery, but he knew as surely as Patrick Henry, born in freedom, that freedom was a natural human right. Henry was suspicious of government as a protector of that right and distrusted the Constitution; Douglass had experienced the tyranny of government but called for a stronger, not weaker, Constitution to protect his freedom. Both would have agreed that the Constitution was created to preserve the rights enumerated in the Declaration of Independence. New issues and times would continue to test American understanding of freedom and the role of the Constitution in defending it.

FOUR
THE SUFFRAGISTS

Angelina Grimké
1805–1879

DELIVER ME FROM THE OPPRESSION OF MEN

I

Freedom, for Angelina Grimké, was escape first of all from the slaveholding family and society in which she had grown up. Looking back on it later, she herself had no explanation for the fact that she felt sickened by the slavery system. Angelina's father was a lawyer, judge, and planter, a veteran of the Revolutionary struggle for American freedom, a distinguished member of Charleston society, and a slave owner. She grew up with the sights and sounds of slavery all around her—and hated it. She said:

> I only wonder that I had such feelings. I wonder when I reflect under what influence I was brought up that my heart is not harder than the nether millstone. But in the midst of temptation I was preserved, and my sympathy grew warmer, and my hatred of slavery more inveterate, until at last I have exiled myself from my

> native land because I could no longer endure to hear the wailing of the slave.[1]

Angelina was the youngest of fourteen children and closest in feelings to her much-older sister Sarah. Once, when Sarah felt insulted by one of the slaves, her father had the slave stripped and tied and had Sarah whip him until he fell on his knees and begged for mercy.[2] Sarah was twelve years older than Angelina and served as a godparent for Angelina at her baptism. They always had a close relationship, and Angelina sometimes even addressed her older sister as "Mother."[3]

Although the family plantation was a hundred miles from Charleston, the Grimké home in Charleston was filled with slaves to serve every purpose. Each of the eleven children was given a slave servant; and, besides that, there were slaves who were cooks and kitchen helpers, nursemaids, chambermaids, waiting maids, body servants, coachmen and stable boys, seamstresses, and washers. Some of these were crippled by blows from Mr. Grimké or his sons, one of whom had a violent temper, and many had been whipped until the blood ran down.[4]

When Angelina was fifteen, Denmark Vesey, a free black man, organized a rebellion in Charleston which was betrayed before it began. Trials were held, and thirty-seven black men were hanged. Angelina later wrote that she hoped for a peaceful end to slavery because "of all things I desire to be spared the anguish of seeing our beloved country desolated with the horrors of a servile war."[5]

Angelina's friends spoke of her as having been "a gay, fashionable girl," but she remembered even as a little girl hearing the groans and cries of slaves being punished, and she once slipped out of the house at night to take some ointment to a female slave who had been whipped.[6]

Sarah moved to Philadelphia with her father when he went there in his final illness to consult a Quaker doctor. During that time, she was befriended by Quakers. She read further in Quaker writings when she returned to Charleston for a while in 1819, and she went to meetings of the Charleston Society of Friends. She went back to Philadelphia in 1822 to become a Quaker and operate a small school. She returned often to Charleston for visits, and she kept up a correspondence with Angelina. In 1827, she returned for a long visit and spent long hours urging and praying for Angelina to renounce her deep commitment to the Presbyterian Church and join her as a Quaker.*

Sarah went back to Philadelphia the next spring, and Angelina joined her a few months later.[7] Like her sister, Angelina also returned to Charleston, hoping

---

* Brought up as an Episcopalian, Angelina had become a Presbyterian during a wave of revival.

to persuade members of her family to see the evil of slavery, but she found little response. "My spirit is oppressed and heavy laden and shut up in prison," she wrote to Sarah. Freedom for her could only be found in the North, and eventually she returned to Philadelphia.[8] Among the Quakers, they discovered a world in which slavery was condemned and women could speak in meeting, but even here they found opposition. The Quakers opposed slavery but were not ready to campaign against it. Women could speak in meeting—so long as the men who controlled the meeting thought their testimony acceptable. Just before Angelina returned to Philadelphia, Sarah wrote in her diary, "Oh my God deliver me from the oppression of men."[9]

II

Even in Quaker society, freedom was rather limited. At first the sisters' reading was limited to Quaker publications; only gradually did Angelina become aware of William Lloyd Garrison and his abolitionist paper, *The Liberator.* In the summer of 1835, there was a wave of anti-abolitionist activity in northern cities, angry demonstrations in New York, New Haven, and Hartford. In Boston, the mayor presided at a public meeting in historic Faneuil Hall in which Garrison and others were denounced by name. Garrison came back from a trip to Canada to find Boston in such turmoil that he went into seclusion in a cottage outside the city.

Angelina Grimké knew instinctively what she must do in response. She endured sleepless nights and hesitations and made prayers for guidance; but on August 30, 1835, she wrote to Garrison to express her support for both his stand for principle and for non-resistance. Without asking her permission, Garrison printed her letter under her name in his newspaper, *The Liberator*, upsetting the Philadelphia Quakers, who were unprepared for such radical activity. Even Angelina's sister, Sarah, thought she had gone too far and asked her to withdraw the letter. Angelina, always the more independent of the two, refused to do so, however, and the letter was later republished in *The New York Evangelist* and other abolitionist papers.

The opposition of other Quakers and of her sister continued for many months; but finally Sarah began to relent, and a friend with whom she was staying expressed sympathy and listened patiently as Angelina agonized as to what she might do. Suddenly the answer came: she would build on her own background to write *An Appeal to the Christian Women of the South*, a carefully reasoned discussion of the Biblical passages often used in support of slavery. Old Testament slavery, she pointed out, was not at all the same as Southern slavery, because "the laws of Moses protected servants in their rights as men and women, guarded them from oppression and defended them from wrong."[10] Southern slavery was not like that at all. Grimké urged Southern women as

"Sisters in Christ" to petition their state legislatures and church officials to end slavery. If those to whom she was writing claimed to be powerless, that made no difference. Grimké urged them, like twentieth-century civil rights workers, to use civil disobedience and passive resistance:

> If for instance, there was a law, which imposed imprisonment or a fine upon me if I manumitted a slave, I would on no account resist that law, I would set the slave free, and then go to prison or pay the fine. If a law commands me to sin I will break it; if it calls me to suffer, I will let it take its course unresistingly.[11]

It was while she was writing the letter that another opening came: an invitation from the American Abolition Society to come to New York and speak to women's groups in a series of parlor meetings. The timing was perfect. In her response, she asked whether the Society would be interested in publishing her *Appeal*. They would indeed, and rushed it into print. Angelina had naïvely hoped to go back to Charleston to follow up her *Appeal* in person, but the mayor told Mrs. Grimké that her daughter would not be allowed off the boat should she come and, if she managed to get into the city, she would be arrested and sent back to Philadelphia. Copies of the *Appeal* were seized by Southern post offices and burned.[12]

Instead of Charleston, Angelina went to New York in the fall of 1836. There were training sessions for abolitionist workers being conducted by Theodore Weld, and Angelina and Sarah were the only women among the seventy being trained. When the three-week training session was over, the sisters stayed on in New York to hold a series of parlor meetings for women of the New York Anti-Slavery Society who wanted to hear their firsthand accounts of slavery. Although Angelina spent "many tearful hours" in prayer as to whether she ought to be speaking in public, she soon discovered that she had a talent for speaking, a musical voice that carried well, and an agreeable manner. The parlors proved to be too small, and a local pastor allowed them to use a room at his church. When the audience outgrew the room, they used the church itself; and when a curious man slipped into a back pew, thus creating a mixed audience, Angelina "did not feel his presence embarrassing at all" and continued to speak "just as though he was not there."[13]

In May 1837, the Grimkés came back to New York to attend the first Anti-Slavery Convention of American Women, held in New York. It was the first of three annual gatherings in which the Grimké sisters joined leading female abolitionists from Boston, New York, and Philadelphia. By now their fame had begun to spread, and the American Anti-Slavery Society sent Angelina and Sarah off on a speaking tour of New England.

A woman speaking in public on any subject was a novel idea in itself, but the citizenry flocked to hear them. In Lynn, over a thousand people turned out, men as well as women; in Lowell, fifteen hundred; in Salem, three talks drew twenty-four hundred listeners.[14] In Woonsocket Falls, the gallery was so crowded that the beams began to crack and the meeting had to be adjourned."[15] Sometimes, as in Salem, the audience was drawn largely from the African American community.[16] It seems likely that the crowds came in large part because no one had heard a woman speak in public before, but what they heard was a woman of extraordinary ability as a speaker. Abolitionist Robert F. Wallcut reported that "Angelina's serene, commanding eloquence . . . enchained attention, disarmed prejudice and carried her hearers with her."[17] Wendell Phillips wrote that "I well remember evening after evening listening to eloquence such as never then had been heard from a woman. She swept the chords of the human heart with a power that has never been surpassed and rarely equalled."[18] Her voice would reach to the farthest corners of a large hall. She herself had not realized that she had such a gift. But she found it easy to do. She responded to the crowds and reported that she found "great openness to hear and ease in speaking."[19]

Alarmed by reports of women in leadership roles and mixed, or "promiscuous," audiences,* the Massachusetts Association of Congregational Ministers issued a pastoral letter calling the Grimkés' lectures "a scandalous offense against propriety and decency." But the sisters were delighted to take on that challenge as well. "The whole land seems roused to discussion of the province of Woman, and I am glad of it," wrote Angelina. Some churches were now closed to them; but there were other venues available, and the crowds continued to come.

The speaking tour came to an end when Angelina contracted typhoid fever, but the tour led to an invitation to address a legislative committee of the Massachusetts State Legislature, and Angelina became the first woman in the United States to address a legislative body. Since the clergy had broadened the debate, Grimké not only spoke against slavery, but also defended women's right to petition both as a moral and religious duty and as a political right. Thus the growing involvement of women in the abolition movement began to have further consequences. As women attempted to speak for the slave but had to fight for their right to be heard, they began to become aware of their own lack of freedom.

The relationship between the two issues came into sharp focus when Catherine Beecher, sister of Harriet Beecher Stowe and Henry Ward Beecher,

* The dictionary definition of "promiscuous" is "composed of all sorts of persons or things," but the word has subsequently come to mean indiscriminate sexual relationships.

published "An Essay on Slavery and Abolitionism with reference to the Duty of American Females." Beecher had worked to provide better educational opportunities for women—but to make them better mothers and housekeepers, not to fit them for the public sphere. Angelina had met with Beecher at her school in Hartford and had thought seriously of joining her faculty. Now Beecher wrote to say that the younger woman had gone too far. Women, Beecher argued, are not without influence, but "their mode of gaining influence and of exercising power should be altogether different."[20] Angelina, in short, should stay home. Angelina responded with a series of letters maintaining that a woman had as much right in the public sphere as a man:

> I believe it is woman's right to have a voice in all the laws and regulations by which she is to be governed. . . . Woman has just as much right to sit on the throne of England, or in the Presidential chair of the United States.

To a friend, she wrote:

> My idea is that whatever is morally right for a man to do is morally right for a woman to do. I know no rights but human rights. I know nothing of men's rights and women's rights.[21]

Nineteenth-century American Society was being transformed from the age-old pattern of an agricultural society in which men and women worked together in defined roles to sustain their families, to an industrial society in which men and women worked less and less together. A growing number of men went to work in offices and factories, while women worked in factories or stayed home to raise children. As wealth increased, more and more women had domestic help and had time to join societies in support of churches and charities. There they learned to speak for themselves and to become advocates. When men resisted women's increasing assertiveness, the issue became one of women's freedom to act as they chose. As Carolyn Williams put it, "From the antislavery conventions of the 1830s arose a women's community committed to overturning racial and sexual oppression."[22] The Grimké sisters came back from their speaking tour for abolition, collected Angelina's letters, and published them as *Letters on the Equality of the Sexes and the Condition of Women*. One thing led to another.

III

While Angelina was recovering her strength after the tour, she fell in love with Theodore Weld, whom she had first met at the New York training sessions. He had sworn not to marry until slavery was abolished, but he made an exception for Angelina.[23] They were married on May 14, 1838, which was Monday of a busy week.

On the same day as the wedding, a new building, Pennsylvania Hall, erected for the use of the Pennsylvania Anti-Slavery Society, was dedicated in Philadelphia. Letters of congratulations were read from former President John Adams and from Theodore Weld, who presumably was unable to attend because he was getting married.

The dedication was an occasion for celebration by abolitionists, but others were angry. The next day, as the Anti-Slavery Convention of American Women met in the hall, messages were circulated around the city calling on "citizens who entertain a proper respect for the right of property" to "interfere, forcibly if they must, and prevent the violation of these pledges (the preservation of the Constitution of the United States), heretofore held sacred." In response, crowds began to gather; by the evening of the sixteenth, when William Lloyd Garrison introduced the first speaker to an audience of three thousand, the crowd had become unruly. As shouts and jeers from outside began to interrupt the speeches, Angelina Grimké challenged them in a remarkable speech punctuated by the noise from the crowd and the sound of rocks breaking the windows.

> Men, brethren and fathers—mothers, daughters and sisters, what came ye out for to see? A reed shaken with the wind? Is it curiosity merely, or a deep sympathy with the perishing slave, that has brought this large audience together? [A yell from the mob without the building.] Those voices without ought to awaken and call out our warmest sympathies. Deluded beings! "They know not what they do." They know not that they are undermining their own rights and their own happiness, temporal and eternal. . . . Those voices without tell us that the spirit of slavery is here, and has been roused to wrath by our abolition speeches and conventions: for surely liberty would not foam and tear herself with rage, because her friends are multiplied daily, and meetings are held in quick succession to set forth her virtues and extend her peaceful kingdom. This opposition shows that slavery has done its deadliest work in the hearts of our citizens.

"As the tumult from without increased," Garrison reported later, "and the brickbats fell thick and fast, [Grimké's] eloquence kindled, her eyes flashed, and her cheeks glowed."[24] The transcript of the speech is punctuated with continuing references to the noises from the crowd of protesters:

> [Just then stones were thrown at the windows,—a great noise without, and commotion within.]
> [Great noise.]
> [A yell from the mob without the building.]
> [Another outbreak of mobocratic spirit, and some confusion in the house.]
> [Shoutings, stones thrown against the windows, &c.]
> [Mob again disturbed the meeting.]

Angelina Grimké was not deterred. "What is a mob?" she asked. "What would the breaking of every window be? What would the levelling of this Hall be? Any evidence that we are wrong, or that slavery is a good and wholesome institution?"

The transcript provides remarkable testimony to Grimké's poise and command as a speaker in circumstances never faced by Patrick Henry or Daniel Webster. It is also remarkable for the way in which Grimké turned around the argument against women as speakers and participants in public affairs. Women's role, the Congregational clergy had argued in denouncing the Grimkés' tour of Massachusetts, is in the home and in dependence on men whose role it is to protect her. But facing the mob, Grimké cited her weakness and defenselessness as her primary weapon.

> A few years ago, and the South felt secure, and with a contemptuous sneer asked, "Who are the abolitionists? The abolitionists are nothing?"—Ay, in one sense they were nothing, and they are nothing still. But in this we rejoice, that "God has chosen things that are not to bring to nought things that are."

Men might have the power; but power, she argued, does not establish right, and women are uniquely able to make that point. The noise and tumult continued until finally the meeting was brought to an end, and the speakers and audience left arm in arm to be sure that none of the black or female members were attacked.

The next day, the mayor came with the police and declared the conference ended and locked the hall. The mob then set fire to the building. When firemen were summoned, some of them sprayed their colleagues and adjacent buildings rather than the fire, and the building was destroyed. In the next few days, the mob continued their riotous behavior, destroying a black orphans' shelter and heavily damaging a black church. The city's official report blamed it all on the abolitionists, saying they had upset the citizens by encouraging "race mixing" and inciting violence.

The Philadelphia Riot is noteworthy for several reasons. One is that it dramatically demonstrates the level of hostility that abolitionism provoked in the

North. Another is Grimké's central role in opening up the "public sphere" to women. It was her example that inspired Abby Kelley Foster and, later, Lucy Stone to become abolition speakers. She also helped inspire hundreds and then thousands of middle-class Northern women to join anti-slavery societies, to circulate petitions, to raise funds, to write anti-slavery poems and polemics, and to contribute to the movement in other ways. These women not only played key roles in the struggle for emancipation, they also provided much of the leadership for the new women's rights movement in the 1840s and 1850s.

Itinerant speaking for abolition was a dangerous occupation for both women and men. Local audiences were often hostile, sometimes violent. There was, for example, an anti-abolition riot in Cincinnati. In Alton, Illinois, as already mentioned, a mob killed the abolitionist newspaper publisher Elijah Lovejoy. The hostility against abolitionists had several sources. One was a concern that abolition would endanger the Union. Another, according to Angelina Grimké, was prejudice, specifically against the mixing of the races, called "amalgamation" by its opponents.

> . . . the North is most dreadfully afraid of Amalgamation. She is alarmed at the very idea of a thing so monstrous, as she thinks. And lest this consequence might flow from emancipation, she is determined to resist all efforts at emancipation without expatriation. It is not because she approves of slavery, or believes it to be the "cornerstone of our republic," for she is as much anti-slavery as we are; but amalgamation is too horrible to think of. . . . Great numbers cannot bear the idea of equality, and fearing lest, if they [blacks] had the same advantages we enjoy, they would become as intelligent, as moral, as religious, and as respectable and wealthy, they [white Northerners] are determined to keep them as low as they possibly can.[25]

Most basically, of course, prejudice arises out of ignorance and finds expression when members of any segment of society feel insecure. Few white people in those days had met an educated African American, but many white people felt insecure amid the rapid changes in their society. A white man might, of course, still have a sense of power in his home and in relation to women; so when a white woman like Angelina Grimké took up the abolition cause, she became a convenient target.

IV

As it turned out, Angelina Grimké Weld's speech in Pennsylvania Hall was her last significant public appearance. Women, she had argued, should not be confined to the roles of housewife and mother; nevertheless, that was her role for most of the rest of her life. It was, however, hardly a traditional family that she and her husband established. She and Theodore moved to a small cottage in Fort Lee, New Jersey, with Sarah along to make an unorthodox third. Theodore was a follower of the "Graham diet," popular with nineteenth-century reformers.* Frequent visitors like Elizabeth Cady Stanton, Henry Stanton, and John Greenleaf Whittier shared their "simple meals." One week Angelina was the cook, the next week it was Sarah. Sarah liked to cook a week's meals in advance, which meant meals were often "cool." Theodore's voice had given out, so he was no longer the eloquent speaker he once had been, but he was deeply involved in abolition work and had an office in New York. Theodore and Angelina felt it would be best if they did the work of the house themselves, he on the outside, she on the inside. Angelina's mother was shocked: "Pray, have you no servants?"

Both Angelina and Theodore continued to write tracts for the abolition movement. As Weld listened to his wife's stories of life in the South, he decided that they should be written down and published. "As a Southerner," Grimké had told the audience in Pennsylvania Hall, "I feel that it is my duty to stand up here to-night and bear testimony against slavery. I have seen it—I have seen it. I know it has horrors that can never be described." Her stories, with others Weld collected, were published under the title *American Slavery As It Is: Testimony of a Thousand Witnesses*.[26] Published in 1839, it sold well and became perhaps the best known of all anti-slavery writings.[27] It remains an invaluable firsthand look at the reality of slavery.

Although she seems to have assumed that she would return to the lecture circuit, the opening somehow never came. There were three children, but Sarah was better with them than Angelina. For a while they ran a school. Angelina was a better teacher than Sarah. From 1854 to 1862, they were part of a commune in Perth Amboy, New Jersey, where again they taught school. Angelina served on the Central Committee for the second and third general conventions for women's rights and sent long messages to both, but did not attend.

With the coming of war, both Theodore and Angelina returned to the work they knew best. Theodore embarked on long lecture tours, and Angelina went to work for the Woman's Loyal League, organizing and coordinating their work in support of the soldiers. She prepared and gave an "Address to the Soldiers," speaking naturally of freedom. This was, she told the soldiers,

> a war of principles . . . and now *all* who contend for the rights of labor, for free speech, free schools, free suffrage, and a free

---

* The Graham diet centered on unsifted bread free of the chemical additives commonly used to give bread a whiter color. Theodore Weld allowed no meat, butter, tea, or coffee, nor tobacco, nor alcoholic drinks.

> government, securing to *all* life, liberty, and the pursuit of happiness, are driven to do battle in defense of these or fall with them.[28]

Angelina was also deeply involved in the effort to persuade Lincoln of the need to put an end to slavery. She helped shape petitions to the President and members of Congress and then went door to door to obtain signatures.

When the war was over, Angelina, Sarah, and Theodore moved to Hyde Park, near Boston, once again to teach school. It was in February 1868 that Angelina noticed an article in *The Anti-Slavery Standard* that took her back to her beginnings in Charleston. An article about how well some ex-slaves were doing when given academic opportunity mentioned a young man named "Grimkie." Angelina guessed it must be her family name and wrote to the student at Lincoln University in Pennsylvania. A prompt reply confirmed that Archibald Henry Grimké was a son of Angelina's uncle and one of his slaves and therefore her nephew. Indeed, there were two such nephews, and Angelina went to visit them and find out about their financial needs. She and Sarah contributed to their support, and the two young men went on to distinguished careers in law and ministry. She had never wanted to break her connection with Charleston and her family, and there was a certain appropriateness to having the connection restored through two young men of mixed racial background.

Largely at a local level, Angelina continued to be involved as well in the struggle for women's suffrage; but just short of her seventieth birthday, she suffered a stroke. Crippled and unable, toward the end, to speak, she lived a few more years and died in October 1879. Sarah had died six years earlier. Theodore Weld died at the age of 92 in 1895 and used his last years to write a valuable biography of Angelina. Wendell Phillips contributed a vital assessment of Angelina's impact:

> Her own hard experience, the long, lonely intellectual and moral struggle from which she came out conqueror, had ripened her power and her wondrous faculty of laying bare her own heart to reach the hearts of others shone forth until she carried us all away captive. . . . It was when you saw she was opening some secret record of her own experience that the painful silence and breathless interest told the deep effect and lasting impression her words were making on minds that never afterward rested in their work.[29]

It was ironic that Angelina should have lost her voice toward the end, since she had done so much to give a voice to others, to set other women free to contribute their voices toward the expansion of human freedom.

Abby Kelley Foster
1811–1887

BLOODY FEET, SISTERS, HAVE WORN SMOOTH THE PATH BY WHICH YOU HAVE COME UP HITHER

I

"Put down your hand," said the chairman of the meeting; "your vote will not be counted."

Abby Kelley had been told to be quiet before, but never had the issues been as clearly stated as they were in a meeting in New Haven, Connecticut, in late May 1840. Henry G. Ludlow, a local pastor, was presiding; and when Abby Kelley stood up to speak, he spelled out his fears very clearly. Dorothy Sterling, one of Kelley's biographers, notes wryly that "The psychosexual undertones of Ludlow's speeches went unnoticed in New Haven in 1840," but they are quite clear to twenty-first-century readers looking back. Ludlow could not have been more clear:

> No woman will speak or vote where I am moderator. It is enough for women to rule at home. It is woman's business to take care of the children in the nursery; she has no business to come into this meeting and by speaking and voting lord it over men. Where woman's enticing eloquence is heard, men are incapable of right and efficient action. She beguiles and blinds men by her smiles and her bland winning voice.

Ludlow told his audience that he would not sit in a meeting where women were allowed to speak and vote. Hat in hand, he stalked down the aisle and left the meeting in the hands of the vice-chairman. Before long, however, he was back to inform the meeting that he would not "sit in a meeting where the sorcery of a woman's tongue is thrown around my heart. I will not submit to PETTICOAT GOVERNMENT. No woman shall ever lord it over me."

Abby Kelley had no particular interest in "lording it" over Henry Ludlow, but she had strong views on the subject of slavery and believed that her views should be heard. "I am bound by duty to God and man to speak," she managed to say, but the majority of the gathering agreed with Ludlow and voted that women should not be allowed to speak or vote.[30]

The Hartford meeting came only days after a calamitous meeting of the American Anti-Slavery Society in New York City that led to a permanent division between the New England and New York Societies. The tension had been building for several years as William Lloyd Garrison attempted to broaden the membership of the Society to include women at every level. There were a number of women's anti-slavery societies in New York and New England and elsewhere, meeting separately from the men to conduct their business. Women's societies were a new thing, and women had little experience organizing and holding meetings and speaking in public. It was only three years earlier, in May 1837, that women had come together in New York for "the first public political meeting of women in America."[31] Only a year after that, the New England Anti-Slavery Society decided to take the next logical step. Women had been coming to their meetings as spectators, but in 1838 the New England leaders decided to enlarge their membership by enrolling women as members. There was a fight over the proposal that took the best part of the meeting's second day, but the forces of change prevailed.

Abby Kelley was one of the new members of the New England Society. As a Quaker, she was accustomed to speaking when the Spirit moved her; so soon she was on her feet to speak, and eventually, as usually happens to people who speak up at a meeting, she was on a committee. Abby Kelley became the catalyst in the division between the Garrisonian abolitionists centered in Boston and the more conservative New Yorkers.

II

Many of the first women involved in the abolition movement were, like Abby Kelley, Quakers. She was born on a farm near the little community of Pelham in western Massachusetts on January 15, 1811, where she not only helped her mother in the house but also helped her father doing chores outside. Perhaps more important, she learned the Quaker reliance on the "inner spirit" as her guide. When she went to Quaker meeting, she would often sit in silence for an hour or more with the rest of the assembled members as they waited for guidance; but when the Spirit came to one of them, man or woman, they stood up to speak and everyone listened. No wonder so many of the first abolitionists were Quaker women, and no wonder they were among the first to insist that they had an equal right to be heard. The women's suffrage movement was born in the abolition movement, and Quakers helped lead the way.

Like her older sisters, Abby was given a basic education at the local district school—but, unlike her sisters, she also attended a Quaker school in Providence, Rhode Island, in 1826 and 1829. She borrowed money from an older sister to pay for the first year, and she earned money for the second year herself by teaching school. In addition to spelling and grammar, algebra, astronomy, and botany, she learned rhetoric and memorized and recited stanzas from such classics as Milton's *Paradise Lost*.[32] When the time came for her to speak, she was better prepared than many.

But she had prepared herself to be a teacher, and after her time at school in Providence, at the age of nineteen, she went back to her parents' home in Millbury, Massachusetts, and taught school to help provide an education to her younger siblings—and, indeed, to subsidize her parents, who seemed unable to break free of debt. By the time she was twenty-five, she had helped her parents attain some security, so she felt free to expand her horizons by taking a position at a Quaker school in Lynn, Massachusetts, a town just north of Boston and four hours by train and coach from Millbury. She had heard William Lloyd Garrison lecture while she had still been in Millbury, so she had been in Lynn only a few weeks before joining the local Female Anti-Slavery Society.

Although it was not considered altogether proper for women to become politically involved, the Boston chapter was petitioning Congress to end slavery in the District of Columbia and, when the Lynn Chapter decided to support them, Abby volunteered to help collect petitions. Rebuffed at many a door by husbands who told them it was "none of their business" and by women unwilling to venture into strange territory, Kelley and her colleagues eventually estimated that they had, nevertheless, gained signatures from almost half the women in town. Having petitioned Congress, Abby also petitioned the local Friends for permission to use the meeting house for abolition meetings and soon was able to welcome William Lloyd Garrison and Henry Stanton. "At length," she wrote, "my whole soul was so filled with the subject that it would not leave me in school hours." By 1835, she was the corresponding secretary of the Lynn Female Anti-Slavery Society.[33]

The anti-slavery movement appealed to women for two particular reasons. In the first place, the notion of women and children being separated, sold as slaves, and condemned to hard labor offended them. It was a Quaker poet, Elizabeth Margaret Chandler, who wrote the often-quoted lines

> Think of the frantic mother,
> Lamenting for her child.
> Till falling lashes smother
> Her cries of anguish wild!
> Shall we behold, unheeding,
> Life's holiest feelings crush'd?
> When woman's heart is bleeding,
> Shall woman's voice be hushed?[34]

In the second place, as the Lynn Society noted at its first annual meeting in 1836: "In this sphere it is not denied that woman may operate with propriety and efficiency."[35] If women wanted to correspond with other female abolitionists and make items to sell at the annual Boston anti-slavery fair, who would complain? Did they not do the same for missionaries at home and abroad? But this modest activity would lead on to areas not yet explored.

Meanwhile, in New York, the Grimké sisters were gaining attention with their firsthand testimony to the evils of slavery, and Abby Kelley invited them to speak in Lynn. In reply, they spoke of a future lecture trip being planned for Massachusetts but invited Abby meanwhile to come to New York in May 1837 for the first women's anti-slavery convention. Abby attended and met for the first time a number of other women like Lucretia Mott. She would have heard of Mott before, but now they met and became friends. Also for the first time she met a significant number of African Americans, since some ten percent of those attending were black. Perhaps even more important, she was there to vote on a radical proposal made by Angelina Grimké that "it is the duty of woman, and the province of woman, to plead the cause of the oppressed in our land, and to do all that she can by her voice, and her pen, and her purse, and the influence of her example," to bring an end to slavery.[36]

Toward the end of June, the Grimké sisters arrived in Lynn to address the Women's Anti-Slavery Society. Abby Kelley chaired an afternoon meeting and escorted the visitors to the Methodist church that evening. The men who had brought the sisters from Boston found seats in the gallery, and then a few more curious men came and a few more until there were almost as many men as women, and over a thousand people, in the church. It was not the first time Angelina Grimké had found herself addressing a "promiscuous" audience, but it was a new thing in Boston. A local reporter wrote that "The audience seemed astonished at the evidence which their own eyes and ears furnished, having never witnessed such a display of talent in a female."[37] Nonetheless, the Grimké sisters had a story to tell, and there were men who wanted to hear it. As they continued their tour around the state, they continued to welcome men into their audience.

The sisters returned to Philadelphia and sent Abby Kelley an invitation to Angelina's wedding, to take place in Philadelphia in May 1838 just before a planned convention of anti-slavery women. The wedding took place as planned and the convention assembled as scheduled, but Philadelphia was no longer the "city of brotherly love" that William Penn had envisioned. The Mason-Dixon line separating North and South was not far away, and many of the merchants were deeply involved in trade for Southern products. The notion of black and white meeting together and women daring to speak in public outraged a number of citizens, and the women found the meeting hall surrounded by a jeering crowd whose anger rose as the evening meeting went on. Even Angelina Grimké, with her New England experience of challenging audiences, was barely able to make herself heard above the tumult.

Abby Kelley had no such experience and had never addressed a "promiscuous" audience, let alone one besieged by rioters; but, true to Quaker tradition, she felt moved to speak as well—and did so. It was not the tumult, she told the audience, that impelled her to speak, but "the still, small voice within which may not be withstood." With volleys of stone crashing against the windows, she could hardly be heard above the tumult, but she used the parable of Dives and Lazarus to compare the wealthy North with the rich man who ignored the poor man, the slave, lying at his doorstep. "Ought we not to raise him up?" she asked. "Is there no one in this hall who sees nothing for himself to do?"

Theodore Weld pushed his way through the crowd to find her afterwards, and told her that she had an obligation to use her abilities as a lecturer. "If you don't," he said, "God will smite you!"[38]

III

Some of God's agents were usually ready to smite Abby Kelley anyway.

She went back to Lynn in time to go to Boston for the next meeting of the New England Anti-Slavery Society. William Lloyd Garrison was hoping to move women from the status of spectators to full membership, and a resolution to do so was adopted before all the members were present. It was not until the second day that the battle began. Abby was appointed to a committee, and immediately a resolution was presented by a group of clergy protesting women's membership in the society. Much of the third day was given over to parliamentary battles. Abby spoke on behalf of the enlarged membership and nudged some of the male members to do so as well. The convention ended with women still official members; but seven clergy signed a protest, and John Greenleaf Whittier joined them in arguing that the issue of women's rights was a distraction from the abolition campaign.[39]

Abby Kelley had been placed on a three-member committee to draw up a statement to the churches; but in both Massachusetts and Rhode Island, many of the clergy refused to read "Miss Kelley's Memorial" to their congregations.

When school began that fall, Kelley resigned her position. She was concerned about her mother's health and needed time to think through her own future. She was being entreated to become a speaker and felt deep urgings to respond positively. After Pennsylvania Hall, however, she knew what she might face.

In mid-September, Kelley went back to Boston for a meeting of the American Peace Society. Garrison and others hoped to move the convention beyond a simple disavowal of war to a complete dissociation from the governments that supported war. She was on a committee that drew up a declaration of sentiments that said:

> We cannot acknowledge allegiance to any human government. . . . Our country is the world, our countrymen are all mankind. . . . As every human government is upheld by physical strength, we therefore voluntarily exclude ourselves from every legislative and judicial body, and repudiate all human politics. . . . There is great security in being gentle, harmless, long-suffering and abundant in mercy. . . . We shall adhere to the doctrines of non-resistance and passive submission to enemies. . . . It will be our leading object to devise ways and means for effecting a radical change in the views, feelings, and practices of society respecting the sinfulness of war. . . .

It was a radical statement, and it got attention. Clergy and politicians denounced it. Abolitionists deplored the idea of withdrawing from the fight to change government through political action. But Ralph Waldo Emerson commended them. Henry Thoreau made use of their ideas a decade later when he wrote "Civil Disobedience." Tolstoy was delighted by it at the end of the century and copied parts of it. Mohandas K. Gandhi was influenced by it in the twentieth century, and so, through him, was Martin Luther King, Jr.[40]

Over the next winter, Kelley spent time with her mother but corresponded with Theodore and Angelina Weld about her feeling of being called. Angelina told her she would learn by doing, but Theodore told her to read as much as she could. She read materials he sent, and even a book on rhetoric. When spring came, she was ready to go to New York for the annual meeting of the American Anti-Slavery Society and to set out on the lecture circuit herself.[41] Kelley became the first woman to speak at the Convention, and there were fierce battles over allowing membership to women; but Gerrit Smith, presiding, carefully said "they" rather than "he" or "she," and the Society remained superficially united when it was over.[42]

During the next year, Abby Kelley traveled in northern Connecticut, encountering bitter opposition in many places, but sometimes also large audiences and support. In May 1840, she went back to New York for the next convention of the Anti-Slavery Society and a showdown over the issue of women's involvement.

The dominant personality in the New York faction was Lewis Tappan, an evangelical Christian who, like the Massachusetts Congregational clergy, read the Book of Genesis as establishing an eternal order of things that put men in charge. Allied with them were many, including women, who believed that the attempt to give women equal status was a distraction from the work of ending slavery. It seemed to them that the situation of Northern women was not in a class with the situation of black slaves, and that it was best to focus on the greater evil. They believed they lost support by widening the fight to include the rights of women.

When William Lloyd Garrison decided to challenge the New Yorkers at the 1840 meeting of the American Anti-Slavery Society, he chartered a boat and two trains to bring down as many of his Boston cohorts as possible, over 450 delegates, and nominated Abby Kelley to serve on the business committee. The voice vote on her nomination was so close that tellers had to be asked to count first one side and then the other. The result was still close, but Abby won by a vote of 557 to 451. The opposition faction then walked out and formed a separate society.[43] The schism continued until the Civil War.

IV

At the New York Convention, Abby Kelley was selected to go to an international meeting in London, but she chose to return to Connecticut and continue her campaign there. "My mission," she said to a Boston gathering, "has been back among the people, among the hills and the hamlets." She spoke of freedom and the need to think of it in terms of the human family. There was a time, she told her audiences, when the United States had hurled its principles across the Atlantic so that "thrones trembled and monarchs blanched with fear." But now America had become a reproach before the world, since it held one-sixth of its population in chains. Nor was it only those seen as enslaved: the abolition campaign, she told her audiences, had revealed just how little freedom most Americans enjoyed. "You were free to be mobbed—free to be slandered and misrepresented to any amount—free to be driven from your place of meeting." So it was that

> The mere existence of slavery in any section of our land endangers the freedom of all. All the great family of mankind are bound up in one bundle. When we aim a blow at our neighbor's rights our own are by the same blow destroyed. Can we look upon the wrongs of millions—can we see their flow of tears and grief and blood, and not feel our hearts drawn out in sympathy? We must dislodge slavery from every place we visit, be willing to withstand the wild waters of the opposition, and be ranked with the poor and the oppressed.[44]

Those who came were moved by her oratory, but often she found bitter opposition. In Cornwall and Canaan in the northwest corner of Connecticut, mobs formed and threw rotten eggs and "the contents of outhouses" through the windows. Once a band marched back and forth outside to drown her out. Once a drunk marched up and down the aisle, breaking glass candle chimneys with a club. Another time, a well-dressed man walked into a private home to shake his fist in her face. She was denounced in pulpits and papers, threatened by mobs, called a Jezebel to her face.[45]

As Abby Kelley continued her campaign, she traveled to New Hampshire, where her path crossed that of another radical abolitionist named Stephen Symonds Foster. Kelley had formally given up her membership in her Quaker meeting when they failed to commit themselves to the cause. Foster was another who had joined the "comeouter" exodus of many abolitionists from the established and cautious churches. He had prepared for ordained ministry at Dartmouth and Union Seminary, but got into trouble in both places because of his pacifism. Foster then joined forces with Parker Pillsbury, another radical, and they perfected the technique of breaking up church services by speaking out in the midst of a service. Practicing non-resistance, Foster had been dragged limply down the aisle and kicked down the steps. Twice he had been thrown out of the second floor of a church building. In four months, he was ejected from churches twenty-four times. He had been jailed. He had spent weeks in bed recovering from his beatings. Kelley had not been treated that roughly, but she understood what he had endured. Foster was thirty-two and Kelley was thirty. They seemed destined for each other.

For a while, however, Foster and Kelley continued on separate paths. Kelley had begun to receive invitations from western New York State and had traveled beside the Erie Canal to the new settlements along that route. In January 1842, Kelley went to Boston for the annual meeting of the Massachusetts Anti-Slavery Society. A reporter wrote of the "sweetly melodious yet trumpet tones" she used in "depicting the wrongs of the colored man."[46]

Kelley's mother died that winter and Abby spent some time settling her mother's estate; but in November of that year, she attended a convention in Utica, New York, and Stephen Foster was there. They might have had much in common, but they spent a good part of the convention arguing fiercely over who should be allowed to vote. Foster wanted to open the vote to everyone present, but Kelley thought only members should have that privilege. William Lloyd Garrison was present and managed to moderate the clash between the two strong-minded members.

After the convention ended, Foster, exhausted by long weeks of travel, went home to New Hampshire to recuperate. Long letters of advice and concern from Abby Kelley followed him.

Letters back and forth continued through the winter and spring of 1843. In May, they were both at the annual convention in New York but were too busy with meetings to see much of each other. That fall, she was back in upstate New York, where another reporter, who had heard Henry Clay and John Randolph, wrote that "we are not alone in saying that *in her line* and *in her way*, no public speaker we have ever heard could have held his audience in fixed attention to an equal degree of absorption."[47]

Now, however, she also had the fixed attention of Stephen Foster. They were together at a convention in Utica and spent time afterward in the home of friends. Abby was concerned that marriage would draw her away from her commitment to the cause of the slaves, as it seemed to have done with Angelina Grimké, but Stephen wrote that "I have no idea of spending another winter alone." He did, nevertheless, spend the winter unmarried and, perhaps in frustration, published a tract in the spring of 1843 denouncing the churches as a *Brotherhood of Thieves*.[48] Abby loved it and sold it at her meetings. In the fall of 1843 and early months of 1844, they traveled together through upstate New York, denouncing the churches and drawing attention wherever they went. That fall, they were both in New Hampshire, though Abby kept a companion with her to prevent scandal and she and Foster were seldom in the same community.

In the fall of 1844, Kelley responded to requests to go to Pennsylvania, and now it was she who was fearing another winter of solitude and entreating Foster to join her in the work. He did come to Pennsylvania and they spent time together, but still Abby had other priorities. She responded to appeals to come to Ohio, and Stephen joined her there in the summer and fall of 1845. In the end, they were married by a mutual exchange of vows before twelve witnesses in New Brighton, Pennsylvania, on December 21, 1845.[49]

At first they continued their abolition campaigns. In the small town of Unionville, Ohio, they were arrested and briefly jailed for selling tracts on Sunday. In the best tradition of non-resistance, they had been carried limply from their house and to the jail and the court. When it developed that tracts were commonly sold on Sunday, they were released. But the campaign was shortened when Abby realized that she was pregnant. Stephen, now that he was married, found himself thinking more and more of a home and a farm. In February 1847, he bought a farm on the outskirts of Worcester, Massachusetts, and it was there that their only child, Alla, was born on May 17.[50]

Stephen Foster, it turned out, was a very good farmer. The land was poor, but he improved it and made it productive. He had been ready to take time away from the endless, grueling campaigning. But Abby was not ready. She had feared that she would be taken away from the cause by marriage, and she was, indeed, enslaved for a while by the infant. Stephen went back to the campaign, but Abby wrote him to say "She does not look up to you as to me, so imploringly for food and the supplying of all her wants, reminding me constantly of her utter dependence and of her incapacity to defend herself. . . . I should feel her absence much." But she also missed the campaign trail and decided to wean the baby early and be back at the work of abolition in the next year. Stephen had a younger sister who could care for the child. "We will see," she wrote a friend, "whether I care so much for my baby as to forget the multitude of broken-hearted mothers."[51]

Less than a year after Alla's birth, Abby was back on the road, going to New York and Philadelphia and returning to New York for the annual convention in May. For the next several years, she and Stephen usually alternated time at home and time on the road, though it was Stephen who was increasingly the one to stay home for the work of the farm. Their marriage, however, was strong, and they worked both in public and private as a team. Abby told a friend: "Had I known how much holier and happier and more useful married life is than single, I should not have tarried so long."[52]

V

The Seneca Falls Convention launching the Women's Rights movement was held in July 1848. Abby Kelley Foster had a year-old baby and was not there. But Abby Kelley Foster, like Angelina Grimké Weld, had been campaigning for women's rights as long as they had been campaigning for abolition. They could not campaign for the rights of the slaves without first asserting their own right as women to stand up in public and express their views. The two causes were inseparable. When the convention met in Seneca Falls, the foundation for the women's suffrage movement had already been laid in the abolition movement. But the meetings in Seneca Falls and Rochester in the summer of 1848 were really local meetings; so was a meeting friends of Abby's held in Salem, Ohio, almost two years later. There was need to raise the campaign to a national movement.

Planning for such a movement began with a meeting at the end of the New England Anti-Slavery Convention on May 30, 1850. That meeting created a planning committee of seven, including Abby Kelley Foster, and a convention was called to meet in Worcester, Massachusetts, in October. Over a thousand men and women—more men than women—including delegates from eleven states responded to the call. Abby Kelley and Stephen Foster were both there.

The essential purpose of the convention was summed up in resolutions presented on the first day and unanimously approved at the end:

> Resolved, That every human being of full age, and resident for a proper length of time on the soil of the nation, who is required to obey law, is entitled to a voice in its enactments; that every such person, whose property or labor is taxed for the support of government, is entitled to a direct share in such government. Therefore,

> Resolved, That women are clearly entitled to the right of suffrage, and to be considered eligible to office . . . and that every party which claims to represent the humanity, civilization, and progress of the age, is bound to inscribe on its banners, Equality before the law, without distinction of sex or color.[53]

Abby Kelley Foster is not recorded as having spoken, but what could she have added to the resolution? She was one of nine women and nine men appointed to the Central Committee to carry on the work of the convention. One year later, when a second convention was held in Worcester, Abby finally did speak her piece clearly and firmly and made it clear why she had not spoken before:

> I did not rise to make a speech—my life has been my speech. For fourteen years I have advocated this cause by my daily life. Bloody feet, sisters, have worn smooth the path by which you have come up hither. [Great sensation.] You will not need to speak when you speak by your everyday life. Oh, how truly does Webster say, Action, action, is eloquence! Let us, then, when we go home, go not to complain, but to work. Do not go home to complain of the men, but go and make greater exertions than ever to discharge your every-day duties. Oh! it is easy to be lazy; it is comfortable indeed to be indolent; but it is hard, and a martyrdom, to take responsibilities. There are thousands of women in these United States, working for a starving pittance, who know and feel that they are fitted for something better, and who tell me, when I talk to them, and urge them to open shops, and do business for themselves, "I do not want the responsibility of business—it is too much." Well, then, starve in your laziness!
>
> Oh, Madam President, I feel that we have thrown too much blame on the other side. At any rate, we all deserve enough. We have been groping about in the dark. We are trying to feel our way, and oh! God give us light! But I am convinced that as we go forward and enter the path, it will grow brighter and brighter unto the perfect day.[54]

VI

Abby Kelley Foster's commitment to women's suffrage, however, remained a background issue as events led up to the Civil War. The Fosters' home in Worcester was a station on the Underground Railroad, and Stephen was arrested in a complicated incident in which he had worked to save a slave catcher from a local mob. Abby committed herself even more fully to the abolition movement; but now, after so many years of speaking, her golden voice became tarnished with the strain and she would frequently turn over the speechmaking to such traveling companions as Susan B. Anthony and Lucy Stone. John Brown's raid, the rise of the Republican Party, and the approach of war also complicated things immensely for those committed to non-resistance and abstaining from politics. Stephen was increasingly willing to countenance violence, and Garrison reconsidered his avoidance of politics. Divisions within the movement became sharp and angry, with Garrison criticizing Abby in a public speech and Abby denouncing the Republican Party.[55]

When war came, Abby was one of the few abolitionists who continued to uphold pacifism. On the other hand, she abandoned her abstinence from politics sufficiently to help gather four hundred thousand signatures to a petition to support the Thirteenth Amendment and abolish slavery.[56] Both Abby and Stephen, however, remained committed to moral reform, while many others had shifted to a concern for military victory. When the Emancipation Proclamation led William Lloyd Garrison to declare victory and stop publishing his paper, Abby Kelley Foster insisted that a mere amendment to the Constitution would not solve the problems of the former slaves. Prejudice remained strong. Frederick Douglass pointed out that the Abolition Society had been founded not simply to end slavery but to elevate the former slaves. "When we have taken the chains off the slave," he said, "we shall find a harder resistance to the second purpose. . . . Slavery is not abolished until the black man has the ballot."[57]

Through the first post-war years, Abby Kelley Foster maintained that the rights of the freed slaves had to take precedence over women's rights; but gradually her concern shifted to center on women's rights. She and Stephen were increasingly limited by health problems, but they were involved in meetings in their area and when they spoke, it was usually to recommend or demand more radical action. "The whip needs a snapper," she would say, or "I don't want harmony. I want truth."[58]

Finally they found a cause that enabled them to make headlines without leaving home, when they refused to pay taxes on their property. In 1872, the hundredth anniversary of the Boston Tea Party was a year away, and great plans were being made to celebrate the centenary of the Declaration of Independence. Abby proposed to the Massachusetts Woman Suffrage Society that in the Spirit of '76 they withhold their taxes on the Revolutionary principle of "No taxation without representation." Two members agreed to support them.

The town was reluctant to create an issue by selling the farm of an elderly couple, but Abby egged them on by suggesting that they schedule a tax sale of the farm for July Fourth. Town officials continued to drag their feet but finally scheduled a sale for February 20, 1874. Once a date was set, the Fosters called for a Convention on Taxation Without Representation to be held in Worcester on the day before the sale. The Convention provided the publicity they had hoped for, and more publicity was garnered when one buyer appeared and the property was sold for one hundred dollars. When Stephen notified the buyer that he would need to remove them by force, he decided it wasn't worth the trouble. The issue simmered for years until finally Stephen's health prevented him from fighting on and he settled his bills.[59] The point, however, had been made: the Revolution was still incomplete: half the population did not yet have the freedom for which the war had been fought. The newspapers were surprisingly sympathetic. "Their deed of heroism has no parallel," said the *New York Post*. There was sympathy, but there were few supporters.

Stephen Foster became an invalid by 1878 and died in 1881. Abby moved to Worcester to live with her younger sister and died in 1887. Lucy Stone said of her, "The world of women owes her a debt which they can never repay. The movement for the equal rights of women began directly and emphatically with her. . . . She had no peer and she leaves no successor."[60]

Elizabeth Cady Stanton
1815–1902

NO JUST GOVERNMENT CAN BE FORMED WITHOUT THE CONSENT OF THE GOVERNED

I

If Angelina Grimké's honeymoon was unusual, so was that of Elizabeth Cady Stanton. Henry Stanton was not the sort of man Elizabeth's father had in mind for his daughter. The announcement of their engagement did not bring "unmixed joy and satisfaction." They had known each other less than a month, but Elizabeth was twenty-four years old and knew her own mind. Henry was ten years older, "engaging, eloquent, dominant, masculine, demanding, charming, and a good dancer," and that seemed good to Elizabeth. Henry was also, however, trained for the ministry, a financially unrewarding profession, and unemployed except as a speaker for the cause of abolition. He was a renowned speaker on the abolition circuit, but that did not impress Elizabeth's father, a distinguished and conservative lawyer.[61]

Elizabeth's friends had warned her of her father's likely reaction, so she took the precaution of informing him by letter so that he could absorb the news in her absence. Henry was off on a speaking tour when Elizabeth finally went home to confront her father alone. The ensuing four months were difficult at best. Elizabeth's brother-in-law weighed in with her father, and Elizabeth finally succumbed to familial pressure and broke the engagement—though not the relationship.

Henry, meanwhile, was deeply involved in the controversy within the American Abolition Society between the Garrisonians and anti-Garrisonians. Garrison believed that the Constitution was immoral and therefore abolitionists should take no part in it by voting, holding office, or serving on juries. On the other hand, they believed that women should have the right to speak and vote and hold office. It was an odd combination of beliefs! To be an anti-Garrisonian meant only that one disagreed with Garrison on the Constitution. Anti-Garrisonians believed that it was possible to work within the system, but anti-Garrisonians were often widely divided on other issues. Thus Elizabeth Cady and Henry Stanton were both anti-Garrisonians, but Henry believed that abolitionists should concentrate on that one issue and not be concerned about women's rights, and Elizabeth felt differently. She had broken her engagement to Henry, but not the relationship, and in the spring of 1840 he faced her with a decision. The two anti-slavery factions had finally divided, and Henry Stanton was chosen by the anti-Garrisonian faction to be a delegate to the first World Anti-Slavery Convention, which was being held in London. He suggested that Elizabeth might like to go with him and consider it a honeymoon.

Elizabeth accepted the challenge, and a wedding was quickly arranged. Only Elizabeth's sister represented her family. The bride had no time for an elaborate wedding dress, and the bride's vow to "obey" her husband was omitted—over the objection of the pastor. Stopping briefly in New York City before leaving, the new couple made a quick visit to Henry's best friend, Theodore Weld, living with his wife, Angelina Grimké, and her sister Sarah in nearby Belleville, New Jersey. Weld, like Stanton, had left the Garrisonian wing of the abolition movement—though not, presumably, over a woman's right to speak in public, since his wife had made a major speech only a few days after their wedding.[62]

Elizabeth had been thoroughly exposed to abolitionist teaching through her cousin, Gerrit Smith, long before she met Henry. One of the wealthiest men in the country, Smith was not only a leading abolitionist but a supporter of almost every good cause, from prison reform to equal rights for women, abolition of the death penalty, and the Greek and Irish revolutions. He was also a vegetarian. Staying with the Smiths, Elizabeth Cady met not only abolitionists but fugitive slaves, temperance advocates, and reformers of every sort. Visiting the Smith household, sometimes for weeks at a time, Elizabeth was inevitably engaged in passionate discussion of every manner of issue—but seems not to have committed herself to any particular cause.[63] That would begin to change with her marriage and the trip to England.

The idea of an international Anti-Slavery Convention had been suggested by American abolitionists, and the original invitation from the English abolitionists had simply asked all abolition societies to send delegates. The British quickly realized, however, that women might be delegated by some American societies, and sent a follow-up request for a list of *male* delegates. Nevertheless, the Garrisonians, among others, sent women as representatives, and the result was that the first session was spent arguing over who should be seated. Wendell Phillips urged strongly that the women should be seated, and Henry Stanton spoke in favor as well, but he was not a Garrisonian and some believed that his heart was not in it. When a voice vote was called for, Henry was thought to have voted against the motion. He had, until the break with Garrison, supported women's participation, but apparently came to agree with the anti-Garrison faction that women's rights were a distraction from the primary question of abolition. The vote was overwhelmingly against seating the women. The women therefore were relegated to a separate section but, as a special concession, allowed to remain for the business meetings.

Elizabeth Cady Stanton was appalled at the course of the debate; and when Garrison, arriving after the vote, chose to sit with the women, he, her husband's adversary, became her hero. Lucretia Mott, a Quaker crusader for abolition and women's rights, was one of the important American leaders present; and she, though twice Elizabeth's age, was glad to meet her. They became fast friends and went together to visit schools, museums, and prisons while the men went about their business. When Lucretia Mott preached a sermon in a Unitarian Chapel, it was the first time Elizabeth Stanton had heard a woman speak in public or preach a sermon. Elizabeth wrote to Angelina Grimké that "my soul finds great delight in her society," and Mott wrote in her diary that "Elizabeth Stanton grows daily in our affections."[64] As for Stanton, she wrote that "Mrs. Mott was to me an entire new revelation of womanhood. I sought every opportunity to be at her side, plying her with questions. . . . I had never heard a woman talk what[,] as a Scotch Presbyterian, I had scarcely dared to think. . . ."[65] After the vote was taken denying women the right to serve as delegates, they walked back to their lodgings arm in arm and "resolved to hold a convention as soon as we got home, and [to] form a society to advocate the rights of women."[66]

It would be eight years before the Seneca Falls Convention was held. Elizabeth Cady Stanton made use of the time not only to start a family but also to lobby for a Married Women's Property Act in Albany, where she was living at the time. Her first public speech, in 1842, was on temperance and made only a passing reference to women's rights.[67]

Moving in 1844 to Boston, she became acquainted with a wide range of reformers, including John Greenleaf Whittier, Bronson Alcott, and Ralph Waldo Emerson. William Lloyd Garrison was *persona non grata* to Henry, but Elizabeth exchanged letters with Garrison nonetheless. She also met Frederick Douglass and broadened his horizons to include women's rights.[68] He would continue to be a valuable ally.

II

In 1847, the Stantons moved back to upstate New York. Away from the varied stimulation of life in Boston, Elizabeth began to feel acutely the limitations of life as a housewife and to look around for a role that would set her free to use her gifts for some larger purpose. When Lucretia Mott came to the area in 1848 for an annual Quaker gathering, the two spent Thursday, July 13, with three other like-minded women. They decided that they could not claim to be much oppressed themselves, but, as Elizabeth put it in a letter to another friend, they had "souls large enough to feel the wrongs of others."[69] Elizabeth had worked already to secure women's property rights in New York State and insisted on the importance of political action and the right to vote. Lucretia Mott was reluctant to press for the vote, fearing that it would make them look ridiculous, but insisted on the importance of economic and social reform. Both agreed, nonetheless, that society needed to be changed. The obvious solution—everyone was doing it—was to issue a statement and call a convention.*

Having agreed on what to do and seeing no reason to delay any longer, they set the opening day for the next Wednesday. It was short notice and, "having no experience in the *modus operandi* of getting up conventions," the planning was less than complete. When they went to the church to begin the meeting, no one had thought to bring a key, and a Stanton nephew had to be hoisted in through a window to open the door from the inside. But there was no lack of response. The pews were quickly filled and the meeting called to order by Lucretia Mott's husband, since none of the women had been able to imagine themselves presiding at a meeting.

* Mott and Cady, of course, had attended the first World Convention on Slavery in 1840, but conventions were held by churches; mission, Bible, and tract societies; abolitionists; temperance advocates; and many others. The first national political conventions were held in 1830 and 1831. The American Colonization Society was formed in 1816 to support colonization of African Americans to Africa, and the first Negro National Convention was held in 1839 to oppose them.

Lucretia Mott, the only woman with experience as a speaker, went first and, surveying "the degraded condition of woman the world over, showed the importance of inaugurating some movement for her education and elevation." Elizabeth Cady Stanton also spoke to the opening session. Revealing her lack of experience as a speaker, some complained that she could not be heard, but she took a good-humored approach to disarm any skeptics in the audience:

> We do not propose to petition the legislature to make our husbands just, generous, and courteous, to seat every man at the head of a cradle, and to clothe every woman in male attire.

In fact, she pointed out, when men wish to be most dignified, "bishops, priests, judges, barristers, and lord mayors of the first nation on the globe, and the Pope of Rome, with his cardinals" resort to the "loose flowing robes" that women ordinarily use, thus tacitly "acknowledging that the male attire is neither dignified nor imposing."

Stanton may have begun with a light note, but she made it very clear that she had serious business on her agenda, and that it had to do with freedom:

> . . . we are assembled to protest against a form of government existing without the consent of the governed—to declare our right to be free as man is free, to be represented in the government which we are taxed to support, to have such disgraceful laws as give man the power to chastise and imprison his wife, to take the wages which she earns, the property which she inherits, and, in case of separation, the children of her love; laws which make her the mere dependent on his bounty. It is to protest against such unjust laws as these that we are assembled today, and to have them, if possible, forever erased from our statute books, deeming them a shame and a disgrace to a Christian republic in the nineteenth century. We have met to uplift woman's fallen divinity upon an even pedestal with man's. And, strange as it may seem to many, we now demand our right to vote according to the declaration of the government under which we live.

So that was the agenda, and if there were some who could not hear her, those who could would have noticed that she could turn a phrase as aptly as Patrick Henry or Daniel Webster. And she could be very clear about her demand for the right to vote:

> The right is ours. Have it, we must. Use it, we will. The pens, the tongues, the fortunes, the indomitable wills of many women are

> already pledged to secure this right. The great truth that no just government can be formed without the consent of the governed we shall echo and re-echo in the ears of the unjust judge, until by continual coming we shall weary him.[70]

Stanton was careful to put their crusade in a larger context. "War, slavery, drunkenness, licentiousness, gluttony" were among the national sins she listed as demanding attention; but these, she argued, could not be dealt with effectively without "some new element, some purifying power, some spirit of mercy and love." And that required the woman's voice because "man cannot fulfill his destiny alone, he cannot redeem his race unaided."

The speech-making over, the convention moved to consider a declaration of rights that had been drawn up in advance. It is significant that they modeled their statement on the Declaration of Independence, although they struggled to find eighteen grievances to match the list made by the founding fathers. It was not, after all, specific grievances that were the root problem, but attitudes and expectations more relevant to agricultural and feudal societies in which roles had been defined by sheer physical strength and biology. They were seeking liberty to live freely in a new industrial world where a growing number of roles would be defined not by physical strength, but by intelligence and skill in interpersonal relationships. Elizabeth Cady Stanton was the principal author and Frederick Douglass, who had made the fifty-mile trip from Rochester to be present, was one of the most effective voices in support. "We hold these truths to be self-evident," they declared "that all men and women are created equal; that they are endowed by their Creator with certain inalienable rights; that among these are life, liberty, and the pursuit of happiness. . . ."[71] To that end, they hoped to amend the Constitution so that it would better reflect the ideals proclaimed in the Declaration of Independence.

The most controversial issue was, as they had known it would be, the right to vote. Even Lucretia Mott had been skeptical, but Elizabeth Cady Stanton insisted on it and, in the end, it was narrowly adopted. Apparently they were well satisfied with their first convention, since they held a second one only two weeks later in Rochester. This time a woman was nominated to preside. Stanton was still nervous about so radical an innovation, but she was overruled and a woman named Abigail Bush presided.

Other such meetings followed on a state and national basis, but Elizabeth Cady Stanton, having set the ball in motion and spoken her piece, was not an important part of it for a number of years. She wrote letters and articles but allowed her family responsibilities to take precedence over meetings and travel. Each of the national conventions held in the 1850s began with a letter from her, but she herself was not there.[72] After she met Susan B. Anthony in 1851, beginning a long, sometimes conflicted friendship, she coached Anthony in speaking and wrote speeches for her. Sometimes Anthony, who lived near Rochester, supervised the children or stirred the pudding while Stanton worked on a speech. "I forged the thunderbolts," Stanton wrote; "she fired them."[73]

Although Stanton stayed away from most meetings herself until 1860, she was briefly involved with the temperance movement. She and Susan B. Anthony organized the New York State Women's Temperance Society in 1851, and Stanton was elected first president in 1852. Over her objection, the meeting voted to open the membership to men. Although she spoke more moderately to the meeting than she might have done, her advocacy of women's rights so offended male temperance leaders that they joined with conservative women at the next meeting and voted her out of office.[74] Yet, being neither single like Anthony nor old enough to be free of her children like Mott, nor wealthy enough to have enough household help, she could not see her way clear to give time to the women's movement directly. It frustrated her, and she wrote to Anthony in 1853: "How much I long to be free of housekeeping and children, so as to have time to think and read and write."[75] Freedom for her was not simply a social cause but a very personal issue. It irritated Anthony that, in spite of such declarations, Stanton continued to have more children, four between 1850 and 1860 to add to the three she had borne before that. "Those of you who have talent to do honor to poor—oh! how poor—womanhood have all given yourselves over to baby-making; and left poor brainless me to do battle alone," complained Anthony.[76]

Though Stanton spoke at no women's conferences in this time, she did respond to urgent requests by going to Albany in 1854 to testify for a bill on women's rights. Her testimony was passionate and eloquent. "Would to God," she told the legislators, "you could know the burning indignation that fills woman's soul when she turns over the pages of your statute books, and sees there how like feudal barons you freemen hold your women."

But the passion was balanced with a careful, even lawyerly, exposition of the law. She had spent time in her father's law offices when she was growing up, and the clerks had teased her with citations of the laws that made women subject to their husbands. She cited "Sec. 1, Bill of Rights, 2 R.S., 301," which provided that "no authority can, on any pretence whatever, be exercised over the citizens of this state but such as is or shall be derived from, and granted by, the people of this state." "So who," she asked, "granted you this authority over women?" She cited the Constitution, Article 2, Section 2, and she cited the case law, "7 Howard's Practice, Reports, 105, Levett agt. Robinson and Witbeck, sheriff, &c.," that said a woman's earnings belong to her husband. She argued that:

> It is not enough for us that by your laws we are permitted to live and breathe, to claim the necessaries of life from our legal protectors—to pay the penalty of our crimes; we demand the full recognition of all our rights as citizens of the Empire State. We are persons; native, free-born citizens; property-holders, tax-payers; yet are we denied the exercise of our right to the elective franchise. We support ourselves, and, in part, your schools, colleges, churches, your poor-houses, jails, prisons, the army, the navy, the whole machinery of government, and yet we have no voice in your councils. We have every qualification required by the constitution, necessary to the legal voter, but the one of sex. We are moral, virtuous and intelligent, and in all respects quite equal to the proud white man himself, and yet by your laws we are classed with idiots, lunatics and negroes; and though we do not feel honored by the place assigned us, yet, in fact, our legal position is lower than that of either; for the negro can be raised to the dignity of a voter if he possess himself of $250; the lunatic can vote in his moments of sanity, and the idiot, too, if he be a male one, and not more than nine-tenths a fool; but we, who have guided great movements of charity, established missions, edited journals, published works on history, economy and statistics; who have governed nations, led armies, filled the professor's chair, taught philosophy and mathematics to the savants of our age, discovered planets, piloted ships across the sea, are denied the most sacred rights of citizens.[77]

Such eloquence increased the pressure on her to take a fuller part in the women's movement, but still she resisted. "My whole soul is in the work," she wrote to Susan Anthony, "but my hands belong to my family."[78] Her understanding of freedom was very personal; her letters speak of "domestic bondage" and being a "household drudge," but also of looking forward to getting the youngest child in school so that she could give herself more fully to the work she longed to do.[79]

The seventh Stanton baby arrived in 1859; but in that same year, Elizabeth's father died, leaving a significant estate to his wife and enough to Elizabeth to give her some financial security for the first time. Henry's income as a lawyer and lecturer was unpredictable and never enough. Now Elizabeth would have some freedom of her own to demand freedom for others. She began the new decade with three major speeches in three months: one to the Judiciary Committee of the New York State Legislature on property rights, one on the right to vote to the American Abolition Society, and one on divorce to the National Women's Rights Convention.[80]

In speaking to the legislature in Albany, Stanton connected the issue of women's rights with the abolition movement, as she had done before, and called her speech "A Slave's Appeal." This time her appeal was answered when the legislature passed a married woman's property act the next day. She made the same connection in the letter she sent to the Tenth National Women's Rights Convention later that spring: "Her bondage, though it differs from that of the Negro slave, frets and chafes her all the same. She too sighs and groans in her chains. . . ." Indeed, she argued that "the prejudice against sex is more deeply rooted and more unreasonably maintained than that against color." And now, beginning to feel free to break her own chains, she went to the American Anti-Slavery Convention and reminded the delegates that women also were slaves. Two days later, she followed up her letter to the women's convention by going herself and introducing ten resolutions about divorce. "Personal freedom," she told the delegates, "is the first right to be proclaimed," but no married woman enjoys such freedom. Marriage should be made a simple contract between equal parties, with equal restraints and privileges on both sides.[81]

Stanton's resolutions caused considerable turmoil and used up one whole session of the convention. When it was over, Wendell Phillips moved to table the resolutions and expunge the entire debate from the records. William Lloyd Garrison was satisfied to table the resolutions and preserve the record—which the convention did. They had wanted her back but were not, perhaps, prepared to deal with her when she came. A year later, Wendell Phillips, as trustee of an endowment, tried to make amends by offering Stanton a three-month trip to Europe to speak about women's rights. She was sorely tempted, but the demands of home and family were still too strong.[82] She did a brief speaking tour in early 1861 in support of abolition, but her most personal involvement in the Civil War came with the New York draft riots. The Stantons had moved to the city, and Elizabeth found herself standing at her doorway in Manhattan prepared to repel rioters. For a few years, the war overwhelmed other concerns; but when it was over, it was possible at last for Elizabeth Cady Stanton to become fully involved in the women's movement.

III

The war was over, but it had transformed American society in such a way that Elizabeth Cady Stanton could not simply pick up the old campaign for women's rights where she had left it and go forward from there. Before the war, she had campaigned for women's rights and the abolition of slavery. Now the slaves were free and a new issue had arisen: for if the slaves were free, were they to be given the vote; and if they were to be given the right to vote, what about women? To the horror of Stanton and her colleagues, Congressional action to enfranchise the former slaves in the Fourteenth Amendment to the Constitution spoke of *male* citizens, making definite what before had simply been assumed. It was the first time any distinction of gender had been enshrined in the Constitution, and it was obviously included because the women's-rights movement had questioned what the authors of the Constitution had assumed. Now it was made explicit.

Stanton was outraged, but she and Susan B. Anthony working together could not convince such old allies as Wendell Phillips that women's suffrage had the same priority as black suffrage. Persuaded that those working for black and female suffrage should work together, they joined in forming an American Equal Rights Association, only to have the AERA then give priority to black suffrage. In 1866, an effort to extend the franchise in the District of Columbia to women as well as African Americans was defeated, and in 1867 a revision of the New York State Constitution failed to include women in the electorate. When Stanton testified before the legislative committee in Albany, Horace Greeley, the chairman of the committee, asked her why women should have the ballot if they could not defend it with a bullet. Her response, that she could send a substitute as easily as Greeley had done in the Civil War, was a neat point but also alienated an important legislator.[83]

Later that same year, the new state of Kansas failed to include women's suffrage in its constitution despite weeks of campaigning by Stanton, Anthony, and others. No actions were taken, but the issue now was being presented to the voters, and in 1872 the Republican Party platform went so far as to say that "the honest demands of any class of citizens for equal rights should be treated with respectful consideration."[84] Why any class of citizens should not automatically have equal rights was not explained.

But perhaps it was progress that a woman's right to vote was now an issue in all these places. The need for education was obviously still a high priority, and that had always been Elizabeth Cady Stanton's chief concern and strength. With Susan B. Anthony and Lucretia Mott at her side as usual, she called together a convention to form a Woman's Suffrage Association in Washington in 1868 and, of course, did a good deal of the speaking. Grace Greenwood, a novelist, gave readers of the *Philadelphia Press* a clear summary of the skills that Stanton brought to the task:

> Her speeches are models of composition, clear, compact, elegant and logical. She makes her points with peculiar sharpness and certainty, and there is no denying or dodging her conclusions. . . . [She is] now impassioned, now playful, now witty, now pathetic. Mrs. Stanton has the best arts of the politician and the training of the jurist, adding to the fiery, unresting spirit of the reformer. She has a rare talent for affairs, management, and mastership. Yet she is in an eminent degree womanly, having an almost regal pride of sex.[85]

Very few speakers have ever been accused of bringing together such an array of talents. Patrick Henry was not remembered as being "playful" as a speaker, nor would one ever have described Daniel Webster as being either "compact" or "witty." As for Stanton's "training" as a jurist, it was acquired secondhand at best in her father's law office. But these skills made her a sought-after speaker and opened opportunities for her to teach and to convert. For ten years, she spent two thirds of her time on the lecture circuit as a paid speaker and celebrity. She spoke about a dozen subjects, ranging from "The Subjection of Women" to "The Bible and Women's Rights." Neither rain nor snow nor gloom of night impeded her as she traveled through snowdrifts in the Midwest on a sled or sat on a trunk on a donkey cart. Like a traveling evangelist, she reported that she "brought many male sinners to repentance," and stirred up some lethargic women "to a state of rebellion against the existing order of things."[86]

It was always an uphill fight. The activists were always a small minority, but Stanton accepted that as inevitable. "[T]he history of the world," she wrote, "shows that the vast majority, in every generation, passively accept the conditions into which they are born, while those who demanded larger liberties are ever a small, ostracized minority, whose claims are ridiculed and ignored."[87] But Stanton persisted in pressing her case for reform, until a vehicle she was traveling in overturned. She finished the tour, but an attack of pneumonia in the fall of 1879 persuaded her that the time had come to retire from the lecture circuit and find new realms to conquer. She attempted to vote in the fall of 1880, explaining to the poll watcher that a recent amendment to the Constitution had declared that "all persons born or naturalized in the United States, and subject to the jurisdiction thereof, are citizens of the United States" and entitled to vote. The poll watcher told her, "I know nothing about the Constitutions, State or national. I never read either; but I do know that in New Jersey, women have not voted in my day, and I cannot accept your ballot."[88]

In 1881, Elizabeth Cady Stanton was sixty-five, and she instructed Susan B. Anthony that she would not stand for reelection as president of the National Woman Suffrage Association. She spent the better part of the next decade working with Anthony on a history of the women's-rights movement and traveling several times to England and France. By 1889, she had, according to one biographer, "survived her husband, outlived most of her enemies, and exhausted her allies."[89] When Susan B. Anthony organized an International Council of Women in Washington to commemorate the fortieth anniversary of the Seneca Falls Convention, Stanton, now seventy-three, made an opening address that stressed the similarities among women of various conditions and nations. They were alike, she told them, "in bondage" whether "housed in golden cages with every want supplied, or wandering in the dreary deserts of life, friendless and forsaken."[90]

She resigned as president of the NWSA in 1892, at the age of seventy-seven, and in her last address laid out a narrow philosophy of freedom in a speech titled "The Solitude of Self."

> The strongest reason for giving woman all the opportunities for higher education, for the full development of her faculties, her forces of mind and body; for giving her the most enlarged freedom of thought and action; a complete emancipation from all forms of bondage, of custom, dependence, superstition; from all the crippling influences of fear—is the solitude and personal responsibility of her own individual life. The strongest reason why we ask for woman a voice in the government under which she lives; in the religion she is asked to believe; equality in social life, where she is the chief factor; a place in the trades and professions, where she may earn her bread, is because of her birthright to self-sovereignty; because, as an individual, she must rely on herself.

She had fought for freedom from oppression without apparently ever envisioning what she had never experienced: a society of free individuals working together toward a common purpose.

Anthony and Stanton had one of their sharpest disagreements as to policy toward the end of the century. Anthony thought they should concentrate on the one issue of the right to vote and let nothing distract themselves or others. But Stanton was unwilling to give up other causes; for all her insistence on the primacy of the suffrage, she could not narrow her interests. In 1895, at the age of eighty, she committed the ultimate outrage by publishing *The Woman's Bible*, a commentary compiled from her own work and that of others, on passages in the Bible dealing with women. "The clergy," she noted with satisfaction, "denounced it as the work of Satan, though it really was the work of Ellen Battelle Dietrick, Lillie Devereux Blake, [the] Rev. Phebe A. Hanaford, Clara Bewick Colby, Ursula N. Gestefeld, Louisa Southworth, Frances Ellen Burr, and myself."[91] In fighting for freedom, she insisted on being free herself to challenge whatever orthodoxies offended her.

Three years later, her autobiography showed her with none of the sharp edges. The story of her public life, she said, would be found in *The History of Woman Suffrage*; the autobiography was "the story of my private life as the wife of an earnest reformer, as an enthusiastic housekeeper, proud of my skill in every department of domestic economy, and as the mother of seven children."[92] Though she had spoken again and again of domestic bondage, she had, after all, found freedom there also.

FIVE

Abraham Lincoln
1809–1865

A NEW NATION, CONCEIVED IN LIBERTY

I

The most important speech Abraham Lincoln ever made was not the Gettysburg Address, but a speech he made on a midwinter evening in New York City at the end of February 1860, a critical election year. Without that speech, there would probably have been no President Lincoln and therefore also no Gettysburg address.

Lincoln had been invited to come to New York to speak in the Plymouth Church in Brooklyn where Henry Ward Beecher had made himself the country's preeminent preacher. Lincoln's prompt acceptance of the invitation was evidence of his willingness to put himself on a national stage and to test his ability to draw support from the sophisticated eastern wing of the Republican Party. He bought a new suit for a hundred dollars from a local tailor and began to research the issues he intended to explore.

Lincoln's thinking about the speech centered increasingly on the historical record of the framing of the Constitution. He visited the nearby State Library to find relevant documents, but several critical resources were even more readily available. In his own library he had a two-volume edition of Jonathan Elliot's compilation of the debates in the state conventions on the adoption of the Constitution* and a one-volume edition of John Sanderson's five-volume *Biography of the Signers to the Declaration of Independence*. In his law office there was a copy of James Kent's four-volume *Commentaries on American Law*. All of these provided the specific historical information he wanted. As he read and thought, he habitually made notes on strips of paper until he was ready to put them together. Sometimes he numbered the strips of paper and saved them in his hat. When he was ready to write, he sat down and assembled the strips and began to write out his speech on a standard pad of blue paper.[1]

A young man in the community** who provided graphic descriptions of Lincoln in his research and writing tells us that Lincoln would sometimes sit motionless for up to half an hour, thinking through what he needed to say and oblivious of everything else. Sometimes he would read sections of his speech to his law partner, William Herndon, who wrote that Lincoln's perception was "slow, cold, clear, and exact" and that he was a "remorseless analyzer of facts, things, and principles."[2] Herndon was increasingly exasperated by Lincoln's focus on his political career at the expense of their legal business, but Lincoln could not completely put aside either his legal career or the press of political concerns. In October, there was a trial in Urbana. In December and January, he appeared before the Illinois supreme court and the U.S. Circuit Court in Springfield. Requests for speeches came from other places than New York and had to be politely refused. One request, from Boston, was turned aside with a long and thoughtful letter widely reproduced in party newspapers, in which he said "Those who deny freedom to others, deserve it not for themselves; and, under a just God, cannot long retain it."[3] In a society without electronic communications, Lincoln's letters were a vital means of communicating his positions.

One study of Lincoln's presidency argues that his pen was "arguably his most powerful presidential weapon."[4]

In spite of all distractions, the New York speech was fully prepared by the time Lincoln left Springfield and made his laborious way to New York on five different trains without sleeping cars or diners. For three days and three nights he took his meals from a picnic basket packed by his wife and slept as best he could, though each night he needed to change trains at one or two o'clock in the morning.[5]

---

* See various references to Elliot in Chapter One.

** Henry Bascom Rankin was a farmhand in the area, and it is not clear how he had the opportunity to observe Lincoln so closely. Modern historians tend to discount his observations, but he obviously knew Lincoln, since Lincoln signed his photograph album and wrote that he was "honored" to do so.

Arriving in New York on Saturday, Lincoln learned that the event had been taken over by the "Young Republicans Club" and transferred to the Cooper Union in Manhattan. This was a newly opened center for working people in New York that was open not only to men and women alike but also to both black and white. Its 1,800-seat auditorium was the largest secular meeting space in the city. The so-called "Young Republicans" (some of whom, like Horace Greeley, age forty-eight, were well into their middle years) had created a series of talks by leading Republican politicians, as much as anything to see what alternatives there might be to New York's "favorite son," Senator William Seward. Informed of the change of venue only after he checked into his hotel, Lincoln spent what time he had in rewriting his speech for a more secular audience, though he did take time to visit Beecher's church in Brooklyn for the Sunday service.[6]

Monday, February 27, 1860 was a relatively mild mid-winter day in New York City,* so a large crowd made their way to the Cooper Union, unsure exactly who this western politician was. The auditorium was only three quarters full, but those present included a good cross section of the city's leading businessmen, politicians, lawyers, editors, and clergy. The sight of Lincoln as he sat on the platform and when he stood to speak only increased their doubts. The expensive new suit was not up to eastern standards, and the tall, gangly figure inside it seemed awkwardly put together as well. The surprisingly high-pitched voice did nothing to re-assure the audience, but the words, as carefully constructed as a lawyer's brief, quickly commanded their attention.[7] This was no fiery polemic, but a carefully researched, thoughtfully organized analysis of the attitudes and intentions of the country's founding statesmen on the subject of slavery. Did their vision for America, Lincoln asked, imagine an expanding or diminishing role for slavery? As his first two words indicated, Lincoln wanted to avoid emotion and get to "the facts."

"The facts with which I shall deal this evening are mainly old and familiar," Lincoln began, "nor is there anything new in the general use I shall make of them. If there shall be any novelty, it will be in the mode of presenting the facts, and the inferences and observations following that presentation." The voice had seemed shrill at first and the midwestern accent was unfamiliar, but the voice quickly modulated into a clear tenor that carried well and the subject matter was laid out simply and clearly. Senator Stephen A. Douglas, in his debates with Lincoln two years earlier, had frequently

---

* Various accounts of the event report weather ranging from "mild" to "blizzard," but meteorological records tell of an "unseasonably warm" 44 degrees in mid-afternoon. There was no precipitation. Holzer, 103.

appealed to the framers of the Constitution for support in arguing that the federal government had no authority to override the will of the people in this matter. "Our fathers," he said, "when they framed the Government under which we live, understood this question just as well, and even better, than we do now" and had given the federal government no such power. In a recent lengthy article in *Harper's New Monthly Magazine*, Douglas had attempted to document his claims about the framers' intentions. Now Lincoln, who had done his own research, quoted Douglas's claim and proposed to lay out the facts concerning it.[8]

There were, he told his audience, thirty-nine men who signed the Constitution. What evidence do we have of their positions on slavery and federal authority? Citing names and dates, Lincoln told his audience that the question of slavery in the "Northwestern Territory" (the future states of Ohio, Indiana, Illinois, Michigan, Wisconsin, and Minnesota) had come up twice before the Constitution was even adopted, and five of the six future signers of the Constitution, sitting as members of the Congress of the Confederation, voted to prohibit slavery there. In the first Congress to sit under the Constitution, an ordinance was passed prohibiting slavery in that territory and sixteen signers of the Constitution were present. Lincoln named each one of them. The ordinance was approved without objection. George Washington, another of the thirty-nine signers, then President of the United States, signed the bill. When Tennessee and Mississippi and Alabama were organized as territories, slavery was there already, but Congress prohibited the importation of slaves to those areas without objection. Case by case, like the careful lawyer he was, Lincoln showed how the federal government had assumed the right under the Constitution to prohibit or limit slavery in its territories. Signers of the Constitution had not objected.

Other actions were cited and the names of other signers of the Constitution. Nowhere in the historical record did Lincoln find any evidence that the signers of the Constitution believed that the federal government had no authority to prohibit slavery in the territories. Summing up his case, the seemingly awkward but eloquent politician told his hearers:

> If any man at this day sincerely believes that a proper division of local from federal authority, or any part of the Constitution, forbids the Federal Government to control as to slavery in the federal territories, he is right to say so, and to enforce his position by all truthful evidence and fair argument which he can. But he has no right to mislead others, who have less access to history, and less leisure to study it, into the false belief that "our fathers who framed the Government under which we live" were of the same

> opinion—thus substituting falsehood and deception for truthful evidence and fair argument. [Applause]

Thus the first section of the address set out to establish the facts in the case. Part Two, slightly shorter, was addressed to the South, taking up charges made in the South that the Republican Party was determined to destroy the Union. In fact, he said, it was the South that was determined to force a new understanding of federal power on the nation.

> Your purpose, then, plainly stated, is that you will destroy the Government, unless you be allowed to construe and enforce the Constitution as you please, on all points in dispute between you and us. You will rule or ruin in all events. . . .
>
> But you will not abide the election of a Republican president! In that supposed event, you say, you will destroy the Union; and then, you say, the great crime of having destroyed it will be upon us! [Laughter.] That is cool.* A highwayman holds a pistol to my ear, and mutters through his teeth, "Stand and deliver, or I shall kill you, and then you will be a murderer!" [Continued laughter.]

The third and shortest part of the speech was addressed to Republicans, presumably the audience of "Young Republicans" in front of him:

> Let us be diverted by none of those sophistical contrivances wherewith we are so industriously plied and belabored—contrivances such as groping for some middle ground between the right and the wrong, vain as the search for a man who should be neither a living man nor a dead man—such as a policy of "don't care" on a question about which all true men do care—such as Union appeals beseeching true Union men to yield to Disunionists, reversing the divine rule, and calling, not the sinners, but the righteous to repentance—[*prolonged cheers and laughter*] such as invocations to Washington, imploring men to unsay what Washington said, and undo what Washington did.
>
> Neither let us be slandered from our duty by false accusations against us, nor frightened from it by menaces of destruction to

* This is not the contemporary "cool," a term of approval. The word implied "controlled or unexcited" in the eighteenth century, "impudent" or "uncaring" in the early nineteenth. This seems to have evolved into "calmly audacious" after 1825 and is apparently Lincoln's meaning here.

> the Government nor of dungeons to ourselves. [*Applause.*] LET US HAVE FAITH THAT RIGHT MAKES MIGHT, AND IN THAT FAITH, LET US, TO THE END, DARE TO DO OUR DUTY AS WE UNDERSTAND IT.

"Three rousing cheers" were given to the orator, according to *The New York Times*, while *The Evening Post* reported a standing ovation, with "the waving of handkerchiefs and hats, and repeated cheers."[9]

An eyewitness that evening said "When Lincoln rose to speak, I was greatly disappointed. He was tall, tall,—oh, how tall! and so angular and awkward that I had, for an instant, a feeling of pity for so ungainly a man." Once Lincoln warmed up, "his face lighted up as with an inward fire; the whole man was transfigured. I forgot his clothes, his personal appearance, and his individual peculiarities. Presently, forgetting myself, I was on my feet like the rest, yelling like a wild Indian, cheering this wonderful man."[10]

The next day, Lincoln traveled up to New England to visit his older son, who was preparing for admission to Harvard at Phillips Exeter Academy—and took advantage of the opportunity to follow a zigzag course that took him to eleven cities for eleven more speeches in eleven days. The speeches were based for the most part on his Cooper Union address and ended with his summons to a "faith that right makes might." From Exeter, New Hampshire on Sunday, March 3, he took time to write home to Mary and tell her that the speech in New York "had gone off passably well." He asked how the two younger sons were doing and told her he hoped to be home again in a week and a day.[11] Back in New York the next Sunday, he went again to the Plymouth Church in the morning and then toured a charity mission in the worst Manhattan slum in the afternoon. He spoke to the children collected for Sunday School, telling them about his own childhood deprivations. Then, turning down invitations to speak in New Jersey, Pennsylvania, and Ohio, he took the ferry across the Hudson and boarded the Erie Railroad for the long, slow trip along New York's snow-covered southern tier, saying a few words to small groups at some of the stations. Changing trains at Toledo and Fort Wayne, he was back in Springfield on March 14, just three weeks after leaving, and facing a mountain of accumulated mail.

II

It was fashionable for many years for American politicians to claim a frontier origin, preferably birth in a log cabin. It began, of course, with Patrick Henry, who was a child of the frontier although Henry never aspired to the presidency and was not born in a log cabin. Andrew Jackson, who broke the string of establishment presidents in 1828, was the first to bring the story of a log-cabin birth to the White House. From Jackson to Garfield, 1828 to 1881, half of the presidents could claim that distinction.* It seemed to symbolize humble origins and an ability to understand the lives of others who lived in similar circumstances. It also testified to the candidate's ability to achieve something of the American dream.

If humble origins were an asset, Lincoln probably had the best claim of any American president. He has been called "one of the least experienced and most poorly prepared men ever elected to high office."[12] Certainly he had a minimum of formal education. Lincoln may have been taught to read by the eighteen-year-old illegitimate nephew of his mother's sister who was living nearby. "I taught him to write with a buzzard's quill which I killed with a rifle," said Dennis Hanks. That would have given Lincoln a head start when he was able to go to a school a mile away for one term. When that school closed, Lincoln was able to go to a school four miles away for a few months, but his attendance was sporadic because, as a young teenager, he had farm chores to perform. The following year, again, he was able to attend at times, but by his own summary "the aggregate of all his schooling did not amount to one year."[13]

Legends of Lincoln the log-splitter have some basis in fact; Lincoln did everything boys and young men needed to do growing up on a farm at the western edge of settlement. He split logs and slaughtered hogs and helped with house-raisings. He clerked at the general store and worked with the blacksmith. In his late teens, he rode a shipment of meat, corn, and flour down the Ohio and Mississippi to New Orleans. But he loved to read and, once he got the hang of it, he read whenever he could. And like Patrick Henry, he would still sometimes go barefoot even as an adult.

Already, as a young adult, Lincoln was seen as a leader. He was nominated for the state legislature when he was only twenty-three, but when volunteers were called for to put down an Indian uprising he took time away from campaigning to serve in the militia. It was customary for volunteer militia units to elect their own captain, and Lincoln was chosen to lead his. He served less than three months, but it provided a useful lesson in leadership and acquainted him with men from other parts of the state. Back on the campaign trail, he traveled around the county, soliciting votes and telling people "My politics are short and sweet, like the old woman's dance." There were four candidates to be chosen but Lincoln finished eighth in a field of thirteen.

After that, he ran a general store for a while with a partner and found himself with time on his hands for reading and for memorizing passages of

* Although William Henry Harrison made the log cabin a symbol of his campaign, he was not born in one. Andrew Jackson was the first President to be born in a log cabin. The others were Zachary Taylor, Millard Fillmore, James Buchanan, Abraham Lincoln, Ulysses S. Grant, and James A. Garfield.

Shakespeare. Years before, he had studied William Scott's *Lessons in Elocution*. Now he went out of his way to get a copy of a standard English grammar and memorized long sections. He served as postmaster for a while and learned to be a surveyor. None of these was ultimately satisfying, but all of them brought him into contact with large numbers of people, an important background for someone interested in politics.

In 1834, Lincoln ran again for the state legislature, and this time he won. When he ran for a second term, he polled more votes than any other candidate. He identified himself as a Whig, the more liberal party and one committed to a program of internal improvements. A newly elected and younger Democrat, Stephen A. Douglas, a foot shorter than Lincoln, led initiatives for canals and railroads that Lincoln and the Whigs were happy to support, but the Panic of 1837 killed most such plans. Also on the legislative agenda were resolutions condemning abolition societies and affirming that slavery was guaranteed by the Constitution. The resolutions were adopted by a vote of 77 to 6, with Lincoln one of the six negative votes. He and his handful of colleagues argued that slavery was bad policy and founded on injustice, but that the work of abolition societies only made the situation worse.

On the positive side, Lincoln was a key member of a coalition that moved the state capital to Springfield, a more central location and closer to Lincoln's base in Sangamon County. Lincoln then moved to the new capital himself and entered a partnership with an older and established lawyer. He would learn the legal business by doing, but he also bought a copy of Blackstone's *Commentaries*, a basic work on the development of English law and important in the development of the American legal system as well. He read, as always, everything on which he could lay his hands.

Among the authors whose work Lincoln read and studied was Euclid, the ancient Greek mathematician, whose definitive summary of geometry had been written well over two thousand years earlier. What Euclid offered Lincoln was a clearly defined, step-by-step, logical analysis of a problem and a method for proving a proposition. Lincoln would use that method to win cases as a lawyer and to construct the speeches that would win him the presidency. David Hirsch, a lawyer, and Dan Van Haften, a mathematician, have published a careful study of Lincoln's use of Euclidian principles,[14] but Garry Wills, writing eighteen years earlier, had already noted that Lincoln "was proud of the mastery he achieved over Euclid's elements, which awed Herndon and others. . . . It was the logical side of language—the principles of order as these reflect patterns of thought or the external world—that appealed to him."[15] Douglas L. Wilson, in his study of Lincoln's rhetoric, also notes "his Euclidian version" of the nation's founding in the Gettysburg address.[16] That analysis was made at the time by such men as Lyman Abbott, a lawyer and Congregational pastor, who said of the Cooper Union speech that it was "as convincing as a demonstration in Euclid's Geometry."[17] [An appendix to this chapter spells out exactly how the Cooper Union speech can be analyzed in Euclidean terms.]

What Lincoln wanted to do as a lawyer, of course, was to prove his case. Apparently he went at his speechmaking with the same objective. Isaac Newton Arnold, who was a lawyer and contemporary of Lincoln, noted that Lincoln was often urged to make more use of his sense of humor and ability to tell amusing stories, but that he refused to do so, saying the issue was too important and that "I do not seek applause, nor to amuse the people, I want to convince them."*

Arnold also noted that

> while Douglas was sometimes greeted with the loudest cheers, when Lincoln closed, the people often seemed solemn and serious, and could be heard, all through the crowd, gravely and anxiously discussing the topics on which he had been speaking.[18]

His private secretary, John Hay, noted that Lincoln could "snake a sophism out of its hole better than all the trained logicians of all schools."[19] Horace Greeley, a frequent critic of Lincoln, admitted that Lincoln's "command of logic was as perfect as his reliance on it was unqualified."[20]

More than simple logic, however, was needed, and Lincoln knew that also. Lincoln's own approach to rhetoric can be seen in his eulogy for the great Kentucky orator Henry Clay, an idol of Lincoln's:

> Mr. Clay's eloquence did not consist, as many fine specimens of eloquence [do], of types and figures—of antithesis and eloquent arrangement of words and sentences; but rather of that deeply earnest and impassioned tone, and manner, which can proceed only from great sincerity and a thorough conviction, in the speaker of the justice and importance of his cause. This it is, that truly touches the chords of human sympathy.[21]

Lincoln's reputation as "Honest Abe" was a critical factor in his ability to persuade others. A contemporary journalist, Noah Brooks, told of meeting an angry old Democrat stamping away from a Lincoln speech, "striking the earth

* In view of Lincoln's fondness for telling stories, it is remarkable how few can be found in his public speeches. In all the Lincoln-Douglas debates there are only two or three stories, and those are brief.

with his cane and exclaiming, 'He's a dangerous man, sir, a d—d dangerous man! He makes you believe what he says in spite of yourself!'"[22]

Lincoln's care for the sound of words was such that he frequently read letters and speeches out loud to anyone who happened to be available, sometimes not asking for comments afterwards. He needed only to hear it for himself. He said to one of his law clerks, "I read by ear. When I have got my thoughts on paper, I read it aloud, and if it sounds all right, I just let it pass." One of his White House clerks reported that it was Lincoln's custom "to read his manuscript over aloud, 'to see how it sounded,' as he could hardly judge of a thing by merely reading it."[23]

One thing Lincoln would not do was speak without careful preparation. By contrast, he sometimes talked about what he called "spread-eagle" speaking. He liked to repeat a description of the style: "He mounted the rostrum, threw back his head, shined his eyes, opened his mouth, and left the consequences to God."[24] That was not Lincoln's manner.

As a young man and occasionally later in his life, Lincoln wrote poetry. It was not remarkable for its quality, but it was evidence of "his strong sense of cadence and sophisticated ear for rhythmic patterns"[25] that would be so evident in his later speeches.

III

After serving four terms in the Illinois legislature, Lincoln did not run again. He needed to give more time to his law practice; and he was getting married in November 1842, to Mary Todd, the daughter of a wealthy Kentucky plantation owner. So he took care of all that and in 1846, when a seat in the United States House of Representatives was open, Lincoln rejoined the political world and was elected to Congress with the understanding that he would serve only one term.

Although the new Congress was elected in the fall of 1846, it did not convene until December 1847, so Lincoln had a full year to plan and prepare. By the time the new Congress arrived, the Mexican War was essentially over and all the Congress could do was pick over the events of that war to praise or condemn. Condemnation of a war after it has been won is not a good way to win elections, so the new Congress was cautious. Nevertheless, investigations were ordered as to what had happened and who was responsible. Lincoln had avoided comment on the war while it was being waged and while he was campaigning, on the theory that he had insufficient information. In Washington, he would have to take sides.

He arrived in the capital in time to receive a message from President Polk announcing that a war that Mexico had begun by shedding American blood on American soil was now over, and nothing remained to be done except to assimilate the territory Mexico had ceded in the Southwest and along the West Coast.

Polk's message triggered a full-scale attack by the Whigs, and Lincoln was one of those leading the charge. He had been in Washington less than a month when he introduced a series of resolutions calling on the President to identify the spot where American blood had been shed and to prove that it had been shed on American soil. Unfortunately, there were very few in Washington who were much interested in questioning the war, now that it was over. Presidents are not easily questioned when they place American troops in harm's way, especially when they can point to victories. Lincoln's resolution was never voted on, and his question about the "spot" became an attack line for his opponents who took to calling him "Spotty Lincoln." Stephen A. Douglas would use that line of attack in his debates with Lincoln ten years later.

Writing to William Herndon, Lincoln argued that the war had been unconstitutional and that the founding fathers had intended to preserve American freedom by preventing an executive from compelling the country to fight. War, he wrote, "is the most oppressive of all Kingly oppressions," and they had therefore "so frame[d] the Constitution that *no one man* should hold the power of bringing this oppression upon us." Patrick Henry would have understood.

IV

Once back in Springfield, Lincoln's clear priority was his law practice. He had no obvious future in politics. Whigs might carry a Congressional district, but they had no prospects for carrying the state. For the time being, he needed to make a living for himself and his family, and opportunities lay open before him. Railroads were criss-crossing the state, binding together not just New York and Chicago and Saint Louis, but very small communities as well. How many people today outside of Illinois could suggest where the Alton and Sangamon Railroad ran? But such lines were being built; and wherever railroads ran, there were property issues to be resolved and a need for lawyers to resolve them.

Working for the Alton and Sangamon Railroad, Lincoln and his partner, William Herndon, established the right of a corporation to change its charter in the public interest and established themselves as leading practitioners of railroad law. Sometimes politicians can do more to advance themselves in the public mind by succeeding in an area outside the political arena. When Lincoln subsequently won a case for the much larger Illinois Central Railroad and asked for a fee of $2,000, the Railroad complained that it was "as much as Daniel Webster himself would have charged." Lincoln therefore consulted with other leading attorneys and submitted a revised bill for $5,000. When the Railroad complained that they lacked funds to pay, Lincoln took them to court and won. He still continued to represent the Illinois Central. He represented other railroads as well, and sometimes their opponents.[26] He was working for his family, not for corporations or their opponents, but whoever would pay him his fee.

The spread of the railroads made another difference for Lincoln: now he could get home on weekends when he was dealing with cases in another town and spend more time with his family. He did not, however, abandon his interest in politics. He advised the Whig candidate for the Congressional seat he had once held, and made speeches for the Whig presidential candidate in 1852. His legal work itself helped him continue to build a constituency, since he traveled a circuit with other judges and lawyers, meeting more and more people, making himself more widely known.

For a short while, Lincoln tried his hand at lecturing, but he was not a success. It was an era in which Ralph Waldo Emerson, Frederick Douglass, and Elizabeth Cady Stanton, among many others, spent months traveling the country, offering their views on a variety of subjects. Stanton did not always talk about women's rights, nor did Douglass always talk about slavery. They were capable speakers, and audiences were glad to listen to them whatever their subject. But Lincoln could not speak about just anything. He made speeches about temperance and alcohol and gave a long and tedious talk on inventions and discoveries, but the response was poor. Lincoln said himself: "I am not a professional lecturer—have never got up but one lecture; and that, I think, rather a poor one."[27] He was not a voice for hire, an instrument that could play any tune. He needed a cause he believed in and an opportunity to address it to be effective as a speaker. That opportunity would come.

In 1858, there was a senator to be elected in Illinois since Stephen A. Douglas was completing his first term, and Lincoln saw an opportunity to return to the political arena. Although it was the Illinois legislature, not the popular vote, that would choose the senator, Lincoln could still campaign in hope that the legislature would notice and would hear from their constituents.

In June, the Republican Party convened in Springfield and formally nominated Abraham Lincoln for the Senate seat held by Stephen A. Douglas. In accepting the nomination, Lincoln spoke some of the most memorable of all his words—but they may have cost him the election. He spoke about the Kansas-Nebraska Act of 1854, with its promise of "popular sovereignty" to determine the policy of the new territories.

> We are now far into the fifth year, since a policy was initiated, with the avowed object, and confident promise, of putting an end to slavery agitation.

> Under the operation of that policy, that agitation has not only not ceased, but has constantly augmented.
>
> In my opinion, it will not cease, until a crisis shall have been reached, and passed.
>
> "A house divided against itself cannot stand."*
>
> I believe this government cannot endure, permanently half slave and half free.
>
> I do not expect the Union to be dissolved—I do not expect the house to fall—but I do expect it will cease to be divided.
>
> It will become all one thing or all the other.
>
> Either the opponents of slavery, will arrest the further spread of it, and place it where the public mind shall rest in the belief that it is in the course of ultimate extinction; or its advocates will push it forward, till it shall become alike lawful in all the States, old as well as new—North as well as South.[28]

It was Lincoln at his very best: clear, concise, Biblical in reference and style. John Nicolay and John Hay, Lincoln's official biographers, thought that this speech was the most carefully prepared of all Lincoln's speeches. He worked on it, off and on, for over a month and tested early versions on his partner and ten or twelve friends.[29] He had looked for a clear and simple image, and found one familiar to most of his hearers from the teaching of Jesus. He had encountered the figure of speech years earlier when he read *Aesop's Fables* and found the fable of the lion and the bulls,** and he had used the Biblical figure fifteen years earlier in urging unity in the Whig Party.[30] But Douglas and others could and did portray the "house divided" speech as a prediction, even advocacy, of civil war. Lincoln had meant no such thing. He believed that Douglas's policies and the recent Dred Scott decision were tending to the spread of slavery; and he believed that if slavery were not allowed to spread, it would eventually die as impractical and immoral. But it was easy to interpret the words otherwise, and the Democrats continued to do so.

V

The campaign had already begun, and the two candidates had even spoken consecutively in Chicago on July 9 and 10 and in Springfield on the afternoon and evening of July 17, when Lincoln sent a brief note to Douglas asking

---

* Saint Mark 3:25.

** A lion seeks to take over a field dominated by bulls and waits until they fight among themselves to take over. In some versions, the motto is "a kingdom divided against itself cannot stand."

whether it would be agreeable to him "to divide time and address the same audiences during the present canvass?" Douglas responded the same day with a much longer note, complaining that he already had a set schedule and Lincoln should have suggested the plan earlier. Nevertheless he agreed to have one such meeting in each of the congressional districts except the two in which both had already spoken. Thus there would be seven debates, two each in August and September and three in October. Each debate would consist of an opening statement of an hour's length, a response of an hour and a half, and a response by the first speaker of a half hour.[31]

The Lincoln-Douglas debates of 1858 are remembered as one of the defining moments in American history, a contest that brought the nation's attention to Abraham Lincoln as a rising star in American politics and led directly to his presidency and leadership in the struggle that reshaped American history and redefined American freedom. All of that may be true, but to read the debates today is a mind-numbing experience. They focus repetitively on minor issues and seldom exhibit even brief flashes of either humor or passion.

Nonetheless, the good people of Illinois, lacking television and cell phones, flocked to them as desert travelers to water. They gathered for the debates by the hundreds and thousands. They came on foot and in farm wagons and in chartered trains. They came from surrounding towns and villages and even adjacent states, across the midwestern prairies from Indiana, and across the Mississippi River from Iowa. They stood for three hours and more to listen, and they went away to talk about what they had heard for days and weeks afterwards.

The first debate took place on August 21 in Ottawa, Illinois, some eighty miles west-southwest from Chicago and just a hundred miles east of the Mississippi River at Davenport, Iowa.* The local paper reported that

> from sunrise till high noon . . . Ottawa was beleaguered with a multiplying host from all points of the compass. Teams, trains and processions poured in from every direction like an army with banners. . . . Military companies and bands of music monopolized the thoroughfares around the courthouse and the public squares.

An estimated twelve thousand people were on hand when the speechmaking began. Six days later, the candidates arrived in Freeport, a hundred miles northwest of Ottawa, with torchlight parades and cannon firing salutes. This time, the crowd was estimated to be a third larger than the one in Ottawa. Two

* The site is marked today by a large boulder with a commemorative plaque and a statue of the two debaters.

weeks later, there were only some fifteen hundred at Jonesboro, three hundred and fifty miles south of Chicago; but three days after that, halfway back to Chicago, there were twelve to fifteen thousand at Charleston.* In Charleston, there were parades featuring thirty-two young ladies on horseback representing the states of the Union. Each candidate had a procession with representative ladies, but the Republican newspaper could only count fifteen young ladies in the Douglas procession and thought some of them were under age.

From Charleston, the debates moved to Sullivan, thirty miles to the east, and then to Galesburg, fifty miles south of Davenport, where the crowds were the largest yet. On October 13, a somewhat smaller but still large crowd welcomed the candidates to Quincy, on the Mississippi River over a hundred miles southwest of Galesburg. From Quincy, the candidates went together by boat one hundred twenty-five miles down the river to Alton, where a somewhat smaller crowd welcomed them with much less excitement. Perhaps even in mid-nineteenth century Illinois, there could be too much of a good thing. And, indeed, the candidates had said what they had to say more than once or twice, and anyone with access to a newspaper would have known by now the principal arguments and perhaps could have recited whole paragraphs that were repeated again and again.

But there were moments to savor. Lincoln, for example, liked to portray himself as the humble challenger up against a leader "of world-wide renown," seen by many as a future President. Lincoln suggested that Douglas's friends, therefore,

> have seen in his round, jolly, fruitful face, post offices, land offices, marshalships and cabinet appointments, chargeships and foreign missions, bursting and sprouting out in wonderful exuberance ready to be laid hold of by their greedy hands. [Great laughter]

On the contrary, Lincoln said, "Nobody has ever expected me to be President. In my poor, lean, lank face nobody has ever seen that cabbages were sprouting out. [Tremendous cheering and laughter]," and therefore Republicans had no choice except "to fight this battle upon principle and upon principle alone." It was a nice way to jibe at his opponent while asserting that he would debate only principles.[32]

Both debaters made it clear that they had no vision of a society in which black and white were equal participants. Douglas repeated his basic

---

* The reports of crowd sizes and related events come from Angle, Paul M. (ed.), *Created Equal? The Complete Lincoln-Douglas Debates of 1858*. Chicago: University of Chicago Press, 1958.

understanding of racial matters a number of times in the debates. At Ottawa, he put it this way:

> For one, I am opposed to negro citizenship in any and every form. I believe this government was made on the white basis. I believe it was made by white men, for the benefit of white men and their posterity forever, and I am in favor of confining citizenship to white men, men of European birth and descent, instead of conferring it upon negroes, Indians, and other inferior races. [Good for you! Douglas forever!][33]

Lincoln was still limited by his lack of exposure to African Americans and even to those relatively few abolitionists who were able to think in terms of full racial equality. But Lincoln had come far beyond Douglas. Lincoln said:

> I have no purpose to introduce political and social equality between the white and the black races. There is a physical difference between the two, which, in my judgment, will probably forever forbid their living together upon the footing of perfect equality; and inasmuch as it becomes a necessity that there must be a difference, I, as well as Judge Douglas, am in favor of the race to which I belong having the superior position. I have never said anything to the contrary, but I hold that, notwithstanding all this, there is no reason in the world why the negro is not entitled to all the natural rights enumerated in the Declaration of Independence—the right to life, liberty, and the pursuit of happiness. [Loud cheers] I hold that he is as much entitled to these as the white man. I agree with Judge Douglas he is not my equal in many respects—certainly not in color, perhaps not in moral or intellectual endowment. But in the right to eat the bread, without the leave of anybody else, which his own hand earns, he is my equal and the equal of Judge Douglas, and the equal of every living man.[34]

As indicated, the transcript of the debates is broken constantly by reference to crowd noises: [Hurrah for Douglas], [Loud applause], [That's the truth], [Hit him again], and so on. Sometimes the candidates would respond to particular comments from the crowd. In spite of the great size of the crowds, there was a sense of intimacy and real engagement of the audience in the event.

Douglas, with a deep baritone, seemed at first to have the better voice, but less ability to use the resources of the English language, less instinct for the music and resonance of words. His voice also carried less well and stood up less well under the strain; by the end it was becoming hard to hear him. Lincoln, on the other hand, seemed to grow more confident as the days went by, and was able to present his essential argument with greater clarity and forcefulness. A Cincinnati reporter wrote that Lincoln's "clear, ringing voice" was "easily heard by those on the outer limits of the crowd."[35]

In the last debate, in Alton, Lincoln was the second speaker and so had one opportunity, an hour and a half long, to present his case. He began, as so often in previous rounds, by dealing with statements made by Douglas that misstated Lincoln's position. He had not, he told his audience, complained of the Dred Scott decision because it "held that a negro could not be a citizen"; he complained of it because he saw it to be part of a scheme to make slavery a nationwide institution. Here Lincoln cited the great Kentucky senator Henry Clay (1777–1852), who had defended slavery while calling it "a great evil." That, Lincoln asserted, had been the prevailing opinion until recent years. The authors of the Constitution had deliberately avoided the word "slave" and spoken always of "persons held to bondage" and used similar phrases, because they understood that slavery was evil and did not believe that it would or should be an enduring aspect of American society. But Douglas had promoted compromises that opened new territory to slavery and refused to state whether he thought it was an evil or not.

Douglas had insisted in his opening speech that slavery was simply one more institution that states should be able to adopt or reject at their discretion, just as Indiana had laws about cranberries and Illinois did not. Lincoln, in reply, was happy to tell Douglas the difference between cranberries and slavery:

> He tries to show that variety in the domestic institutions of the different States is necessary and indispensable. I do not dispute it. I have no controversy with Judge Douglas about that. I shall very readily agree with him that it would be foolish for us to insist upon having a cranberry law here, in Illinois, where we have no cranberries, because they have a cranberry law in Indiana, where they have cranberries. I should insist that it would be exceedingly wrong in us to deny to Virginia the right to enact oyster laws, where they have oysters, because we want no such laws here. I understand, I hope, quite as well as Judge Douglas, or anybody else, that the variety in the soil and climate and face of the country, and consequent variety in the industrial pursuits and productions of a country, require systems of laws conforming to this variety in the natural features of the country. I understand quite as well as Judge Douglas, that if we here raise a barrel of flour more than we want, and the Louisianians raise a barrel of sugar more than

> they want, it is of mutual advantage to exchange. That produces commerce, brings us together, and makes us better friends. We like one another the more for it. And I understand as well as Judge Douglas, or anybody else, that these mutual accommodations are the cements which bind together the different parts of this Union; that instead of being a thing to "divide the house"—figuratively expressing the Union—they tend to sustain it; they are the props of the house tending always to hold it up.
>
> But when I have admitted all this, I ask if there is any parallel between these things and this institution of slavery? I do not see that there is any parallel at all between them. Consider it. When have we had any difficulty or quarrel amongst ourselves about the cranberry laws of Indiana, or the oyster laws of Virginia, or the pine-lumber laws of Maine, or the fact that Louisiana produces sugar, and Illinois flour? When have we had any quarrels over these things? When have we had perfect peace in regard to this thing which I say is an element of discord in this Union? We have sometimes had peace, but when was it? It was when the institution of slavery remained quiet where it was. We have had difficulty and turmoil whenever it has made a struggle to spread itself where it was not. I ask, then, if experience does not speak in thunder-tones, telling us that the policy which has given peace to the country heretofore, being returned to, gives the greatest promise of peace again.[36]

It was in the final minutes of his hour and a half that Lincoln seemed to become most passionate about the basic issue, insisting that it was not a matter of indifference, as Douglas claimed, but a clear matter of right and wrong.

> I have stated upon former occasions, and I may as well state again, what I understand to be the real issue of this controversy between Judge Douglas and myself. . . . The real issue in this controversy—the one pressing upon every mind—is the sentiment on the part of one class that looks upon the institution of slavery as a wrong, and of another class that does not look upon it as a wrong. The sentiment that contemplates the institution of slavery in this country as a wrong is the sentiment of the Republican party. It is the sentiment around which all their actions, all their arguments, circle; from which all their propositions radiate. They look upon it as being a moral, social, and political wrong; and while they contemplate it

> as such, they nevertheless have due regard for its actual existence among us, and the difficulties of getting rid of it in any satisfactory way, and to all the constitutional obligations thrown about it. Yet having a due regard for these, they desire a policy in regard to it that looks to its not creating any more danger. They insist that it, as far as may be, be treated as a wrong, and one of the methods of treating it as a wrong is to make provision that it shall grow no larger. They also desire a policy that looks to a peaceful end of slavery some time, as being a wrong. . . .

And, again, Lincoln insisted that it was slavery itself that threatened the Union, because an institution that denied freedom to some threatened the freedom of all.

> Has anything ever threatened the existence of this Union save and except this very institution of slavery? What is it that we hold most dear amongst us? Our own liberty and prosperity. What has ever threatened our liberty and prosperity save and except this institution of slavery? If this is true, how do you propose to improve the condition of things by enlarging slavery—by spreading it out and making it bigger? You may have a wen or cancer upon your person, and not be able to cut it out lest you bleed to death; but surely it is no way to cure it, to engraft it and spread it over your whole body. That is no proper way of treating what you regard as a wrong.
>
> [Judge Douglas] says he "don't care whether it is voted up or voted down" in the Territories. . . . He may say he don't care whether an indifferent thing is voted up or down, but he must logically have a choice between a right thing and a wrong thing. He contends that whatever community wants slaves has a right to have them. So they have if it is not a wrong. But if it is a wrong, he cannot say people have a right to do wrong.
>
> He says that, upon the score of equality, slaves should be allowed to go into a new Territory like other property. This is strictly logical if there is no difference between it and other property. If it and other property are equal, his argument is entirely logical. But if you insist that one is wrong and the other right, there is no use to institute a comparison between right and wrong.

Lincoln's peroration was certainly the most effective statement in the long series of debates. The fundamental issue was human freedom:

> That is the real issue. That is the issue that will continue in this country when these poor tongues of Judge Douglas and myself shall be silent. It is the eternal struggle between these two principles—right and wrong—throughout the world. They are the two principles that have stood face to face from the beginning of time; and will ever continue to struggle. The one is the common right of humanity, and the other the divine right of kings. It is the same principle in whatever shape it develops itself. It is the same spirit that says, "You toil and work and earn bread, and I'll eat it." No matter in what shape it comes, whether from the mouth of a king who seeks to bestride the people of his own nation and live by the fruit of their labor, or from one race of men as an apology for enslaving another race, it is the same tyrannical principle. . . .
>
> Whenever the issue can be distinctly made, and all extraneous matter thrown out, so that men can fairly see the real difference between the parties, this controversy will soon be settled, and it will be done peaceably too. There will be no war, no violence. It will be placed again where the wisest and best men of the world placed it.[37]

But Douglas could not be made to see it. In his final half hour, he could only repeat what he had been saying for well over three months:

> All you have a right to ask is that the people shall do as they please; if they want slavery, let them have it; if they do not want it, allow them to refuse to encourage it. My friends, if, as I have said before, we will only live up to this great fundamental principle, there will be peace between the North and the South.[38]

The issue that emerged most clearly in the debates was "popular sovereignty," a slogan Douglas used again and again. In 1859, Douglas used it as the theme for a long article in a national magazine in an apparent attempt to cast himself as a centrist candidate for president.

"Popular sovereignty" is a wonderful slogan—but what does it mean? That question lay behind Patrick Henry's objection to the Constitution. Henry believed in popular sovereignty so long as it was exercised at a state level, but not at a national level. So, if a majority of Virginians wanted to enslave African Americans, they must be free to do so even if a majority of the citizens of the United States thought it was morally wrong. Both Lincoln and Douglas believed in government "of the people, by the people, and for the people," but people in different parts of the country have different interests. Can there be different laws for Maine and California? If so, why not for individual counties? If so, why not for each town, each block, each family? But the freedom of one family to build a skyscraper may well impinge on the freedom of their neighbors to enjoy sunshine and fresh air. If residents of the South were free to own human beings as property, why should they have to give up their property to travel in the North?

In 1858, popular sovereignty at a national level would probably have outlawed slavery, and the issue for the Southern states was whether they could remain in union with a majority who were likely to limit their freedom to treat people as property. The Dred Scott decision, in fact, opened the possibility that the Supreme Court would rule that the Constitution permitted slavery everywhere. If so, New England might have seceded and a President Stephen Douglas or President Jefferson Davis might have attacked New England to force slavery on them.

Thus the meaning of "popular sovereignty" was the fundamental issue facing the nation in the middle of the nineteenth century. Occasionally the Lincoln-Douglas debates did concern themselves with that issue and, when they did, the debates became a compelling example of the democratic process at work.

When the debates were over, the maneuvering to choose the next senator went on backstage as legislators sorted out their choices. Republicans had won fifty percent of the popular vote but only forty-six percent of the seats in the legislature, so Douglas was chosen to serve a second term. Lincoln said he was glad he had made the race, since "It gave me a hearing on the great and durable question of the age, which I could have had in no other way; and though I now sink out of view and shall be forgotten, I believe I have made some marks which will tell for the cause of civil liberty long after I am gone."[39] Lincoln resolved that he would now focus on his "private business" and would decline invitations to speak.

VI

Lincoln might have wished to focus on his "private business," but the debates had made him a national figure and he could no longer avoid being invited to speak in Iowa, Wisconsin, Indiana, and Kansas. Newspapers here and there began mentioning him as a possible presidential candidate. Lincoln himself insisted that he was unqualified, and to all outward appearance he was. He had almost no formal schooling and had never held an administrative position; but Douglas had never been an administrator either, and Americans have frequently chosen presidents whose whole experience was in the legislative branch of government. Truman, Kennedy, Johnson, Nixon, and Obama would be recent examples of presidents without significant executive experience.

But perhaps the voters understand that the presidency is not first of all about executive ability, but rather that indefinable quality called leadership which is often seen in the use of language to draw together and inspire and provide a sense of unity and purpose. Lincoln seemed, to more and more Americans, to have that indefinable quality.

Lincoln did manage to abstain from politics for almost a year, but in September 1859 a senate race in Ohio drew both Lincoln and Douglas back into the arena to contend for their party and candidate. This time there was no direct confrontation; but since neither was himself a candidate, he was somewhat freer in his use of language. When Douglas remarked that in a contest between a negro and a crocodile, he was for the negro, but in a contest between a negro and a white man, he was for the white man, Lincoln suggested that Douglas was equating the black man with reptiles. Douglas and his friends, Lincoln argued, were steadily undermining the position of black Americans and preparing the way for making slavery legal everywhere.[40]

Perhaps the most important event in Ohio was a speech Lincoln made in Cincinnati on the last night before he returned to Illinois. In the days since the Illinois debates, Lincoln had continually been sharpening his arguments. In Illinois, he had failed to get Douglas to say whether slavery was right or wrong and had drawn attention to that fact. Now, in Ohio, he stressed it yet again: "There is not a public man in the United States, I believe, with the exception of Senator Douglas, who has not at some time of his life, declared his opinion whether the thing is right or wrong."[41]

Early in his speech, Lincoln took advantage of his position across the Ohio River from Kentucky to address himself to those nearby Southerners. "I often hear it intimated," he told them, "that you mean to divide the Union whenever a Republican, or anything like it, is elected President of the United States. . . . Well, then, I want to know what you are going to do with your half of it?" He reminded the Kentuckians that if they were no longer a part of the Union, there would be no need for Northerners to adhere to the Fugitive Slave Law. And suppose there were war: "Will you make war upon us and kill us all?" Lincoln asked. They should remember that "there are not so many of you as there are of us."[42]

Douglas had argued that the states of the Midwest were free because the voters had chosen against slavery. Lincoln argued that it was the Congressional laws provided for the Northwest Territory that had preserved them as free states. From Cincinnati, he could look across the river at Kentucky and ask: What made the difference? Parts of Kentucky lie north of some parts of Ohio. The two states have very much the same soil and climate, but the one had slavery and not the other. Likewise Missouri and Illinois, on two sides of the Mississippi, were much alike in climate and soil, but there were ten thousand slaves in Missouri and none in Illinois. Again, it was Congressional action that had set one in the direction of freedom and the other toward slavery. So Douglas was wrong in suggesting that the Constitution allowed each state to choose for itself. "The people of these United States are the rightful masters of both congresses and courts," Lincoln told the cheering crowd. We must not use that power to overthrow the Constitution, "but to overthrow the men who pervert that Constitution."[43]

The election in Ohio, along with elections in Pennsylvania, Iowa, Indiana, and Minnesota, took place on a Friday in mid-October, and Republican candidates were successful everywhere. Lincoln had spent that week in the courtroom in the town of Clinton, fifty miles northeast of Springfield. He got back to Springfield on early Saturday evening to find a brass band and a cheering crowd outside his house. He needed to speak to them, but first he took a quick look at the mail. There was a telegram from New York inviting him to come and speak. It would be his first major speech in the East and an obvious opening to life on the national stage. One member of the New York committee wrote to the editor of the Springfield paper to lobby Lincoln to come. "We want to hear a speech from him, such a one as he delivered in Cincinnati. . . ." So the effort made in Ohio had been worth it. The speech in Cooper Union would make Abraham Lincoln a national figure.

VII

There was still a strong tradition in 1860 that presidential candidates should not campaign for office.* The office should seek them, not they the office. The candidate should be humble and not flaunt his virtues in public. For Lincoln it was good strategy as well. "My name is new in the field," he wrote a supporter, "and I suppose I am not the first choice of a very great many. Our policy then is to give no offense to others—leave them in a mood to come to us, if they shall be compelled to give up their first love."[44]

The 1860 presidential election would be about freedom, about liberty, not simply and most obviously freedom for the millions of human beings held in slavery but freedom also for the nation to live up to its founding declarations; but the candidates would not be free to speak to their fellow citizens about their beliefs and goals. Of course, they could speak about other things. Lincoln could, for example, go to Bloomington to jibe at Congressional Democrats for supporting legislation to prevent polygamy in the territories while claiming they had no power to control slavery.[45] He could resurrect his failed lecture on

* In fact, it continued to stand as an unwritten rule until William Jennings Bryan's 1896 campaign, with the only notable exceptions being Stephen Douglas in this election and Horace Greeley in 1872.

"Inventions and Discoveries" for a Springfield audience. He could respond to a friend in Connecticut who wrote to tell him of recent electoral success in that state as a result—his friend believed—of Lincoln's speeches there. But when the friend asked how he could help forward Lincoln's nomination, Lincoln was atypically incoherent:

> As to the Presidential nomination, claiming no greater exemption from selfishness than is common, I still feel that my whole aspiration should be, and therefore must be, to be placed anywhere, or nowhere, as may appear most likely to advance our cause.[46]

Perhaps the most effective campaigning, however, was being done through the reprinting and distribution of the Cooper Union address. Horace Greeley had rushed out an edition of it in pamphlet form while Lincoln was still traveling in Connecticut, offering it at four cents a copy and ten dollars for a thousand. It quickly went through four editions. Not long after Lincoln was back in Springfield, his home town newspaper, assuming partisans would want it available for distribution, had it available at twenty-five cents for a dozen and a dollar for a hundred. Other editions appeared in Washington, Detroit, and Chicago.

In spite of all that, Senator (and former Governor) Seward of New York was still the odds-on favorite when the 1860 Republican National Convention, held that year in Chicago, assembled in a hastily built convention hall known as the "Wigwam." *Harper's Weekly* published a picture of the candidates, showing Seward in a large central medallion surrounded by much smaller pictures of ten other candidates. Lincoln's picture was one of four in the bottom row. But Lincoln had hometown advantage, and his supporters made good use of it. They printed extra tickets to distribute to his supporters, seated them where they could make the most noise, and arranged for Seward's supporters to be seated in a remote corner of the hall.

The *Chicago Press and Tribune* published a banner editorial the day before the Convention, headed THE WINNING MAN: ABRAHAM LINCOLN.[47]

The Second National Convention of the Republican Party assembled on Wednesday, May 16, and moved to nominations and balloting on Friday the 18th. Senator Seward was the frontrunner and favorite, but he captured only 173 votes on the first ballot, fewer than expected, and Lincoln with 102 votes was a surprisingly strong second. Ten other candidates were far behind. On the second ballot, Seward gained only eleven votes, while Lincoln picked up 79 and was only three votes behind. It was obvious, then, that Lincoln would win and with 231.5 on the third ballot, he needed only a vote and a half more (for a majority 233 of the 465 voters present). Four Ohio delegates quickly shifted their votes and then over a hundred more votes followed, to make the final tally 349 for Lincoln and 111 for Seward.

Lincoln had spent the morning playing handball with friends. In the afternoon, he went to his law office and read telegrams brought in by an editor from the *Illinois State Journal*. When the second ballot made it clear that he would be chosen, he walked over to the office of the *Journal* to await the result of the third ballot. When that telegram came, he accepted congratulations from his fellow handball players who had given up their game to hear the news. "Gentlemen," he told them, "you had better come up and shake my hand while you can—honors elevate some men." Then he excused himself to walk home and tell his wife—who, he said, "is probably more interested in this dispatch than I am."[48]

Lincoln was strongly inclined to go to Chicago to accept the nomination but was told not to by his advisers. Instead, he waited for an official committee to travel to Springfield and advise him of the nomination. He would spend the months until election day attempting to work at his law practice and sending off letter after letter declining invitations to speak, refusing to issue statements, and behaving as candidates were expected to behave.

The Democrats had met in April in Charleston, South Carolina, and had been unable to agree on a candidate after 57 ballots. Eventually the rival factions would meet separately. Northern Democrats nominated Stephen A. Douglas in Baltimore in June, and Southern Democrats nominated John C. Breckinridge of Kentucky, also meeting in Baltimore in June. To complicate matters further, a new Constitutional Union Party nominated John Bell of Tennessee.

Lincoln continued to maintain his silence during the ensuing campaign, allowing the continued printing and distribution of the Cooper Union Address to speak for him. Douglas, on the other hand, abandoned tradition in the belief that it was too important a time for candidates to keep silent and campaigned in twenty-three states. He finished second among the four major candidates in the popular vote with 29.5%, but he finished last in the Electoral College, carrying only Missouri, a slave state, and New Jersey, a free state. Lincoln, with no votes in the South,* won just under 40% of the popular vote and a clear majority in the Electoral College.[49]

VIII

No sooner was the election over than the South Carolina legislature called for a convention to consider their relationship with the Union. Surely this might have seemed a time for Lincoln to speak, to reassure the South that he had no

---

* Lincoln's name was not on the ballot at all in ten Southern states.

intention to interfere with their distinctive institution, to use his eloquence to call for unity. But everyone whose advice he valued recommended against it. For one thing, he had no official position as yet. The Electoral College would not meet until December 5 and the result would not be officially certified until February 13. Besides that, Lincoln, like many others, found it impossible to believe that secession was really a serious threat. Why would intelligent people leave a country that had prospered so greatly under its Constitution? The great majority of the people in the South were not slaveholders. Why would they risk their lives and security for an institution that was of no benefit to them? It seemed to Lincoln that he had said again and again all that could be said to assure the South that he posed no threat to their "property." But he had also, in his Cooper Union speech, addressed the South as "you":

> Your purpose, then, plainly stated, is that you will destroy the Government, unless you be allowed to construe and enforce the Constitution as you please, on all points in dispute between you and us. You will rule or ruin in all events. . . .

He had "lightened" the passage by comparing the South to a "highwayman" holding "a pistol to my ear." The audience had laughed, but it is hard to speak that way of comrades who are fundamentally still one family.

So Lincoln busied himself with the task of building an administration and responding to all the letters and telegrams and well-wishers that surged into Springfield. Even when the time came to board the train to Washington to begin his preparation, he was reluctant to speak. By that time, six states had officially seceded and more were on the verge of doing so. But Lincoln had said all he could say and done all he could do as someone still without an official position.

The time would come when he must speak, and he had been working long and hard on an inaugural address, beginning to work on it as soon as the election was over and secluding himself in some available space on the third floor of the building where his brother-in-law had a store. He had already memorized most of Daniel Webster's great Second Reply to Hayne with its refrain of "Liberty and Union," and it was much in his mind as he thought about what to say himself. He also obtained a collection of previous inaugural addresses and studied it.[50]

When Lincoln was satisfied with his handwritten text, which may have been the third or fourth draft, he took it to the state printer, who locked himself and a compositor into the office, made copies, and put them in a safe until Lincoln could correct them. Lincoln wrote "First Edition" on his copy and went through it carefully, dropping several paragraphs and changing the wording to soften the tone. Some paragraphs were literally cut out and pasted in a new location. Apparently there were three more printed editions, some of which, atypically, were shown to friends and advisers, before Lincoln was satisfied.[51]

The Congress had not yet certified the Electoral College vote on February 11, but Lincoln needed to get to Washington to begin the work of a new administration. This time, a train had been chartered for the trip and he would not need to change trains in the middle of the night. Friends and neighbors were there at 7:55 in the morning as the President-elect climbed the steps to his private car and turned to say a few last words with the simplicity that was characteristic of his best addresses. If it seems strange that he would speak to his friends as "these people," it may be because he spoke extemporaneously and then attempted to write down what he had said afterward at the request of a reporter. Finding it difficult to write well on a moving train, he passed the paper to his secretary and dictated the rest, but he was no longer addressing his friends: he was recreating it with a national audience in mind.[52]

> My friends—no one, not in my situation, can appreciate the feeling of sadness at this parting. To this place, and the kindness of these people, I owe everything. Here I have lived a quarter of a century and have passed from a young to an old man. Here my children have been born, and one is buried. I now leave, not knowing when, or whether ever, I may return, with a task before me greater than that which rested upon Washington. Without the assistance of the Divine Being, who ever attended him, I cannot succeed. With that assistance I cannot fail . . . let us confidently hope that all will yet be well. To His care commending you, as I hope in your prayers you will commend me, I bid you an affectionate farewell.[53]

The journey took twelve days, and the train moved over eighteen different railroads, stopping at cities and towns along the way to let the crowds that had gathered see their new President and hear him say a few words. Now, at last, he allowed himself to speak briefly about national affairs. He had, perhaps, more questions than answers. He spoke aloud some of the questions he was turning over in his mind as he traveled. He had memorized much of Webster's reply to Hayne and he knew that the same issue remained: "Shall the Union and shall the liberties of this country be preserved to the latest generation?"[54] What, he asked, did the South have to fear? Would he not be justified in holding or even retaking forts that belonged to the national government? These were simply questions, he noted; no decisions had been made. He would seek for a peaceful resolution of the crisis but, he told the New Jersey legislature in Trenton, "It may be necessary to put the foot down firmly."

The inaugural address, which he had worked on so long, would provide his first chance to address the whole nation. He had entrusted his son, Robert, age seventeen, with the case containing the latest draft of the inaugural address and, perhaps for the first time, lost his temper with him when he learned that Robert had entrusted it to a hotel porter. The porter in turn had thrown it on a pile of luggage behind the hotel desk, forcing Lincoln to burrow through a pile of unclaimed baggage to retrieve it.

On arriving in Washington ten days before the inauguration, he gave a copy to William Seward, who had been his chief rival for the nomination and who he had now asked to be his Secretary of State. Seward sent back a ten-page letter telling Lincoln that he approved of the speech in general: "The argument is strong and conclusive, and ought not to be in any way abridged or modified." Yet there were modifications of language that Seward believed would be helpful: ". . . something besides or in addition to argument is needful to meet and remove prejudice and passion in the South, and despondency in the East. Some words of affection—some of calm and cheerful confidence." Seward then offered forty-nine specific suggestions of changes in language designed to soften the tone and "soothe the public mind." Working with Seward's comments, Lincoln revised his speech, adopting some of the suggestions and reworking others in his own way. It made a great speech stronger in many ways, but it remained Lincoln's own.

Addressed almost entirely to the people and politicians of the Southern states, Lincoln's first inaugural was one last plea for unity. Lincoln was clear as to what he considered his duty as President. He would not surrender federal property in the South, and he would do his best to continue the role of the federal government in, for example, delivery of the mail. But he would do nothing to aggravate the situation. If the situation were to deteriorate, it would not be his doing. Most especially, as he had often said before to the irritation of abolitionists, he would do nothing to interfere with the institution of slavery where it existed. Speaking slowly and clearly, as he always did, he told the South exactly what he had told them when he spoke in Cincinnati:

> I have no purpose, directly or indirectly, to interfere with the institution of slavery in the States where it exists. I believe I have no lawful right to do so, and I have no inclination to do so.

More specifically, he spelled out at some length his position on the fugitive slave laws which he believed were so much a part of the Constitution that he had no choice but to obey them. Beyond that, he pleaded with the South to take more time to think about what they were doing:

> Before entering upon so grave a matter as the destruction of our national fabric, with all its benefits, its memories, and its hopes, would it not be wise to ascertain precisely why we do it? Will you hazard so desperate a step while there is any possibility that any portion of the ills you fly from have no real existence? Will you, while the certain ills you fly to are greater than all the real ones you fly from, will you risk the commission of so fearful a mistake?
>
> My countrymen, one and all, think calmly and well upon this whole subject. Nothing valuable can be lost by taking time.

Freedom itself was at stake, he suggested. Where factions could split away over one issue or another, there could be no lasting security, and without security there could be no real freedom.

> A majority held in restraint by constitutional checks and limitations, and always changing easily with deliberate changes of popular opinions and sentiments, is the only true sovereign of a free people. Whoever rejects it does of necessity fly to anarchy or to despotism. Unanimity is impossible. The rule of a minority, as a permanent arrangement, is wholly inadmissible; so that, rejecting the majority principle, anarchy or despotism in some form is all that is left.

The closing paragraph was, as is so often the case with the great orations, the one that appealed most directly to the emotions and used phrases that would be long remembered. Surprisingly, it was not at all the ending Lincoln had first planned, but one based on a new paragraph suggested by Seward. Lincoln had planned to say:

> In your hands, my dissatisfied fellow countrymen, and not in mine, is the momentous issue of civil war. The government will not assail you, unless you first assail it. You can have no conflict, without being yourselves the aggressors. You have no oath registered in Heaven to destroy the government, while I shall have the most solemn one to "preserve, protect and defend" it. You can forbear the assault upon it; I can not shrink from the defense of it. With you, and not with me, is the solemn question, "Shall it be peace, or a sword?"

That, Seward suggested, was too aggressive by far. He suggested a whole new ending:

> I close. We are not, we must not be aliens or enemies but fellow countrymen. Although passion has strained our bonds of affection too hardly they must not, I am sure they will not be broken. The mystic chords which, proceeding from so many battle fields and so many patriot graves, pass through all the hearts and all the hearths in this broad continent of ours, will yet again harmonize in their ancient music when breathed upon by the guardian angel of the nation.

That was certainly better than Lincoln's proposed ending, but Lincoln then took Seward's paragraph and rewrote it, making it warmer and more personal. Seward's rather abrupt "I close" became the expressive "I am loath to close." The complex third sentence, "Although passion has strained our bonds of affection too hardly they must not, I am sure they will not be broken," was polished and simplified to "Though passion may have strained, it must not break our bonds of affection." The obscure "mystic chords" became "mystic chords of memory." "Countrymen" became "friends," while "the guardian angel of the nation" became, out of Lincoln's memory of Shakespeare (Sonnet 144), "the better angels of our nature," making it personal instead of national.

> I am loath to close. We are not enemies, but friends. We must not be enemies. Though passion may have strained, it must not break our bonds of affection. The mystic chords of memory, stretching from every battlefield and patriot grave to every living heart and hearthstone all over this broad land, will yet swell the chorus of the Union, when again touched, as surely they will be, by the better angels of our nature.[55]

The newspapers, North and South, responded predictably to praise or excoriate, but George Templeton Strong, a New York lawyer and diarist, wrote that the speech was "unlike any message or state paper of any class that has appeared in our time. . . . [It] seems to introduce one to a man and to dispose one to like him."[56]

IX

Oddly, the Congress went home after the inauguration. The pattern of meetings of Congress had been created to meet the needs of citizen-legislators who were mostly farmers. Fewer of them were farmers by 1861, but the settled custom prevailed: it was March 1, time to plant the crops whether there was a war on or not. It was probably convenient for Lincoln also that he could learn something about administration without members of Congress looking over his shoulder to complain and second-guess. Nevertheless, the Congress would be needed to authorize wartime expenditures, so Lincoln summoned them to return for a special session to begin on July 4. Meanwhile, on his own authority, he expanded the army by ten regiments and ordered the enlistment of 18,000 sailors for the navy.

Beyond the obvious physical measures to be taken, however, there was need of a statement that would clarify administration goals. Seward nagged Lincoln relentlessly about the need for a statement of policy; and as the summer session of Congress approached, Lincoln spent more and more time by himself, drafting such a statement. In the long, discouraging months of war that led to a turning point at Gettysburg in July 1863, Lincoln made no other significant speeches; but he did issue statements, and these lacked only an audience and a speaker to be ranked with the great speeches Lincoln did make.

Lincoln seems always to have written for the ear. Albert Chandler, a cipher operator in the War Department, was often present when Lincoln received telegrams and sat down to write a response. His writing, Chandler reported, was "slow and apparently somewhat labored," and he would whisper words and phrases or even speak them aloud as he worked.[57] William O. Stoddard, an assistant secretary, remembered coming into the office once and being asked by Lincoln if he, Lincoln, could read him something aloud. "I can always tell more about a thing after I've heard it read aloud," Lincoln said, "and know how it sounds. Just the reading of it to myself doesn't answer as well either." When Stoddard asked whether he could read the letter aloud, Lincoln answered, "No, no; I'll read it myself. What I want is an audience. Nothing sounds the same when there isn't anyone to hear it and find fault with it."[58] Stoddard said of Lincoln, "He was more an orator than a writer."[59]

Three written documents from the time between the inauguration and Gettysburg deserve to be included among Lincoln's speeches. Two of them were messages to the Congress which, in more recent times, would have been read by the President himself.* In Lincoln's time, it was customary to send the message to Congress and have it read by a clerk, but it was designed to be spoken aloud and Lincoln instructed the clerk as to how it should be read. The third document was a letter written to Horace Greeley; but it, too, was a public statement such as might today have been made in an interview with a reporter. All of them, as we know from such accounts as those already mentioned, were written for the ear.

The message delivered to Congress on the Fourth of July, 1861, made, surprisingly, no reference to the anniversary even though Lincoln made a

---

* Washington and Adams had delivered their messages to Congress in person, but Jefferson thought it smacked too much of kings addressing their subjects and sent his messages. Not until Woodrow Wilson became President was the older pattern restored.

very practical comparison between the cost of winning freedom then and maintaining it now:

> A debt of $600,000,000 now is a less sum per head than was the debt of our Revolution when we came out of that struggle, and the money value in the country now bears even a greater proportion to what it was then than does the population. Surely each man has as strong a motive now to preserve our liberties as each had then to establish them.

More important than the financial cost, Lincoln insisted, was the importance of the American experiment in freedom, not just to Americans but to the whole world. The southern states, he said, "have forced upon the country the distinct issue, 'Immediate dissolution or blood.'"

> And this issue embraces more than the fate of these United States. It presents to the whole family of man the question whether a constitutional republic, or democracy—a government of the people, by the same people—can or can not maintain its territorial integrity against its own domestic foes. It presents the question whether discontented individuals, too few in numbers to control administration according to organic law in any case, can always, upon the pretenses made in this case, or on any other pretenses, or arbitrarily without any pretense, break up their government, and thus practically put an end to free government upon the earth. It forces us to ask, Is there in all republics this inherent and fatal weakness? Must a government of necessity be too strong for the liberties of its own people, or too weak to maintain its own existence?

Here Lincoln looked for a way of putting the issue more plainly than that of "maintaining a constitutional republic, or democracy." Those are technical terms, but Lincoln used another phrase that he would return to at Gettysburg. More clearly and simply, it is "a government of the people, by the same people." Daniel Webster had used a similar phrase in his debate with Senator Hayne—"It is, sir, the people's Constitution, the people's government, made for the people, made by the people, and answerable to the people."[60] Lincoln had studied that speech, and it must have been in his mind as he wrote his own speech.

As he had stated this theme toward the beginning of his address, he returned to it toward the end. Noting that some of the seceding states had followed Jefferson's example by adopting declarations of independence, Lincoln pointed out that:

> unlike our good old one signed by Washington, they omit "We, the people," and substitute "We, the deputies of the sovereign and independent States." Why? Why this deliberate pressing out of view the rights of men and the authority of the people?

Quickly, he answered his own question:

> This is essentially a people's contest. On the side of the Union it is a struggle for maintaining in the world that form and substance of government whose leading object is to elevate the condition of men; to lift artificial weights from all shoulders; to clear the paths of laudable pursuit for all; to afford all an unfettered start and a fair chance in the race of life. Yielding to partial and temporary departures, from necessity, this is the leading object of the Government for whose existence we contend.

It was over a year later that Lincoln came back to the issue of policy, in responding to an open letter published by Horace Greeley, the New York editor, in his *Tribune*. Greeley was complaining that there had been as yet no proclamation ending slavery. Abolitionists had been fuming about this ever since Lincoln's inauguration, and now they had found a prominent spokesman to press the issue for them. Lincoln responded immediately in an open letter to the Washington newspaper *The National Intelligencer*. This, too, although reprinted as a letter, is clearly an oral document, to be read aloud as if Lincoln himself were speaking to every reader:

> As to the policy I "seem to be pursuing," as you say, I have not meant to leave any one in doubt. I would save the Union. I would save it the shortest way under the Constitution. The sooner the national authority can be restored the nearer the Union will be "the Union as it was." If there be those who would not save the Union unless they could at the same time save Slavery, I do not agree with them. If there be those who would not save the Union unless they could at the same time destroy Slavery, I do not agree with them. My paramount object in this struggle is to save the Union, and is not either to save or destroy Slavery. If I could save the Union without freeing any slave, I would do it, and if I could save it by freeing all the slaves, I would do it, and if I could save it by freeing some and leaving others alone, I would also do that. What I do about Slavery and the colored race, I do because I believe it helps to save this Union, and what I forbear, I forbear because I do not

believe it would help to save the Union. I shall do less whenever I shall believe what I am doing hurts the cause, and I shall do more whenever I shall believe doing more will help the cause. I shall try to correct errors when shown to be errors; and I shall adopt new views so fast as they shall appear to be true views. I have here stated my purpose according to my view of official duty, and I intend no modification of my oft-expressed personal wish that all men, everywhere, could be free. Yours,

A. Lincoln.

The driving rhetoric of the letter is such that one critical point may easily be overlooked. The whole emphasis is on saving the Union, but at the end Lincoln reminds his readers *and listeners* that this is his purpose "according to my view of official duty" and then reminds them, too, of his " oft-expressed personal wish that all men, everywhere, could be free."[61] He might have added that he had also often stated his belief that slavery could not survive if it were not permitted to expand.

X

Whether the Union could be saved, however, remained very much in doubt. While Grant and others won important victories in the West, the eastern commanders were bedeviled by doubts and seemingly unable to move. Sometimes when they did move, as at Fredericksburg in December 1862, the result was disastrous for the North. Outnumbering Lee's army by three to two, the Northern forces lost twice as many killed and injured and drew back. Six months later, when Lee attempted to win a decisive victory by invading Pennsylvania, he was stopped at Gettysburg in a battle that left some 50,000 casualties, the majority on the Southern side.

In the words of the poet Steven Vincent Benét, there had been "two crab-armies fumbling for each other,/ As if through a fog of rumor and false report"; but when it was over and Lee drew back, there was only one possible outcome. "Each dusty road," wrote Benét, "leads to Appomattox now."[62]

Historians and military experts still argue about how much of a defeat the Battle of Gettysburg was for the Southern cause, but it is indisputable that the Northern side took courage from it and that Lincoln's Gettysburg Address at the dedication of the military cemetery remains a landmark definition of the objective for which the war was waged.

Legends persist about Lincoln writing the Address on a piece of scrap paper or on the back of an envelope while traveling north from Washington on the train. These are nonsense. Lincoln was never one to write a speech at the last minute. Again and again, he began his meticulous planning weeks or even months in advance, typically as soon as he agreed to take part in an event. How long he had to prepare for Gettysburg is unclear. Edward Everett, the principal orator, was invited on September 23 and asked to be present for the dedication, to be held on October 23. Everett said he could not be ready until November 23, so that date was set. Lincoln had it on his calendar by October 30,[63] but the formal invitation was sent on November 2.[64] Lincoln rarely traveled away from Washington to make speeches, and now he was told that Everett would be the speaker of the occasion and Lincoln asked only to make "a few remarks." So his acceptance of this invitation indicates its importance in his eyes, that he saw these "few remarks" as an important opportunity. Surely, then, with little time to work and an important statement to be made, he did not leave it to be written on the train. The best evidence is that Lincoln had not only written the speech before then, but that it had gone through at least three drafts.[65] Always in Lincoln's mind was a far larger audience than would be present in Gettysburg. What he said would be read; and because his speech was brief, it would be on the front news pages nationwide.

The importance it had in Lincoln's eyes is indicated also by the fact that he overrode the arrangement made by Secretary of War Stanton for a morning train. Lincoln knew how easy it would be for things to go wrong at the last minute and wanted to be sure of his arrival in time. He went to Gettysburg, as a result, on the previous afternoon. The Governor of Pennsylvania, less cautious and coming from only thirty miles away, failed to arrive in time for dinner with six other governors; his trip took nine hours. Lincoln not only arrived in time, but left himself opportunity the evening before to work on his speech. Several witnesses spoke of seeing Lincoln at work on his Address and of seeing him go to Secretary of State Seward's room to confer with him about his speech. It seems likely that Lincoln spent another hour working on his speech the next morning.[66] All this, it should be remembered, had to do with a text of 272 words; but Woodrow Wilson, half a century later, said "If I am to speak for ten minutes, I need a week for preparation . . . if an hour, I am ready now."[67]

Invidious contrasts are also made between the President's brevity and the main speaker's longevity. But it was expected that Everett would speak for at least two hours. The audience would have felt shortchanged with less. Lincoln, on the other hand, had been asked only for "remarks." His task was to make those few remarks serve his purpose: to sum up as clearly and memorably as possible the vital importance of the cause for which so very many had died. That he achieved his purpose has never been seriously doubted. Everett's task was to memorialize the fallen; Lincoln's was to ensure "that these dead shall not have died in vain," but that "the living" be dedicated "to the unfinished work" and that the nation experience "a new birth of freedom."

For that purpose, Lincoln employed all the considerable skill that he had learned and developed over so many years of private study and public oratory. He would give his speech the feel of an imperishable Biblical text* with his opening words: "Fourscore and seven years ago. . . ." Lincoln did not normally count that way. In his First Inaugural, he had said "It is seventy-two years since the first inauguration of a President under our National Constitution." He did not say "threescore years and twelve." But this time he wanted to be remembered.

From that beginning, Lincoln, who had always been fond of alliteration, went on to a sentence dominated by the letter "f":

> *Four* score and seven years ago
> our *fathers* brought *forth* . . .

What exactly "our fathers" brought forth had been, of course, a critical issue in the Lincoln-Douglas debates and the Cooper Union Address. Lincoln sums it up here in a brief phrase echoing the Declaration of Independence: "a new nation dedicated to the proposition that *all* men are created equal." In the Lincoln-Douglas debates, the meaning of that phrase had been debated: did it mean all men of whatever color, or all *white* men? Lincoln had always been clear that there could be no racial division within that statement, that our fathers had never thought it was limited to *some* men. Now that proposition is raised up as a central purpose for the existence of the country.

The long final sentence again sets out Lincoln's understanding of the purpose of the war. It was no narrow vision, but a struggle to preserve for all the earth a special kind of government. He had tried to describe it in his first address to the Congress, and he elaborated on that definition now. He had said, in July of his first year in office, that the rebellion of some states against the whole "presents to the whole family of man the question whether a constitutional republic, or democracy—a government of the people, by the same people—can or can not maintain its territorial integrity against its own domestic foes." Now he would conclude his address with that same idea, but enriched by an additional phrase: "that this nation, under God, shall have a new birth of freedom . . . and that government of the people, by the people, for the people, shall not perish from the earth."

The added phrase "for the people" is critical. It is sometimes hard for elected representatives and other employees of the government to remember that they are employees not "of the government, to serve the government," but "of the people" and, most critically, "for the people."

---

* "Biblical language" here always means the English of the King James Version of 1611, the only Bible Lincoln and almost all his hearers knew.

Lincoln added just two words to his written text when he spoke: "under God." If it was a sudden impulse, he never regretted it, since he approved that phrase in every edition that came to his attention. Strikingly, the addition comes just before the idea of "a new birth of freedom." Rebirth, being born again, is a basic tenet of Christianity, but of many other religious traditions as well. The phrases belong together.

Edward Everett's task had been to recall the battle that had been fought and the heroism of the fallen. He did it well. Lincoln's task was far harder: to refocus the nation's understanding of its past and its vision of the task ahead. Garry Wills has written, "Lincoln does not argue law or history. He *makes* history."[68] It could not have been better done.

XI

But the war was not over. Indeed, the war was going so badly by the summer of 1864 that Lincoln was planning ahead for the very likely need to make a transition to a new administration. Union armies had been successful in the West, but in the East, in the arena visible to New Englanders and New Yorkers and the major East Coast cities, there was no evidence of progress. Lincoln had replaced his do-nothing generals with Ulysses S. Grant, and Grant was making every effort to move his army forward; but in two weeks in May he had lost 32,000 men—and Lee was still there. Further fighting in June brought the casualty list to almost 100,000. Mary Lincoln told her husband what many in the country were also saying: "Grant is a butcher and is not fit to be at the head of an army."[69] When Lee sent a small force under Jubal Early through the Maryland Wilderness toward Washington in July 1864, Lincoln was forced to take troops away from Grant to defend the capital.

At the end of August, with radical Republicans planning to nominate their own candidate, the news from the war suddenly brightened. Sherman had captured Atlanta and Admiral Farragut had captured Mobile, the last significant port on the Gulf of Mexico. When the radicals of the Republican Party attempted to draw in the Northern governors, they were roundly rejected as being out of touch. Lincoln moved quickly to reunite the party, and in November he won reelection by 400,000 votes, carrying all but three of the twenty-two states participating in the election.

After that, things went better. Sherman gave Savannah to Lincoln for Christmas, and by Inauguration Day in March Lincoln could be thinking about a way to bring warring peoples together in "a new birth of freedom." After four grueling years of warfare, Lincoln found himself turning more and more to expressions of faith, never more so than in his brief talk to the nation that day from the Capitol steps. He began by noting how different the situation was from what he had faced four years earlier. Then there had been a fear of impending war. "All dreaded it, all sought to avert it"; but, said Lincoln, echoing the Calvinist faith he had been exposed to while growing up, "the war came." Human beings can plan, but God's plan controls events. In spite of human hopes and plans, "the war came."

In early September 1862, Lincoln had sat down after a particularly difficult day to sort out his thoughts on paper as he so often did. No doubt he formed many of the words with his lips as he wrote. His thoughts were centered on a divine purpose behind the events in which he was involved. What he wrote that day was unknown at the time and only discovered years after his death, but the thoughts he wrote then formed a background for the Second Inaugural Address more than a year and a half later. With thoughts inevitably shaped by the Calvinist theology so dominant on the American frontier, a theology centered on thoughts of a purposeful God with a predestined plan for each individual and nation, he had written: "The will of God prevails . . . it is quite possible that God's purpose is different from that of either party . . . I am almost ready to say . . . God wills this contest, and wills that it shall not end yet."

On the eve of victory, Lincoln could look back and attempt to see what God's purpose had been. Perhaps it would help to reconcile the warring parties if they could look to God's purpose rather than their own:

> Both read the same Bible and pray to the same God, and each invokes His aid against the other. . . . The prayers of both could not be answered. That of neither has been answered fully. The Almighty has His own purposes.

In commenting on his speech some days later to New York politician Thurlow Weed, Lincoln said he thought the speech "would wear as well—perhaps better than anything I have produced" but that it seemed not to be "immediately popular." Why was it not? Lincoln understood why: "Men are not flattered by being shown that there has been a difference of purpose between the Almighty and them. . . . But to deny it . . . is to deny there is a God governing the world."[70]

God's purpose may not be clear, but it is certain; and Lincoln, who in early manhood had been very skeptical of the Christianity he had been exposed to, nevertheless wrestled mightily with the God he sought to understand; and he came to believe that there was a purpose in the events he had been part of, even though he himself could glimpse it only dimly. He did understand, however, that those who respond to God's purpose are not freed from pain, as that purpose is worked out in human events:

> Fondly do we hope, fervently do we pray, that this mighty scourge of war may speedily pass away. Yet, if God wills that it continue

> until all the wealth piled by the bondsman's two hundred and fifty years of unrequited toil shall be sunk, and until every drop of blood drawn with the lash shall be paid by another drawn with the sword, as was said three thousand years ago, so still it must be said "the judgments of the Lord are true and righteous altogether."

But if mere human beings cannot fully discern the shape of history, they can deal charitably with those other human beings who are equally doing their best according to the light they are given. Lincoln's final paragraph brings cataclysmic events down to a very personal level, while keeping an eye on the ultimate vision of a lasting peace, and not one just for Americans but for the whole world. The last paragraph may be his finest:

> With malice toward none, with charity for all, with firmness in the right as God gives us to see the right, let us strive on to finish the work we are in, to bind up the nation's wounds, to care for him who shall have borne the battle and for his widow and his orphan, to do all which may achieve and cherish a just and lasting peace among ourselves and with all nations.[71]

It has been a temptation to stop here and let Lincoln have the last word; but this book is designed to show sources and connections, so it must be noted how this passage is soaked in Biblical language and imagery. So, for example, to "put away malice" is a particularly common injunction in the New Testament epistles,* and to "bind up wounds" is a phrase found both in the Psalms and in the Gospels.** A concern for the widow and orphan is prominent in the prophets and the New Testament as well.*** Most importantly, "charity" in the King James Version is not giving to the poor, but an attitude toward others that enables unity.****

---

* See, for example, Ephesians 4:31 and I Peter 2:1.

** See Psalm 147:3 and the Parable of the Good Samaritan in Luke 10:34.

*** "Widows" and "orphans" were important concerns of the prophets and New Testament, usually as "the fatherless" and "widows." See Isaiah 1:17 and James 1:27.

**** Lincoln would have had in mind especially the 13th chapter of Paul's First Epistle to the Corinthians: "And though I bestow all my goods to feed the poor, and though I give my body to be burned, and have not charity, it profiteth me nothing. Charity suffereth long, and is kind; charity envieth not; charity vaunteth not itself, is not puffed up, Doth not behave itself unseemly, seeketh not her own, is not easily provoked, thinketh no evil; Rejoiceth not in iniquity, but rejoiceth in the truth; Beareth all things, believeth all things, hopeth all things, endureth all things. Charity never faileth. . . ." Two modern definitions based on Paul's are worth noticing: "Love is not patronizing and charity isn't about pity, it is about love. Charity and love are the same—with charity you give love, so don't just give money but reach out your hand instead."—Mother Teresa. "A bone to the dog is not charity. Charity is the bone shared with the dog, when you are just as hungry as the dog."—Jack London

Most strikingly, at this critical moment in American history when decisions needed to be made for very local and immediate problems, Lincoln held up a concern not simply for peace in his own country but also for peace with "all nations." He never thought in narrow terms. He had spoken of that larger focus in the last speech of his debates with Senator Douglas. Again, in his first message to Congress in 1861, he had struck that same note. It was present in the last words of the Gettysburg Address. He never forgot that the American experiment was an example and inspiration to other nations and people in their various struggles for freedom. He understood even in those days of high borders and narrow concerns that without international peace, there could be no real and lasting freedom either for Americans or for others.

Analysis of Part III of Lincoln's Cooper Union Address in terms of Euclidean demonstration

Lincoln's speech at Cooper Union is actually three speeches combined into one. The first part asks what understanding the signers of the Constitution had of the use of federal legislation to regulate slavery in the territories in order to show that Stephen A. Douglas was wrong. The second part speaks to the South and tells them that the Dred Scott decision was wrong. The third part asks whether it is possible to yield to Southern demands, but insists that slavery is wrong. Each of the three sections of the address can be analyzed according to Euclidean principles. The following spells out the Euclidean demonstration of Part III.

Element One. Enunciation: The Enunciation states what is *given* and what is being *sought*.

GIVEN: A few words now to Republicans. It is exceedingly desirable that all parts of this great confederation shall be at peace, and in harmony, one with another. Let us Republicans do our part to have it so. Even though much provoked, let us do nothing through passion and ill temper. Even though the Southern people will not so much as listen to us, let us calmly consider their demands and yield to them if, in our deliberate view of our duty, we possibly can.

SOUGHT: Judging by all they say and do, and by the subject and nature of their controversy with us, let us determine, if we can, what will satisfy them.

Element Two. Exposition: The exposition takes separately what is given and prepares it in advance for use in the investigation.

Will they be satisfied if the Territories be unconditionally surrendered to them? We know they will not. In all their present complaints against us, the Territories are scarcely mentioned. Invasions and insurrections are the rage now. Will it satisfy them if, in the future, we have nothing to do with invasions and insurrections? We know it will not. We so know, because we know we never had anything to do with invasions and insurrections; and yet this total abstaining does not exempt us from the charge and the denunciation.

The question recurs, what will satisfy them? Simply this: We must not only let them alone, but we must somehow convince them that we do let them alone. This, we know by experience, is no easy task. We have been so trying to convince them from the very beginning of our organization, but with no success. In all our platforms and speeches, we have constantly protested our purpose to let them alone; but this has had no tendency to convince them. Alike unavailing to convince them is the fact that they have never detected a man of us in any attempt to disturb them.

Element Three. Specification: The specification takes separately the thing that is sought and makes clear precisely what it is.

These natural—and apparently adequate—means all failing, what will convince them? This, and this only: cease to call slavery wrong, and join them in calling it right. And this must be done thoroughly—done in acts as well as in words. Silence will not be tolerated—we must place ourselves avowedly with them. Senator Douglas's new sedition law must be enacted and enforced, suppressing all declarations that slavery is wrong, whether made in politics, in presses, in pulpits, or in private. We must arrest and return their fugitive slaves with greedy pleasure. We must pull down our Free State constitutions. The whole atmosphere must be disinfected from all taint of opposition to slavery, before they will cease to believe that all their troubles proceed from us.

Element Four. Construction: The construction adds what is lacking in the given for finding what is sought.

I am quite aware they do not state their case precisely in this way. Most of them would probably say to us "Let us alone, do nothing to us, and say what you please about slavery." But we do let them alone—have never disturbed them—so that, after all, it is what we say that dissatisfies them. They will continue to accuse us of doing, until we cease saying.

I am also aware that they have not, as yet, in terms, demanded the overthrow of our Free-State constitutions. Yet those constitutions declare the wrong of slavery, with more solemn emphasis than do all other sayings against it; and when all these other sayings shall have been silenced, the overthrow of these constitutions will be demanded and nothing be left to resist the demand. It is nothing to the contrary, that they do not demand the whole of this just now. Demanding what they do, and for the reason they do, they can voluntarily stop nowhere short of this consummation. Holding, as they do, that slavery is morally right and socially elevating, they cannot cease to demand a full national recognition of it, as a legal right and a social blessing.

Element Five. Proof: The proof draws the proposed inference by reasoning scientifically and by the propositions that have been admitted.

Nor can we justifiably withhold this, on any ground save our conviction that slavery is wrong. If slavery is right, all words, acts, laws, and constitutions against it are themselves wrong, and should be silenced and swept away. If it is right, we cannot justly object to its nationality—its universality; if it is wrong, they cannot justly insist upon its extension—its enlargement. All they ask, we could readily grant, if we thought slavery right; all we ask, they could as readily grant, if they thought it wrong. Their thinking it right, and our thinking it wrong, is the precise fact upon which depends the whole controversy. Thinking it right, as they do, they are not to blame for desiring its full recognition, as being right; but, thinking it wrong, as we do, can we yield to them? Can we cast our votes with their view, and against our own? In view of our moral, social, and political responsibilities, can we do this?

Wrong as we think slavery is, we can yet afford to let it alone where it is, because that much is due to the necessity arising from its actual presence in the nation; but can we, while our votes will prevent it, allow it to spread into the National Territories, and to overrun us here in these Free States? If our sense of duty forbids this, then let us stand by our duty, fearlessly and effectively. Let us be diverted by none of those sophistical contrivances wherewith we are so industriously plied and belabored—contrivances such as groping for some middle ground between the right and the wrong, vain as the search for a man who should be neither a living man nor a dead man—such as a policy of "don't care" on a question about which all true men do care—such as Union appeals beseeching true Union men to yield to Disunionists, reversing the divine rule, and calling not the sinners, but the righteous to repentance—such as invocations to Washington, imploring men to unsay what Washington said, and undo what Washington did.

Element Six. Conclusion: The conclusion reverts to the enunciation, confirming what has been proved.

Neither let us be slandered from our duty by false accusations against us, nor frightened from it by menaces of destruction to the Government nor of dungeons to ourselves. LET US HAVE FAITH THAT RIGHT MAKES MIGHT, AND IN THAT FAITH LET US, TO THE END, DARE TO DO OUR DUTY AS WE UNDERSTAND IT.

SIX

William Jennings Bryan
1860–1925

YOU SHALL NOT CRUCIFY MANKIND UPON A CROSS OF GOLD

I

William Jennings Bryan was born to be a speaker.* One of his earliest memories was of standing on a small table to recite, for his mother, passages he had memorized. His father was a lawyer who served twelve years in the Illinois State Senate from 1852 to 1864.** William thought first of becoming a minister, then decided to be a farmer, but before long he settled on being a lawyer like his father. With that in mind, he went to a preparatory academy and then to Illinois College in Jacksonville, Illinois, and entered every speaking contest provided. In his first year at the prep school, he recited Patrick Henry's famous speech in a contest but won no prize—or even mention. Nothing daunted, he entered again in his second year and won third prize. In his first year of college, he won a second prize,

* Bryan was born just five days before Abraham Lincoln came back to Illinois from his trip to New York and New England, centered on his Cooper Union speech.
** As a Democrat, Bryan's father presumably voted to send Stephen A. Douglas to the United States Senate rather than Abraham Lincoln.

and in his sophomore and junior years won first prize. When his class graduated, he delivered the valedictory address. Bryan then spent two years at a law school in Chicago and returned to Springfield to enter a legal partnership and marry. Three years later, in 1887, he moved to Lincoln, Nebraska, to join a friend in a law firm there.

Bryan had been in Nebraska less than a year when he became involved in local politics and made twenty-five speeches supporting the Democratic candidate for Congress. His candidate was defeated—only one Democrat had ever won an election in Nebraska—so in 1890 Bryan was nominated himself, and although there seemed little chance that he would win, he challenged his Republican opponent to a series of eleven debates. A the end of the series, Bryan expressed appreciation that they had been able to carry on their debate in a "fair and friendly manner" and apologized if he had offended his opponent in any way. He then surprised his opponent by presenting him with a copy of Gray's "Elegy"* and expressed the hope that "whether the palm of victory is given to you or to me, [we will] remember those of whom the poet says:

> Far from the madding crowd's ignoble strife,
> Their sober wishes never learned to stray,
> Along the cool sequestered vales of life
> They keep the noiseless tenor of their way."

Somehow that brief stanza summed up for Bryan the whole purpose of government; and there, at the very beginning of his career, he expressed his views as clearly and forcefully as he would ever do:

> These are the ones most likely to be forgotten by the Government. When the poor and weak cry out for relief they, too, often hear no answer but "the echo of their cry," while the rich, the strong, the powerful are given an attentive ear. For this reason is class legislation dangerous and deadly. It takes from those least able to lose and gives to those who are least in need. The safety of our farmers and our laborers is not in special legislation, but in equal and just laws that bear alike on every man. The great masses of our people are interested, not in getting their hands into other people's pockets, but in keeping the hands of other people out of their pockets. Let me, in parting, express the hope that you and I may be instrumental

* One of the most quoted poems ever written, Thomas Gray's "Elegy Written in a Country Churchyard" (1751) contains such familiar phrases as "paths of glory," "celestial fire," "far from the madding crowd," and "kindred spirit."

> in bringing our Government back to better laws which will give equal treatment without regard to creed or condition. . . .

Bryan had simplified his oratorical style since his college days, and a local paper said of him "His style is so different from that of any other public speaker. . . . (He uses) no high sounding phrases, demagogic appeals to passion or prejudice or . . . tragic gestures. . . . He thoroughly believes what he says and his entire lack of artfulness makes him invincible."[1]

The issues facing the Congress in the last decade of the century were economic problems, and the focus was on the income tax and tariffs. The subject of tariffs on imported goods had been an issue in American life almost from the beginning. Manufacturers generally supported tariffs to protect their industries from foreign competition, while farmers especially opposed them as making American products more expensive. Bryan summed up the tariff issue in his campaign speeches by calling it "a cow fed by western farmers and milked by eastern factory owners." A bumper crop of corn in 1889 had depressed prices and left farmers ready to support someone who understood their needs. Bryan spent less than $200 on the campaign but defeated his opponent by over sixty-seven hundred votes, a margin of ten percent.

So Bryan went to Washington and served on committees and waited for the right moment to make his first speech. That moment came after almost a year, in the course of a debate on tariffs. Bryan had prepared carefully for the moment, but it was mid-afternoon before his opportunity came and Congressmen had begun to slip away to the early dinners that were the Washington pattern. Bryan began slowly to deal with some of the technical issues, but every technical detail was embellished with anecdotes and illustrations and gentle jibes at the opposition. Congressmen began to drift back and the gallery began to fill. After an hour, Bryan suggested that he should conclude, but there were cries of "Go on! Go on!" So he did, for two more hours, yielding several more times to the cries of "Go on!"

Why, he asked, should there be a protective tariff on wool? He had specific numbers memorized, and balanced them with humor:

> Is it because of the importance of the industry? The gentleman from Maine, Mr. Dingley, said that it was one of the most universal of all the industries of the farm and when I tried to call his attention to the fact that only a small proportion of our people own sheep he did not care to be further interrupted. The fact is, Mr. Chairman, that last year the value of sheep in this country was only $108,391,444 while the value of live stock upon the farm was $2,329,787,770; that is, the value of sheep was less than one

> twentieth the value of all the live stock. The wool crop last year was valued at about $70,000,000 while the value of the corn, wheat, and oats raised that year without mentioning the other crops of the farm amounted to $1,582,184,206. Three items of the farm amounted to twenty times the value of the wool clip. Out in Nebraska there was a time when we had almost one sheep for each man woman and child. We look back to it as the mutton age of Nebraska. But alas that happy day has passed! The number of sheep has continually decreased until now if every woman in the State named Mary insisted upon having a pet lamb at the same time we would have to go out of the State to get lambs enough to go round.

He also had a story to help make his point:

> It was said by a French writer that Robinson Crusoe was a protectionist, that when he was on the island all alone he started to make a canoe by hollowing out a log with a broken stone. Just about the time he commenced, some boards floated up to the shore and the thought came to him, "I will take these boards and make myself a canoe out of them," but the protective idea came to him and he said, "No, if I do that I will lose the labor I put into the log." So he kicked the boards away from the shore and went on hacking at the log with the broken stone.

Bryan was probably not original in talking about the government taking money out of people's pockets, but he made it sound original by adding two modifying words, "crying up":

> Whenever you see the Government by operation of law send a dollar singing down into one man's pocket you must remember that the Government has brought it crying up out of some other man's pocket. You might just as well try to raise a weight with a lever without a fulcrum as try to help some particular industry by means of taxation without placing the burden upon the consumer.

When he was interrupted with a question, as he frequently was, he had exactly the right answer:

> MR. MCKENNA: Do you really believe that the protective policy is similar to the pickpocket's policy of putting a man's hand into another man's pocket and extracting money from it?

> MR. BRYAN: Yes, that is my belief.
>
> MR. MCKENNA: Now, then, one other question: . . . If that is so, how do you justify your position not in economics but in morality for reporting a bill which leaves 39 per cent taxes on woolen clothing?
>
> MR. BRYAN: Mr. Chairman, if I found a robber in my house who had taken all I had and I was going to lose it all or else get one half back, I would take the half. I will ask the gentleman from California whether he would refuse to give the people any relief because he could not give all that he wanted to give?

He quoted Supreme Court decisions; he cited the cost of particular items such as tin plate ten years ago and today; he cited manufacturers who had testified that they could make more products at better prices if not for the tariff; and he pointed out that the manufacturers who pleaded for the protection of the tariff "are the ones who build their stately palaces, who give their banquets which rival in magnificence the banquets of ancient times." And always there was the flashing wit. The official transcript shows that he was interrupted some fifty times by laughter.[2]

Finally, after some three hours, he did conclude with partisan praise for the Democratic Party that seeks to protect the real "home industry" of this country.

> When some young man selects a young woman willing to trust her future to his strong right arm and they start to build a little home, that home which is the unit of society and upon which our Government and our prosperity must rest, when they start to build this little home and the man who sells the lumber reaches out his hand to collect a tariff upon that, and the man who sells paints and oils wants a tariff upon them, the man who furnishes the carpets, table cloths, knives, forks, dishes, furniture, spoons—everything that enters into the construction and operation of that home—when all these hands, I say, are stretched out from every direction to lay their blighting weight upon that cottage and the Democratic Party says "Hands off, and let that home industry live," it is protecting the grandest home industry that this or any other nation ever had.

The protection of American freedom, he pointed out, was more than a matter of armies:

> We cannot put our safety in expensive fortifications along a seacoast thousands of miles in extent nor can we put our safety in a great standing army that would absorb in idleness the toil of the men it protects. A free government must find its safety in happy and contented citizens who, protected in their rights and free from unnecessary burdens, will be willing to die that the blessings which they enjoy may be transmitted to their posterity.
>
> The day will come, Mr. Chairman, the day will come when those who annually gather about this Congress seeking to use the taxing power for private purposes will find their occupation gone, and the members of Congress will meet here to pass laws for the benefit of all the people. That day will come, and in that day, to use the language of another, "Democracy will be king! Long live the king!"[3]

The *New York Times* reported: "His voice is clear and strong, his language plain, but not lacking in grace. He uses illustrations effectively and he employs humor and sarcasm with admirable facility."[4] The Congressional record also shows a different side of Bryan's oratory from the set speech on the public stage. In Congress he had to be ready for interruptions and questions, but he had an ability to turn a question to his own advantage as he did in a debate on the income tax in January 1894. When Bryan pointed out that most of the countries of Europe had much higher income taxes, he was interrupted by another member, who got more of a response than he might have expected:

> MR. WEADCOCK: The gentleman will allow me to suggest that at Monte Carlo such a man would not pay any income tax at all.

Bryan was ready for him:

> Then, Mr. Chairman, I presume to Monte Carlo he would go, and that there he would give up to the wheel of fortune all the wealth of which he would not give a part to support the government which enabled him to accumulate it.
>
> Are there really any such people in this country?
>
> Of all the mean men I have ever known, I have never known one so mean that I would be willing to say of him that his patriotism was less than two per cent deep.
>
> There is not a man whom I would charge with being willing to expatriate himself rather than contribute from his abundance to the support of the government which protects him.

> If we have people who value free government so little that they prefer to live under monarchical institutions, even without an income tax, rather than live under the stars and stripes and pay a 2 per cent tax, we can better afford to lose them and their fortunes rather than risk the contaminating influence of their presence....

As usual, Bryan had some lines of poetry memorized that were exactly right for the situation:

> If we are to lose some of our "best people" by the imposition of an income tax, let them go with the poet's curse ringing in their ears:
>
> Breathes there the man with soul so dead
> Who never to himself hath said,
> This is my own, my native land!
> Whose heart hath ne'er within him burned,
> As home his footsteps he hath turned
> From wandering on a foreign strand!
> If such there breathe, go, mark him well;
> For him no minstrel raptures swell;
> High though his titles, proud his name,
> Boundless his wealth as wish can claim
> Despite those titles, power, and pelf,
> The wretch, concentered all in self,
> Living, shall forfeit fair renown,
> And, doubly dying, shall go down
> To the vile dust from whence he sprung,
> Unwept, unhonored, and unsung.*

After two terms in Congress, the opportunity came in 1894 to run for the Senate, though now Bryan would be encountering the full weight of Nebraska's Republican history. His opponent would be James Thurston, chief counsel for the Union Pacific Railway, the epitome of arrogant capitalism. But Senators were not yet elected directly; Bryan needed a majority in the state legislature; and that was an impossible goal. Bryan won 73% of the popular vote—though many Republicans may have abstained from voting to emphasize that it was a meaningless referendum. The legislature chose Thurston to represent them in Washington. But across the nation, people were beginning to see in Bryan a possible candidate for the presidency in 1896. Bryan obviously had such

* The poem is from *The Lay of the Last Minstrel* by Sir Walter Scott.

an idea himself, since he spent the next year and a half traveling widely and speaking about the gold standard to all who would listen.[5]

II

The most famous speech in the history of American political conventions was made by one of the youngest men in the hall. William Jennings Bryan went to the Democratic Party convention of 1896 as a former member of Congress and delegate from the State of Nebraska. He had no special role and no certainty that he would have an opportunity to speak. He knew he was likely to be nominated for president or vice-president, but candidates traditionally were not even at the conventions that nominated them and were not expected to speak.

Bryan hoped he might be made chair of the committee on resolutions; but he discovered that a senior delegate wanted that position, so Bryan deferred to him. Bryan was, after all, only thirty-six years old and barely old enough to be a legal candidate for president. After the resolutions committee had completed its work, however, the chair of the committee asked Bryan to manage the floor debate on the platform being presented. That gave him the opportunity to make the closing speech summing up the party's position on the major issues. Since Bryan had been speaking on those subjects for months, he needed no time to write a speech. He would be repeating arguments he had often made before and, in particular, phrases like "a cross of gold" that he had often used elsewhere.

In his opening remarks, Bryan staked an immediate claim to the moral high ground. He might be young, he was saying, but the issues are too important to let that make a difference:

> I would be presumptuous, indeed, to present myself against the distinguished gentlemen to whom you have listened if this were a mere measuring of abilities; but this is not a contest between persons. The humblest citizen in all the land, when clad in the armor of a righteous cause, is stronger than all the hosts of error. I come to speak to you in defense of a cause as holy as the cause of liberty—the cause of humanity.

Briefly, Bryan summed up the national debate over the gold standard, an issue creating division in both parties. The country had been in depression, and many Americans believed that the country's economic troubles were a result of relying on a limited supply of gold instead of using gold and silver together. Bryan had worked with the silver forces to convince others throughout the country, so that they could come to this convention "not to discuss, not to debate, but to enter up the judgment already rendered by the plain people of this country." It was the ordinary people, farmers and factory workers, who Bryan claimed to represent. The gold forces claimed to represent "businessmen," but Bryan wanted the delegates to understand that farmers and factory workers also were businessmen. In his memoirs, he said he considered this passage the most important one presented and regretted that it had been given so little attention:[6]

> When you [turning to the gold delegates] come before us and tell us that we are about to disturb your business interests, we reply that you have disturbed our business interests by your course. We say to you that you have made the definition of a business man too limited in its application. The man who is employed for wages is as much a business man as his employer; the attorney in a country town is as much a business man as the corporation counsel in a great metropolis; the merchant at the cross-roads store is as much a business man as the merchant of New York; the farmer who goes forth in the morning and toils all day, who begins in the spring and toils all summer, and who by the application of brain and muscle to the natural resources of the country creates wealth, is as much a business man as the man who goes upon the Board of Trade and bets upon the price of grain. . . . We come to speak of this broader class of business men.

Bryan had learned to steer away from the more emotional language once prized by orators, but he could not resist a reference to

> the hardy pioneers . . . who have made the desert blossom like a rose . . . who rear their children near to Nature's heart, where they can mingle their voices with the voices of the birds—out there where they have erected schoolhouses for the education of their young, churches where they praise their Creator, and cemeteries where rest the ashes of their dead—these people, we say, are as deserving of the consideration of our party as any people in this country. It is for these that we speak.

As Bryan continued, he was surprised to find the audience "seemed to rise and sit down as one man. At the close of a sentence it would rise and shout, and when I began upon another sentence, the room was as still as a church." He was able to single out a few delegates whose faces were especially responsive and focus on them, seeing his own face reflected in theirs. It was, he wrote later, something absolutely unique in his experience.[7] As he went on with his speech, he wanted the delegates to understand that there were many Americans who felt that their voices had not been heard:

> We have petitioned, and our petitions have been scorned; we have entreated, and our entreaties have been disregarded; we have begged, and they have mocked when our calamity came. We beg no longer; we entreat no more; we petition no more. We defy them!

Bryan went on to speak briefly about the other planks of the platform: the income tax, life tenure in government offices, the tariff; but the gold standard was "the paramount issue." He would devote the bulk of his speech to that issue, but first he would take time to have a little fun with the delegates and poke fun at the Republicans. A few months previously, he told the delegates, everyone expected William McKinley, the Republican candidate, to be elected, but how is it now?

> Why, the man who was once pleased to think that he looked like Napoleon—that man shudders today when he remembers that he was nominated on the anniversary of the Battle of Waterloo. Not only that, but as he listens, he can hear with ever-increasing distinctness the sound of the waves as they beat upon the lonely shores at St. Helena.

The delegates roared their appreciation, and Bryan moved on to mock the Republicans for trying to have it both ways on the gold standard by promising to adopt bimetallism if there could be international agreement. Why, he asked them, would you do that if the gold standard is good? And why would you put America at the mercy of an international agreement and international bankers? The Republicans, he argued, are the party of the wealthy, who believe prosperity flows down from the rich to the poor and that

> . . . if you will only legislate to make the well-to-do prosperous, their prosperity will leak through on those below. The Democratic idea, however, has been that if you legislate to make the masses prosperous, their prosperity will find its way up through every class which rests upon them.
>
> You come to us and tell us that the great cities are in favor of the gold standard; we reply that the great cities rest upon our broad and fertile prairies. Burn down your cities and leave our farms, and your cities will spring up again as if by magic; but destroy our farms and the grass will grow in the streets of every city in the country.

It had not been a long speech as convention speeches go, fewer than three thousand words and not much more than twenty minutes in length. Even today, American churchgoers would not be much surprised by a Sunday sermon that long; some would consider it too short.* But Bryan had made his point: silver versus gold was not so much the issue as was the growing sense of disenfranchisement of the western farmers and the factory workers in the growing cities. The gold standard was simply a convenient symbol of the oppression of the poor by the rich, and Bryan would hold that symbol up as he stepped forward a few inches and launched into a summary that would become one of the most famous passages in the history of American oratory:

> We care not upon what lines the battle is fought. . . . If they dare to come out in the open field and defend the gold standard as a good thing, we will fight them to the uttermost. Having behind us the producing masses of this nation and the world, supported by the commercial interests, the laboring interests and the toilers everywhere, we will answer their demand for a gold standard by saying to them: You shall not press down upon the brow of labor this crown of thorns, you shall not crucify mankind upon a cross of gold.**

As Bryan began his last sentence, he raised his hands above his head with the fingers spread to form a crown and brought them slowly down to symbolize a crown of thorns. As he completed the sentence, he stepped back from the podium and stretched his arms straight out as if crucified himself. He held the pose for five long seconds and then left the stage to walk back to his delegation as the convention hall erupted around him. Delegates stood on their chairs and waved their arms, their hats, their canes, their coats, and their umbrellas. They danced, they sang, they cried. They tore up their state standards and carried them to the Nebraska delegation. They picked up the orator and carried him around on their shoulders. In a spontaneous demonstration that would be copied less spontaneously by convention delegates for a hundred years afterwards, they processed around the hall while the band played. William Allen White, the Pulitzer prize-winning Kansas newspaper man, wrote: "Through the nerves of the telegraph that speech thrilled a continent, and for a day a nation was in a state of mental and moral catalepsy."[8]

---

* Martin Luther King, Jr.'s "I Have a Dream" speech was half as long, but a typical Sunday sermon of King's would have been more like five thousand words.

** http://www.authentichistory.com/1898. The Cross of Gold speech was recorded in 1921, twenty-five years after it was given. The recording equipment was still inadequate, and the speaker's voice was also twenty-five years older.

The nomination came on the fifth ballot the next day. Bryan had been too busy to shave that morning; but when it seemed clear that he would be nominated, he went to the hotel barbershop and found his life in danger from a barber so excited, he could hardly handle the razor.[9]

III

During the campaign, William McKinley, the Republican nominee, followed, at least in form, the time-honored precedent of maintaining a dignified silence in public. Guided by Marcus ("Mark") Hanna, his manager, however, he did make speeches almost daily, sometimes a dozen speeches a day, but only from his front porch in Ohio. Delegations of citizens from every walk of life were brought to his home day by day, and thousands made the journey to stand on his lawn and hear the candidate.

Bryan meanwhile abandoned the tradition entirely and traveled the country by train, speaking wherever the train stopped. As usual, the Democrats had a minimal budget and little recourse to the captains of industry, while Mark Hanna had compiled an enormous war chest for McKinley. Starting with a gift of $250,000 from John D. Rockefeller and Standard Oil, Hanna added gifts from New York Life of $50,000 and from western railroads totaling $174,000. Eventually he had over three and a half million dollars, the largest political war chest ever assembled, to use as needed, and nothing was left to chance. A speakers' bureau in Chicago deployed an army of 1,400 orators to speak on request. By mid-September, a hundred million pieces of literature had been distributed. By election day, twice that number had been sent out in at least nine languages ranging from Norwegian to Hebrew. In addition to the usual campaign practices, factory owners in New England posted signs that warned their workers that their factories would be closed down the day after the election if Bryan won.[10]

In support of Bryan, the best the Democrats could find was newspaper publisher William Randolph Hearst, who raised money from friends and eventually turned over some $40,000 to the national committee. Meanwhile, Bryan traveled east to make an acceptance speech in New York's Madison Square Garden. An overly long introductory speech and stifling heat discouraged some who left early as a result and gave the hostile press a chance to speak of the event as a failure, but most of the audience sat through the two-hour event and emerged enthusiastic. As Bryan journeyed back to the Midwest, crowds too large for the buildings welcomed him in Columbus, Toledo, and South Bend.

The industrial East, however, was safe McKinley country, the West and South equally safe for Bryan. The election would be fought and won in the old "Northwest Territory" from Ohio to Minnesota, which both candidates could claim as their home country. McKinley was born and brought up in

Ohio, where he still lived, and Bryan was born and brought up in Illinois. After a few days at home in Nebraska, Bryan was on the road again, traveling through Kentucky, Tennessee, and North Carolina, then up through Washington, D.C. and New York to Boston, where he spoke to a crowd of seventy-five thousand. The largest part of his time, however, was spent in the states in the Ohio and Mississippi valleys. By election day, he had traveled over eighteen thousand miles and made over six hundred speeches. For much of the time, Bryan made his own arrangements, bought his own tickets, and often carried his own luggage.

In New York, Bryan explained to the ordinary people of that city why his focus on financial policy affected them:

> This great city is built upon the commerce of the nation and must suffer if that commerce is impaired. You cannot sell unless the people have money with which to buy, and they cannot obtain the money with which to buy unless they are able to sell their products at remunerative prices. Production of wealth goes before the exchange of wealth; those who create must secure a profit before they have anything to share with others. You cannot afford to join the money changers in supporting a financial policy which, by destroying the purchasing power of the products of toil, must in the end discourage the creation of wealth.

He built his closing appeal on the Statue of Liberty, which had been set in New York's harbor less than ten years earlier, and on the freedom it stood for, not only to Americans but to the rest of the world.

> It is true that a few of your financiers would fashion a new figure—a figure representing Columbia, her hands bound fast with fetters of gold and her face turned toward the East, appealing for assistance to those who live beyond the sea—but this figure can never express your idea of this nation. You will rather turn for inspiration to the heroic statue which guards the entrance to your city—a statue as patriotic in conception as it is colossal in proportions. . . . That figure—Liberty enlightening the world—is emblematic of the mission of our nation among the nations of the earth. With a government which derives its powers from the consent of the governed, secures to all the people freedom of conscience, freedom of thought and freedom of speech, guarantees equal rights to all, and promises special privileges to none, the United States should be an example in all that is good, and the leading spirit in every movement which has for its object the uplifting of the human race.[11]

But many Americans were not convinced. Perhaps Bryan's decision to make the gold standard the central issue asked too much of voters who would have to understand and support an economic theory that divided the experts. Perhaps the lives of western farmers and eastern factory workers were so different they failed to see what they had in common.* Perhaps the focus on the abstract issue of monetary policy meant that Bryan seemed not to address the more tangible and immediate issues that affected most Americans. Perhaps the lingering depression that had begun in the previous Democratic administration left people ready for a change—though Democratic President Grover Cleveland supported the gold standard.** Some thought that the rising price of wheat during the summer had made the difference. When the votes were counted, McKinley had 7,036,638 to Bryan's 6,467,946 and 271 electoral votes to Bryan's 176.[12] Bryan sent a telegram to McKinley "to extend my congratulations. We have submitted the issues to the American people and their will is law." No losing candidate for president had ever sent such a message, and McKinley was quick to acknowledge it and express appreciation "with all best wishes for your health and happiness."[13] But the fight was not over. Even in losing, Bryan had drawn more votes than any previous winning candidate. It was close enough that he saw reason to hope for better things in another four years.

IV

Two weeks after the election of 1896, William Jennings Bryan went to Denver to launch his campaign for 1900. By then, he would be forty years old and still the youngest president the country has ever had. Even before McKinley had been inaugurated, Bryan had published a collection of his speeches under the suggestive title "The First Battle," and it was selling at the rate of over a thousand copies a day.[14]

A very different battle intruded, however, on Bryan's plans. The restive population of Cuba was drawing increasing attention from Americans. The United States had pressed Spain to grant the Cubans self-government, and Spain had yielded to every American demand or at least accepted arbitration. McKinley had no interest in a war, but there were newspapers happy to use the rebellion to sell papers; and when an American battleship, the *Maine*, exploded in Havana harbor, they were sure the Spanish government was responsible. On April 11, 1898, McKinley asked the Congress for authority

* While Bryan won 48.3% of the rural vote and only 40.6% of the urban vote, the larger differences were regional. Bryan was strong in the West and the South, both in rural and urban areas: McKinley was strong in New England and the old Midwest, in rural and urban areas alike.

** Bryan thought the failures of the Cleveland administration were critically important and said "I have borne the sins of Grover Cleveland." Coletta, 197.

to intervene in Cuba if necessary, and two weeks later the Congress took it upon itself to declare war.

Bryan had opposed the war but, like McKinley, saw nothing to gain by resisting popular pressure for intervention. When Congress acted, however, Bryan wrote to McKinley offering his services. Receiving no reply, he offered himself to the Governor of Nebraska to serve in the state's national guard. As in Lincoln's day, it was still the custom for national guard regiments to elect their own officers, so Bryan became a colonel and found himself encamped in Florida awaiting a call to action that never came. Two weeks after they arrived in Florida, Spain sued for peace, but the Nebraska regiment was kept in Florida for four more months. There were some who thought McKinley was being cautious about Spain, and some who thought he was more interested in keeping Bryan in Florida until the fall elections were over.

Mustered out in December, Bryan quickly found himself with a real fight on his hands. Although the Congress had specified that the United States had no territorial designs on Cuba, it had said nothing about the Philippines, and those islands also had fallen to American forces. There were many who believed acquisition of the islands was simply a further extension of America's "manifest destiny," and others who saw it as a first step toward acquiring a colonial empire like that of the English, the French, and the Dutch, and dangerous to the future of America.

The administration proposed a treaty with Spain to end the war, establish an independent Cuba, and make the Philippines an American territory. To the surprise of many, Bryan supported the treaty, feeling that to oppose it left the country at war and might make the Democratic Party responsible. Furthermore, he felt that bringing the Philippines under American control would make it easier to give the islands their independence than if it were necessary to force Spain to create a republic there later.

So the treaty was signed and the war ended, but the Philippines were not given independence and Americans found themselves involved in a war with the same Filipinos who had been fighting Spain for independence and who continued their struggle against the United States. By the time of the Democratic convention of 1900, it had become a major issue between the parties. Bryan was easily renominated for President in early July and officially accepted the nomination a month later, in front of a gathering of fifty thousand in (inappropriately) Military Park, Indianapolis.

In a speech three times as long as his Cross of Gold Speech, Bryan began by saying that the election would be "a contest between Democracy on the one hand and plutocracy on the other" because "the Republican party is dominated by those influences which constantly tend to substitute the worship of mammon for the protection of the rights of man." But ninety percent of the speech that followed had to do with what Bryan called "the menace of imperialism" and, more specifically, the American occupation of the Philippine Islands.

Once again, the question could be asked whether Bryan had chosen a theme that was a secondary concern for the average citizen, who had more immediate concerns than American policy on the other side of the world. Bryan did his best to make the connection:

> Imperialism would be profitable to the army contractors; it would be profitable to the ship owners, who would carry live soldiers to the Philippines and bring dead soldiers back; it would be profitable to those who would seize upon the franchises, and it would be profitable to the officials whose salaries would be fixed here and paid over there; but to the farmer, to the laboring man and to the vast majority of those engaged in other occupations it would bring expenditure without return and risk without reward.

Bryan then reviewed the various reasons people gave for occupying the Philippines: that it would bring Christianity to the islands, that we could not yield land won at the price of American blood, and finally that it was simply America's destiny.

Bryan's deep commitment to Christian faith was well known, and it enabled him to reject out of hand what he called the "gun-powder gospel." A good many Protestants saw the occupation of the Philippines as a chance to evangelize Roman Catholics, but Bryan would have none of it. It was, he pointed out, "a sufficient answer to say that a majority of the Filipinos are now members of one branch of the Christian church." Furthermore, "If true Christianity consists in carrying out in our daily lives the teachings of Christ, who will say that we are commanded to civilize with dynamite and proselyte with the sword? . . . Compare, if you will, the swaggering, bullying, brutal doctrine of imperialism with the golden rule and the commandment 'Thou shalt love thy neighbor as thyself.'"

Some, Bryan went on, suggested that "the naval victory at Manila made the permanent acquisition of those islands necessary" and that "The shedding of American blood in the Philippine islands . . . (made) it imperative that we should retain possession forever." No, said Bryan, "we won a naval victory at Santiago, but that did not compel us to hold Cuba. . . . American blood was shed at San Juan Hill and El Caney, and yet the president has promised the Cubans independence. . . . Better a thousand times that our flag in the Orient give way to a flag representing the idea of self-government than that the flag of this republic should become the flag of an empire."

As to destiny, Bryan was scornful:

> When our opponents are unable to defend their position by argument they fall back upon the assertion that it is destiny, and insist that we must submit to it, no matter how much it violates our moral precepts and our principles of government. This is a complacent philosophy. It obliterates the distinction between right and wrong and makes individuals and nations the helpless victims of circumstance.
>
> Destiny is the subterfuge of the invertebrate, who, lacking the courage to oppose error, seeks some plausible excuse for supporting it. . . . The Republicans say that this nation is in the hands of destiny; Washington believed that not only the destiny of our own nation but the destiny of the republican form of government throughout the world was entrusted to American hands. Washington was right. The destiny of this Republic is in the hands of its own people, and upon the success of the experiment here rests the hope of humanity.

But Bryan was at his eloquent best in his closing paragraphs, in which he held up a different vision from that of the imperialists. He had invoked the founding fathers in his opening paragraphs: Washington, Jefferson, and especially Patrick Henry, whose "passionate appeal, 'Give me liberty or give me death,'" Bryan suggested, might well prove an inspiration to the Filipinos. At the end, like Martin Luther King, Jr. sixty-three years later, Bryan held up his dream of what America might become:

> I can conceive of a national destiny surpassing the glories of the present and the past—a destiny which meets the responsibilities of today and measures up to the possibilities of the future.
>
> Behold a republic, resting securely upon the foundation stones quarried by revolutionary patriots from the mountain of eternal truth—a republic applying in practice and proclaiming to the world the self-evident propositions that all men are created equal; that they are endowed with inalienable rights; that governments are instituted among men to secure these rights, and that governments derive their just powers from the consent of the governed.
>
> Behold a republic in which civil and religious liberty stimulates to earnest endeavor and in which the law restrains every hand uplifted for a neighbor's injury—a republic in which every citizen is a sovereign, but in which no one cares to wear a crown.

> Behold a republic standing erect while empires all around are bowed beneath the weight of their own armaments—a republic whose flag is loved while other flags are only feared.
>
> Behold a republic increasing in population, in wealth, in strength and in influence, solving the problems of civilization and hastening the coming of an universal brotherhood—a republic which shakes thrones and dissolves aristocracies by its silent example and gives light and inspiration to those who sit in darkness.
>
> Behold a republic gradually but surely becoming the supreme moral factor in the world's progress and the accepted arbiter of the world's disputes—a republic whose history, like the path of the just, "is as the shining light that shineth more and more unto the perfect day."

Undoubtedly there were millions who heard Bryan that year whose ancestors had come, or who themselves had come, precisely because of that vision; yet political campaigns are more likely to be determined by immediate economic issues, and even by the amount of money spent convincing the electorate that their immediate welfare and security are threatened by the opposition candidate. What the voters knew was that the last Democratic administration had ended in a depression and that times were now better. What McKinley and his colleagues promised, and could advertise widely with the funds available to Mark Hanna, was most simply a change from the administration responsible for the depression and rejection of Bryan's "radical" theories, and that hit much closer to home than an appeal to America's moral values.

Like Adlai Stevenson (whose grandfather was Bryan's running mate) in his two campaigns against Eisenhower fifty years later, Bryan had an enormous following of deeply committed admirers, but prosperity and security outvoted oratorical skill and an appeal to American moral values. Contemporary analysts tried to understand Bryan's unique appeal. Kansas newspaperman William Allen White, who shared many of Bryan's middle American values but not his attachment to the Democratic Party, interviewed him in depth and looked inside his home, where he found a library heavy in moral values and light in political and economic analysis. He saw Bryan as a man of naïve values and limitless charm with a smile as "clear and steadfast and cheerful as the sunrise" and "breezy amiability," but he saw "no more reason for electing an orator to office than a fiddler. Both talents arouse the emotions."

In a similar way, Willa Cather, a fellow Nebraskan and author of books based in the Midwest, found much to admire and much to question. She admired the working partnership between Bryan and his wife but disliked his earnest piety, imparted "with a glance as penetrating as a searchlight." White and Cather saw the limits in Bryan's imagination and moralism but were not impressed by the commitment and vision that had so often been lacking in the safer candidates frequently chosen by the major parties.[15]

Bryan faced the same long odds in 1900 as in 1896: a generally prosperous economy and a "safe" candidate with the built-in advantage of the incumbent. Mark Hanna and McKinley promised voters "a full dinner pail"—something very specific and tangible. They also offered an exciting new candidate for vice-president in the young Theodore Roosevelt, only a year and a half older than Bryan, fresh from his triumphs in the Spanish American War. Bryan campaigned harder than ever, making a hundred speeches in New York alone, but Roosevelt campaigned even harder, making more speeches than Bryan and traveling more miles. In the end, Bryan fell short again. He showed gains in New York and Illinois, though he lost them both, but he lost even his own state and won fewer states and fewer total votes than in 1896. Afterwards, Bryan compiled a book entitled *The Second Battle*, but it sold poorly and there were few who envisioned a third campaign.

Bryan could, however, create an image of himself as the conscience of America. He continued in demand as a speaker and, with his brother's help, he began to publish a weekly newspaper called *The Commoner*. There were columns of humor and practical advice, but a steady diet as well of speeches and articles by Bryan himself. Nevertheless, there was no likelihood of a third run in 1904. McKinley was assassinated less than a year after his reelection, leaving the popular and energetic Theodore Roosevelt plenty of time to establish himself before the next election cycle. To make it more difficult, Roosevelt took on many of the issues that Bryan cared about, initiating an antitrust suit against a major corporation and forcing employers to accept arbitration in a coal strike. He also created national parks and set to work building the Panama Canal. The Democrats, seeking, perhaps, to appeal to Americans worn out by Roosevelt's dynamism and Bryan's energy, chose the most colorless candidate available, Alton B. Parker, an appeals judge from upstate New York, a foe of active government and an ineffective public speaker.

Bryan was at the Democratic convention and did his best to support a platform embodying his concerns in an oration that brought tears to the eyes of his long-time supporters. The young Baltimore writer and rising star H. L. Mencken had never heard Bryan before, and though he would be remembered for his attacks on Bryan twenty years later, he wrote that Bryan's speech was the best political speech he had ever heard. "I listened to it," he wrote, with "my eyes apop and my reportorial pencil palsied. . . . What a speech, my masters! What a speech!"[16]

Judge Parker accepted the nomination with a firm commitment to the gold standard and proceeded to establish his credentials as the anti-Bryan.

The Democrats had failed to win with Bryan and therefore chose a different approach. The result was certainly different, but not in the way they had hoped. Parker polled a million votes fewer than Bryan and lost every state outside the South by double-digit margins.

Bryan began his third campaign almost immediately. Parker and Roosevelt both had announced that they would not run again in 1908, so the field was clear and Bryan knew what he wanted. Economic issues, he said, were always moral issues, and he hoped to appeal to the moral sense of the nation. Immoral business combinations should be abolished, a board should be set up to resolve labor problems, and the Philippines should be set free. First, however, Bryan and his wife would travel around the world. In 1905, they took ship from San Francisco to see Japan. From Japan they moved on to Korea and China and the Philippines, then the Dutch East Indies, Singapore, Burma, and India. By the springtime, they were in the Middle East visiting Egypt, Palestine, Syria, and Turkey. In western Europe, they were surprised by the popular attachment to the monarchies in Germany, England, Scandinavia, and elsewhere. In England, they were introduced to J. P. Morgan, who pretended not to recognize the name Bryan. They shook hands and moved away. The king, on the other hand, asked to meet Bryan, and Bryan found him to be a very genial man.

The Bryans were in England on the Fourth of July, and Bryan was invited to address the American Society. It gave him an opportunity to elaborate on his vision of America's role in the world. Americans had pondered America's relationship to the world since John Winthrop spoke about the "city on a hill," but travel was now much faster and communications almost instantaneous, giving that relationship a new urgency. Bryan had been thinking about it as he traveled, and his talk to the Americans in London provided an opportunity to share his thoughts with other Americans. He used as his text a poem of Rudyard Kipling's with the title "The White Man's Burden." Kipling's poem is looked at today as an unfortunate expression of European imperialism and racism; but, in fact, Kipling is arguing against the kind of imperialism that exploited the less developed areas of the world for the white man's benefit and suggesting that with empire comes responsibility. Bryan did not quote the theme-setting first lines, which make it clear that Kipling saw colonialism as a burden that involved hardship and service to others:

> Take up the White Man's burden,
> Send forth the best ye breed
> Go bind your sons to exile
> To serve your captives' need;

Bryan quoted instead the second verse, which says the same thing in different words:

> Take up the White Man's burden—
> In patience to abide,
> To veil the threat of terror
> And check the show of pride;
> By open speech and simple,
> An hundred times made plain,
> To seek another's profit
> And work another's gain.

With that poem for his text, Bryan went on to talk about the responsibility western nations needed to recognize:

> No one can travel among the dark-skinned races of the Orient without feeling that the white man occupies an especially favored position among the children of men, and the recognition of this fact is accompanied by the conviction that there is a duty inseparably connected with the advantages enjoyed.
>
> There is a white man's burden—a burden which the white man should not shirk even if he could, a burden which he could not shirk even if he would. That no one liveth unto himself or dieth unto himself, has a national as well as an individual application. Our destinies are so interwoven that each exerts an influence directly or indirectly upon all others.

Bryan was speaking at the very dawn of the twentieth century and beginning to suggest the need to move beyond the age of empire building into a new era of shared gifts and shared responsibilities. To do that, he points to the language of his day and suggests a need to move beyond it; yet the distance we have come since then, through two world wars and a cold war, makes it hard to appreciate. When Bryan speaks of "the so-called inferior races," we cringe at the phrase and hardly notice that Bryan is rejecting it with the adjective "so-called." Speaking to American businessmen in England, Bryan was suggesting that the comforts of the late Victorian world bring with them a responsibility:

> It is a false civilization, not a true one, that countenances the permanent separation of society into two distinct classes, the one encouraged to improve the mind and the other condemned to hopeless ignorance. Equally false is that conception of international

> politics which would make the prosperity of one nation depend upon the exploitation of another. While no one is farsighted enough to estimate with accuracy the remote, or even the immediate, consequences of human action, yet as we can rely upon the principle that each individual profits rather than loses by the progress and prosperity of his neighbors, so we cannot doubt that it is to the advantage of each nation that every other nation shall make the largest possible use of its own resources and the capabilities of its people.
>
> Society has passed through a period of aggrandizement, the nations taking what they had the strength to take and holding what they had the power to hold. But we are already entering a second era—an era in which the nations discuss not merely what they can do, but what they should do, considering justice to be more important than physical prowess. In tribunals like that of The Hague the chosen representatives of the nations weigh questions of right and wrong, and give a small nation an equal hearing with a great and a decree according to conscience. This marks an immeasurable advance. But is another step yet to be taken? Justice, after all, is cold and pulseless, a negative virtue.
>
> The world needs something warmer, more generous. Harmlessness is better than harmfulness. But positive helpfulness is vastly superior to harmlessness, and we still have before us a larger, higher destiny of service.

Bryan was a late Victorian himself, but one with a conscience; and it seems likely, to use a very trite phrase, that he gave his audience "something to think about." In ten years, Bryan's vision also would be challenged with the outbreak of World War I and all the grim and unimagined challenges of the twentieth century.

From England, the Bryans traveled through more of western Europe before embarking for home from Gibraltar. Bryan used the voyage to work on a speech that he would give when he was home again after a year abroad.

V

Bryan was welcomed home in a tumultuous gathering at Madison Square Garden that included two senators and a crowd of twelve thousand. Blinking back tears while the audience cheered and cheered, Bryan took the opportunity to tell his audience everything he had been thinking about while traveling the world. "Like all travelers who have visited other lands," he told them,

> I return with delight to the land of my birth, more proud of its people, with more confidence in its Government, and grateful

> to the kind Providence that cast my lot in the United States. . . . My love for our form of government has been quickened as I have visited castles and towers, and peered into dark dungeons, and I am glad that our nation, profiting by the experience of the past and yet unhampered by traditions and unfettered by caste, has been permitted to form a new center of civilization on new soil and erect here a government "of the people, by the people and for the people."[17]

It might have been a time to tell stories and share good feelings, but Bryan had had time not only to reflect on the uniqueness of America, but also to ponder its future, to think about what needed to change in a constantly changing world, and to bring Americans closer to the vision of freedom. Of the fifty-three paragraphs of his speech, three were introductory, six had to do with peace and imperialism, and thirty-eight dealt with the immediate practical issues that Bryan wanted to put forward in the next election. Naturally, there were reporters on hand ready to distort and misinterpret all of it.

The image of a city on a hill was not mentioned, but it underlay some of his opening comments.

> I also return more deeply impress than ever before with the responsibility that rests upon our nation as an exemplar among the nations, and more solicitous that we . . . may present a higher ideal than has ever before been embodied in a national life and carry human progress to a higher plane than it has before reached.[18]

America could not do that, however, while acting like a colonial power:

> We have given the monarchist a chance to ridicule our Declaration of Independence and the scoffer has twitted us with inconsistency.[19]

It was time to give the islands their independence and move on. Now Bryan's focus was on domestic issues, and especially those that had to do with economic justice. It was time to amend the Constitution to allow for an income tax that would "make it possible for the burdens of the Federal Government to be apportioned among the people in proportion to their ability to bear them." There was a need also for economic regulation. Bryan said he was often asked "Why can't a business man conduct his business to suit himself?"

> I answer without hesitation that he has no right to conduct his own business in such a way as to deprive his employees of the right to

> life, liberty and the pursuit of happiness. To support this position I need only refer to the laws regulating the safety of mines, the factory laws fixing the age at which children can be employed, and usury laws establishing the rate of interest.[20]

He saw a need for an eight-hour day so parents could have time with their children and adults had time to educate themselves and participate intelligently in the work of democracy.[21] And he was concerned about the way corporations were free to spend their money to influence government policy, an issue that remains unresolved over a century later:

> No important advance can be made until this corrupting influence is eliminated, and I hope that the Democratic party will not only challenge the Republican party to bring forward effective legislation on this subject, but will set an example by refusing to receive campaign contributions from corporations and by opening the books so that every contributor of any considerable sum may be known to the public before the election. . . . Contributions should be individual, not corporate, and no party can afford to receive contributions even from individuals when the acceptance of those contributions secretly pledges the party to a course which it cannot openly avow. In other words, politics should be honest. . . .[22]

The power of corporations to control the economy was an increasing issue and one that Theodore Roosevelt had addressed himself. But Bryan felt there was more to be done. He quoted the younger John Rockefeller, who had said, in a moment of blatant honesty, that to grow an American Beauty Rose it was necessary to pinch off ninety-nine buds so that the one hundredth bud could receive the full benefit of the sun and the soil. In like manner, he urged, the smaller businesses must be pinched off so that the largest and most successful can achieve their full potential. Bryan suggested that the businessmen whose businesses were thus "pinched off" might feel differently about the issue.[23]

The issue that attracted the most attention of the press, however, was the railroads. Lacking airlines and superhighways, the railroads controlled the flow of goods in the economy and generally had no competition. Bryan had no doubt that the government might need to own at least the major interstate railroads, to keep them from draining the country's whole wealth into their pockets.

> I have already reached the conclusion that railroads partake so much of the nature of a monopoly that they must ultimately become public property and be managed by public officials in the interest of

> the whole community in accordance with the well-defined theory that public ownership is necessary where competition is impossible.

The discussion of the railroads was carefully phrased, confined to the main interstate carriers, and only part of a much larger discussion. Bryan's primary focus, again an issue unresolved a century afterwards, was on the way wealth was accumulating in the pockets of the few at the expense of the many. He called it "plutocracy," rule by the wealthy. It was the theme of his closing flourish:

> Plutocracy is abhorrent to a republic; it is more despotic than monarchy, more heartless than aristocracy, more selfish than bureaucracy. It preys upon the nation in time of peace and conspires against it in the hour of its calamity. Conscienceless, compassionless and devoid of wisdom, it enervates its votaries while it impoverishes its victims. It is already sapping the strength of the nation, vulgarizing social life and making a mockery of morals. The time is ripe for the overthrow of this giant wrong. In the name of the counting-rooms which it has defiled; in the name of business honor which it has polluted; in the name of the home which it has despoiled; in the name of religion which it has disgraced; in the name of the people whom it has opprest, let us make our appeal to the awakened conscience of the nation.

As he did so often, he added a favorite piece of poetry, this time from the Scottish bard Robert Burns:

> And, O, may Heaven their simple lives prevent
> From luxury's contagion, weak and vile;
> Then, tho unearned wealth to wickedness be lent,
> A virtuous populace will rise and stand
> A wall of fire around their much loved land.

The morning papers the next day were not charmed by the poetry or distracted by the other issues raised. BRYAN OUT FOR GOVERNMENT OWNERSHIP was a typical headline.[24] Republicans were delighted to be able to denounce Bryan as a Socialist, and Democrats were embarrassed to find that their once and future candidate was dividing a party that had no other obvious leader. Complicating matters further was President Theodore Roosevelt, who was accused of "stealing lumber from Bryan's woodpile." Roosevelt, too, saw the danger of uncontrolled corporate greed; and over the next year, as reform-minded Republicans won a number of races, some began to speak of a Roosevelt-Bryan merger. Roosevelt went so far as to seat Bryan next to himself at a White House dinner, but he never overcame his patrician dislike for the prairie orator and continued to label him a "demagogue and agitator" even while adopting many of Bryan's goals.[25]

Roosevelt, however, did not choose to run for reelection in 1908, having served the better part of two terms. William Howard Taft, Roosevelt's chosen heir, was less committed to his causes than Roosevelt understood, and Bryan spent a good part of the campaign quoting Roosevelt with approval and challenging Taft to commit himself to his predecessor's program. The issue, as the Democratic convention defined it, was: Shall the People Rule? Bryan expanded on it in his acceptance speech:

> Our platform declares that the overshadowing issue which manifests itself in all the questions now under discussion, is "Shall the people rule?" No matter which way we turn; no matter to what subject we address ourselves, the same question confronts us: Shall the people control their own Government and use that Government for the protection of their rights and for the promotion of their welfare? or shall the representatives of predatory wealth prey upon a defenseless public, while the offenders secure immunity from subservient officials whom they raise to power by unscrupulous methods?

Every one of the specific issues confronting the country was, as Bryan saw it, a question of whether the people or the plutocrats would have their way:

> "Shall the people rule?" I repeat, is declared by our platform to be the overshadowing question, and as the campaign progresses, I shall take occasion to discuss this question as it manifests itself in other issues; for whether we consider the tariff question, the trust question, the railroad question, the banking question, the labor question, the question of imperialism, the development of our waterways, or any other of the numerous problems which press for solution, we shall find that the real question involved in each is, whether the Government shall remain a mere business asset of favor-seeking corporations or be an instrument in the hands of the people for the advancement of the common weal.[26]

As it turned out, however, the people were distracted by conflicting goals and issues and came to believe that Taft was simply a much larger, somewhat friendlier version of Roosevelt. He had the further advantage of being a new face, and Bryan was definitely not. Bryan also continued to depend on his own oratory in a world increasingly informed by newspapers. There were more voters than in 1904, when the Democratic candidate inspired no one; but half a million fewer voters came to the polls than eight years earlier. The electorate was content to stay with the party in power, and Taft won a popular majority of well over a million votes and 321 out of 483 electoral votes.[27]

The 1908 election was notable also for technological reasons: it featured the first recorded speeches by the candidates. The technology was still primitive and involved recordings made in Bryan's library with the candidate speaking slowly into the horn of an instrument that recorded the speech on a cylinder or disk. Ten such speeches, limited to four minutes, were recorded and can be found today online, where those who are interested can hear them; but the voice quality is flat and thin and quite unlike the descriptions of Bryan's rich, full baritone.[28]

VI

Once the election was over, the news was better. The Republicans fell into a vicious internal fight. Roosevelt's progressives felt that Taft and his followers had abandoned the fight to reform the economic and political structure of the country. Democrats watched with amusement and reaped a harvest in the next midterm elections. Bryan had some justification for claiming that victory was the result of his years of evangelism for the reform cause, and certainly the Democratic party was now committed to reform in a way that it had not been when a young orator electrified them in 1896.

Bryan remained, if not the leader, certainly the conscience of the party. He was also free to return to the Chautauqua circuit that had been part of his summer employment since 1904. Beginning late in the nineteenth century, the Chautauqua movement filled a similar role to that of the lyceum movement earlier in the same century. It provided speakers and entertainers mostly to the small towns that had no access to the resources of the larger towns and cities. William Jennings Bryan was one of the greatest stars of the movement from 1904 until his death. After the election defeat of 1908, Bryan focused more on religion and morality. One of his most popular lectures was titled "The Prince of Peace." "Government," he told his hearers,

> affects but a part of the life which we live here and does not deal at all with the life beyond, while religion touches the infinite circle of existence as well as the small arc of that circle which we spend on earth. No greater theme, therefore, can engage our attention. If I discuss questions of government I must secure the coopera-tion of a majority before I can put my ideas into practise, but if,

> in speaking on religion, I can touch one human heart for good, I have not spoken in vain no matter how large the majority may be against me.[29]

Unquestionably, Bryan touched a number of hearts with this lecture, which he gave in countless American communities as well as in Mexico and Canada, Tokyo, Manila, Bombay, Cairo, and Jerusalem. He had had long conversation with Leo Tolstoy in Russia,[30] and he quoted Tolstoy as saying that faith rests on "man's consciousness of his finiteness amid an infinite universe and of his sinfulness; and this consciousness . . . man can never outgrow." Bryan's lecture might be described as intended to reinforce that consciousness in his hearers by suggesting analogies and telling stories that would enable them to be more aware of the mystery of life. Bryan's very presence would also, of course, tend to deepen the faith of his hearers, for here was a great man who had traveled the world and discoursed with great philosophers and had now come to their small town to share his faith with them. Bryan's faith would be put on public display in a very different way toward the end of his life; but in his planned statement to the Scopes Trial court—never made for various reasons—he used some of the same arguments that he had used for many years in his talk on "The Prince of Peace."

Bryan was, however, still a politician, and he had one more major role to play on the national stage. In one of the more surprising evolutions in American political history, a college professor named Woodrow Wilson, who had gained national prominence in his battle as president of the college to reform Princeton University, emerged as the Democratic candidate for president in 1912. His battles at Princeton had made him a dark-horse candidate for president while he was still in the academic world; but when he left the college and was elected Governor of New Jersey, he became a significant political figure. Wilson had refused to support Bryan in 1896; but Bryan played a major role in gaining the nomination for Wilson in 1912, and Wilson, in gratitude, made Bryan his Secretary of State.

The Secretary of State in those days was not the administrator of a very large office. There were only 157 Washington-based employees, and not many more than four hundred worldwide; so even though Bryan had never been an administrator, the position was not an enormous challenge in that respect. In other respects, the challenge was much greater. In the first place, it was a position in which oratory was not very useful, and in the second place it made Bryan the assistant to someone with an ego as large as his own. The potential for conflict was clear on Inauguration Day, when Wilson finished his brief inaugural address and the crowd set up a chant for Bryan to speak also. Bryan waved the demand away and shook hands with Wilson, but the point had been made: there were many who still saw Bryan as their leader.

Bryan came to the State Department position with a greater background in international relationships than Wilson. He had met world leaders in their own countries and had spoken in Japan and India and England, among others. He also had his own agenda. In particular, Bryan came as an apostle of peace with the idea that America could take a lead in the search for peace by initiating a series of bilateral treaties, in which countries would pledge to submit all disagreements to international arbitration and to begin no hostilities until a full year after doing so. The idea had come to him after his meeting with Leo Tolstoy, and it had been one of the two conditions he had made with Wilson for accepting the position.[31]

Bryan's second condition was that he be excused from serving alcoholic beverages at diplomatic functions. Wilson had no objection, and the result was that at the first such occasion, grape juice and spring water were the only beverages available. The Russian ambassador admitted that "he had not tasted water for years," but he had drunk some claret before coming and so survived without difficulty.[32]

Bryan and Wilson were an odd couple. "Bryan," one biographer has written, "learned from people. Wilson learned from books."[33] The political commentator Walter Lippmann thought Bryan was "irresistibly funny. . . . He moves in a world that has ceased to exist. . . . His virtues, his habits, his ideas are the simple, direct, shrewd qualities of early America." Wilson, on the other hand, knew there was a new world of industry on which the power of government needed to be brought to bear.[34] Nevertheless, they worked well together at first. Bryan was willing to follow Wilson's lead and came to enjoy Cabinet meetings. Treasury Secretary William McAdoo said that Bryan was "quick to grasp a point, equipped with a fine and wholesome sense of humor, patient in argument, always willing to listen to the other side of a question . . . an excellent counsellor and loyal friend."

Bryan's "experience" in foreign affairs would hardly have prepared him for the variety of complex issues that quickly confronted him: a civil war in Mexico, tension between Colombia and Panama, German interest in acquiring a port in Haiti, tensions between Japan and China, a revolution in China, Japan's unhappiness with legislation discriminating against Japanese residents of California, and the question of Philippine independence. Pressed hard by the Japanese government, Bryan had to make the long train trip to the West Coast to negotiate with the California legislature about discriminatory legislation. The Californians were unwilling to back off, but Bryan could at least tell the Japanese government that he understood their anger and had done the best he could. Often the best Washington could hope for was to pour oil on troubled waters. At least none of these problems escalated into a major confrontation.

With approval from Wilson and the Senate, Bryan publicized his plan for bilateral nonaggression treaties and received word from a number of major powers that they accepted the idea in principle. Britain, France, Russia, Austria, Germany, and Italy were among those signaling support, and before long thirty nations had signed treaties. Unfortunately, Germany, Japan, Austria, and Turkey refused to sign because it was not in their interest, and even those that did still had other treaties already committing them to military action in certain circumstances—which shortly took place. The German refusal was based on the fact that they had a much larger standing army than their neighbors, and a cooling-off period might allow their neighbors to offset that advantage.[35] Of course, Germany's refusal to sign one of the peace treaties left the United States free to enter a war with Germany without a need to cool off.

The Wilson administration had been in office less than a year and a half when a Serbian nationalist assassinated Archduke Francis Ferdinand, heir to the Austro-Hungarian throne, and the peace of Europe collapsed in deadly warfare. Bryan immediately was ready with suggestions for mediation; but Wilson's foreign-policy adviser, Edward House, thought it better to wait until the belligerents themselves were looking for a way out, and Wilson repeatedly turned down Bryan's various suggestions for mediation.[36]

Wilson and Bryan agreed that the United States should be strictly neutral, but had great difficulty agreeing on what constituted neutrality. To allow American firms to sell munitions or foodstuffs equally to all the belligerents did not have a neutral result, since the British navy controlled the shipping lanes. It seemed to many that Wilson's "neutrality" did, in fact, favor the Allied nations. Wilson was an admirer of the English parliamentary system of government, preferring it to the American Constitution, and while Bryan was campaigning for the Democratic ticket in the fall of 1914, in the early days of the war, decisions were made that seemed to lean in the Allied direction. America might have contested British naval policies, for example, that gave them control of shipping, but to do so would very likely have required the United States to take military actions that would have favored Germany. Both Wilson and Bryan agreed that making loans to belligerents should not be allowed, since lack of money would hasten the end of the war, but by March 1915, they decided to allow credits to belligerents. Again and again, technical issues arose that were resolved in the Allies' favor. American neutrality prevented submarines being built for the belligerents, but submarine parts were sold to Canada for assembly there.[37] Domestic considerations also influenced decisions. Exporting foodstuffs gave aid to the Allies, since they controlled shipping, but Bryan was reluctant to carry his neutrality that far since an embargo would have hurt American farmers.

The attempt to maintain a neutral stance began to come apart more rapidly in May 1915, when the Germans torpedoed the *Lusitania*, a British-owned passenger liner carrying 128 American passengers, off the coast of Ireland.

When it was discovered that the ship was also loaded with munitions, Bryan felt both sides were at fault, but Wilson would not issue a statement that blamed both sides equally as Bryan preferred to do. Bryan, therefore, resigned from the Cabinet, giving up his considerable restraining influence on the administration. "I believe," he said, "I can do more on the outside to prevent war than I can on the inside."[38]

The "outside" was, of course, the Chautauqua meetings and lecture circuit, but it was also now more Florida than Nebraska. Mary Bryan's arthritis had worsened to the point that walking was difficult. They had begun to build a house in Florida in 1912, and by 1916 they had abandoned the cold winds of Nebraska for the sunshine and warmth of the South.

But Bryan could not abandon the career to which he had given his life. Traveling coast to coast, he exhorted the crowds to work for neutrality. At an international exposition in San Francisco, he told a crowd of fifty thousand that "Across the seas, our brothers' hands are stained in brothers' blood. The world has run mad. They need a flag that speaks the sentiment of the human heart, a flag that looks toward better things than war. Force begets force," he told them; "love begets love." When the speech was over, the exposition had arranged for an imitation torpedo boat to attack an imitation battleship moored in the harbor and "blow it to bits," blowing up Bryan's message in the process.[39] Meanwhile, Wilson moved for "preparedness" by asking Congress to authorize a hundred new warships and an increase in the army from one hundred thousand to four hundred thousand.[40] But at the same time, Wilson was signing laws to support labor, increase the income tax, and restrain corporations.

When the Democratic Convention of 1916 assembled and Wilson observed tradition by remaining in Washington, Bryan was there as a reporter but not scheduled to speak. The galleries, however, set up a chant of "Bryan! Bryan! Bryan!" and finally the chair had no alternative except to call him forward. In an hour-long speech interrupted forty times by applause, Bryan hailed Wilson's domestic achievements and told them: "I join with the American people in thanking God that we have a President who does not want this nation plunged into war." Every one of the twelve hundred delegates came forward at the end to line up and shake his hand.[41] In the campaign that followed, Bryan, as usual, spoke four or five times a day and in twenty states, mostly in the West and mostly in areas where his support for women's suffrage and prohibition would be useful. Wilson lost all the states Bryan failed to visit but won by an eyelash when the western votes were counted.[42]

Once past the election, Bryan resumed his opposition to Wilson's steady drift toward war. But when Germany removed the limits on its U-boats and the Congress overwhelmingly approved Wilson's request for a declaration of war, Bryan supported the war effort—though he campaigned more enthusiastically for prohibition and women's suffrage. Those, too, followed quickly on the end of the war, with the ratification of two amendments to the Constitution: prohibition in January 1919, and women's suffrage in August 1920.

William Jennings Bryan was a speaker, as usual, at the 1920 Democratic Convention. There were many who hoped he would be a candidate again—he was "only" sixty years old—but he was beginning to be concerned about his health and told friends he would only be a candidate if the Republican Party were to split again. Waving aside the microphone—Bryan had no need of these modern gadgets to make himself heard—he told the delegates what he thought the Party should do. He thought, first of all, that they should stand firm for prohibition:

> Are you afraid that we shall lose some votes? O my countrymen, have more faith in the virtue of the people! If there be any here who would seek the support of those who desire to carry us back into bondage to alcohol, let them remember that it is better to have the gratitude of one soul saved from drink than the applause of a drunken world.

He urged them as well to rejoice in the women's suffrage amendment. And he told them to work for ratification of the treaty that Wilson had brought back from Europe, even if it had to be modified to be accepted. Wilson would refuse to accept modifications and lose the fight, with the result that the League of Nations came into being without America and lost whatever opportunity there was to build a better and more lasting peace. Bryan, unlike Wilson, felt it was better to compromise than lose what Americans had fought for, and he was ready even to amend the Constitution again to make ratification easier:

> Shame on the man, democrat or republican, who talks of making a partisan question of this great issue, with the world on fire. [Applause.] Who will give a guarantee of the futures? Who can give us assurance that Europe will not drift back into war while we are discussing reservations? How pitiful the difference between the reservations that have been discussed in the senate for a year when you compare them with the large provisions in that treaty.
>
> If I could secure ratification without reservations and give to Woodrow Wilson the honor of it I would gladly go to the scaffold today. But I cannot do it, my friends; nobody can do it. We are confronted by a constitutional provision, requiring a two-thirds' vote, that enables a minority to obstruct ratification. I want to

> take it out of the way. I am not willing to share responsibility for what may occur. I, like these gentlemen, believe in God. Someday I shall stand before his judgment bar; and when I appear there, there shall not be upon my hands the blood of people slaughtered while I talked politics. [Applause.]
>
> Just one word more on this subject, my friends. I have not been able in the short time given to say all I would like. [Voices of "Go on."] Would you know how anxious I am to bring peace to this distracted world? I will tell you. Our allies owe us nearly $10,000,000,000. I am willing for our government to use all of it, if necessary, to purchase peace, universal and perpetual. [Applause.] I would rather that we should give up every dollar of it than invite another war. Give us a chance to lift the burden from the back of the toilers of the world and they will bow down and thank God for the Stars and Stripes that set a world free. . . . Is it not worth while to place in the hands of Woodrow Wilson the standard of civilization and allow America to lead in the conquest of the world for universal peace? Some day the song the shepherds heard at Bethlehem will be sung in every land. Why not make it the international anthem now? [Great applause.]

World peace was what mattered most to Bryan—but, as usual, he had more than one issue on his mind. He and his brother had published a paper for years to take his ideas to the people. Now he wanted a party newspaper to serve that purpose:

> I want some way of getting information to every voter; I want them to know the facts when they come to vote; I want them to hear the arguments pro and con; let them know the truth, and the truth will make them free. . . . We want it so that they will not sell a congressman's position on the bargain counter. We want it so that they cannot open the door of the United States senate with a golden key. We want it so that Wall street will not be able to build a barrier in front of the White House, over which a candidate can climb only with the aid of bales of bills. We must open the way between our children and the stars. That will be worth more than a ten-million-dollar campaign fund.

Corporations were a relatively new phenomenon in American life, and Americans were only beginning to understand their power to influence the Congress, a power which would only grow greater over the next century. Bryan saw clearly that the difficulty was the ability of corporate officers to evade responsibility for corporate actions.

> I ask you, next, to adopt the profiteering plank. . . . I want you to help us take the profiteer's hand out of the provision basket and out of the wardrobe of the people. I want you to help us to declare for a law that will empower the judge to send to the penitentiary the officers of a corporation that profiteers, and not merely fine the corporation. [Applause.]
>
> Be not frightened; time and again in history the timid have been afraid, but they have always found that they underestimated the number of those who had not bowed the knees to Baal. The Bible tells us of a time when the great Elisha was told by his servant that the enemy was too great for them. The prophet answered: "Fear not they that be with us are more than they that be against us."* And then, he drew aside the veil and on the mountain top the young man could see horses and chariots that had been invisible before. In just a few days another state will ratify the suffrage amendment, and then on the mountain top you will see the women and the children, our allies in every righteous cause. We shall not fall. [Great and prolonged applause.][43]

As Bryan stepped back from the speaker's stand, a great shout went surging up into the vaulted dome of the roof in an endless sea of sound. . . . Bryan, tears streaming down his face, was called back to the edge of the platform again and again, until the chair of the convention banged his gavel relentlessly and threatened to clear the gallery.

When they went on about their business, they voted down every one of Bryan's proposals by an overwhelming margin. They loved him still but, like the rest of the country, they were tired of fighting and ready to relax and let reform and peace and things like that wait for another day.

Bryan had one remaining battle to fight.

VI

Charles Darwin published *On the Origin of Species* in 1859. The controversy over it continues. For some, it seemed to provide answers to the mystery of life. For others, it was a brilliant insight into the method of the Creator. And for others still, it posed a stark, black-and-white question: "Is the Bible true?" None of these was central to the mind of William Jennings Bryan.

---

* 2 Kings 6:16.

Bryan had never been a profound thinker or theologian. Bryan was a very practical man; he cared about consequences. His very simple goal was to make the world a better place. It seemed to him that teaching evolution would not do that. Indeed, it seemed to him that it was likely to make the world more dangerous.

As Darwin's theory* filtered down into the schoolrooms of America where children came to learn about their world, there were many—then as now—to whom it seemed that this new teaching was dangerous. Bryan gave a series of lectures in the spring of 1922 at a Presbyterian seminary in Richmond, Virginia. In the longest of the talks, titled "The Origin of Man," Bryan cited Tolstoy's teaching that Christianity was a practical faith because it taught human beings how to live in harmony with each other. If, on the other hand, human beings were simply another species of animal, and animals indeed evolved by conflict with each other, what reason was there to care for the weak and the helpless?[44] Bryan was less interested in the science than the practical outcome of it. In subsequent months, Bryan gave similar talks in other colleges and universities in Vermont, New York, and Wisconsin. Prominent clergy like New York's Harry Emerson Fosdick responded by suggesting that Bryan was mistaken in connecting his faith to obsolete scientific opinions.

The issue came to a head when a substitute high school teacher in Dayton, Tennessee, John Thomas Scopes, agreed to let himself be used in a test case to determine the legality of a state law prohibiting the teaching of evolution. The case, brought to trial in the summer of 1925, became a national and international media spectacle when Bryan agreed to assist the prosecution team and Clarence Darrow, once a supporter of Bryan's, agreed to help the defense. Much of the testimony presented was, of course, technically irrelevant since there was obviously a law that Scopes had broken. The judge, nevertheless, permitted Bryan and Darrow to examine each other in a series of exchanges that did credit to neither party.

> DARROW: Do you claim that everything in the Bible should be literally interpreted?

---

* It was a "theory" not in the common colloquial meaning of the word, but rather in the scientific meaning: in science, the term "theory" refers to "a well-substantiated explanation of some aspect of the natural world, based on a body of facts that have been repeatedly confirmed through observation and experiment" [National Academy of Sciences, 1999]. Theories must also meet further requirements, such as the ability to make falsifiable predictions with consistent accuracy across a broad area of scientific inquiry, and production of strong evidence in favor of the theory from multiple independent sources.

BRYAN: I believe everything in the Bible should be accepted as it is given there. Some of the Bible is given illustratively; for instance, "Ye are the salt of the earth." I would not insist that man was actually salt, or that he had flesh of salt, but it is used in the sense of salt as saving God's people.

DARROW: But when you read that Jonah swallowed the whale—or that the whale swallowed Jonah, excuse me, please—how do you literally interpret that?

BRYAN: When I read that a big fish swallowed Jonah—it does not say whale.

DARROW: Doesn't it? Are you sure?

BRYAN: That is my recollection of it, a big fish. And I believe it, and I believe in a God who can make a whale and can make a man, and can make both do what He pleases.

DARROW: Mr. Bryan, doesn't the New Testament say whale [Matthew 12:40]?

BRYAN: I am not sure. My impression is that it says fish, but it does not make so much difference. I merely called your attention to where it says fish, it does not say whale.

DARROW: But in the New Testament it says whale, doesn't it?

BRYAN: That may be true. I cannot remember in my own mind what I read about it.

DARROW: Now, you say the big fish swallowed Jonah, and he remained how long—three days—and then he spewed him up on the land. You believe that the big fish was made to swallow Jonah?

BRYAN: I am not prepared to say that; the Bible merely says it was done.

DARROW: You don't know whether it was the ordinary run of fish or made for that purpose?

BRYAN: You may guess; you evolutionists guess.[45]

Finally the judge decided that it was time to get back to the simple question of the guilt or innocence of John Scopes. That was easy enough: the jury was asked for a verdict and properly pronounced Scopes guilty. He was fined one hundred dollars, but the verdict was overturned on a technicality. As a result, Bryan never had the opportunity to make a coherent statement of his position. That statement was later released, and it raises points all too often overlooked. Bryan's statement was lengthy (fourteen thousand words) and complex, but in it the final issue raised is one of consequences. Bryan quoted a passage from Darwin's book *The Descent of Man*, in which the author wrote:

> With savages, the weak in body or mind are soon eliminated; and those that survive commonly exhibit a vigorous state of health. We civilized men, on the other hand, do our utmost to check the process of elimination; we build asylums for the imbecile, the maimed and the sick: we institute poor laws and our medical men exert their utmost skill to save the life of every one to the last moment. There is reason to believe that vaccination has preserved thousands who from a weak constitution would formerly have succumbed to smallpox. Thus the weak members of civilized society propagate their kind. No one who has attended to the breeding of domestic animals will doubt that this must be highly injurious to the race of man. It is surprising how soon a want of care, or care wrongly directed, leads to the degeneration of a domestic race; but, excepting in the case of man himself, hardly anyone is so ignorant as to allow his worst animals to breed.[46]

Bryan was appalled by this analysis of the progress of civilization:

> Darwin reveals the barbarous sentiment that runs through evolution and dwarfs the moral nature of those who become obsessed with it. Let us analyze the quotation just given. Darwin speaks with approval of the savage custom of eliminating the weak so that only the strong will survive, and complains that "we civilized men do our utmost to check the process of elimination." How inhuman such a doctrine as this! He thinks it injurious to "build asylums for the imbecile, the maimed and the sick" or to care for the poor. Even the medical men come in for criticism because they "exert their utmost skill to save the life of everyone to the last moment." And then note his hostility to vaccination because it has "preserved thousands who, from a weak constitution would, but for vaccination, have succumbed to smallpox!" All of the sympathetic

> activities of civilized society are condemned because they enable "the weak members to propagate their kind." . . . Could any doctrine be more destructive of civilization? And what a commentary on evolution! He wants us to believe that evolution develops a human sympathy that finally becomes so tender that it repudiates the law that created it and thus invites a return to a level where the extinguishing of pity and sympathy will permit the brutal instincts to again do their progressive (?) work! . . . Let no one think that this acceptance of barbarism as the basic principle of evolution died with Darwin.[47]

Bryan's concern, as already stated, was with outcomes: not "What do Christians believe?" but "What difference does it make?" Evolution seemed to him to be making the wrong kind of difference, and in his time it often did. If humanity moves upward through conflict and struggle, the First World War was part of the process. Beyond even that was the enthusiasm, scarcely remembered now, in the first half of the twentieth century for "eugenics," the theory and practice of improving the quality of the human race by sterilizing or castrating selected populations, typically prisoners and those with reduced mental abilities. Even after the Second World War, a majority of the states had such laws on the books and in some, California in particular, thousands of sterilizations were carried out. Adolf Hitler's deliberate elimination of whole populations of Jews, gypsies, and the mentally incompetent put the science of eugenics in a different light; after World War II, states backed away from their programs and repealed their laws. It should be remembered that Hitler's intention to eliminate the weak and sick was clearly stated in *Mein Kampf*, published in the same year as the Scopes Trial.

Bryan correctly saw, in the way evolution was often taught, a plan for the improvement of the human race diametrically opposed to everything he had stood for throughout his life. That was what, however ineptly, he was arguing against in Dayton. That aspect of Bryan's life has been largely misunderstood and forgotten. The lasting difference William Jennings Bryan made was in taking a stodgy and ineffectual Democratic Party and giving it a sense of purpose, dedicated to reform, and concerned for those Americans whose freedom was being constrained by economic forces.

Bryan's health had been declining for several years before the Dayton trial, and that ordeal apparently consumed whatever energy he had left. A medical exam four days later showed his blood pressure and other physical signs in a normal range, but he died peacefully the next day while taking a nap.[48]

SEVEN

Franklin Delano Roosevelt
1882–1945

THE ONLY THING WE HAVE TO FEAR IS FEAR ITSELF

I

There are two traditions as to when and where Franklin Delano Roosevelt made his first public speech. One source claims it was when he was eighteen years old and spending a summer at the family vacation home on Campobello Island in the Canadian Bay of Fundy. Somehow Roosevelt had been made secretary-treasurer of a group formed to lay out a new golf course and was called on to explain the plan to summer residents who objected to it. Afterwards, Horace Gray, an Associate Justice of the Supreme Court, complimented Roosevelt on the clarity and simplicity of his presentation and counseled him to stick to that style of public speaking.[1]

The other source tells us that he made his first speech while on his honeymoon in Scotland. Eleanor had been asked to open a flower shop, a ceremony that involved snipping a ribbon and making a few remarks. She agreed to snip the ribbon but was clear that making speeches was not something she did; she was willing to deal with the ribbon if Franklin would deal with the oratory. Roosevelt had been an editor of his college newspaper and not active in debate societies of any sort, but he was willing to help out if he could. He spent the evening working with paper and pencil and the next day made his debut as a speaker. He told the audience that he and Eleanor both had some traces of Scottish ancestry and that he had had a Scottish nurse when he was a child who rewarded good behavior with a piece of Scottish shortbread. Having established that bond with his hearers, he made some tentative observations about the differences between Scottish and American gardens and sat down to polite applause.[2] In later years, as her husband's career expanded his invitations to speak beyond his time available and Eleanor became deeply involved in various causes, it would more often be Eleanor who would take on speaking engagements for Franklin.

Both stories would seem to agree that Franklin Delano Roosevelt, unlike Daniel Webster, William Jennings Bryan, and many other earlier politicians, had not looked for opportunities to speak in public during his early years. Roosevelt took a required course in public speaking at Harvard, but, unlike Webster, Lincoln, and Bryan, he had not studied elocution. He did, however, show an early interest in politics. While Roosevelt was making his way through Groton and Harvard, a distant cousin, Theodore Roosevelt, had been building a career in public office, and by the time Franklin Roosevelt was at Harvard, Theodore Roosevelt was in the White House. In 1902, Cousin Teddy's daughter Alice turned eighteen and made her debut at the White House. Franklin took the train down from Boston, partied until two A.M., visited the new home of the Library of Congress, took tea at the White House, and went to a reception given by the Austrian ambassador. It was, he reported to his mother, "one of the most interesting and enjoyable three days I have ever had." It seemed to him that he might like a similar career himself. In his junior year at Harvard, he was chosen to be editor of the *Harvard Crimson* and, although he had completed the requirements for a degree in three years, he stayed on to serve as editor in his senior year. His editorials generally focused on sports and immediate college issues, but he also wrote editorials urging students to get involved in politics.

Theodore's branch of the Roosevelt family, centered on Oyster Bay, Long Island, had traditionally been Republicans, although he did not fit comfortably into the party of William McKinley. Franklin's branch of the family lived in Hyde Park, on the Hudson, and although its members were inclined to be Democrats, Franklin had no strong convictions one way or another. It was Theodore's brand of Republicanism that made an impression on his younger cousin and shaped Franklin's brand of Democracy.

Graduating from Harvard with a "gentleman's C," Franklin Roosevelt moved on to Columbia Law School, as his cousin had done, and dropped out without graduating as Theodore had also done. Unlike Theodore, however, Franklin did take and pass the New York bar exam.[3] The time in law school, as both Roosevelts understood, counted for much less than "connections" and on-the-job training. Connections brought Franklin to an unpaid staff position at the prestigious New York law firm of Carter, Ledyard, and Milburn, where staff members with a few years of experience showed him how to file papers and carry out other low-level duties. In his abundant spare time, he could sail at the Yacht Club, golf in suburban Westchester and rural Dutchess counties, and socialize with people whom it was useful to know. Quite freely, he acknowledged to friends that he had his eye on the Presidency. He knew how his cousin had gotten there and saw no reason why he could not follow the same course himself.[4]

The path Theodore had followed had begun with a seat in the New York State Assembly, and Franklin, three years out of law school in 1910, decided the time had come for him to find an Assembly seat for himself. Unfortunately, an Assembly seat was not available; but there was an opening in the State Senate. Democrats had seldom won elections in Dutchess County, but the local Democratic Party was happy to have the Roosevelt name on the ticket and Franklin was undeterred by local history. The local Congressman was also a Democrat, a rarity in upstate New York, and he was willing to tutor the novice. Roosevelt learned one lesson from the Congressman that he never forgot: speak to your audience as "My friends. . . ." His goal was, in fact, simply to establish himself as a friend of neighbors he hardly knew. Platitudes would serve until he knew them and their concerns better:

> For every new face that I have met it has been impressed upon me that here we have a population that is truly American in the best sense of the word: a people alive, a people desirous of progress and of real representation and of honest, efficient government.

His opponent, however, took every opportunity to deride Roosevelt as an ignorant newcomer in their midst, and that gave Roosevelt a bit more to work with. Years later he recalled:

> I had a particularly disagreeable opponent and he called me names . . . and I answered him in kind. And the names I called him were worse than the names he called me. So we had a joyous campaign.[5]

But Roosevelt always had joyous campaigns. He loved being on stage, and it showed. Eleanor thought he looked nervous when she went to hear him; but, if so, he overcame it quickly and the electorate liked what it saw and heard.[6] Besides, after seven years of Theodore Roosevelt, his chosen successor, William Howard Taft, had left the public disenchanted with the Republican Party, and

1910 was a good year for Democrats. Roosevelt surprised the experts with an upset victory and took his place in the State Senate. Theodore had upset the Assembly by working for reform, and Franklin upset the Senate by opposing and defeating the entrenched power of Tammany Hall. A place in the sun in Albany led quite naturally to a place at the next national Democratic Convention, where Roosevelt worked for the nomination of Woodrow Wilson and heard William Jennings Bryan speak when he threw his support to the New Jersey governor.

When Woodrow Wilson was elected President in 1912, Roosevelt was perfectly placed to be offered and accept the position that had been Theodore's first Washington job: Assistant Secretary of the Navy. Josephus Daniels, the new Navy Secretary, knew nothing about ships but something about Washington; Roosevelt, on the other hand, knew much more about ships. He was not only a summer sailor, he had collected and read thousands of books on naval matters. He and Daniels made a good team, with the younger man working to update naval procedures and the older man handling the more political aspects of the job. When war broke out in Europe, Daniels and Roosevelt realized that the American navy was unprepared for a twentieth-century war, and they worked to expand and modernize America's naval forces. To follow his cousin's career more exactly, Roosevelt should have resigned when America entered the war in order to lead a cavalry charge against the Germans, but Wilson vetoed any such idea and Roosevelt had to be content with a tour of the battlefront. At least it enabled him to say, afterwards, "I have seen war." His time in the Navy Department also brought him into contact with the labor unions that worked in the shipyards, and he took their side in disputes with the admirals and Congress over wages. He didn't always win those fights, but he did build a useful reputation for himself as a friend of labor.

When the war ended two years before the next national election, Roosevelt had to give serious attention to his future, since there was little possibility of the Democrats returning to power. He talked of forming a partnership with friends to establish himself as a New York lawyer and politician-in-waiting. The Democratic Convention in the summer of 1920, however, decided that his name could add interest to the national ticket and, remembering how another Roosevelt had helped another national ticket twenty years earlier, nominated him for vice-president on a ticket with Governor James Cox of Ohio. In keeping with tradition, Roosevelt accepted the nomination from his home in New York, but his speech was national news, carried in newspapers everywhere. The themes of unity, patriotism, and peace were hardly exciting, but Americans had emerged from the war fearful of communism and ready to withdraw from the world scene. Patriotism and a desire for unity were in short supply. Roosevelt urged his fellow citizens to think carefully about their priorities:

> Much has been said of late about good Americanism. It is right that it should have been said. And it is right that every chance should be seized to repeat the basic truths underlying our prosperity and our national existence itself. But it would be an unusual and much to be wished-for thing, if in the coming presentation of the issue a new note of fairness and generosity could be struck.
>
> Littleness, meanness, falsehood, extreme partisanship: these are not in accord with the American spirit. I like to think that in this respect also we are moving forward. Let me be concrete. We have passed through a great war, an armed conflict which called forth every resource, every effort, on the part of the whole population. The war was won by Republicans as well as by Democrats. Men of all parties served in our armed forces. Men and women of all parties served the government at home. They strived honestly, as Americans, not as mere partisans. Republicans and Democrats alike worked in administrative positions, raised Liberty Loans, administered food control, toiled in munitions plants, built ships. The war was brought to a successful conclusion by a glorious common effort—one which in the years to come will be a national pride.
>
> Even if a nation entered the war for an ideal, so it has emerged from the war with the determination that this ideal shall not die. It is idle to pretend that the declaration of war of April 6, 1917, was a mere act of self-defense, or that the object of our participation was solely to defeat the military power of the central nations of Europe. We knew then as a nation, even as we know today, that success on land and sea could be but half a victory. The other half is not won yet. The cry of the French at Verdun, "They shall not pass" and the cheer of our own men in the Argonne, "We shall go through," these were essential glories, yet they are incomplete. To them we must write the binding finish—it shall not occur again—for America demands that the crime of war shall cease.[7]

Wilson's campaign for the League of Nations had been defeated, but Roosevelt still believed that it was "a practical solution to a practical problem" and that for Americans to reject it would be to reject their own values. The country, however, had had enough of idealism and international concerns for a while, and the Democratic ticket lost overwhelmingly.

II

At the age of 38, Franklin Roosevelt had established himself as a national leader in the Democratic Party and might have been a leading candidate for the Senate or for governor, if not the national ticket again, had not disaster struck in the following summer. Vacationing as usual at Campobello, Roosevelt woke up one morning to find a weakness in one leg that quickly involved the other leg as well and gradually crept up his body so that even his arms and hands began to grow limp. It took some time before a diagnosis of poliomyelitis could be made, and longer still before Roosevelt could reorient his life around this new reality. It was six months before he could be fitted for the heavy leg braces he would need for the rest of his life, and over a year before he made the first visit back to his office in Manhattan. It had been, he said, "a grand and glorious occasion," although his crutches had slipped and he had fallen on the marble floor on his way to the elevator.[8] He was not easily discouraged.

The next several years, dominated by the struggle to rebuild the strength of his legs, were also a time in which Roosevelt learned important lessons about his country, his fellow citizens, and economics on a personal level. He discovered a rundown resort at Warm Springs, Georgia, where he could relax and let the warm water support him. A car fitted with hand controls freed him to travel the countryside and chat with the local farmers. For the first time, he understood how the price of cotton controlled human lives and the way world circumstances prevented a whole section of the country from paying a living wage to its schoolteachers and left farmers struggling with poverty, illness, and despair. "I began to learn economics at Warm Springs," he said years later when he came back to Georgia to dedicate a new schoolhouse.[9] Roosevelt had always valued the human bonds formed through his relationship with the public; now he understood more deeply the suffering that so many endured helplessly—and they knew that he also understood what it meant to suffer. Raymond Moley said of him, "I've been amazed with his interest in things. It skips and bounces through seemingly intricate subjects, and maybe it is my academic training that makes me feel that no one could possibly learn much in such a hit or miss fashion. I don't find that he has read much about economic subjects. What he gets is from talking to people. . . ."[10]

Even in Warm Springs, Roosevelt kept in touch with his party. His name came up when people talked about candidates for governor or senator as early as 1922, but Roosevelt told them he wasn't ready. He played a key role, however, in persuading Al Smith to run for governor that year. Smith had served a two-year term from 1918 to 1920 but then lost his bid for reelection. He had been thriving financially in private life and was reluctant to run again, but Roosevelt published an open letter to Smith that was critical in persuading him to accept the nomination. He won in 1922 and then twice more, in 1924 and

1926. In 1924, Roosevelt stepped back into the spotlight when he placed Smith's name in nomination for the presidency at Madison Square Garden in New York. He had marked off the fifteen-foot distance from the chair on the dais to the podium on the floor of the library in his Manhattan house and walked it over and over to rehearse his path. When the time came, he took a crutch in each hand, placed it under each arm, and in full view of twelve thousand spectators, his legs sheathed in steel braces, his teeth clenched in a smile, he walked forward, grasped the podium with both hands, and waited for the cheers to subside.[11]

The speech that followed was remarkable mostly for the fact that it was done at all. Although primarily an encomium for Al Smith, it was significant also for the vision Roosevelt held up for the party and country. Speaking for the first time to a national convention, he used words and phrases like "progressive," "vision," "the common people," and "the aspirations of the average man" as opposed to the forces of "privilege." These would be familiar terms in Roosevelt's speeches over the next twenty years. The closing paragraph, however, like much that went before it, was standard convention fare:

> I present to you—the one above all others who has demonstrated his power, his ability to govern; this leader whose whole career gives convincing proof of his power to lead; this warrior whose record shows him invincible in defense of right and in attack on wrong; this man, beloved by all, trusted by all, respected by all; this man who all admit can bring us an overwhelming victory this year—this man of destiny whom our State proudly dedicates to the nation—our own ALFRED E. SMITH![12]

The double emphasis on "power" is surprising since Americans like to think of themselves as free of control by others, but perhaps Roosevelt was influenced in his choice of words by his own feeling of limited power. Mark Sullivan, a conservative journalist, called Roosevelt's speech "a noble utterance" and said it "belongs with the small list of really great convention speeches."[13] Yet today the speech is remembered, if at all, only for the title of "the Happy Warrior" that Roosevelt bestowed on the nominee. The phrase came from a poem by William Wordsworth and was given to Roosevelt in a first draft by Judge Joseph Proskauer, a key Smith adviser.[14] That phrase would be remembered, but so too would Roosevelt's simple physical presence. That presence, representing as it did enormous handicaps overcome, with the confidence he projected and the quality of his voice, made a lasting impression on those who were there.

The *New York Times* said, "The most popular man in the convention was Franklin D. Roosevelt. . . . Whenever word passed around the floor that Mr. Roosevelt was about to take his seat in the New York delegation, a hush fell over the Garden. On his appearance each time there was a spontaneous burst of applause."[15]

The convention itself was remembered only for Roosevelt's speech and the dreary, endless polling that went on through 103 ballots before nominating John W. Davis of West Virginia, "who had left few marks on the public record that anyone could object to."[16] In the election that followed, Calvin Coolidge amassed almost twice as many votes as Davis, who carried only the solid South. Robert La Follette of Wisconsin carried his own state on a Progressive ticket and took over half as many votes nationally as Davis. William Jennings Bryan died that summer; so when the election was over, Smith and Roosevelt were the leading Democrats left standing and Roosevelt, lacking Smith's Roman Catholic faith and harsh New York accent, was the more attractive to many in the party. But Roosevelt saw little chance of a Democrat winning while prosperity continued, so he was content to work again for Smith's nomination.

In 1928, Roosevelt put Smith in nomination when the Democrats assembled in Houston for the first convention in the South since the Civil War. Walking to the podium without a cane and only his son's arm for support, Roosevelt told the delegates that Smith was "loved by little children [and] dumb animals."[17] Twenty names were placed in nomination, but Smith was chosen on the first ballot. Nationally, however, Smith's religion and opposition to prohibition raised enormous questions with many voters, and Smith was overwhelmed by six million votes in November, carrying only half the states even in the once-solid South.

Roosevelt had known as well as anyone that it was not a good year to be a Democratic candidate; but when New York State Democrats asked him to run for governor, he was unable to resist the challenge of what seemed to everyone else a doomed campaign. At first, Roosevelt campaigned simply for Smith. He told New Yorkers what he had heard, in his visits to Warm Springs in Georgia, that was being said about Smith's religious affiliation in the South; and he told voters how, ten years earlier, he had seen American boys being carried back from the battlefront on stretchers:

> and somehow in those days people were not asking to what church those boys belonged. . . . If any man or woman, after thinking of that, can bear in his heart any motive in this year which will lead him to cast his ballot in the interest of intolerance and of a violation of the spirit of the Constitution of the United States, then I say solemnly to that man or woman, "May God have mercy on your miserable soul."[18]

Somehow it was national issues rather than state issues that interested Roosevelt. He spoke of the need for government-guaranteed pensions for the elderly and for legislation to protect the interests of labor. The Republicans claimed to be the friends of labor, but "How dare they say that?" Roosevelt asked: "How do grown up and ostensibly sane political leaders perjure themselves that way?" He spoke about the need for national legislation to protect farmers also. Smith finally wired Roosevelt's staff to remind them that "He is not running for President but for Governor. . . . And tell him to stick to state issues!"[19]

It is, of course, the national vote that normally determines winners and losers at the local level. When the voters went to the polls in November, Smith lost even New York, but Roosevelt ran far ahead of the national ticket in the state and managed a margin of twenty-five thousand votes out of over four million cast. By the time he ran for reelection two years later, the stock market had crashed and taken down the Republican party with it.

Herbert Hoover had accepted the Republican nomination in 1928, proclaiming that the nation was nearing "a final triumph over poverty." His inaugural address spoke of "liberation from widespread poverty."[20] By the time the midterm elections came, all that had vanished and Roosevelt was reelected with a margin of 730,000, twice the largest margin ever before recorded in the state. So the way was open for Roosevelt to be nominated for president in 1932. He had a solid majority of the Convention votes on the first ballot, but it still required four ballots to reach the two thirds called for by Convention rules. Breaking with the precedent that required a candidate to stay home and wait for word from the Convention, Roosevelt chartered an airplane to take him from New York to Chicago to accept the nomination in person and dramatize his ability to provide strong and innovative leadership in a time of crisis. "These are unprecedented and unusual times," he told the delegates:

> I have started out on the tasks that lie ahead by breaking the absurd tradition that the candidate should remain in professed ignorance of what has happened for weeks until he is formally notified of that event many weeks later.
>
> My friends,* may this be the symbol of my intention to be honest and to avoid all hypocrisy or sham, to avoid all silly shutting of the eyes to the truth in this campaign. You have nominated me and I know it, and I am here to thank you for the honor.

Claiming the mantle of "the great indomitable, unquenchable, progressive soul" of Woodrow Wilson, he warned the delegates of the danger of

* Roosevelt continued to use the greeting he had learned to use twenty years earlier in Dutchess County.

"radicalism" and told them that "ours must be a party of liberal thought, of planned action, of enlightened international outlook, and of the greatest good to the greatest number of our citizens." He insisted that he would speak to them in plain language about the country's problems:

> Let us look a little at the recent history and the simple economics, the kind of economics that you and I and the average man and woman talk. . . . Let us talk economics that the figures prove and that we can understand. . . . Let us use common sense and business sense.

He emphasized the importance of fair prices for farmers, still half the population of the country, and the need to lower mortgage rates; but he had no specific proposals to accomplish these goals except to protect farmers from international competition by tariffs. Yet he denounced tariffs which, he said, "have isolated us from all the other human beings in all the rest of the round world." Only at the end did he provide the words that would become the usual label for all his years in office, saying:

> I pledge you, I pledge myself, to a new deal for the American people.[21]

Finally, of course, what mattered was not the specific proposals that the candidate made so much as the impression he created of a dynamic leader who understood their problems and was their "friend." That was all projected over the great new medium of radio, which enabled a candidate to address not crowds of five thousand or fifty thousand but a nation of one hundred twenty-five million, of whom forty million would vote that fall.

An aspect of Roosevelt's projection of confidence and his joy in campaigning was his use of humor. More truly than Al Smith, Roosevelt was always a "Happy Warrior." One example from the 1932 campaign was a speech in late August in Columbus, Ohio, in which Roosevelt suggested that the Republicans were living in an "Alice in Wonderland" world:

> The poorhouse was to vanish like the Cheshire cat. A mad hatter invited everyone to "have some more profits.". . . A cynical Father William in the lower district of Manhattan balanced the sinuous evil of a pool-ridden stock market on the end of his nose. A puzzled, somewhat skeptical Alice asked the Republican leadership some simple questions:
>
> "Will not the printing and selling of more stocks and bonds, the building of new plants and the increase of efficiency produce more goods than we can buy?"

> "No," shouted Humpty Dumpty. "The more we produce, the more we can buy."
>
> "What if we produce a surplus?"
>
> "Oh, we can sell it to foreign consumers."
>
> "How can the foreigners pay for it?"
>
> "Why, we will lend them the money."
>
> "I see," said little Alice, "they will buy our surplus with our money. Of course, these foreigners will pay us back by selling us their goods?"
>
> "Oh, not at all," said Humpty Dumpty. "We set up a high wall called the tariff."
>
> "And," said Alice at last, "how will the foreigners pay off these loans?"
>
> "That is easy," said Humpty Dumpty; "did you ever hear of a moratorium?"[22]

The impression of a dynamic leader was strengthened by Roosevelt's determination to campaign across the country. He had used radio effectively as Governor of New York, and it was readily available to him as a candidate for president, but he drew strength from contact with people and needed also to test at least some of his ideas in public forums. Industrial unemployment was the visible face of the depression, but farmers had been struggling ever since the end of the war. Indeed, with the exception of wartime prosperity, they had been struggling since the end of the previous century. Their need lay behind William Jennings Bryan's appeal against the gold standard.

Roosevelt stopped in Topeka, Kansas, to talk about farm problems and to paraphrase Lincoln by saying "This nation cannot endure if it is half boom and half broke." The problem, Roosevelt believed, was agricultural overproduction, and the solution lay in voluntary planning with government guidance. In Salt Lake City, he talked about the railroads, which also suffered from oversupply and needed government help in planning. In Seattle, he talked about how tariffs had disrupted international trade, and in Portland he talked about a national perspective on the development of hydroelectric power. In short, unfettered competition had run the nation into the ground, and government intervention and guidance were needed to get back on the right track. Nevertheless, Roosevelt insisted that part of the problem was too much government spending and the lack of a balanced budget. The differences between Hoover and Roosevelt were perhaps more a matter of attitudes than policies. In Portland he defined it as a matter of openness to change, and he believed that change was part of American tradition. "My friends," he said, "my policy is as radical as American liberty. My policy is as radical as the Constitution of the United States."[23]

The issue facing the country, which Roosevelt would define in one way and Hoover in another, was, as it had always been in American history, the definition of freedom. Roosevelt did not clearly define that issue until later in his years in office, but Hoover was clear as to what it meant to him: it meant that the government should not intrude on individual lives.

When the Congress voted in 1931 to allow veterans to borrow against money not due them until 1945, Hoover vetoed it on the grounds that such an outlay "breaks the barrier of self-reliance and self-support in our people." The battle against unemployment was to be fought by "the resolution of our people to fight their own battles in their own communities,"[24] not by the federal government, since that would weaken "the sturdiness of our national character." Hoover's point of view has been part of a continuing debate over the best way to strengthen and preserve that liberty that Patrick Henry demanded. "Economic freedom," Hoover said, "cannot be sacrificed if political freedom is to be preserved."[25] To place responsibility with the federal government would be, Hoover believed, to "lay the foundation [for] the destruction of [people's] liberties."[26]

That philosophy had not prevented Hoover from creating new governmental structures to rescue the banking system and increase the money supply. Government intervention to save banks was different from intervention to help individuals. The measures Hoover took were finally insufficient, but they did lay the groundwork for the stronger measures taken by the next administration.

Roosevelt, meanwhile, as Governor of New York State in 1931, did concern himself with individuals and secured the creation of a Temporary Emergency Relief Administration. Like Hoover (and conservatives to this day), he was fearful of creating a class of citizens permanently on "the dole," but he argued that government must extend temporary relief "not as a matter of charity, but of social duty; the State accepts the task cheerfully because it believes in that close relationship with its people which is necessary to preserve our democratic form of government."[27]

Roosevelt presented the plan to expend state moneys on public works for the employment of residents of the state as "temporary," and probably thought of it that way. Years later, in Washington, when the Social Security system was proposed to him, he still worried about "the dole." But a key adviser, Samuel Rosenman, regarded the original message as a landmark in the history of governmental social thinking in the United States and credited it with establishing the principle "that it is the duty of government to use the combined resources of the nation to prevent distress and to promote the general welfare of all the people." On this basis, he argued that the New Deal had its origins in Albany.[28]

III

More important than any specific policies was the attitude with which Roosevelt approached his task. That attitude was summed up so memorably in his inaugural address that it even provided material for a Google commercial message on television eighty years later.* "I am certain," said the new president,

> that my fellow Americans expect that on my induction into the Presidency I will address them with a candor and a decision which the present situation of our people impel. This is preeminently the time to speak the truth, the whole truth, frankly and boldly. Nor need we shrink from honestly facing conditions in our country today. This great Nation will endure as it has endured, will revive and will prosper. So, first of all, let me assert my firm belief that the only thing we have to fear is fear itself—nameless, unreasoning, unjustified terror which paralyzes needed efforts to convert retreat into advance.

What transcripts seldom show and commentators fail to appreciate is the brief pause Roosevelt made in the key sentence: "The only thing we have to fear is [pause] fear itself." The tactical pause put additional emphasis on the word that followed it: fear. His skill as an orator drove home the key word. Roosevelt would go on to discuss specific issues to be dealt with, but none of them made as great a difference as the emotional approach the president took to the task at hand and the emotional attitude with which the public faced the economic crisis, shifting from fear to confidence.

It may be worth remembering that Roosevelt's predecessor, Herbert Hoover, who was there to hear that speech, had also told Americans that there was no reason to fear the future. In his own inaugural address, four years earlier, Hoover had said:

> Ours is a land rich in resources; stimulating in its glorious beauty; filled with millions of happy homes; blessed with comfort and opportunity. In no nation are the institutions of progress more advanced. In no nation are the fruits of accomplishment more secure. In no nation is the government more worthy of respect. No country is more loved by its people. I have an abiding faith in

---

* In an ad for Google Nexus 7, viewers saw a boy, at a loss for words to speak to a potential girlfriend, overcoming his fears with the help of Roosevelt's words: "The only thing we have to fear is . . . fear itself. . . ."

> their capacity, integrity and high purpose. I have no fears for the future of our country.[29]

It is noteworthy that Roosevelt said "we" and Hoover said "I." Roosevelt was always reaching out to include others. Hoover was an engineer by profession and had been paid always for his own expertise and individual opinion. Thus, when the stock market crashed only seven months after his inauguration as president, fear was rampant and Hoover was unable to speak in a way that would help Americans overcome their very natural fears. Less than two weeks after the crash, the head of a leading financial service wired Hoover about "the wave of fear now sweeping investors" and advised him that "a public statement from you regarding [the] psychology of [thc] present situation would save untold suffering and unnecessary loss." A few days later, Hoover, in his first public statement after the crash, began by describing the numerous meetings he had held with "business leaders and public officials." Perhaps he thought Americans would be relieved to know that the president himself was involved in an effort to stabilize the markets. They might also be relieved to hear that the alarming ups and downs in the market were the result of "overoptimism" and "over pessimism" (to use Hoover's terminology), and that these were "unjustified."[30]

Hoover's statement, however, failed to connect that analysis with his response. His choice of language would have seemed to indicate a clear understanding that the crash was not simply the inevitable result of economic forces, but that emotions such as "overoptimism" and "over pessimism" were deeply involved. Indeed, at an off-the-record press conference in mid-November, Hoover said "We are dealing here with a psychological situation to a very considerable degree. It is a question of fear." But he went on to say: "I do not believe that words ever convince a discouraged person in these situations." He added that he was working with businesses and organizations and "I don't want to talk about it." A few days earlier, he had said "My own experience has been that words are not of any great importance in times of economic disturbance. It is action that counts."[31]

Action, however, in Hoover's view should not come from the government. Roosevelt, on the other hand, was clear that government should act. He was not an economist, and even economists disagreed as to what needed to be done; but he and his advisers had a number of ideas and were willing to try them and see what worked. He was, one biographer wrote, "a politician, not an ideologue; he served people, not causes."[32] Meanwhile, and perhaps more important, Roosevelt could and would deal with the fear that he, like Hoover, believed was "unjustified." Such fear "paralyzed needed effort." Roosevelt knew something about paralysis and what could be done by determined effort. He set out to reassure and unite the nation with the best weapons at his command: his confidence and his voice.

Only days after his inaugural address, he sat down to use the radio for the first in a series of "Fireside Chats." It was a technique he had already put to good use in Albany; now, more than ever, it was a way to rebuild shattered confidence in the government. Radio made all speech more intimate, but this was not a public speech that the radio audience could listen to: it was a "chat," an informal conversation with the individual listener. This first chat was principally about the "bank holiday" that Roosevelt and the Congress had declared just five days after his inauguration, closing all banks from March 6 to March 10 to try to keep even more banks (than the over five thousand that already had) from going out of business:

> I want to talk for a few minutes with the people of the United States about banking—with the comparatively few who understand the mechanics of banking but more particularly with the overwhelming majority who use banks for the making of deposits and the drawing of checks. I want to tell you what has been done in the last few days, why it was done, and what the next steps are going to be.

He spoke for a while about the way the Congress, Republicans and Democrats together, had acted to make the needed supply of money available. He admitted that not every bank would be reopened and there might be some individual losses,

> but there will be no losses that possibly could be avoided; and there would have been more and greater losses had we continued to drift. I can even promise you salvation for some at least of the sorely pressed banks. We shall be engaged not merely in reopening sound banks but in the creation of sound banks through reorganization.

In closing, he thanked his listeners for their confidence and support:

> After all, there is an element in the readjustment of our financial system more important than currency, more important than gold, and that is the confidence of the people. Confidence and courage are the essentials of success in carrying out our plan. You people must have faith; you must not be stampeded by rumors or guesses. Let us unite in banishing fear. We have provided the machinery to restore our financial system; it is up to you to support and make it work.
>
> It is your problem no less than it is mine. Together we cannot fail.

There were three more chats that first year and two, three, or four in most of the twelve years of his presidency. There was one just after December 7, 1941, and one just before and another just after the D-Day invasion of Europe on June 6, 1944.

As one expert on Roosevelt's use of radio put it:

> For Franklin Delano Roosevelt, the essence of political leadership in a democracy was teaching. His radio talks to the nation that came to be called fireside chats did not preach or exhort, as his cousin Theodore Roosevelt's speeches did. FDR's explained in direct, simple, calm language a certain problem and what the administration proposed to do about it. These talks constituted a new genre in U.S. political literature, and they also fashioned a new relationship between the president and the people. The country's foremost civic educator called the room where he met reporters for his biweekly press conferences his "schoolroom," the budget, his "textbook," his speeches, "seminars."[33]

To work with him in developing this new approach to presidential leadership, Roosevelt had a shifting staff of speechwriters. Woodrow Wilson was the last president to write all his speeches himself, but Roosevelt was the first to make the writing of speeches a team project.* Samuel Rosenman, a former New York State Assemblyman, was always a critical member of a shifting team that included at different times Louis Howe, a newspaper man who had worked with Roosevelt since his earliest days in Albany; Raymond Moley, a Barnard College professor who came to Roosevelt first as an adviser on criminal justice; Harry Hopkins, an important administrator in Albany and Washington relief programs; and Robert Sherwood, a distinguished author and playwright.

Roosevelt may have expanded the role of speechwriter beyond what it had been before, but he did not simply delegate speechwriting to others. On the five or six nights a month set aside for the purpose, Roosevelt and his writers would come together at 7:15 in the president's study for drinks, which Roosevelt mixed from a tray on his desk. Half an hour was allowed to enjoy the drinks and casual conversation. Then, at precisely 7:45, dinner was provided on a portable extension table that accommodated six. When dinner was over, Roosevelt seated himself on a sofa near the fireplace and read aloud the latest draft of

---

* Judson Welliver, "literary clerk" during the Harding administration from 1921 to 1923, is generally considered the first presidential speechwriter in the modern sense—someone whose job description includes helping to compose speeches. *White House Ghosts* by Robert Schlesinger, whose father wrote speeches for John F. Kennedy, describes the evolution of the craft.

whatever speech was under consideration. A secretary took down revisions and addenda as they were dictated. Working together, Roosevelt and his writers deleted phrases, sentences, paragraphs, and even whole pages, replacing them with new material or discarding them entirely. New material might come from Roosevelt's own speech file, a collection of material copied from his reading, newspaper clippings, correspondence, and miscellaneous items that he had been accumulating for many years. Often there were suggestions submitted by members of Congress and others. Sometimes a call went out to advisers not present, such as the Pulitzer Prize-winning poet Archibald MacLeish, who Roosevelt had installed at the Library of Congress.[34]

The president would go to bed eventually, but the team might continue to work through the night—Rosenman relied on Coca-Cola, Hopkins on coffee, and Sherwood on whiskey to keep alert[35]—so as to be able to leave a new draft on the president's breakfast tray the next morning. Responding to any further criticism from Roosevelt, work would continue during the day and again that evening and the next through a dozen or more drafts until there was an agreed text for the president's use. All of it had been studied and criticized and read aloud by Roosevelt so that he was thoroughly familiar with it by the time he needed to deliver it.

Critically important to the success of the fireside chats—and Roosevelt's speeches generally—were his voice and his ability to project intimacy and confidence. Roosevelt's voice has been called "cultivated," which may refer to the hint of Harvard in his accent. The letter "r" tended to disappear, so that "war" became "wau" and "fear" became "feah." John F. Kennedy had a similar accent, and in both cases it added interest without being too distinctively provincial. Roosevelt's voice was also called "resonant." A *New York Post* reporter wrote: "He speaks with a strong clear voice, with a tenor note in it which rings—sings, one is tempted to say—in key with . . . [an] intangible, utterly charming and surely vote-winning quality."[36] Mark Sullivan said of him that with his voice, "he could recite the Polish alphabet and it would be accepted as an eloquent plea for disarmament."[37] He "knew how to strike upon every chord of human emotion," and with "the timing of a great actor, he spoke slowly, reassuringly and meaningfully."[38] Letters came thanking him for his "delivery so crystal clear, so deliberate, so straight from the heart" and the "conviction . . . strength . . . [and] confidence" that came through to the listener.[39]

Rosenman was firm in the belief that "more than any other president—perhaps more than any other political figure in history—Franklin D. Roosevelt used the spoken and written word to exercise leadership and to carry out policies."[40]

Against this background it may be useful to look again at Roosevelt's first inaugural address. Long after the event, Raymond Moley claimed initial authorship, and one important study of the speech supports Moley's claim.[41] Although the existing "first draft" is in Roosevelt's writing, Moley claimed later, when he had become an opponent of the New Deal and angrily severed his ties with Roosevelt, that it was a copy of a text he presented to the president-elect and that Roosevelt destroyed it after he had copied it. If so, it came into being differently than Roosevelt's White House speeches in having begun without Roosevelt's input.

Of the first one hundred and fifty-three words of the speech as given, only thirty-three are in the existing first draft—and that first draft, apparently, was written out by Roosevelt after he and Moley had spent the evening reworking it. It is also of interest that the first phrase of the speech as given, "This is a day of national consecration," was not in the text that Roosevelt took with him to the Inauguration but was added at the last minute, and the word "national" was ad libbed as the new president spoke.

The existing first draft is also lacking its best-known line: "The only thing we have to fear is fear itself." That line is sometimes attributed to Louis Howe; but it is also true that shortly before his first inauguration, Franklin Roosevelt was given an anthology of Henry David Thoreau's writings, in which can be found the thought "Nothing is so much to be feared as fear." Eleanor Roosevelt has testified that Thoreau's book was in Roosevelt's hotel suite as he reworked his inaugural address in the last days before the inauguration. But Thoreau's sentence itself had antecedents in similar sentences from the Duke of Wellington (circa 1832), Francis Bacon (1623), and Michel de Montaigne (1580).

The great nineteenth-century preacher Phillips Brooks once said that "preaching . . . has in it two essential elements: truth and personality."[42] Others clearly helped Roosevelt define the truth as he understood it, but without his personality through which to proclaim it, the message would not have been heard. Whoever else may have worked on the speech and whatever sources, ancient and modern, may have been employed, it was, in the end, Roosevelt's speech.

IV

Historians write about Roosevelt's first "hundred days" as a remarkable and transformative period by which new presidents have been measured ever since, but never again in peacetime has a Congress been so easily persuaded of the need to act together in a positive way. The most effective measures were those that created jobs, the Civilian Conservation Corps and the Works Progress Administration in particular. In that same period, Congress approved a Federal Emergency Relief Administration, the Tennessee Valley Authority, and a national industrial recovery bill. A Farm Relief Act established an Agricultural Adjustment Administration, and on his own authority Roosevelt took the nation off the gold standard. Some Republicans pointed to the way in which Russia, Italy, and Germany had recently forsaken freedom to turn to dictators like Stalin, Mussolini, and Hitler and warned that America was on the same path; but Roosevelt had made clear in his inaugural address that he had no such aspirations, although Congress as a whole was too shocked by the seriousness of the situation to mount any effective opposition.

The pace of change slackened after the first three months; not until 1935 was the most lasting change of all, the Social Security system, adopted.

Roosevelt accepted renomination in 1936 with a speech that envisioned a continuing reformation of American society and made clear, perhaps for the first time, how the very meaning of freedom had been transformed by the radical changes that had taken place:

> For too many of us the political equality we once had won was meaningless in the face of economic inequality. A small group had concentrated into their own hands an almost complete control over other people's property, other people's money, other people's labor—other people's lives. For too many of us life was no longer free; liberty no longer real; men could no longer follow the pursuit of happiness.
>
> Against economic tyranny such as this, the American citizen could appeal only to the organized power of government.

Speaking to the convention in Philadelphia, Roosevelt recalled the Declaration of Independence, signed there as a statement of freedom from political royalists, and spoke of the need for freedom now from "economic royalists."

> The royalists of the economic order have conceded that political freedom was the business of the government, but they have maintained that economic slavery was nobody's business. They granted that the government could protect the citizen in his right to vote, but they denied that the government could do anything to protect the citizen in his right to work and his right to live.
>
> Today we stand committed to the proposition that freedom is no half-and-half affair. If the average citizen is guaranteed equal opportunity in the polling place, he must have equal opportunity in the market place.

Referring to the rise of dictatorships in Europe, Roosevelt suggested that other nations had given up political freedom for the promise of economic security: "They have sold their heritage of freedom for the illusion of a living. They have yielded their democracy." Thus he could summon Americans to "a war for the survival of democracy" and tell them "We are fighting to save a great and precious form of government for ourselves and for the world." Most memorably, he challenged Americans to be thankful for the challenge they faced:

> To some generations much is given. Of other generations much is expected. This generation of Americans has a rendezvous with destiny.[43]

Debate continues, of course, over the legacy of the New Deal. After four years, the Depression still continued. The unemployment rates went from 23.6% in 1932 to 16.9% in 1936 and 14.6% in 1940.[44] These were still unacceptable numbers, but the evidence of real improvement, combined with Roosevelt's unquenchable optimism, led to a landslide victory in 1936 and an easy win in 1940 in spite of the tradition against a president serving three terms. Republicans were divided between those who totally opposed the New Deal and those prepared to adopt many of its measures, recognizing that the public had no desire to return to the dark days following the Crash. Both were easy targets for Roosevelt's rhetoric, the first for their unwillingness to change and the second for their "me-tooism."

At Syracuse, New York, in September 1936, Roosevelt was in top form, laughing with the audience as he mocked the Republican Party.

> Let me warn you and let me warn the Nation against the smooth evasion which says, "Of course we believe all these things; we believe in social security; we believe in work for the unemployed; we believe in saving homes. Cross our hearts and hope to die, we believe in all these things; but we do not like the way the present Administration is doing them. Just turn them over to us. We will do all of them, we will do more of them, we will do them better; and, most important of all, the doing of them will not cost anybody anything."

Roosevelt went on to the most sweeping presidential victory ever, winning every state but Maine and Vermont. Inauguration Day in 1937 came in January instead of March because the Constitution had been amended to shorten the time between the election and inauguration from four months to two. No one, apparently, had stopped to think about outdoor ceremonies in Washington in January, so officials and the crowd stood in a cold, driving rain for the ceremony. Undeterred by the weather, Roosevelt challenged the country to see how much remained to be done:

> I see millions of families trying to live on incomes so meager that the pall of family disaster hangs over them day by day.
>
> I see millions whose daily lives in city and on farm continue under conditions labeled indecent by a so-called polite society half a century ago.
>
> I see millions denied education, recreation, and the opportunity to better their lot and the lot of their children.
>
> I see millions lacking the means to buy the products of farm and factory and by their poverty denying work and productiveness to many other millions.
>
> I see one-third of a nation ill-housed, ill-clad, ill-nourished.

Ever the optimist, however, Roosevelt told the crowd that

> It is not in despair that I paint you that picture. I paint it for you in hope—because the Nation, seeing and understanding the injustice in it, proposes to paint it out. . . . The test of our progress is not whether we add more to the abundance of those who have much; it is whether we provide enough for those who have too little.[45]

But the Supreme Court had overruled some key parts of the New Deal, and Roosevelt had begun pondering how he could work around that obstacle. His overwhelming victory in the election encouraged him to think he could press ahead with more radical changes and—still an obsession—balance the budget. Cutting back on job programs to balance the budget, however, reduced his leverage, and newly reelected conservative members of Congress from the South were beginning to feel that they could safely challenge the president. When Roosevelt tried to resolve his problem with the Court by asking Congress to create a retirement age for the justices and let him appoint an additional justice for every one past that age, it touched off a full-scale rebellion. Eventually one justice switched his vote to sustain such programs as Social Security, and Roosevelt was able to move ahead with his program actually strengthened because the traditional nine-member court had now affirmed them.

The greater challenge to Roosevelt's leadership, however, was developing in international events. Even before Roosevelt won a second term, new violence had broken out abroad. In October 1935, Mussolini invaded Ethiopia and demonstrated the inability of the U.S.-less League of Nations to deal effectively with such acts of aggression. In Asia, Japan was pressing south into the heart of China. In Spain, a bloody civil war broke out in July 1936 and drew in troops and arms from Italy and Germany for the rebel "Nationalists," while Russia and

Mexico offered similar assistance in support of the "Loyalist," or "Republican," side. In March 1938, Hitler invaded and annexed Austria and immediately began pressing claims to German-speaking regions of Czechoslovakia.

Realizing that America, at the very least, would need to be able to protect itself where its interests might be threatened and that a strong current of isolationism in the country would make it difficult to prepare to meet these threats, Roosevelt went to Chicago in October 1937 to call attention to the situation and suggest an appropriate response. America is peaceful and prospering, he told his audience, but we need to be aware of conditions elsewhere:

> [A]s I have seen with my own eyes, the prosperous farms, the thriving factories and the busy railroads, as I have seen the happiness and security and peace which covers our wide land, almost inevitably I have been compelled to contrast our peace with very different scenes being enacted in other parts of the world.
>
> It is because the people of the United States under modern conditions must, for the sake of their own future, give thought to the rest of the world, that I, as the responsible executive head of the Nation, have chosen this great inland city and this gala occasion to speak to you on a subject of definite national importance.

What should be done? Roosevelt was not ready to suggest specific plans. He simply repeated in various ways the single theme: we need to prepare. But he offered one more specific suggestion, still without any details: a "quarantine" of aggressor nations:

> It seems to be unfortunately true that the epidemic of world lawlessness is spreading.
>
> When an epidemic of physical disease starts to spread, the community approves and joins in a quarantine of the patients in order to protect the health of the community against the spread of the disease.

The stirring conclusion also was vague in its implications:

> There must be positive endeavors to preserve peace. America hates war. America hopes for peace. Therefore, America actively engages in the search for peace.[46]

The speech was widely praised by isolationists and interventionists alike, each group reading it as favorable to their side. Overseas also, people read into the speech what they wanted to hear. British Prime Minister Neville Chamberlain hailed it publicly as "a clarion call" but privately said "it was very difficult to discover its meaning." Probably Roosevelt had formed no clear ideas but wanted to see how the public and foreign leaders would react and so gauge how far and how hard he could push toward support of the British and French.

The Supreme Court fight had consumed an enormous amount of time and energy, and Roosevelt emerged from it looking less like an indomitable force. In the midterm elections of 1938, he still saw himself in terms of 1936 and thought he was strong enough to purge uncooperative members of his own party. Instead, Republicans picked up eight seats in the Senate and eighty-one in the House. Democrats still had a comfortable majority in both houses of Congress, but Roosevelt could no longer count on the support of the conservative Democrats he had failed to purge and would have a harder task getting legislation passed than in his first six years.

Even in those circumstances, Roosevelt could still enjoy himself on the campaign trail. Only a month after the midterm elections, he went to North Carolina and spoke to students at the University. "You undergraduates," he said,

> who see me for the first time have read your newspapers and heard on the air that I am, at the very least, an ogre—a consorter with communists, a destroyer of the rich, a breaker of our ancient tradition. . . . You may have heard, for six years, that I was about to plunge the nation into war; that you and your little brothers would be sent to the bloody fields of battle in Europe; that I was driving the nation into bankruptcy; and that I breakfasted every morning on a dish of grilled millionaire!

He threw his head back and smiled broadly as he went on to say:

> Actually, I am an exceedingly mild-mannered person, a practitioner of peace, both domestic and foreign, a believer in the capitalistic system, and for my breakfast, a devotee of scrambled eggs![47]

Sometimes that ability to laugh at himself counted for more than specific programs.

V

When Roosevelt gave his annual State of the Union message in 1939, Europe was clearly on the brink of war, and Roosevelt's first priority was to point out the importance of American military preparedness.

> All about us rage undeclared wars—military and economic. All about us grow more deadly armaments—military and economic. All about us are threats of new aggression military and economic.
>
> . . . the world has grown so small and weapons of attack so swift that no nation can be safe in its will to peace so long as any other powerful nation refuses to settle its grievances at the council table.
>
> We have learned that survival cannot be guaranteed by arming after the attack begins—for there is new range and speed to offense.
>
> We have learned that God-fearing democracies of the world which observe the sanctity of treaties and good faith in their dealings with other nations cannot safely be indifferent to international lawlessness anywhere. They cannot forever let pass, without effective protest, acts of aggression against sister nations—acts which automatically undermine all of us.

In addition, Roosevelt insisted, domestic unity was vital. The Spanish Civil War had made clear the many cross-currents that made unity so difficult. Many Italian Americans were admirers of Mussolini, and therefore of Franco when Mussolini supported him. Roman Catholics, alarmed by the Communist support for the Loyalist cause, tended to support Franco even though a victory for Franco was, in effect, a victory for Hitler. Roman Catholics and Italian Americans were an important part of Roosevelt's base in the cities of the Northeast, but so were non-Roman Catholic liberals who increasingly rallied around the Loyalists. Even isolationists were divided: a leading isolationist senator, Gerald Nye, a Republican from North Dakota, was prepared to lift the arms embargo for the Loyalists and maintain it for the Nationalists. Roosevelt undoubtedly had all this in mind in saying:

> In meeting the troubles of the world we must meet them as one people—with a unity born of the fact that for generations those who have come to our shores, representing many kindreds and tongues, have been welded by common opportunity into a united patriotism. If another form of government can present a united front in its attack on a democracy, the attack must and will be met by a united democracy. Such a democracy can and must exist in the United States.[48]

These were generalities. Roosevelt followed them up with specific requests for $525 million in new money for the army and navy, the largest part of it for airplanes. Undeterred, Hitler declared Czechoslovakia a German protectorate in March. Roosevelt responded by asking for revisions of the neutrality act, which Congress had passed in 1935. To be neutral in a conflict between democracies and dictatorships was, said Roosevelt, to assist the aggressor. He had no intention, he insisted, of sending American troops to Europe; but to enforce an arms embargo was to render assistance to the dictatorships. He called the Senate leaders to the White House to meet with himself and Secretary of State Cordell Hull. Nevertheless, the isolationists in the Senate could not be swayed; and without some support from that bloc, Roosevelt was unable to move.

The Spanish Civil War was less ominous than Hitler's continuing aggression. As first Austria, then Czechoslovakia, were brought under the dictator's control, Roosevelt continued to search for ways to negotiate peace while also working to find what openings he could to help arm the western democracies in spite of neutrality acts and arms embargoes passed by Congress. Charles A. Lindbergh, a leading isolationist, had been given a tour of German air force installations and reported that the Germans had more airplanes than all the democracies combined. Roosevelt looked for ways to expand American output drastically. To assist the British and French, Roosevelt even proposed sending airplane parts across the border to Canadian plants for assembly.

War broke out in Europe in September 1939, and Roosevelt's reaction was very different from Wilson's in 1914. Wilson had made every effort to be not only neutral but impartial. Roosevelt insisted on American neutrality, but two days after Britain and France declared war on Germany he sat down for a Fireside Chat to state his position. "Every battle that is fought," Roosevelt said, "does affect the American future." Nonetheless, he was clear that he would do everything possible to keep America at peace and American soldiers at home. "I hate war," Roosevelt said. "This nation will remain a neutral nation, but I cannot ask that every American remain neutral in thought as well. Even a neutral has a right to take account of facts. Even a neutral cannot be asked to close his mind or his conscience."[49]

Isolationism remained a powerful force in the country, and Lindbergh, "the Lone Eagle" and an American icon for his solo flight across the Atlantic in May 1927, was one of the most effective isolationist leaders. In June 1940, Roosevelt went to the University of Virginia to try to explain to undergraduates why such a stance was no longer feasible. The repeated term "lone island" was a deliberate reference to Lindbergh, the "Lone Eagle":

> Some indeed still hold to the now somewhat obvious delusion that we of the United States can safely permit the United States to become a lone island, a lone island in a world dominated by the philosophy of force.
>
> Such an island may be the dream of those who still talk and vote as isolationists. Such an island represents to me and to the

> overwhelming majority of Americans today a helpless nightmare of a people without freedom—the nightmare of a people lodged in prison, handcuffed, hungry, and fed through the bars from day to day by the contemptuous, unpitying masters of other continents.[50]

Freedom, Roosevelt insisted, was at stake in the growing international crisis.

1940 was, of course, an election year; and a few days after Roosevelt's speech in Virginia, the Republican Convention nominated Wendell Willkie, a businessman who had once voted for Roosevelt. Willkie was corporate counsel for Commonwealth & Southern, a firm in competition with the Tennessee Valley Authority created by the New Deal. He was an internationalist and supporter of a number of New Deal policies, but he was opposed to what he believed was unfair government competition with private businesses such as his. He challenged Roosevelt to a serious of "public forums," but Roosevelt, attempting to avoid campaigning in a national emergency, ignored the suggestion.

Roosevelt was so obviously the front runner for the Democratic nomination that he could hold back until the last minute and then actually threaten not to run unless the convention accepted his choice of a vice president. In his speech accepting the nomination, Roosevelt framed his willingness to serve a third term as a matter of "public duty."

> Like most men of my age, I had made plans for myself, plans for a private life of my own choice and for my own satisfaction, a life of that kind to begin in January 1941. These plans, like so many other plans, had been made in a world which now seems as distant as another planet. Today all private plans, all private lives, have been in a sense repealed by an overriding public danger. In the face of that public danger all those who can be of service to the Republic have no choice but to offer themselves for service in those capacities for which they may be fitted.
>
> Those, my friends, are the reasons why I have had to admit to myself, and now to state to you, that my conscience will not let me turn my back upon a call to service.
>
> The right to make that call rests with the people through the American method of a free election. Only the people themselves can draft a President. If such a draft should be made upon me, I say to you, in the utmost simplicity, I will, with God's help, continue to serve with the best of my ability and with the fullness of my strength.[51]

The summer of 1940 was, indeed, a time of national emergency. France had collapsed under the weight of German arms, and Roosevelt's advisers thought the odds were three to one that Great Britain would be invaded and defeated before the summer was over. They were discussing how to cope with an expected German attack on the weak and undefended countries of South America, aware that German bombers based in Britain would be able to attack East Coast American cities.

Roosevelt, in his role of military leader, went to Ogdensburg, New York, on the same date that Willkie chose to make his acceptance speech. He found 94,000 troops, five anti-aircraft guns, and just over one hundred airplanes. Hitler that summer was sending 1,800 planes a day to attack Britain. Willkie attacked Roosevelt for failing to prepare adequately to defend America; but it seems unlikely, especially as the leader of the more isolationist party, that Willkie himself could have done much more. Somewhat inconsistently, Willkie also accused Roosevelt of wanting to draw America into war. When Roosevelt managed to find a way to send some over-age American destroyers to Britain in return for some British bases in the Western Hemisphere, Willkie denounced it as "the most arbitrary and dictatorial action ever taken by any President in the history of the United States."

In mid-October, with some three weeks left before the election, Roosevelt decided to make a series of five speeches "to correct misstatements." He could not, of course, resist the temptation to have some fun as well. In planning a speech for Madison Square Garden, Roosevelt's speechwriters noticed that the names of some of the Republican leaders in Congress who had opposed Roosevelt's efforts to support Great Britain by, for example, repealing the arms embargo, had an enchanting rhythm: Martin, Barton, and Fish. Roosevelt invoked the trio once; and when he repeated the names a few minutes later, the audience joined in. When Roosevelt moved on to speak in Boston a few days later, that audience was ready immediately to take up the refrain at each mention of Martin and repeat the names with him a number of times. The Boston accent, like the president's, made it even more effective as "Mah-tin, Bah-ton, and Fish!" In a time of crisis, it gave campaign audiences—and indeed the chief campaigner—a chance to relax and enjoy the campaign.

At the end of the campaign, Roosevelt outlined a vision for America based on specific freedoms, "the right of free speech, free religion, free assembly and the right . . . to choose the officers of their own Government in free elections." Two months later, he would build on that pattern to enunciate "The Four Freedoms" in his State of the Union message. The campaign speech had little specific to say, focusing instead on America's future in the broadest terms:

I see an America devoted to our freedoms—unified by tolerance and by religious faith—a people consecrated to peace, a people confident in strength because their body and their spirit are secure and unafraid.

There is a great storm raging now, a storm that makes things harder for the world. And that storm, which did not start in this land of ours, is the true reason that I would like to stick by those people of ours until we reach the clear, sure footing ahead.

We will make it—we will make it before the next term is over.

We will make it; and the world, we hope, will make it, too.

When that term is over there will be another President, and many more Presidents in the years to come, and I think that, in the years to come, that word "President" will be a word to cheer the hearts of common men and women everywhere.

Our future belongs to us Americans.

It is for us to design it; for us to build it.

In that building of it we shall prove that our faith is strong enough to survive the most fearsome storms that have ever swept over the earth.

In the days and months and years to come, we shall be making history—hewing out a new shape for the future. And we shall make very sure that that future of ours bears the likeness of liberty.

Always the heart and the soul of our country will be the heart and the soul of the common man—the men and the women who never have ceased to believe in democracy, who never have ceased to love their families, their homes and their country.

The spirit of the common man is the spirit of peace and good will. It is the spirit of God. And in His faith is the strength of all America.

In the election, Roosevelt carried all but eight states in the Midwest plus Maine and Vermont and took 54% of the popular vote.

There was time for a brief vacation in the Caribbean after the election. Roosevelt came back with new proposals for Congress to assist the British by lending and leasing equipment America could provide that the British could not pay for. He unleashed the full range of persuasive means at his command: press conferences, Fireside Chats, radio talks, and always, of course, the personal meetings with legislators. It was at a press conference in mid-December that Roosevelt employed one of his most successful figures of speech to help Americans think about what came to be called the "Lend-Lease" program. Speaking very informally, Roosevelt asked the reporters to see it as a way to "eliminate the dollar sign."

> That is something brand new in the thoughts of practically everybody in this room, I think—get rid of the silly, foolish old dollar sign.
>
> Well, let me give you an illustration: Suppose my neighbor's home catches fire, and I have a length of garden hose four or five hundred feet away. If he can take my garden hose and connect it up with his hydrant, I may help him to put out his fire. Now, what do I do? I don't say to him before that operation, "Neighbor, my garden hose cost me $15; you have to pay me $15 for it." What is the transaction that goes on? I don't want $15—I want my garden hose back after the fire is over. All right. If it goes through the fire all right, intact, without any damage to it, he gives it back to me and thanks me very much for the use of it. But suppose it gets smashed up—holes in it—during the fire; we don't have to have too much formality about it, but I say to him, "I was glad to lend you that hose; I see I can't use it any more, it's all smashed up." He says, "How many feet of it were there?" I tell him, "There were 150 feet of it." He says, "All right, I will replace it." Now, if I get a nice garden hose back, I am in pretty good shape.
>
> In other words, if you lend certain munitions and get the munitions back at the end of the war, if they are intact—haven't been hurt—you are all right; if they have been damaged or have deteriorated or have been lost completely, it seems to me you come out pretty well if you have them replaced by the fellow to whom you have lent them.
>
> I can't go into details; and there is no use asking legal questions about how you would do it, because that is the thing that is now under study.

Roosevelt was improvising again, as he had done in the depths of the Depression. What mattered was enabling the country to see where he was trying to go and why. At the end of December, he turned again to the "Fireside Chat" format, but with a difference. "This is not a fireside chat on war," Roosevelt told his listeners; "it is a talk on national security." Recalling the crisis America had faced eight years earlier, he told the country:

> Never before since Jamestown and Plymouth Rock has our American civilization been in such danger as now. . . . The Nazi masters of Germany have made it clear that they intend not only to dominate all life and thought in their own country, but also to enslave the whole of Europe, and then to use the resources of Europe to dominate the rest of the world.

Roosevelt went on to discuss very clearly the need to build "the planes, the tanks, the guns, the freighters which will enable [the people of Europe] to fight for their liberty and our security." America, he said "must be the great arsenal of democracy." Production of luxury goods would need to be cut back for this purpose, and management and labor would need to work together without work stoppages. Already, he reported, "Manufacturers of watches, of farm implements, linotypes, cash registers, automobiles, sewing machines, lawn mowers, and locomotives are now making fuses, bomb-packing crates, telescope mounts, shells, pistols, and tanks." It was a speech that dealt with all the specifics of a nation going to war that Roosevelt had been unable to talk about during the campaign. It was a call for a "national effort . . . with absolute confidence that our common cause will greatly succeed."[52]

Eight days later, he employed his 1941 State of the Union message to the same purpose. He made it clearer than ever that it was not a time for neutrality. In spite of strong isolationist sentiment, Roosevelt was increasingly clear that he was committed to working with Great Britain to oppose German aggression. He had spoken freely of Britain in his "Fireside Chat on War." With the Congress, he was less specific; but there could have been no mistaking Roosevelt's meaning when he said "[W]e are committed to full support of all those resolute people everywhere who are resisting aggression." That commitment, he said again, would require major changes in America's industrial base to enable mass production of everything from planes to ships. To change from producing what he called "implements of peace" to what he called "implements of war" would be "no small task." The hardest part, he told the Congress, would be constructing the factories and shipyards where ships and planes could be built.

What he needed from Congress was "funds sufficient to manufacture additional munitions and war supplies of many kinds, to be turned over to those nations which are now in actual war with aggressor nations. . . . They do not need manpower, but they do need billions of dollars' worth of the weapons of defense."

In all honesty, he told the Congress, the Europeans will shortly be unable to pay for all this in ready cash, but "We cannot, and we will not, tell them that they must surrender merely because of present inability to pay for the weapons which we know they must have." He was not suggesting a loan, because the weapons produced would be used, in effect, to defend America and might eventually need to be used by Americans to defend themselves.

Meanwhile, Roosevelt said, America must continue to work for justice and opportunity at home. There must be:

> Equality of opportunity for youth and for others.
> Jobs for those who can work.

> Security for those who need it.
> The ending of special privilege for the few.
> The preservation of civil liberties for all.
> The enjoyment of the fruits of scientific progress in a wider and constantly rising standard of living.

The speechwriters had worked through four drafts of this speech when Roosevelt told them that he had an idea for a peroration or summary and proceeded to dictate the passage on the "Four Freedoms" that was incorporated into the speech almost as dictated. All of this, he concluded, was part of his vision for America's future and

> . . . a world founded upon four essential human freedoms.
>
> The first is freedom of speech and expression—everywhere in the world.
>
> The second is freedom of every person to worship God in his own way—everywhere in the world.
>
> The third is freedom from want, which, translated into world terms,* means economic understandings which will secure to every nation a healthy peacetime life for its inhabitants—everywhere in the world.
>
> The fourth is freedom from fear, which, translated into world terms, means a world-wide reduction of armaments to such a point and in such a thorough fashion that no nation will be in a position to commit an act of physical aggression against any neighbor—anywhere in the world.

"Freedom from fear," of course, echoed Roosevelt's inaugural address and grounded human freedom at home or abroad in the same need for security. "That is no vision of a distant millennium," Roosevelt concluded. "It is a definite basis for a kind of world attainable in our own time and generation," and indeed it was a picture of the world that he had ever more clearly imagined since his first inaugural address in 1932.[53] It would become the basis of the Atlantic Charter signed by Roosevelt and Churchill later in the year, a prominent element in American wartime propaganda, and the basis of the United Nations Universal Declaration of Human Rights. The Four Freedoms were referenced in George W. Bush's address to a joint session of Congress after the 9/11 attack.

---

* The fifth draft said "international terms" for the third and fourth freedoms, but "world terms" was penciled in and incorporated in the sixth draft.

VI

Churchill had been hoping that the United States would declare war on Germany and Italy much sooner than Roosevelt thought possible. Facing a powerful isolationist bloc in the Congress, Roosevelt felt it important to move forward slowly and carefully so as not to provoke more opposition than necessary. Both leaders, however, recognized that an unprepared country could be most helpful, meanwhile, by providing as much arms and equipment as could be spared. Even there, Roosevelt had to be careful, since the generals and admirals were unhappy about sharing America's limited armory with others.

The Japanese attack on Pearl Harbor brought that phase to an abrupt end. As Roosevelt had done what he could to support Britain in Europe, so he had done what he could to support Chiang Kai-shek in Asia. He had sent equipment to the Chinese and had appealed to the Japanese government time and again to halt its continuous expansion. In early December 1941, he had sent a personal appeal for peace to the Emperor of Japan. Meanwhile, the Japanese ambassador and a special envoy had been meeting with Secretary of State Cordell Hull. They had drawn up a formal reply to Roosevelt's appeal and indeed were scheduled to present it to Secretary Hull at one o'clock on December 7. That meeting was postponed at the last minute to two P.M., and by that time Hull had been advised of the Japanese attack. He told the Japanese envoys, after they had handed him their reply, that in all his fifty years of government service he had "never seen a document that was more crowded with infamous lies and falsehoods" and ordered them from his office.

Roosevelt spent the afternoon with his military advisers and then took a brief call from Churchill. Late in the afternoon, he called in his secretary and told her to sit down so he could dictate his message to the Congress. Speaking slowly and distinctly, specifying punctuation and paragraphs, he dictated his message and then showed it to Cordell Hull and Harry Hopkins. Hull suggested an elaboration of details, but Roosevelt thought not. Hopkins suggested a closing sentence that Roosevelt added. Later, a few minor changes were written in—"a date which will live in world history" was changed to "a date which will live in infamy"—and the manuscript was re-typed for use the next day. He ate a light dinner and spent the evening meeting first with his Cabinet, then with Congressional leaders. Other briefings ran beyond midnight.[54]

At noon on Monday, the president went to Congress to read his brief statement. He began calmly and deliberately as if he were reading a news item from the paper:

> Yesterday, December 7, 1941 . . .

then his voice rang out across the room in front of him and across the country by radio:

> . . . a date which will live in infamy—the United States of America was suddenly and deliberately attacked by naval and air forces of the Empire of Japan.

The treachery of "false statements and expressions of hope for continued peace" made those actions worse: "Always will we remember," he said, "the character of the onslaught against us." There was a brief summary of what had happened:

> The attack yesterday on the Hawaiian Islands has caused severe damage to American naval and military forces. Very many American lives have been lost. In addition American ships have been reported torpedoed on the high seas between San Francisco and Honolulu.

Other attacks were listed in the last twenty-four hours against Malaya, Hong Kong, Guam, the Philippine Islands, Wake Island, and Midway Island. Roosevelt's conclusion was brief and to the point:

> Hostilities exist. There is no blinking at the fact that our people, our territory, and our interests are in grave danger.

The last paragraph was handwritten at the end of the final draft, a last-minute addition by Harry Hopkins.[55]

> With confidence in our armed force—with the unbounded determination of our people—we will gain the inevitable triumph—so help us God.

It remained only to ask the Congress to act as the Constitution required.

> I ask that the Congress declare that since the unprovoked and dastardly attack by Japan on Sunday, December seventh, a state of war has existed between the United States and the Japanese Empire.[56]

Congress acted immediately and unanimously—with one dissent. Jeannette Rankin, the first woman to serve in Congress and a lifelong pacifist, had also voted against the First World War.

At last, the inevitable clash between dictatorships and democracies, between tyranny and freedom, would need to be fought out and resolved by force of arms.

In that struggle, the great voices and oratorical skills of Franklin Roosevelt and Winston Churchill would play significant parts in defining the task and encouraging not only the soldiers and sailors who did the fighting, but also the civilians whose work producing arms and equipment was equally essential.

Roosevelt spoke next to the nation in his annual State of the Union Address, which provided the opportunity for the president to define the consequences of the Japanese attack for Americans. It also provided an opportunity for the president to spell out for the enemy exactly what they would be facing.

> I have just sent a letter of directive to the appropriate departments and agencies of our Government, ordering that immediate steps be taken.
>
> First, to increase our production rate of airplanes so rapidly that in this year, 1942, we shall produce 60,000 planes, 10,000 more than the goal that we set a year and a half ago. This includes 45,000 combat planes—bombers, dive bombers, pursuit planes. The rate of increase will be maintained and continued so that next year, 1943, we shall produce 125,000 airplanes, including 100,000 combat planes.
>
> Second, to increase our production rate of tanks so rapidly that in this year, 1942, we shall produce 45,000 tanks; and to continue that increase so that next year, 1943, we shall produce 75,000 tanks.
>
> Third, to increase our production rate of anti-aircraft guns so rapidly that in this year, 1942, we shall produce 20,000 of them; and to continue that increase so that next year, 1943, we shall produce 35,000 anti-aircraft guns.
>
> And fourth, to increase our production rate of merchant ships so rapidly that in this year, 1942, we shall build 6,000,000 deadweight tons as compared with a 1941 completed production of 1,100,000. And finally, we shall continue that increase so that next year, 1943, we shall build 10,000,000 tons of shipping.
>
> These figures and similar figures for a multitude of other implements of war will give the Japanese and the Nazis a little idea of just what they accomplished in the attack at Pearl Harbor.
>
> And I rather hope that all these figures which I have given will become common knowledge in Germany and Japan.

Such a task, of course, would cost money and require the use of materials which would no longer be available for normal peacetime use. That was one reason for all the numbers. It was a long speech, long on both specifics and exhortation. Americans, Roosevelt said, would need to guard against complacency, defeatism, and division. Finally, he put the task in terms of the American heritage of faith:

> We are inspired by a faith that goes back through all the years to the first chapter of the Book of Genesis: "God created man in His own image." We on our side are striving to be true to that divine heritage. We are fighting, as our fathers have fought, to uphold the doctrine that all men are equal in the sight of God.[57]

Roosevelt might not have been thinking of America's own shortcomings in that last respect, but the war would bring significant progress in that way as well.

A month later, it was time for another Fireside Chat. It was Washington's Birthday, and Roosevelt wanted people to see a parallel between Washington's struggle to gain American freedom and the new struggle they were engaged in for freedom for others.

> The present great struggle has taught us increasingly that freedom of person and security of property anywhere in the world depend upon the security of the rights and obligations of liberty and justice everywhere in the world.

Roosevelt also wanted to explain the strategy that would focus attention first on Europe rather than Asia. He asked Americans to get out their maps and study them as he walked them around the globe. "Look at your map," he instructed his listeners. "Look at the vast area of China. . . . Look at the vast area of Russia . . . Look at the British Isles, Australia, New Zealand, the Dutch East Indies. . . ." He wanted Americans to understand that they were engaged in a world war and therefore needed to think in terms of linking the resources and needs of these far-flung places.

To those around him, as had often been true in times of crisis, Roosevelt seemed unnaturally calm. Some of his responses, however, suggested that he, too, was not unfearful of forces beyond his control. It was true that a Japanese submarine had surfaced off the coast of California and had lobbed some shells at Santa Barbara. That hardly justified rounding up 110,000 people of Japanese ancestry, more than half of whom were American citizens, and herding them into "relocation centers" in remote parts of Arizona, Colorado, Montana, and elsewhere. Fear itself was a central factor in a number of decisions made in the first weeks and months of the war.

Other principles, too, were lost sight of in the emergency. Roosevelt and Churchill had issued an Atlantic Charter in August 1941, stating agreed principles that united them in a common cause. They stated that "they respect the right of all peoples to choose the form of government under which they will live; and they wish to see sovereign rights and self government restored to those who have been forcibly deprived of them"; but when Roosevelt suggested that this might be a good time to begin moving India in that direction as a Dominion within the British Empire, that the Indian people might be more supportive of the Allied cause if they could see self-government at the end of the day, Churchill gave Roosevelt a lesson in practical imperial priorities. Applying the Charter to Africa and Asia, Churchill told Roosevelt, "requires much thought." Roosevelt decided that he needed Churchill at the moment more than India, and that he would give the matter more thought himself.[58] The Atlantic Charter, Churchill told the House of Commons later, did not apply to the British Empire.[59]

If Churchill was reluctant to reshape the British Empire, Roosevelt was happy to tell Americans about the way the war was reshaping their country. In a Fireside Chat just before the 1942 midterm elections, he reported what he had seen on a low-key inspection tour of the country:

> I was impressed by the large proportion of women employed—doing skilled manual labor running machines. As time goes on, and many more of our men enter the armed forces, this proportion of women will increase. Within less than a year from now there will probably be as many women as men working in our war production plants.
>
> In some communities, employers dislike to employ women. In others they are reluctant to hire Negroes. In still others, older men are not wanted. We can no longer afford to indulge such prejudices or practices.[60]

Not until after the midterm elections of 1942—in which the Republicans made significant gains, but not enough to gain control of either House of Congress—did Roosevelt have positive news from the battlefront to report to the nation. Africa was probably not an area most Americans had thought about in relation to a war being fought in Asia and Europe; but the British lifeline through the Mediterranean was threatened by a German army in North Africa, and a landing by American troops was a critical first step in rolling back that threat. The American forces landed in Algiers and Morocco moved east against German troops in Libya, while British troops won a major victory against German forces in Egypt. "This is not the end," said Churchill. "This is not even the beginning of the end. It is, perhaps, the end of the beginning."[61]

Some of that "beginning" involved getting the divergent positions of the Allies sorted out: how to unify the Free French forces, and how to negotiate

British interest in the Mediterranean Theater with American and Russian interest in an invasion of France. To build on that beginning, Roosevelt suggested a meeting with Churchill and Stalin. Stalin, whose troops had just broken the German siege of Stalingrad, told Roosevelt he couldn't leave Russia, but Roosevelt and Churchill did meet in Casablanca and agreed at least that unconditional surrender was their goal and that a Western Front would be opened "at as early a date . . . as transportation facilities can be provided." Stalin was far from satisfied, but it was the best Roosevelt could do at that time.[62]

By the summer of 1943, the war had a brighter look. Allied armies had invaded Sicily, and American forces were beginning to push back against the Japanese in the Pacific. The second front in France was still almost a year away, but Roosevelt used a substantial portion of a Fireside Chat that summer to talk about post-war policy and the treatment of returning soldiers. Every member of the armed forces should have, he said, "mustering-out pay large enough in each case to cover a reasonable period of time between his discharge and the finding of a new job." There should be "unemployment insurance" and "an opportunity to get further education or trade training at the cost of the Government." There should also be "improved and liberalized provisions for hospitalization, for rehabilitation, for medical care of disabled members of the armed forces and the merchant marine," and "sufficient pensions for disabled members of the armed forces." Assurances that their government was already thinking in these terms were, of course, helpful immediately in terms of the troops' morale, but it was encouraging also to those at home to think that the end of the war was in sight.[63]

In September, Roosevelt was able to announce that Italy had surrendered and, finally, at a meeting of the three leaders in Teheran in late November 1943, Stalin got the specific commitment he had been demanding: a promise that western forces would invade France in May 1944. On Christmas Eve 1943, Roosevelt was able to offer a very positive outlook on the year ahead:

> I can say to you that at last we may look forward into the future with real, substantial confidence that, however great the cost, "peace on earth, good will toward men" can be and will be realized and ensured. This year I can say that. Last year I could not do more than express a hope. Today I express a certainty—though the cost may be high and the time may be long.

Roosevelt also made the first of several statements about the Russian dictator that would be exploited by Republican politicians for years afterwards as evidence of naïveté or worse. He said at one point that having dealt with Hoover and Huey Long and other American politicians, he was sure he could deal with Stalin.[64]

> To use an American and somewhat ungrammatical colloquialism, I may say that I "got along fine" with Marshal Stalin. He is a man who combines a tremendous, relentless determination with a stalwart good humor. I believe he is truly representative of the heart and soul of Russia; and I believe that we are going to get along very well with him and the Russian people—very well indeed.

More important than individual relationships, of course, would be structures to maintain peace. Already Roosevelt was beginning to point people toward the need for a new international structure more effective than the League of Nations—and with American participation. With more colorful language than was usual in his talks, Roosevelt dismissed those who imagined America could exist in isolation:

> There have always been cheerful idiots in this country who believed that there would be no more war for us if everybody in America would only return into their homes and lock their front doors behind them.[65]

The State of the Union message in January 1944 was primarily a report on the military situation; but Roosevelt was always looking ahead, and he took some time to think about the shape of the American economy after the war:

> It is our duty now to begin to lay the plans and determine the strategy for the winning of a lasting peace and the establishment of an American standard of living higher than ever before known. We cannot be content, no matter how high that general standard of living may be, if some fraction of our people—whether it be one-third or one-fifth or one-tenth—is ill-fed, ill-clothed, ill-housed, and insecure.
>
> This Republic had its beginning, and grew to its present strength, under the protection of certain inalienable political rights—among them the right of free speech, free press, free worship, trial by jury, freedom from unreasonable searches and seizures. They were our rights to life and liberty.
>
> As our Nation has grown in size and stature, however—as our industrial economy expanded—these political rights proved inadequate to assure us equality in the pursuit of happiness.

> We have come to a clear realization of the fact that true individual freedom cannot exist without economic security and independence. "Necessitous men are not free men."* People who are hungry and out of a job are the stuff of which dictatorships are made.
>
> In our day these economic truths have become accepted as self-evident. We have accepted, so to speak, a second Bill of Rights under which a new basis of security and prosperity can be established for all—regardless of station, race, or creed.

Roosevelt then listed what he saw as these basic rights, including workers, farmers, and businessmen in his vision. In what has been called "the most radical statement he ever uttered," Roosevelt called for every American to have a useful and remunerative job, a decent home, adequate medical care, protection in old age and times of unemployment, and a good education. All these rights, he said, provide security, and in a post-war world these rights would need to be established. Without them, he added, there could not be lasting peace in the world.[66]

In June, the long-awaited D-Day invasion of France began. Roosevelt had distributed a prayer through the newspapers so that when he announced D-Day, everyone could join in saying the prayer with him:

> My fellow Americans: Last night, when I spoke with you about the fall of Rome, I knew at that moment that troops of the United States and our allies were crossing the Channel in another and greater operation. It has come to pass with success thus far.
>
> And so, in this poignant hour, I ask you to join with me in prayer:
>
> Almighty God: Our sons, pride of our Nation, this day have set upon a mighty endeavor, a struggle to preserve our Republic, our religion, and our civilization, and to set free a suffering humanity.
>
> Lead them straight and true; give strength to their arms, stoutness to their hearts, steadfastness in their faith.

It was a long prayer, longer than those he would have heard in his local Episcopal Church, but it reflected the Elizabethan English of the Book of

---

* The phrase comes from Vernon v. Bethell (1762), an English property law case, where it was affirmed that there could be no clog on the equity of redemption. In justifying this rule, Lord Henley made the famous observation that "necessitous men are not, truly speaking, free men, but, to answer a present exigency, will submit to any terms that the crafty may impose upon them."

Common Prayer even though it did not include or end with a specifically Christian invocation.

> With Thy blessing, we shall prevail over the unholy forces of our enemy. Help us to conquer the apostles of greed and racial arrogancies. Lead us to the saving of our country, and with our sister Nations into a world unity that will spell a sure peace, a peace invulnerable to the schemings of unworthy men. And a peace that will let all men live in freedom, reaping the just rewards of their honest toil.
>
> Thy will be done, Almighty God. Amen.[67]

D-Day was on June 6. Roosevelt gave one last Fireside Chat six days later. The war was raging in Europe and the Pacific, and that had to be Roosevelt's first concern. But he could not ignore the fact that it was an election year and that he felt unable to step back and let someone else lead America to the impending victory. He accepted the party's nomination at the end of June in words very similar to those he had spoken four years earlier:

> I am sure that you will understand me when I say that my decision, expressed to you formally tonight, is based solely on a sense of obligation to serve if called upon to do so by the people of the United States.
>
> I shall not campaign, in the usual sense, for the office. In these days of tragic sorrow, I do not consider it fitting. And besides, in these days of global warfare, I shall not be able to find the time. I shall, however, feel free to report to the people the facts about matters of concern to them and especially to correct any misrepresentations.

He closed by quoting "the greatest wartime President in our history," Abraham Lincoln, who had set the goal for the United States, a goal in terms as applicable today as they were in 1865—terms which the human mind cannot improve:

> . . . with firmness in the right, as God gives us to see the right, let us strive on to finish the work we are in; to bind up the Nation's wounds; to care for him who shall have borne the battle, and for his widow, and his orphan—to do all which may achieve and cherish a just and lasting peace among ourselves, and with all Nations.[68]

Roosevelt had said he would correct any "misrepresentations," and one misrepresentation he corrected joyfully was a story being spread around that he had taken his dog with him on a trip to Alaska and, after leaving the dog behind by mistake, that he had sent a destroyer back to collect the dog—at enormous cost to the taxpayer. Roosevelt told a meeting of the Teamsters' Union that this was typical of the unfair attacks on himself and his family:

> These Republican leaders have not been content with attacks on me, or my wife, or on my sons. No, not content with that, they now include my little dog, Fala. Well, of course, I don't resent attacks, and my family doesn't resent attacks, but Fala does resent them. You know, Fala is Scotch, and being a Scottie, as soon as he learned that the Republican fiction writers in Congress and out had concocted a story that I had left him behind on the Aleutian Islands and had sent a destroyer back to find him—at a cost to the taxpayers of two or three, or eight or twenty million dollars—his Scotch soul was furious. He has not been the same dog since.[69]

The Republican Party had nominated one of Roosevelt's successors as governor of New York. Thomas E. Dewey had made his reputation as a district attorney attacking organized crime and corruption in New York City. He was only forty-two years old in 1944, but he had a marvelous speaking voice and supported much of what Roosevelt had done, both domestically and internationally, but accused the administration of being allied with corrupt big-city bosses and American communists.

Roosevelt carried thirty-six states; but Dewey, losing by three and a half million votes, still came closer than Hoover or Landon or Willkie had done and put himself in position to try again four years later.

Saying that it was inappropriate to have a celebratory inauguration with the nation at war, Roosevelt took the oath of office for the fourth time in a simple ceremony in January 1945 on the north portico of the White House. His speech was the second shortest inaugural address in history at fewer than six hundred words,* but Roosevelt still gave it his full attention. He gave his speechwriters two drafts: the first was a one-page typed summary of his thoughts, and the second was a three-page draft titled "Other Thoughts for Inaugural Speech." Working with Roosevelt's drafts, Archibald MacLeish prepared a draft, Rosenman prepared two drafts, and Sherwood wrote one. These drafts were brought together in a final address that went through three more drafts, a total of ten to reach the finished product. Sherwood said afterwards: "He worked it over with more care and interest than he had shown in the preparation of any speech in more than two years."[70] Roosevelt may have

* George Washington's second inaugural address at 134 words holds the record.

been thinking of the American failure to continue working with other nations at the end of the First World War and determined to do what he could to shape public opinion for a better result this time. "We have learned lessons," he said,

> at a fearful cost—and we shall profit by them.
>
> We have learned that we cannot live alone, at peace; that our own well-being is dependent on the well-being of other nations far away. . . .
>
> We have learned to be citizens of the world, members of the human community.

Acknowledging God's blessing, Roosevelt closed with a brief word of prayer "for the vision to see our way clearly—to see the way that leads to a better life for ourselves and for all our fellow men—to the achievement of His will to peace on earth."[71]

High on Roosevelt's agenda for the new year was one more meeting with Stalin to plan the final defeat of Germany, to draw Russia into the Pacific war, and to lay a foundation for the United Nations. It may have been his sense of adventure that drew him to Yalta, or the fact that his father had been there many years before, but his advisers were unanimously opposed to the site and Churchill said ten years of research could not have found a worse place. Yalta, in the Crimea, had been a favorite winter resort of the Tsars. It had been ravaged by the communist revolution, adopted by the commissars, looted by the Germans, and only partially rehabilitated since being reclaimed by the Soviets. But Stalin still would not leave Russia, and Yalta seemed to Roosevelt like the best available venue. In early February, he traveled to Malta by ship, flew on to the nearest airfield to Yalta, and then traveled the last eighty miles by car over narrow, winding mountain roads.

One subject of much debate was the occupation of Germany. The British wanted France included; Stalin thought that was unreasonable. Stalin wanted permanent dismemberment of Germany; Churchill and Roosevelt wanted to wait on that. Churchill and Stalin wondered how long America would participate in an occupation program; Roosevelt thought two years might be the maximum.

Poland was an intractable issue. There were two provisional governments, one in exile in London and one, Russian-sponsored, on the ground in Eastern Europe. Each was deeply opposed to the other. The Yalta communiqué spoke blithely of uniting the two factions and holding "free and unfettered elections" as soon as possible. But Russian troops occupied Poland, and a truly free election seemed unlikely.

A priority for the Americans was a commitment by the Soviet Union to join the war against Japan. Roosevelt did not expect a usable atomic bomb to be ready until the fall at least, and there was no way of knowing how effective it might be. Planning had to proceed on the basis of an invasion of the Japanese home islands at a cost of tens of thousands of American lives. A secret codicil to the Yalta agreements called for Russian involvement in the Pacific war within "two or three months" of German surrender. That, in the opinion of Roosevelt and the American generals, was worth all the rest.[72]

Concerns about the president's health had been growing, especially late in the previous year and among those he met with at Yalta. Churchill said that he appeared "very tired . . . placid and frail. I felt that he had a slender contact with life."[73] The long sea voyage home helped; but when he went to report to Congress, he did so from his wheelchair for the first time and began by apologizing for doing so.

Roosevelt's report to Congress was lengthy and dealt with both the specific issues and the general atmosphere of cooperation. He talked at length, with frequent ad-libs, about the need for a new international organization and the conference that would be held in San Francisco to create a specific structure. This time, unlike the time at the end of the First World War, the Congress would be fully represented by a bipartisan delegation. Toward the end, Roosevelt departed from his text to make a very personal appeal:

> The Conference in the Crimea was a turning point—I hope in our history and therefore in the history of the world. There will soon be presented to the Senate of the United States and to the American people a great decision that will determine the fate of the United States—and of the world—for generations to come.
>
> There can be no middle ground here. We shall have to take the responsibility for world collaboration, or we shall have to bear the responsibility for another world conflict. . . .
>
> For the second time in the lives of most of us this generation is face to face with the objective of preventing wars. To meet that objective, the Nations of the world will either have a plan or they will not. The groundwork of a plan has now been furnished, and has been submitted to humanity for discussion and decision. . . .
>
> No one can say exactly how long any plan will last. Peace can endure only so long as humanity really insists upon it, and is willing to work for it—and sacrifice for it.
>
> Twenty-five years ago, American fighting men looked to the statesmen of the world to finish the work of peace for which they fought and suffered. We failed them then. We cannot fail them again, and expect the world again to survive.

The departure from his text was probably not helpful, however heartfelt it may have been. Roosevelt's delivery was hesitant, and he seemed to lose his place in returning to the text when he went back to it. In the following days he continued to work hard and welcome important visitors such as the Canadian Prime Minister, Mackenzie King, and Princess Juliana of the Netherlands, but he tired more easily. There was added stress in the fact that Harry Hopkins, Roosevelt's primary foreign policy adviser, was dying of cancer, so reports that the Russians were breaking their Yalta commitments had to be dealt with by others less familiar with the history.[74]

By mid-March, it was obvious to all who saw him that he was not well. He was not eating much, was losing weight, and appeared gray and drawn. A visit to Warm Springs seemed the best tonic and, indeed, simply being there made him feel enough better to get behind the wheel of his car to drive himself to "the Little White House." His appetite improved and his color returned, at least in the morning. He worked on a speech for a Jefferson Day address to be delivered on April 13 and added, as he often did, his own peroration. After the last typed sentence, "The only limitation to our realization of tomorrow will be our doubts of today," he wrote "Let us move forward with strong and active faith."

The next day began, as usual, with the president sitting in a comfortable chair signing papers while an artist worked on a watercolor portrait. At about 1:15 that afternoon, he said "I have a terrific headache" and slumped over. The doctor arrived a few minutes later to find him unconscious and breathing heavily. With assistance from others, they got him into bed, but there was nothing that could be done. He died two hours later. Edward R. Murrow broadcast from London that Churchill had tears in his eyes as he said "One day the world and history will know what it owes to your President." Stalin sent a message that an autopsy should be done to determine whether he had been poisoned.[75]

As Lincoln had been carried back to Illinois in a funeral train in early April just eighty years earlier, so a funeral train carried Roosevelt's body back to Washington, slowing at stations for the mourners along the way. The funeral service was conducted by Bishop Angus Dun in the East Room of the White House. At Mrs. Roosevelt's request, he included the famous phrase "The only thing we have to fear is fear itself."[76]

EIGHT

Adlai E. Stevenson
1900–1965

A FREE SOCIETY IS A SOCIETY WHERE IT IS SAFE TO BE UNPOPULAR

I

The decade between 1950 and 1960 occupies an odd place in American mythology. The previous decade was a time of traditional heroics, when battles were fought and enemies were clearly defeated. The weapons were different, of course, from those of previous wars. The appearance of the atomic bomb at the end of the war transformed international relationships forever by creating a weapon that even moderately rational human beings could never use again. Yet, if ever the issues were clearly defined, they were in the war against Hitlerism. The decade after 1960 was, by contrast, a time of moral confusion and radical social upheaval. That decade began with a striking new voice calling the nation to self-sacrifice and a moral crusade, but ended with illusions shattered and old certainties increasingly questioned.

In contrast to those turbulent decades, the time between, the decade of the fifties, is often seen as a time of peace and security. General Dwight D. Eisenhower presided over the era as President Eisenhower with his famously winning smile and a slogan which said nothing of policies or principles but simply "I Like Ike." He could act decisively when necessary, as he did when he sent troops to Little Rock to enforce court-ordered segregation of the schools, but he delegated effectively and was seen as often on the golf course as in the Oval Office. The long-running television sitcom (1952–1966) *Ozzie and Harriet* seemed to define the era with its portrayal of a comfortably middle-class suburban family of four. We look back on the decade as a time when the country was at peace and values were secure.

In fact, the decade of the fifties was an era of almost constant tension and conflict. In 1954, the Supreme Court ruled in the case of *Brown v. Board of Education* (347 U.S. 483) that "separate educational facilities are inherently unequal." The ruling that *de jure* racial segregation was a violation of the Equal Protection Clause of the Fourteenth Amendment of the United States Constitution opened the door to a time of bitter contests not only in the South but in Northern school districts on Long Island and elsewhere, as Americans were finally compelled to deal with their racial divisions in a substantive way. The decade began with three years of war in Korea, included the brutal crushing of independence in Hungary by the armies of the Soviet Union, and ended with a deepening conflict in Vietnam. Between those major struggles, there was a constant testing of positions by East and West in Africa and Asia as well as Central America and Europe. Fear of atomic weapons led to measures involving ordinary Americans in a number of ways. Children were taught to take shelter under school desks in the event of an atomic attack, and the city of Madison, Wisconsin issued guides for evacuation. Fear, rather than security, may actually have been the dominant emotion of the era, and that fear was centered on the specter of communism both abroad and at home. Senator Joseph McCarthy epitomized that fear by accusing various government officials, named and unnamed, of being "card-carrying communists," and the House Un-American Activities Committee made similar headlines with its investigations.

The decade of the fifties was remarkable also for the lack of an eloquent voice in London or Washington to enunciate principles and goals. Roosevelt's commanding voice was gone from American politics, and Eisenhower was famous more for the garbled syntax of his news conferences (sometimes thought to be intentional obfuscation) than for any eloquent summons to greatness. Winston Churchill was serving a second term as Prime Minister in Great Britain in the first years of the decade but was crippled by a stroke and no longer able to bring his eloquence to bear in a leadership role.

The most eloquent voice of the era belonged to Adlai Stevenson of Illinois, whose campaigns for the presidency in 1952 and 1956 led to decisive defeats. Yet his eloquence inspired legions of thoughtful Americans and led directly to the idealism of John F. Kennedy's "New Frontier" (a term actually used in a Stevenson speech in his 1952 campaign) of 1960 with its Peace Corps volunteers, and Lyndon Johnson's "Great Society" with its attack on poverty and its espousal of civil rights legislation.

Americans in the twenty-first century are quite accustomed to campaigns for the presidency that begin almost before the ballots of the last election are counted. Candidates begin visiting Iowa and New Hampshire at least four years in advance of any actual voting, and whoever finally emerges from the ordeal as the nominee of a party has already become a familiar presence on television and in the "social media." It seems hardly possible from that perspective that the Democratic National Convention in 1952 should have chosen a man who had raised no campaign funds and contested no primaries, and that the Convention did so in relatively short order. It took only three ballots for the delegates to turn away from Tennessee Senator Estes Kefauver, who had won twelve out of fifteen primaries, and choose instead the little-known Governor of Illinois, Adlai Stevenson.

Stevenson dramatically summed up the challenge of those years in one of his most memorable campaign speeches, what he called a "Fireside Speech," on September 19, 1952.

> Today there is less communication among great groups of men than there was in the roadless world of a thousand years ago. We can no more communicate with half of mankind than we can raise the dead. The while the anti-Christ stalks our world. Organized communism seeks even to dethrone God from his central place in the Universe. It attempts to uproot everywhere it goes the gentle and restraining influences of the religion of love and peace. One by one the lamps of civilization go out* and nameless horrors are perpetrated in darkness. All this is done by an enemy of a kind that we have never faced before. He is primitive but he is also advanced. He goes with a piece of black bread in his hand,** but in his mind he carries the awful knowledge of atomic energy. He is careful, cool, calculating, and he counts time, not impatiently as we do, not by the clock, but by decades, in terms of centuries. Much of what he is trying to do today his ancestors were attempting to do four

* The reference is to a remark attributed to British Foreign Secretary Sir Edward Grey, on the eve of the First World War in 1914: "The lamps are going out all over Europe; we shall not see them lit again in our life-time."

** White bread with all the natural vitamins and minerals removed (often replaced by chemical "enrichment") was the standard in mid-century America.

> hundred years ago.* . . . Long ago, we asserted a great principle on this continent: that men are, and of right ought to be, free. Now we are called upon to defend that right against the mightiest forces of evil ever assembled under the sun.

Looking back, the speech may seem overly dramatic, and there is much to criticize in it, from the notion that there were no roads a thousand years ago when in fact there were many, to the easy assumption that the United States is a defender of Christian values; but it seems to sum up the fearfulness of the times and the sense of being involved in a struggle that might go on for decades (as it did) or for centuries. Most important, however, is the reference to the Declaration of Independence, which Stevenson cites as a seminal document in a worldwide contest between freedom and tyranny. The elegance of his language and his insistence on fundamental principles of human dignity and freedom were central to the way in which Stevenson became so influential a voice for his time.

II

Probably no childhood story clearly foreshadows future eloquence, but the childhood and youth of Adlai Stevenson seem especially unmarked by indications of a future leader. From all accounts, Adlai Stevenson had the most ordinary sort of childhood available to a child in the upper social levels of a small midwestern city. One biographer says "he seemed born to American politics,"[1] and it is true that his grandfather, Adlai E. Stevenson I, had been Vice President of the United States; but that was before Adlai E. Stevenson II was born, and that grandfather died when the young Adlai was fourteen. More influential was his other grandfather, William O. Davis, the publisher of Bloomington, Illinois's influential newspaper, the *Daily Pantagraph*. Stevenson's parents, Lewis Stevenson and Helen Davis, grew up in the comfortable surroundings of their own parents' achievements and seem not to have felt a need to accomplish anything in particular themselves. Lewis did a number of things, some of them quite well, but never really settled into a career. He did serve one term as Secretary of State in Illinois but lost a bitter campaign for reelection and moved on to other things such as an attempt, ultimately unsuccessful, to get American rights to German technology for lighter-than-air aircraft.[2]

---

* This must have puzzled Stevenson's listeners—and the reference is still unclear. The Council of Trent would have been meeting in those years in an attempt to reform the Roman Catholic Church so as to enable it to deal more effectively with the Protestant Reformation. Did Stevenson mean to equate either side in that struggle with the dangers of communism?

Lewis and Helen spent summers in a posh resort in northern Michigan and often went to Florida for the winter. They spent so much time in Europe when Adlai was eleven that he was enrolled in a school in Switzerland. His parents fought frequently, but they loved Adlai and did their best to provide him with financial security and a good education.[3]

The definition of a "good education" had more to do with the quality of the school than with Adlai's achievements. When he did spend time in the Bloomington school system, he was a distinctly mediocre student, getting his best marks in deportment. His parents were determined that he should go to Princeton; but when he applied for admission at the age of sixteen, he was turned down. To remedy his failure, his parents sent him to Choate, a good boarding school in Connecticut; but when he applied to Princeton again at the end of a year, he was again turned down. Two years at Choate finally improved his performance enough to get him admitted to Princeton in the fall of 1918. Woodrow Wilson had attempted to reshape Princeton in the mold of an Oxford college ten years earlier, but John Kenneth Galbraith taught there before World War II and found the students "deeply anti-intellectual" and giving priority to coming from "a reasonably acceptable preparatory school [and] a substantial family . . . with a commitment to sound personal hygiene."[4] Stevenson found his role at Princeton in writing for the school newspaper, *The Daily Princetonian*. He never learned to spell, but he did like to write. There were thirty-seven candidates for two positions on the editorial board, and they were expected to write an article a day. By the end of his freshman year he had won one of those two places, and by his senior year he was managing editor.[5] That was certainly an accomplishment, but managing editor was the second most important position. He joined the second best social club and graduated squarely in the middle of his class academically.

Like Theodore and Franklin Roosevelt and many other future politicians, Stevenson went on to law school; but Harvard, unlike Princeton, was hard work. He had no particular interest in the law and flunked out after two years.[6] He went back to Bloomington to take on the role of managing editor of the family newspaper, the *Daily Pantagraph*. His grandfather had left the paper to his three children and grandchildren in a will that lacked enough precision to prevent family quarrels and, eventually, legal proceedings. While the courts debated the issues, Stevenson enjoyed himself writing reports of everything from a tornado to the Scopes trial. The tornado elicited dramatic prose about "a moment's elemental wrath" and the suffering of the victims, while the Scopes trial led him to write about the nature of free speech and a free press. The unpleasantness of the legal proceedings, however, made it difficult to work with the cousin who was business manager of the paper. So, after two years of newspaper work, Stevenson decided to leave the tensions behind, finish his law degree at Northwestern University, and accept a position with a leading Chicago law firm.

Before settling into his new career, Stevenson took one last trip to Europe as "foreign correspondent" for the *Chicago Herald-American*, which introduced him to an Italy transformed by Mussolini and a Russia transformed by Lenin. The same tactics were on display in both nations, and Stevenson was repelled by what he saw. Of the Italian experiment, he wrote: "One wonders how much freedom you can take away before you begin to tyrannize." Years later he told a friend that in Russia, "I never knew whether or not I was being followed, but I did know that people were afraid to be seen talking to me. . . . I felt that I had seen at first hand what Communism really meant, in terms of terror and brutality."[7]

Back home in Chicago in the autumn of 1926, Stevenson settled in to his new career "without the least eagerness," but he married well (in social terms), joined all the right clubs, and kept himself on the fringes of political life without quite getting in. He turned down a chance to run for the state legislature, sat in the gallery when the Democratic convention came to Chicago to nominate Franklin Delano Roosevelt for president in 1932, and served as Roosevelt's campaign treasurer for the western United States. He and Ellen went to Washington for the inauguration, and before the year was out he found himself co-opted for a position as special assistant to the general counsel of the newly established Agricultural Adjustment Administration. If he wanted experience in government, helping create guidelines for a new agency was an ideal way to gain it. He finished his first day's work at two A.M. the next day. Infighting among the bureaucrats was intense, and within six months Stevenson moved to the Federal Alcohol Control Administration, also a new agency dealing with new problems. His salary went from $5,000 to $7,500, but he gave it only six months before going back to his law firm in the fall of 1934 with a wealth of experience in Washington ways.[8]

Stevenson had already become involved in the Chicago Council on Foreign Relations, a beacon of internationalism in the center of midwestern isolationism. Over the next few years, it would provide him with something to do more interesting and challenging than settling wills and estates. Shortly after returning from Washington, he was elected to a two-year term as Council president. Anyone who was anyone, normally six or seven hundred people, went to the Council luncheons as religiously as they went to the Chicago Symphony. The middle years of the decade were a time of growing international tensions and, as Stevenson put it, "the Council thrives on trouble." Speakers included such luminaries as radio correspondent Edward R. Murrow, philosopher Bertrand Russell, and the former president of Czechoslovakia, Edvard Beneš.

The Council gave Stevenson a broad exposure to foreign affairs and gave the visiting speakers some exposure to Stevenson, whose introductions were carefully thought out, graceful, witty, and substantive. He introduced an author speaking on the civil war in Spain by recommending that people who were on the fence should read her book "if there is a fence or anyone still on it." In introducing Edward R. Murrow, he suggested that there had been two triumphs at Munich, that of Adolph Hitler and that of the Columbia Broadcasting System. Recalling how Murrow had brought the voices of the principal actors to America, he went on to ponder the role of radio in the new age of rapid communications:

> [M]ore important than these spectacular demonstrations of the reportorial possibilities of radio are the implications in radio propaganda, the weapon of the twentieth century that knows no frontiers, no obstacles in time, space, and expense; which has been used with such telling effect already and is destined to play such a significant part in the world of tomorrow.[9]

To think about foreign affairs, of course, involves thinking about domestic affairs, since we instinctively measure one by the other. A judgment on events in Italy is most easily made by contrasting Italian tyranny with American freedom. When Stevenson spoke about the prospects for democracy abroad at the Bloomington Unitarian Church in 1939, he provided his definition of democracy in America. "What we really *want*," he said, "is individual freedom; what we *talk* about is democracy." Democracy, he admitted, is often frustrating with its competition among various interest groups, slowness to respond, narrow defeats for good causes, and failure to choose the best candidates. His suggestions for improvement centered on better education for citizens and a commitment to moral values, patience, and industry. His concern centered on honest government and individual liberty more than systemic reform.[10]

The great advantage of the role Stevenson played in those years was that he could acquire broad exposure to foreign affairs and significant individuals while remaining above the fray. That all changed when Hitler unleashed his juggernaut on the western democracies, overwhelming the French and leaving Britain standing alone. It was, after all, only twenty years since America had come to the aid of the British and French in World War I. The Senate had rejected Woodrow Wilson's proposed League of Nations in favor of non-alignment, but many Americans thought that had been a wrong choice and believed that their judgment was vindicated by the course of European events.

With war looming again, Roosevelt moved quickly to build nonpartisan support for Great Britain by appointing Republicans Henry Stimson and Frank

Knox to serve as Secretaries of War and Navy, but Americans began to choose up sides nonetheless. America First, representing isolationist sentiment, was organized in Chicago with Robert E. Wood, the chairman of the Sears Roebuck Company, as its chairman, Robert McCormick of the Chicago *Tribune* as its loudest voice, and Charles Lindbergh, Henry Ford, and Norman Thomas among its best known members and advocates. To advance an internationalist viewpoint, William Allen White, the nationally known Kansan editor of the *Emporia Gazette*, organized a Non-Partisan Committee for Peace through Revision of the Neutrality Law. That committee became known as the White Committee, and Stevenson led a group that organized a Chicago chapter.[11]

Now Stevenson was no longer able to stand apart from a bitter and divisive struggle. When he debated the issues with a personal friend, Clay Judson, before the League of Women Voters and then the Chicago Bar Association, most of his audience, many of them personal friends, was on the other side. When he wrote to the *Tribune*, they printed his letter under the title "America Second." The debate became increasingly vicious as the White Committee was called a front for Jews, a "mass murder committee," warmongers, and professional bleeding hearts. Friends said he was trying to kill their sons. Stevenson retaliated by calling the isolationists "appeasers" and "defeatists," but he saw no moral or practical alternative to the internationalist position.[12] Paraphrasing Abraham Lincoln, he told his audiences that he did not believe "a world that has obliterated time and space can exist half slave and half free."[13] Biographer John Bartlow Martin wrote: "Adlai Stevenson now suddenly stood at the heart of a great and searing national issue, and he focused all his energies on it. He had found his issue, and found himself."[14]

Riding home one day on the commuter train, Stevenson read a letter that said there was no longer a halfway position: one was either an isolationist or an interventionist. Stevenson had begun to believe that already; and Frank Knox, who had known Stevenson when he was publisher and co-owner of the *Chicago Daily News*, had been urging him to come to serve in the Navy Department with him. Finally, therefore, in July 1940, Stevenson moved back to Washington as Principal Attorney in the Office of the Secretary of the Navy. George Ball, who held important positions in the Kennedy and Johnson administrations, wrote later that Stevenson "became a one-man recruiting office for the United States government . . . helping even casual acquaintances find appropriate assignments in the public service . . . from his deeply held conviction that the government needed and deserved the best talents the nation could produce."[15]

With the outbreak of war, Stevenson's role in coordinating the work of the Navy Department with other offices became critically important. He began writing speeches for Knox and delivering speeches of his own that won high praise. He represented the Navy on a committee on war information that included representatives of the White House and departments of State, Justice, Army, and Navy and made major contributions to the coordination of information policies. Writers like Walter Lippmann and Arthur Krock turned to him for information on Navy policy and war strategy. Although civil rights was never an area that Stevenson cared about deeply, he told Knox that the Navy needed to have Negro officers and suggested a plan to recruit them, which Knox duly implemented.[16] In late 1943, the Foreign Economic Administration needed information on the chaotic situation in Italy and asked for the loan of Stevenson to go to Italy and bring back a report in six weeks. That journey gave Stevenson a firsthand look at the battlefront and the task of rebuilding a shattered economy. The 122-page report helped pave the way for the Marshall Plan and has been cited as "a model that was studied in connection with reconstruction and foreign aid for many nations."[17]

Stevenson's varied experience in wartime Washington and visiting battlefronts in Europe, Africa, and Asia made a lasting impact. To a group of Chicago lawyers, he said:

> I've travelled during this war in the Pacific, the Caribbean, South America, West Africa and the Mediterranean, and . . . no one has enough food, enough clothing, enough anything, except in the United States of America. And now all these people—black, brown, yellow, white—have seen our forces move thru; have seen our healthy boys, their clothes, their food, and their equipment. It makes you wonder about tomorrow. Are they envious; is more and worse trouble in the making, or is there a great opportunity to improve their lot and ours at the same time? The demand is there; is the wisdom here?[18]

To a friend, he said:

> While I was in Italy I saw a public-opinion poll in which seven out of ten Americans said they didn't want their boys to enter public life. Think of it! Boys could die in battle, but parents didn't want their children to give their living efforts toward a better America and a better world. I decided then that if I ever had a chance I'd go into public life.[19]

Knox died of a heart attack in April 1944 and was replaced by James Forrestal. Forrestal and Stevenson had none of the chemistry that had enabled him to work so well with Knox; and although he was offered various other positions, he decided the time had come to go back to Illinois.[20] He had told a Chicago audience a year earlier that "The problems of war are dwarfed by the problems of peace."[21] There were opportunities in Illinois for him to play a part in solving those problems.

III

Stevenson was ready for Illinois, but Illinois was not yet ready for him. He had been away too long; and when he had been in Illinois, he had built his support primarily among independents. Illinois politics, however, were largely controlled by a well-established machine that favored loyal partisans. Washington, on the other hand, kept calling. There were jobs available: Assistant Secretary of State, Assistant Attorney General, positions on the Securities and Exchange Commission or the Federal Communications Commission, for example. All these he declined, but he did at last accept an offer to work with Archibald MacLeish, the poet and Librarian of Congress, who wanted help with a public information program about the development of plans for the United Nations.

The initial organizing conference for the United Nations, with 285 delegates from fifty nations and some 2,600 reporters, was held in San Francisco in April, May, and June of 1945. At the request of journalists James Reston and Arthur Krock, Stevenson was brought in to be their "official leaker" of information. That in turn led to his appointment as minister to the September meeting in London of a preparatory commission for the first General Assembly meeting the following year. When Edward Stettinius, American Ambassador to the UN, was felled by a gallstone attack, Stevenson wound up presiding over Executive Committee meetings as decisions were made about the division of authority within the organization. Most of those he dealt with, such as Andrei Gromyko of Russia, Jan Masaryk of Czechoslovakia, and Wellington Koo of China, held the rank of Ambassador or higher. A reporter during the 1952 campaign remarked that Stevenson was the only American he knew who was on a first-name basis with the dour Gromyko.[22] Stevenson called it an "ordeal" but said that he "enjoyed it immensely."

He stayed on as chief of the American delegation when the Preparatory Committee met again in November to make further critical decisions. A Chicago reporter wrote that while others took the spotlight, it was Stevenson who did most of the legwork and a large part of the brainwork. "Time and again he broke impasses between the powers when agreement seemed impossible." When the first General Assembly meeting was held in January 1946, Stettinius was back, but Stevenson stayed on as "senior adviser" to the U.S. delegation.[23] He had hoped to be a delegate, and those he had worked with were surprised when he was not, but those positions went to senior senators and people like

Eleanor Roosevelt who had more influence and name recognition than he.[24] At the end of that session, he was offered the post of Ambassador to Argentina but went home to Illinois instead.[25]

Back in Illinois, he resumed his involvement with the Council on Foreign Relations and spoke frequently about his experience in the creation of the United Nations and his vision of the future. He saw South America and the colonial areas of Africa and Asia as "the battleground in the new Thirty Years' War of ideas." "Food is a better weapon than cannons," he said; "there is room for us all, but in the new era that dawned over Hiroshima we will have to wage peace with all the zeal and urgency of war, all of us."[26]

The next two years were a scattered mix of work for his law firm, attempts to buy the *Chicago News*, more work at the United Nations in New York, and speeches on foreign affairs. He was given honorary degrees by two Illinois colleges and told the students at Illinois Wesleyan in his hometown of Bloomington:

> The United Nations is only a spade; it won't work by itself. . . . The weeds that smothered the League of Nations will smother it if the garden is neglected. You are the gardeners. We are all the gardeners, we who know that science has outdistanced philosophy, that there will be no victors in another war, that jealousy, suspicion and intolerance are at last armed with weapons which in one burst of universal fury can fulfill Kant's grim prophecy that "the world will be the graveyard of the human race." This is a time for thinking, for discipline self-imposed by free men, for vision, for purpose, for example. It's a threshold, a threshold to something very bright or very dark. It's morning. It's exciting. It's a good time to be alive, and awake.

Later that spring, he took part in a radio debate with Governor Kim Sigler of Michigan on the question: "Should the Communist Party be banned in America?" Stevenson was opposed to the idea:

> In the first place, you would drive the Communist Party underground, and surely everyone knows it is best to keep your adversary where you can see him. In the second pace, it would be a confession of weakness. Democracy is strong; let's act that way. . . . And thirdly, suppression is a dangerous precedent. If in a moment of nervous anxiety we outlaw a political party to protect democracy, who knows what liberties may be sacrificed to the same end and then where is our freedom, our democracy? Let us not adopt

> Fascism to defeat Communism. . . . But even more important than these common-sense reasons for opposing the legislation are some fundamental principles. This is the land of the free.[27]

Clearly he had found the voice that would thrill so many Americans when they began to hear it a few years later. Meanwhile, however, he found himself out of the mainstream of events and unclear as to a focus for his energies. On February 5, 1947, he wrote in his diary:

> Am 47 today still restless; dissatisfied with myself. What's the matter? Have everything. Wife, children, money, success, but not in law profession. Too much ambition for public recognition; too scattered in interests; how can I reconcile life in Chicago as lawyer with consuming interest in foreign affairs and desire for recognition and position in that field. Prospect of Senate nomination sustains, & sometimes troubles, even frightens me. Wish I could at least get tranquil & make Ellen happy and do go[od] humble job at law.[28]

IV

1946 was a bad year for Democrats. Truman had not yet gained his footing, and Americans had trouble seeing him as a leader after twelve years of Roosevelt. Republicans swept to power in both houses of Congress in the elections that year and began to push back against the legislation of the New Deal. Democrats, of course, were unwilling to accept the need for a change after their long years of power, and began to organize in new ways to reclaim their position. On a national level, liberals organized Americans for Democratic Action, and in Illinois they organized Independent Voters of Illinois. Those organizing were, to some extent, young leadership coming back from the war and determined to replace the old guard.

In Illinois, there was an "old guard" that was already prepared for change. Jake Arvey, the Democratic leader of Chicago's Cook County, was, on the one hand, "the very incarnation of the big city boss" and, on the other, a shrewd, principled leader who had returned from the war determined to find good candidates who could win elections. Working on the theory that good candidates might draw more votes than bad candidates, Arvey forced out the inept mayor of Chicago and won with a reform-minded candidate. Seeing that his formula worked, Arvey decided to back University of Chicago professor Paul H. Douglas for the Senate. Friends of Stevenson meanwhile were supporting him as a candidate for the Senate, but the incumbent Republican Senator was a war hero and Arvey wanted Douglas, also a veteran, to run for the Senate. Arvey wanted a candidate for governor in the same liberal mold as Douglas and, on a trip to Washington, Secretary of State James F. Byrnes told him he had a gold nugget available in Stevenson. Arvey went back to Chicago, arranged a meeting with Stevenson, and was suitably impressed. The result was that Stevenson was nominated for governor and reluctantly accepted nomination to that position rather than for the Senate.

Ten days later, Arvey and Stevenson went to Springfield on the train to meet the Democratic State Central Committee, and Stevenson was told he would need to make a statement. Withdrawing to the club car, he wrote what he proposed to say on the back of telegram forms and showed it to Arvey. "Don't change a word," Arvey told him. He had been looking for a different kind of candidate, and now he knew he had what he wanted. Stevenson had written:

> I want to win because I believe that we must and we can give this state better, wiser, thriftier government. I believe with all my heart and mind that as citizens of the Republic, not as Democrats, but as citizens of the richest, strongest, healthiest Republic on earth, we must restore popular esteem and confidence in the democratic system at all levels, municipal, state, and national. . . .
>
> I believe that the people are wise and just; they are very tolerant, very forgiving. But once aroused by prolonged abuse they are merciless to their betrayers. It will not be enough to arouse them, it will not be enough to win the election. You have to deserve, you have to win the people's confidence, not once, but constantly. . . . We will keep the people's confidence not by our words but by our works.

"We can go with him," one of the committee members told Arvey; "he's got class."[29] But neither the committee nor Arvey believed they had a chance to win. Odds-makers offered ten to one against Stevenson. Arvey tried desperately to get Eisenhower to run for president as a Democrat to strengthen the ticket; but when Eisenhower finally rejected the Democratic Party, Arvey accepted the candidates he had rather than those he wanted and gave his support to what he assumed was a losing Truman-Barkley-Stevenson ticket. As the campaign went on, more and more evidence of corruption in the governor's office came to light, and Stevenson proved to be an excellent campaigner. One campaign aide reported:

> The man has the strongest self-control, both mentally and physically, that I have ever witnessed. In my car he would sit by the hour with a fat brief case propped up on his lap, while he would draft his next speech, or a few press releases. . . . He never missed

> a chance to acquire more facts and he was always exploring possible information by asking questions of everyone who was near him.[30]

Newsweek reported: "The friendly, earnest candidate visited almost every lunch wagon and curbstone . . . making as many as a dozen speeches in a single night."[31] The *New York Times* said that "Political observers with the caravan report that Mr. Stevenson's chatty, persuasive style of delivery and his infectious grin have introduced a 'new look' in Illinois campaigning that is winning audiences."[32] He became an early advocate of equal pay for women for equal work, and he supported a Fair Employment Practices Commission, a constitutional convention to revise the state constitution, a long-range road-building program, and a drastic overhaul of the state's welfare system and mental hospitals.[33]

From a motel room, Stevenson wrote a friend about his experience:

> It's been an amazing experience, and I've come to wonder how anyone can presume to talk about "America" until he's done some political campaigning. Perhaps it's the secret, perhaps the curse, of American political success, the illusive [*sic*] business of finding your way to the heart of the average man, when there is no such thing, and when, unhappily, the human heart is often an organ encased in a pocket book, and not a text book, let alone a Bible. I've seen Illinois in a capsule, the beauty of the south, the fruit belt, the coal fields, the oil fields, the great industrial area around East St. Louis, and everywhere the rich, black, fecund earth stretching away and away. It gives you a great feeling of pride and power. Shut your eyes a moment and let the fetid, hot places, the scorched islands, the arid, the cold, the small, all the places of the world where men struggle to live and love and breed, dance through your head. Then open your eyes and look at Illinois, and murmur "thrice-blessed land." Exult in the power, majesty, wealth, might of it, and then come back to life with a start when a political pal with a cigar says, "Pardon me, Governor, but. . . ."[34]

How many writers, even professional writers, could produce such a paragraph at the end of a tiring day?

The opposition consistently portrayed Stevenson as a "striped pants diplomat" on the theory that no right-thinking citizen would vote for a diplomat, especially anyone in striped pants! Stevenson finally began telling audiences that he didn't actually own a pair of striped pants. But the strongest charge the incumbent, Governor Dwight H. Green, could make was that Stevenson had been mostly out of Illinois for twelve years and was a supporter of the United Nations. Green, on the other hand, was attacked by the St. Louis *Post-Dispatch* for "commercialized gambling and its attendant gangsterism and graft." Stevenson himself spoke of "gangsters and hoodlums with back-door keys to the State House" and "new revelations of kickbacks and shakedowns." He spoke in Bloomington of the values he had grown up with: "that good government and good citizenship are one and the same . . . that what was wrong between private citizens is doubly immoral between public officials and private citizen . . . that good government is good politics."[35]

When the votes were counted, Stevenson became only the fourth Democrat to be elected Governor of Illinois since the Civil War and gained the largest plurality—with 57% of the vote and a margin of 572,067—in the history of the state. The size of Stevenson's victory carried Harry Truman to victory in Illinois by an eyelash (33,612) and helped Truman gain an equally unexpected victory over Thomas E. Dewey.

In his inaugural address, Stevenson called for the measures he had been advocating during the campaign. He wanted a more active government, but not necessarily a larger one. He wanted to put more power in the hands of independent agencies, "to *enlarge* freedom, and avoid the creeping paralysis of bureaucratic control of the details of economic life." A year later, he spoke of the danger of "the heavy hand" of "a monster state" and told a Jackson Day Dinner that the only thing worse than neglect and too little government is "paternalism and too much government." His efforts to reduce the cost of government were legendary. He complained about the high cost of brochures printed by state agencies and turned off extra lights in the governor's mansion. Such frugality, along with a thriving economy and a surplus inherited from his predecessor, enabled Stevenson to increase state aid to schools, raise the salaries of government workers, and increase spending on highway construction.[36]

Other aspects of Stevenson's ambitious agenda fared less well. Too many vested interests opposed amending the state constitution, and Stevenson may not have been sufficiently committed to civil rights legislation. He did order desegregation of the National Guard, and he banned discrimination by food vendors in state parks. When a mob attacked a black family who attempted to move into the white suburb of Cicero, Stevenson ordered in the National Guard and won praise from black leaders for his handling of the situation. But Stevenson was capable of telling racist jokes and never really understood the issue. He worked hard at the tasks he had set, but he had never before headed a business or governmental organization at any level, and most of his experience was in foreign affairs. He looked forward to a second term in which he would be able to work on issues with more experience behind him.[37]

That, of course, never happened. Only a few months after his inauguration, Stevenson flew to Washington to meet with President Truman. The announced purpose was to discuss taxes and the legislative session in Illinois, and economic and international affairs in general. But why would a newly inaugurated president have wanted to have a general discussion with a newly installed governor unless he were thinking abut the future? Stevenson's unexpected and landslide victory had gotten attention, and Truman continued to ask Illinois visitors: "How is your governor doing?"[38] Here and there a columnist or two, looking ahead to 1952, suggested that Stevenson's was a name to bear in mind.[39]

In the fall of 1949, Stevenson went to New York to take part in the laying of the cornerstone of the United Nations building and to speak at a *Herald Tribune* forum. It was his first public speech to a national audience, and he was nervous about it. He wrote it out first in longhand and then had it typed and then retyped. The final copy was heavily marked up; Stevenson consistently worked over his speeches up to the last moment. He had been asked to speak about "What Kind of Democrat I Am," but he began by saying he didn't think people were much interested in party labels. "I think government should be as small in scope and as local in character as possible," he said. But he wanted, inevitably, to speak from an international viewpoint:

> I'm an internationalist. . . . I think that peace is the most important unfinished business of our generation; that we are going to be in this brutal cold war for a long time to come. . . . I don't like any interference with free markets, free men, and free enterprise. I like freedom to succeed, or to fail. But I also know that there can be no real freedom without economic justice, social justice, equality of opportunity and a fair chance for every individual to make the most of himself. And I know there is little the man on the assembly line or the plow can do to affect the chain of events which may close his factory or foreclose his mortgage.[40]

In December, he was in Washington for dinners and meetings and made a long and thoughtful speech on state and federal relationships at a dinner for the Hoover Commission on government organization.[41] In 1950, he sent the state police on raids of some three hundred gambling houses. He said that there had been

> a breakdown of local law enforcement, the breakdown of decency in government in many parts of the state, the triumph of greed, corruption and, perhaps worst of all, cynicism. In ordering these

> raids I did not feel like the joyful exhilaration of a knight in shining armor tilting with the forces of darkness. I felt more like a mourner at a wake. For something had died in Illinois, at least temporarily. And what has happened in Illinois is by no means unique.[42]

Newscaster Eric Sevareid did a special report about Stevenson and said "He is that rare creature, a reformer who was elected with the support of the hard-bitten political machine. . . . And therefore his position today is a rare one, exposed, dangerous, and exhaustingly difficult. But his ultimate record will be of consequence not only to this hitherto graft-ridden state, but perhaps to other Midwest states struggling to clean their political stables. Every governor in the land, like every crook in Illinois, is watching Stevenson."[43]

One of the most remarkable scenes they witnessed was Stevenson's veto of a bill that would make it a felony to belong to any subversive group and would require a loyalty oath of all public employees and candidates for office. In a day when politicians competed to see who was most strongly anti-communist, Stevenson refused to go along. No one, he said, disagreed about the evil of communism, but the proposed bill seemed designed to do more harm that good. It required someone wanting to teach school to prove that she or he was not a communist. Local prosecutors were required to present to grand juries all information obtained, including, presumably, unsubstantiated allegations. "I can see nothing but great peril," Stevenson said, "to the reputations of innocent people. I know full well," he concluded,

> that this veto will be distorted and misunderstood. . . . But I must in good conscience protest against any unnecessary suppression of our ancient rights as free men. Moreover, we will win the contest of ideas that afflicts the world not by suppressing these rights but by their triumph. We must not burn down the house to kill the rats.[44]

V

Truman and others also were watching Stevenson, especially after the New Hampshire primaries in 1952. Truman had kept silent about his intentions and had not campaigned in New Hampshire. An incumbent president traditionally didn't need to campaign in New Hampshire, because no one would be foolish enough to challenge him. In 1952, however, Senator Estes Kefauver of Tennessee did campaign in New Hampshire and won. He won most of the primaries that year, because there was really no competition; other candidates were too old, too awkward, or too regional in their base of support. Kefauver had made his reputation in televised investigations into organized crime, and there was broad support for his campaign. Party leaders, however, were nervous about Kefauver because his investigations had uncovered links between organized crime and big-city political machines.

President Truman had already decided privately not to run again; after the New Hampshire primary in February 1952, he announced that intention publicly. He had already met secretly with Stevenson in January to urge Stevenson to run for the nomination. Stevenson said "no" to Truman but left the door open. When the convention met that summer, "draft Stevenson" committees had done what they could. Stevenson had not stood in their way, but he had continued to say "no" in public.

The Democratic Convention of 1952 met in Chicago, and Stevenson as host governor welcomed the delegates to Illinois. Now he was truly on a national stage, and the delegates were exposed to a kind of rhetoric they had not heard before: clear, confident, commanding, reminding them of the tradition they represented and its place in the American drama. One biographer calls it "the best speech he ever made."[45] It was only fourteen minutes long and was interrupted twenty-seven times by applause and shouts of "We want Stevenson." He welcomed them to Illinois and told the delegates what freedom meant in the Midwest:

> Here on the prairies of Illinois and the Middle West, we can see a long way in all directions. We look to east, to west, to north and south. Our commerce, our ideas, come and go in all directions. Here there are no barriers, no defenses, to ideas and aspirations. We want none, we want no shackles on the mind or the spirit, no rigid patterns of thought, no iron conformity. We want only the faith and conviction that triumph in free and fair contest.

He told them about the history of the party in Illinois, how they had elected only three Democrats as governor before him since the Civil War, but one was Roman Catholic, one was Protestant, and one was Jewish. "That, my friends, is the American story," he told them, "written by the Democratic Party, here on the prairies of Illinois in the heartland of the nation."

He ridiculed the Republican Party, at whose convention, he said, "For almost a week pompous phrases marched over this landscape in search of an idea." Conversely, "the millions of mankind . . . see in us . . . an understanding of a world in the torment of a transition from an age that has died to an age struggling to be born." "This is not the time," he continued,

> for superficial solutions and endless elocution, for frantic boast and foolish word. For words are not deeds and there are no cheap and painless solutions to war, hunger, ignorance, fear, and to the new

> imperialism of Soviet Russia. Intemperate criticism is not a policy for the nation; denunciation is not a program for our salvation. Words calculated to catch everyone may catch no one. . . .

If Stevenson was critical of Republicans, he was critical of his own party as well:

> Where we have erred, let there be no denial; where we have wronged the public trust, let there be no excuses. Self-criticism is the secret weapon of democracy, and candor and confession are good for the political soul. But we will never appease, nor will we apologize for our leadership in the great events of this critical century from Woodrow Wilson to Harry Truman! Rather will we glory in these imperishable pages of our country's chronicle.

What the delegates heard was exactly what he told them they needed: "not bombast, abuse, and double talk, but a sober message of firm faith and confidence." He called on them to make their decisions that way: by "earnest thought and prayerful deliberation."[46] It was, on balance, a rather more serious address than might have been expected, but the delegates loved it and launched a spontaneous demonstration. On the platform, Jake Arvey turned to a neighbor and said: "No one will believe me when I tell them this is all spontaneous. He asked me not to have anything like this and I kept my word."[47]

They knew they did not want the candidates they were offered, but what about this man who seemed to embody their highest estimation of who they were or wanted to be? Stevenson's welcoming speech was given on Monday afternoon; balloting did not begin until Friday, but the delegates had not forgotten the impression Stevenson had made. He was a close second even on the first ballot; midway through the third ballot, Kefauver came forward to withdraw. As one campaign aide put it, "Never had such a reluctant candidate been chosen by a convention that no one controlled."[48]

The third ballot was taken Friday evening and lasted until well after midnight. It was two A.M. on Saturday before President Truman came to the podium with Adlai Stevenson and Stevenson began his acceptance speech. For all his unwillingness to be a candidate, he had never found himself able to issue the traditional "Sherman statement": "If nominated, I will not run; if elected, I will not serve." Whether at Stevenson's initiative or his own, an aide, Carl McGowan, had been working on an acceptance speech since earlier in the week. Drawing on things Stevenson had said before and knowing how Stevenson thought, he had drafted a statement, and Stevenson had been working it over. By the time he knew he would need it, McGowan said it had become substantially Stevenson's speech, more so than most of the speeches he made later in the campaign. It was only slightly longer than the speech he had made to welcome the delegates at the beginning of the week, but it took longer to deliver because the interruptions of applause were longer and louder. He began with a self-effacing modesty that was very much in character:

> Mr. President, ladies and gentlemen of the convention, my fellow citizens:
>
> I accept your nomination and your program. I should have preferred to hear those words uttered by a stronger, a wiser, a better man than myself. But after listening to the President's speech, I even feel better about myself. None of you, my friends, can wholly appreciate what is in my heart. I can only hope that you understand my words. They will be few.

Oddly, for a man who seldom went to church, he began and ended with Biblical quotations. They were his additions; McGowan disliked them and wished he had eliminated the first one especially.

> I have asked the Merciful Father—the Father of us all—to let this cup pass from me, but from such dread responsibility one does not shrink in fear, in self-interest, or in false humility. So, "If this cup may not pass from me except I drink it, Thy will be done."

He spent a good part of the speech in generalities about the glorious history of the Democratic Party and the divisions evident in the Republican Party, all of which was mightily cheered, before coming to his peroration and the one line that people would always remember: "Let's talk sense to the American people." That it seemed so memorable a statement speaks volumes about what people expected from their candidates, but Stevenson had his eye on the work to be done when the election was over. There was also a darkness in Stevenson's vision that may have been appropriate to the early days of the Cold War but was not calculated to excite partisan enthusiasm:

> . . . even more important than winning the election is governing the nation. That is the test of a political party, the acid, final test. When the tumult and the shouting die, when the bands are gone and the lights are dimmed, there is the stark reality of responsibility in an hour of history haunted with those gaunt, grim specters of strife, dissension, and materialism at home and ruthless, inscrutable, and hostile power abroad.

The ordeal of the twentieth century, the bloodiest, most turbulent era of the whole Christian age, is far from over. Sacrifice, patience, understanding, and implacable purpose may be our lot for years to come. Let's face it. Let's talk sense to the American people. Let's tell them the truth, that there are no gains without pains, that there—that we are now on the eve of great decisions, not easy decisions, like resistance when you're attacked, but a long, patient, costly struggle which alone can assure triumph over the great enemies of man, war, poverty, and tyranny, and the assaults upon human dignity which are the most grievous consequences of each.

Let's tell them that the victory to be won in the twentieth century, this portal to the Golden Age, mocks the pretensions of individual acumen and ingenuity, for it is a citadel guarded by thick walls of ignorance and of mistrust which do not fall before the trumpets' blast or the politicians' imprecations or even a general's baton. They are—They are, my friends, walls that must be directly stormed by the hosts of courage, of morality, and of vision, standing shoulder to shoulder, unafraid of ugly truth, contemptuous of lies, half truths, circuses, and demagoguery. . . .

That, that, I—I think, is our ancient mission. Where we have deserted it, we have failed. With your help, there will be no desertion now. Better we lose the election than mislead the people, and better we lose than misgovern the people. Help me to do the job in this autumn of conflict and of campaign. Help me to do the job in these years of darkness, of doubt, and of crisis which stretch beyond the horizon of tonight's happy vision, and we will justify our glorious past and the loyalty of silent millions who look to us for compassion, for understanding, and for honest purpose. Thus, we will serve our great tradition greatly. . . .

And finally, my friends, in this staggering task that you have assigned me, I shall always try "to do justly, to love mercy, and to walk humbly with my God."[49]

VI

Stevenson went back to Springfield the next day to be greeted by a crowd of twenty-five thousand that moved him to tears. The next day, he slipped out of the executive mansion at nearly midnight and made the short walk to Lincoln's home, where the caretaker let him in to sit for an hour in Lincoln's rocker and ponder the road ahead. He never told anyone why he had done it or what it meant, except to say that he had come away with a deep calm about the task ahead of him.[50]

Unlike most candidates, Stevenson had not been campaigning for the nomination and so had no campaign staff or organization except for his local supporters. He had three months until the election, and a major speech to give to the American Legion in just over three weeks. Neither he nor his staff had any real idea of what a national campaign involved. They found a house they thought would serve nicely for the press, with work space downstairs and bedrooms upstairs. Eventually that proved adequate only for Bill Flanagan, Stevenson's press secretary; reporters found space where they could.

The idea of Springfield as campaign headquarters was probably a bad one. Springfield was simply not a big enough city to provide the facilities needed. It came to look like a disaster area, like a city recovering from a tornado. There was tension from the beginning between Truman and those around him, who thought Stevenson should rely on experienced professionals, and Stevenson and his staff, who believed he had accomplished what he had precisely because he had not relied on experienced professionals. It was the independents they wanted to recruit, and they wanted to show their independence by doing things differently. Stevenson chose, for example, not to go to the annual Al Smith dinner in New York presided over by Cardinal Spellman that all candidates who wanted Roman Catholic votes always went to. Jake Arvey told him he dared not turn it down, but he did. Those who wanted an independent-minded candidate were impressed, but the professionals were alarmed.

Eventually, the campaign shaped up as a three-headed dragon, with Democratic national headquarters in Washington, Volunteers for Stevenson in Chicago, and his personal staff in Springfield.

One of Stevenson's greatest concerns was that he would be unable to write all his own speeches. That being inevitable, Carl McGowan went to work to assemble a staff of writers and was able to recruit four Pulitzer Prize winners, including Arthur Schlesinger, Jr. and John Kenneth Galbraith, both Harvard professors, John Fischer, the editor of *Harper's* magazine, Eric Hodgins, an editor of *Fortune*, and Bernard DeVoto, an eminent historian. Secretaries worked at a long table in the middle of a large room while the writers worked at desks around the periphery. Four adjoining bedrooms enabled those who were tired to sleep while work went on around the clock. First one, then another, and finally four writers had to be hospitalized briefly when they collapsed from exhaustion. McGowan did final editing of drafts and passed them on to Stevenson, who always re-worked material in whatever time was available. Somehow the end result almost always sounded uniquely like Stevenson.[51]

When the campaign was over, Stevenson published a collection of fifty speeches made during the campaign, including the welcome address to the

Convention and his acceptance speech. They address issues as diverse as Farm Policy, World Policy, the Role of Labor, Tidelands Oil, Religion and Politics, the New South, and many more. Clearly, no single individual could hope to write speeches on so many subjects in the space of three months; but clearly also, all these topics are of interest to some part of the electorate and should be addressed by a candidate if it is possible. A candidate can, of course, address such interest groups by saying "Your concerns are important to me and I will work hard to satisfy you," but Stevenson preferred to say something substantive even if he knew it might challenge his audience's point of view.

Even before the Democratic Party had chosen its candidate, there were some speaking dates on the calendar because they provided an opportunity for the candidate to speak to important segments of the electorate. As said above, Stevenson took the risk of offending Roman Catholics by not attending the Al Smith dinner in New York. He took the risk of offending veterans precisely by attending an American Legion convention in August and speaking his mind, but he decided to take that risk. He told them, for example, that there were "groups who seek to identify their specific interests with the general welfare" and that "I intend to resist pressure from veterans, too, if I think their demands are excessive or in conflict with the public interest." He pointed out that there were now millions of veterans and asked "if we were all to claim a special reward for our services, who would be left to pay the bill?" Probably most veterans and most Americans would have agreed with that general sentiment, but to say it to a veterans' convention was to challenge them in a way that most politicians would not have thought useful. The Legion had adopted resolutions calling for victory in Korea and the removal of Secretary of State Dean Acheson. Eisenhower had spoken to the convention two days earlier and had called for a more aggressive foreign policy, especially in relation to Eastern Europe.

Stevenson was speaking in one of those eras when some politicians were making a living by proclaiming their Americanism and attacking that of others. Senator McCarthy was looming on the horizon and about to make his name a synonym for such behavior. He had already published a book the previous year, in which he accused General George C. Marshall of treason. The American Legion was sometimes prone to support such behavior. Stevenson challenged that activity head on:

> What can we say for the man who proclaims himself a patriot, and then for political or personal reasons attacks the patriotism of faithful public servants? I give you, as a shocking example, the attacks which have been made on the loyalty and the motives of our great wartime chief of staff, General Marshall. To me this is

> the type of "patriotism" which is, in Dr. Johnson's phrase, "the last refuge of scoundrels."*

"The anatomy of patriotism," Stevenson went on to say, "is complex." He might have said the definition of freedom or liberty is complex, more complex than Patrick Henry or earlier Americans could have realized. Stevenson chose to focus attention on freedom of thought and speech as areas currently under attack. "To strike freedom of the mind with the fist of patriotism," he told the Legionnaires, "is an old and ugly subtlety."

> And the freedom of the mind, my friends, has served America well. The vigor of our political life, our capacity for change, our cultural, scientific, and industrial achievements, all derive from free inquiry, from the free mind, from the imagination, resourcefulness, and daring of men who are not afraid of new ideas. Most all of us favor free enterprise for business. Let us also favor free enterprise for the mind. For, in the last analysis, we would fight to the death to protect it.[52]

He went on to talk about the danger of communism and denounce it in strong language.

> Communism is abhorrent. It is strangulation of the individual; it is death for the soul. Americans who have surrendered to this misbegotten idol have surrendered their right to our trust. And there can be no secure place for them in our public life.

But fear of communism, Stevenson told the Legionnaires, did not justify repression. The next sentence was written in by Stevenson in longhand:

> The tragedy of our day is the climate of fear in which we live, and fear breeds repression. Too often sinister threats to the Bill of Rights, to freedom of the mind, are concealed under the patriotic cloak of anti-communism.

Stevenson went on to be even more specific about the ways in which the fear of communism could become a threat to American freedom. He talked about

---

* When Eisenhower toured Wisconsin with McCarthy, he said he agreed with McCarthy's goals but disagreed with his methods. A draft version of Eisenhower's speech had included a strong defense of General Marshall, but that was deleted at the advice of conservative aides who feared losing Wisconsin.

schoolteachers and the danger to their freedom when they were attacked by "self-appointed thought police or ill-informed censors." Such activities, he said, do nothing to "stop communist activity" but only "give the communists material with which to defame us."[53]

Carl McGowan and others thought the Legion address was the high point of the campaign. It certainly established Stevenson's credibility with liberals who were worried about the impact of McCarthy's tactics on the quality of American life.

Richard Nixon, Eisenhower's vice-presidential candidate, attacked Stevenson two days later for having "made light of the menace of communism" and having "demonstrated a shocking lack of understanding of the problem of subversion."[54]

It may be that Stevenson wasn't expecting to win a lot of votes from the American Legion anyway. He was less aggressive in speaking to farmers about farm policy or to labor unions about labor policy, but the American Legion was not the only interest group he challenged. In fact, when he went to Los Angeles to talk about political morality, he challenged the general public. Whose fault is it, he asked, when we get less than the best in public servants; and he answered very bluntly, "It is the fault of you, the people. Your public servants serve you right; indeed, often they serve you better than your apathy and indifference deserve."

A critical issue at the time was that of the tidelands, offshore areas that might hold considerable oil and mineral wealth. The Supreme Court had ruled that the federal government had jurisdiction, and a Congressional bill giving the states authority had been vetoed by President Truman. Governor Allan Shivers of Texas requested a meeting with Stevenson to fill him in on the issue, and Stevenson spent a good deal of time getting other opinions. Shivers went to Springfield and made his case, but Stevenson said he thought the Supreme Court ruling should be accepted, though a legislative solution might still be possible. Shivers went back to Texas and announced that he could not support Stevenson. It was that sort of thing that made Stevenson an icon in some quarters, but it might have cost him not only Texas votes but also Texas money, and the election.[55]

Not unique to Stevenson because it had become common usage at the time, but noteworthy because of what it indicated about the change in American life since Patrick Henry's time, was Stevenson's frequent use of the term "the free world":

> The building of free-world strength does more than just restrain Soviet aggression. Its effect is to make the free world itself, both because of its freedom and because of its strength, a potent counter-attraction to Soviet power.[56]

Neither Stevenson nor anyone else stopped to define the term "free world," and it was used generally in simple contrast with the countries under communist control, but it seemed to indicate a remarkable change in international life, from a time when America was unique in defining itself in terms of freedom, to a time when a wide variety of nations did so. Some, of course, like Batista's Cuba or Trujillo's Dominican Republic, which were considered American "allies," hardly qualified as free; but any nation taking shelter under the umbrella word "freedom" raised expectations by so doing. Indeed, the American example was so far-reaching in its impact that even communist countries called themselves "people's democracies."

Freedom, of course, was the issue also in civil rights: when would America face the fact that people of color were denied the freedom of equality not only by law and custom in the South, but by employers and real estate agents and personal prejudice in the North? Stevenson referred to the lack of equal rights and opportunities due to race as "the fire hazard in our basement," and it would blaze up in the not very distant future. It was a question Stevenson had to face carefully, since the Democratic Party relied on the still "Solid South" for its support in winning elections. In the event, Stevenson only carried nine states, all of them south of the Mason-Dixon Line. When he went to Texas and made a speech about freedom, he talked about freedom from communism and made no reference to civil rights. He did devote one speech to civil rights early in the campaign, in New York, and talked about the progress that had been made in creating Fair Employment Practices laws. "I have been talking about methods," he said; "about goals, there can, of course, be no disagreement."[57] In fact, there was substantial disagreement about goals, and Stevenson must have known it, but it was not a subject about which he felt strongly.

Stevenson also felt it was important to take the same stance in the South that he took in the North. In fact, he made a better speech in Virginia about civil rights than he had made in New York. He also laid out again his belief in integrity:

> I should justly earn your contempt if I talked one way in the South and another elsewhere. . . . The political abuse of the problem of discrimination in employment, the exploitation of racial aspirations on the one hand and racial prejudices on the other, all for votes, is both a dangerous thing and a revolting spectacle in our political life. It is always better to reason together than to hurl recriminations at one another.[58]

Stevenson had won election as Governor of Illinois by ceaseless campaigning, by making speeches wherever he could find an audience. He went about the business of campaigning for the presidency in the same way. After the formal opening of his campaign on Labor Day in Detroit, he launched his first campaign tour and made thirty speeches in eight western states in eight days. He almost always refused to make the same speech twice, even when he was making ten speeches on the same day. No wonder he needed speechwriters! But the need for so many speeches meant that Stevenson was not always able to review them carefully before delivery and, with speechwriters who tended to be somewhat more liberal than he, Stevenson sometimes found himself on the verge of making a statement with which he was not quite comfortable. He would sometimes pause in mid-sentence staring blankly at the lectern and try to work his way around to phrases with which he was more comfortable.

The insistence on a different speech every time caused problems, and some of his staff wondered whether the failure to repeat phrases and so drum in key ideas contributed to a lack of focus in the campaign.[59] On the other hand, the combination of Stevenson's thoughtful style with talented speechwriters made for speeches to be remembered. Many years later, one historian wrote: "Americans can still afford to read what Stevenson said at that time, for he was confronting the major issues of the modern world, the fate of all mankind. A reader . . . will find . . . much matter still worth thinking about, and periodically memorable passages, soaring to eloquence. The speeches are still a pleasure to read and to quote."[60]

Stevenson's final major speech, on the Saturday before the election, was made in Chicago's Stadium and played variations on a pattern Franklin D. Roosevelt had used more than once:

> I see an America where no man fears to think as he pleases, or say what he thinks. I see an America where slums and tenements have vanished and children are raised in dignity and self-respect. . . .
>
> I see an America where no man is another's master—where no man's mind is dark with fear.
>
> I see an America at peace with the world. I see an America as the horizon of human hopes. This is our design for the American cathedral, and we shall build it brick by brick and stone by stone, patiently, bravely, and prayerfully.[61]

Stevenson would use the same litany in his campaign four years later—and perhaps it lay behind Martin Luther King's "I have a dream. . . ."*

Americans, however, were not looking for thoughtful speeches that fall so much as a reassuring figure. The thought of a menacing communist Russia

* William Safire's Political Dictionary traces the pattern back to Robert Ingersoll in 1876.

with atomic weapons was not something Americans had learned to live with, and Eisenhower had made his reputation in defeating a powerful enemy. Sixty-one million Americans voted that fall, and fifty-five percent voted for Eisenhower. Stevenson's total was greater than any candidate except Roosevelt—barely, in 1936—had ever before received, three million votes more than Truman had collected four years earlier in winning.[62] Stevenson had lost, but he had changed many lives. Richard N. Goodwin, a college senior who would go on to serve Presidents Kennedy and Johnson, wrote: "He told an entire generation there was room for intelligence and idealism in public life."[63]

VII

There had been no time to think what he would do next, but Stevenson was still Governor of Illinois for a few more weeks, and he was deluged with some 300,000 letters that he believed should be answered. He could not possibly answer them all himself, but letters from Albert Einstein, Winston Churchill, Carl Sandburg, John Steinbeck, and Helen Keller were among those that did need a personal response. He made speeches to raise funds to pay off election costs, attended a state dinner given in his honor by President Truman with the entire Cabinet and Chief Justice of the Supreme Court, spoke to the annual Gridiron Club of Washington reporters and others, and had lunch and meetings with Congressional leaders and the newly inaugurated President Eisenhower. Then he left on a trip around the world paid for by *Look* magazine in return for ten articles to be published on his return. Triumphal welcomes in twenty-nine countries led Stevenson to ask "Haven't they heard who won the election?" But his reputation as a thoughtful leader had spread abroad, and he had little opportunity for the reflective time he had hoped for.

Stevenson, perhaps surprisingly, began his trip by traveling west, first to Hawaii and then to Japan. He made a thoughtful speech to the largest turnout in the history of the Japan-American Society, and at eight o'clock the next morning met with university students and faculty who, he was told, were eighty percent inclined toward Marxism. When a student asked him "Just what is democracy, anyway?" he responded without a prepared text:

> Democracy is honest disagreement. It is the right to hold the opinion you believe in, and to fight for it with self-respect and determination. The virtue of democracy is not cold order. It is the heat of men's minds rubbing against each other, sending out sparks. It is liberty with responsibility. It is a struggle that never ends and is always worth the fight.[64]

American leaders had been talking about freedom and democracy in world-wide terms for a long time; as Stevenson traveled through Korea, the Philippines, Vietnam, and India, he had the opportunity to see what that meant at ground level. In one of his articles for *Look* magazine, he wrote that many of the leaders he met

> still look to revolutionary, democratic America for inspiration and encouragement. But their countries are poor and backward. Their peoples know little of democracy and the blessings of human freedom, but they want to eat every day, and they mean to do it. The next few years will tell whether these leaders can make democracy work in this great new area of decision, Asia.[65]

In Europe especially, he found concerns about America's tolerance for McCarthy. He told foreign audiences that he would deal with that when he was back home. In one of his *Look* magazine articles, he wrote that "McCarthyism had done America more harm in eight months than Soviet propaganda had done in eight years."[66]

While Stevenson was traveling, other leading Democrats were talking among themselves about a way forward. Eisenhower's overwhelming victory had not translated into a vigorous new administration. Rather, at least from the Democratic point of view, it had magnified the divisions in the Republican Party between East Coast moderates and middle-American conservatives, while putting Eisenhower's lack of clear direction in a national spotlight.

In response, former Air Force Secretary Thomas K. Finletter and others brought together experts in various fields to conduct seminars and help develop position papers. These were made available to Stevenson for use in making speeches so that the country would be reminded that there was an alternative with clear ideas. By the spring of 1956, a staff of twenty based in Chicago was doing research, clipping newspaper and magazine articles, and organizing Stevenson's past speeches and expressions of opinion.[67] Over the next several years, papers were produced that fed into speeches by Stevenson, especially during the 1956 campaign. After 1956, a Democratic Advisory Council continued the work and prepared position papers that became the basis for legislation in the Kennedy and Johnson administrations.[68]

Republican divisions also manifested themselves as Senator McCarthy became increasingly extreme in his charges of communist influence in the government. What angered and disgusted Adlai Stevenson was the fact that the Republican National Committee was sponsoring a series of talks around the country on the theme of "Twenty Years of Treason" and that other Republican leaders were taking up the charge that the Democratic Party was a party of "war, crisis, subversion, and treason." Even a moderate and previously responsible leader like former presidential candidate Thomas E. Dewey made a speech in which he said that the words "'Truman' and 'Democrat' meant military failure, diplomatic failure, death and tragedy."

In February 1954, Stevenson went to Miami to speak on "Crusades, Communism, and Corruption." The speech had gone through eight drafts but was delivered from a longhand text. Stevenson held nothing back in his response to the Republican attacks.

> We are witnessing the bitter harvest from the seeds of slander, defamation and disunion planted in the soil of our democracy. . . There is a peace still to be won, an economy which needs some attention, an atom to be controlled, all through the delicate, sensitive and indispensable processes of democracy, processes which demand, at the least, that people's vision be clear, that they be told the truth, and that they respect one another.

From that perspective, he went on to say:

> It is wicked and it is subversive for public officials to try deliberately to replace reason with passion, to substitute hatred for honest difference. . . . When one party says that the other is the party of traitors who have deliberately conspired to betray America, to fill our government services with Communists and spies, to send our young men to unnecessary death in Korea, they violate not only the limits of partisanship, they offend not only the credulity of the people, but they stain the vision of America and of democracy for us and for the world we seek to lead. That such things are said under the official sponsorship of the Republican Party in celebration of the birthday of Abraham Lincoln adds defamation to desecration. . . . When demagoguery and deceit become a national political movement, we Americans are in trouble; not just Democrats, but all of us.[69]

Stevenson proceeded to provide a bill of particulars:

> Our State Department has been abused and demoralized. The American voice abroad has been enfeebled. Our educational system has been attacked; our press threatened; our servants of God impugned; a former President maligned; the executive departments invaded; our foreign policy confused; the President himself

> patronized and the integrity, loyalty and morale of the United States Army assailed.

And how, he asked, has all this been possible?

> The answer is inescapable: because a group of political plungers has persuaded the President that McCarthyism is the best Republican formula for political success.

There had been important Democratic party leaders, Senators Lyndon Johnson, Richard Russell, and even Hubert Humphrey, who had feared that Stevenson's speech might have negative consequences for Democratic candidates in the elections that fall. But the result was very different. The Republican National Committee consulted with the president and announced that Vice President Nixon would reply on behalf of the party. At a press conference the next day, President Eisenhower commended Republican Senator Ralph Flanders of Vermont for accusing McCarthy of "doing his best to shatter" the Republican party. Nixon followed up by repudiating his friend, Senator McCarthy, and accusing him of "reckless talk and questionable method."

It would still be several months before the Senate itself would take up charges against McCarthy, but in September a Senate panel unanimously recommended censure, and in December it voted 67 to 22 to condemn his conduct. The reign of fear was brought to an end, and it was the defeated candidate who had led the way while the president and those in power held back.[70]

The year 1954 was an important opportunity for Stevenson to assert himself again in the election process. Early in the year, he gave a series of lectures at Harvard on "A Troubled World," which provided an overview of the challenges facing America at mid-century. Americans, he said, need to cultivate "a new attitude toward the problems of life itself":

> Americans have always assumed, subconsciously, that all problems can be solved; that every story has a happy ending; that the application of enough energy and good will can make everything come out right. . . . Our first job, it seems to me, is to school ourselves in cold-eyed humility; to recognize that our wisdom is imperfect and that our capabilities are limited. . . . So the first step in learning our new role in world affairs . . . has to be taken by individual Americans, in the privacy of their own homes, hearts and souls. It involves a recognition that we are never going to solve many of the hard problems of the world, but will simply have to learn to live with them, for years and maybe for centuries.

It was the sort of thoughtful statement at which he was best and which his supporters most admired, but exactly the sort of thing that led Republicans to talk about "eggheads." Three days later, he spoke at Princeton and deplored "the growth of the popularity of unreason, of anti-intellectualism." Later that spring, he spoke at Columbia University and dealt with more practical issues:

> Too many of our people still dwell in wretched slums or on worn-out land. Once again our top-soil, our national skin, is blowing away out on the plains. Our schools and our hospitals are over-crowded; so are our mental institutions and our prisons. Too many of our cities are wasting away from neglect. And how can we boast of our high estate when more than one of ten citizens still do not enjoy fully equal opportunities?[71]

Later that year, he was still more direct as he joined in the off-year election campaign and made eighty speeches in thirty-three different states. Democrats gained seventeen seats in the House and two in the Senate. It was obvious to most observers that the nomination would be his in 1956 if he wanted it.

Meanwhile, Stevenson was growing more and more concerned about the dangerous steps the administration was taking in foreign affairs. There were off-shore Chinese islands claimed both by the communist regime on the mainland and the nationalist regime on Taiwan. Both parties felt themselves locked in a dangerous confrontation: the Democrats because the Republicans had made such loud claims of how the Democrats had "lost" China, and the Republicans because, having made such claims, they could hardly lose an inch of Asian soil themselves. In March 1955, the president requested authority from Congress to defend Taiwan and "closely related localities," and Secretary of State John Foster Dulles announced that such defense would "require the use of atomic missiles." Eisenhower backed that up with the remark that "I see no reason why they [atomic weapons] shouldn't be used just exactly as you would use a bullet or anything else."

Stevenson conferred closely with Congressional leadership and made a widely publicized radio speech on the subject of America's role in the world. Pointing out that the United States holds only six percent of the world's population and was rapidly alienating its natural allies, he asked: "Are we prepared to face the prospect of war in the morass of China, possibly global war, standing almost alone in a sullen world?" He closed with a plea for reason:

> Let us stop slandering ourselves and appear before the world once again, as we really are, as friends, not as masters, as apostles of principle, not of power; in humility, not arrogance; as champions

> of peace, not harbingers of war. For our strength lies, not alone in our proving grounds and our stockpiles, but in our ideals, and their universal appeal to all men who are struggling to breathe free.[72]

The next day, Secretary Dulles told the press that Stevenson's sentiments were exactly those of the administration. He had provided the administration with the cover it needed to back away from an uncomfortable position from which it had seen no easy escape.

VIII

Adlai Stevenson was careful of the sensibilities of Congressional leadership in his role as "nominal leader" of the Democratic Party, but exercised it effectively both through the study groups and position papers that enabled him to speak to important issues and through his willingness to challenge the Republican Party and the president on critical issues. Because of that leadership and because no one else was eager to challenge President Eisenhower, it was assumed that Stevenson would be his party's nominee again in 1956. All that changed when Eisenhower suffered a severe heart attack on September 23, 1955, after playing twenty-seven holes of golf. Suddenly, Estes Kefauver, Averell Harriman, and others found the nomination much more interesting. For Stevenson, it meant a round of primaries that he had hoped to avoid. State primaries inevitably involved local issues, all of them arousing local passions. "I'm not running for sheriff," Stevenson complained to his staff, but primary elections would inevitably involve issues largely irrelevant to the presidency.[73]

In January 1956, Eisenhower announced that he was returning to his job, and assumptions about the fall election began to change again. By that time, the fight for the Democratic nomination had become more of a contest than anyone had imagined, and mostly because Stevenson insisted on being himself and saying what he believed rather than what people wanted to hear. He began his campaign on friendly ground in California and crowded his schedule to demonstrate his vigor in contrast with Eisenhower's uncertain health, but that meant that he came to the most important speech of the trip, to the California Democratic Council, poorly prepared. Stevenson's friend and biographer John Bartlow Martin called the speech "a political disaster." It was thoughtful and "lofty," and no one liked it. Kefauver spoke that same day and unleashed a barrage at the Republicans that delighted his audience. After that, Stevenson was playing catch-up and unable to satisfy anyone. Labor groups, African Americans, Jewish groups, and others all wanted a strong commitment to their cause, but it was Stevenson's nature to look for ways to resolve conflicts, not create them. As a result, no one was satisfied.

The first primary was in Minnesota, and supporters had laid out a grueling schedule. But still, Stevenson and his supporters were expecting to coast to victory, so the speeches he made never mentioned Kefauver. Kefauver won 56 percent of the votes and almost all the delegates to the convention. After that, Stevenson had no choice but to campaign flat-out until November.

Fighting for his political life though he was, Stevenson took on one critical issue in April, when he called for a moratorium on testing of atomic weapons. Scientists were becoming increasingly concerned by the fallout of radiation from such tests, but both the United States and Russia had insisted that they were necessary. Atomic Energy Commissioner Thomas E. Murray had testified before a Congressional committee in favor of suspending tests, saying he saw no reason for the United States to have bigger weapons than it already possessed. "I deeply believe," Stevenson said,

> that if we are to make progress toward the effective reduction and control of armaments, it will probably come a step at a time. And this is a step, it seems to me, we might now take, a step which would reflect our determination never to plunge the world into nuclear holocaust, a step which would reaffirm our purpose to act with humility and a decent concern for world opinion.

He further proposed centering foreign policy on economic development rather than military alliances. "It is time," he said,

> to regain the initiative; to release the warm, creative energies of this mighty land; it is time to resume the onward progress of mankind in pursuit of freedom and peace.[74]

Stevenson returned to the test-ban proposal in his speech to the American Legion after the conventions were over. Eisenhower had raised the possibility himself in a letter to the Chairman of the Atomic Energy Commission, Admiral Lewis Strauss, but he refused to comment on Stevenson's proposal himself, leaving Nixon to call it "the height of irresponsibility and absurdity" and for Dewey to call it "an invitation to national suicide." Two years later, however, Eisenhower decreed a moratorium on tests, and formal negotiations for a test ban treaty began.

In the end, Stevenson won the primaries. He narrowly defeated Kefauver in Florida after staging the first televised debate between candidates, and he defeated Kefauver by two to one in California. Kefauver withdrew before the convention, and the delegates, given freedom to choose a vice-presidential candidate without Stevenson's dictation of a choice, elected Kefauver to run with Stevenson.

Stevenson was at his best in his acceptance speech. He called for a "New America . . ."

> . . . after an interval of marking time and of aimless drifting, we are on the threshold of another great, decisive era. History's headlong course has brought us, we devoutly believe, to the threshold of a new America, to the America of the great ideals and noble visions which are the stuff our future must be made of.
>
> I mean a New America where poverty is abolished and our abundance is used to enrich the lives of every family.
>
> I mean, my friends, a New America where freedom is made real for all without regard to race or belief or economic condition.
>
> I mean a New America which everlastingly attacks the ancient idea that men can solve their differences by killing each other.[75]

Once again, Stevenson assembled a staff of speechwriters of exceptional ability. Some, like Arthur Schlesinger, Jr., were veterans of the first Stevenson campaign. Others were new recruits. Together they provided a variety of skills: Schlesinger was a prize-winning historian; Robert Tufts had worked on policy planning at the State Department; William Lee Miller was a theologian, political reporter, and academic; John Bartlow Martin was a journalist. W. Willard Wirtz, who had worked on the first campaign and taught law at Northwestern and Iowa, emerged as the head of the speech staff. Like Stevenson, he took his time in making decisions and tended toward moderation. Speeches were carefully drafted and edited and worked over by the candidate.* The same team planned the schedule and made the arrangements with each host.

In addition to the Washington staff, a less formally organized group including Herman Wouk, John Gunther, and Alan Lerner met together at the home of Cass Canfield, chairman of the executive committee of Harper and Brothers. Stevenson met with them on occasion and outlined his needs while they, in turn, gave him ideas and sent him material ranging from brief quotations to thirty-page speeches.[76]

There were, however, other Stevenson supporters who thought the issue was not the quality of the speeches but the entire manner of presenting the candidate. These advisers believed that the "egghead" jibes of the first campaign pointed to a communication problem: that the same eloquence that delighted

---

* The statistically minded might be interested to learn that in fifteen major campaign speeches, Stevenson made 976 corrections, or an average of 65 changes per speech. Three quarters of the changes were additions; about twenty percent of the additions were to amplify a point, and another twenty-five percent were to simplify a point. More of this information is available in Windes, 41.

a part of the electorate only confused others. They believed that Eisenhower had made more effective use of the new medium of television to communicate with the electorate, and that Stevenson needed to learn to use it well also. In the words of one historian of the era:

> Where Stevenson appeared to make a fetish of reason, Eisenhower recognized that effective communication depended more on stimulating a sense of shared emotion. His highly effective spot advertisements on television identified with the needs and yearnings of ordinary voters.[77]

Stevenson, however, was not easily converted to new ways. He hated the feeling of being "packaged" and could not overcome the suspicion that there was something unethical about talking to a camera in simplified formulas. He did what he could to accommodate his advisers, but he continued to disparage the merchandising of "candidates for high office like breakfast cereal."

Strong and substantive speeches still marked Stevenson's campaign. On Labor Day, the traditional opening day of a Democratic campaign, he told a Detroit audience:

> I say it is wrong that 14 million of our fellow Americans live today in families whose income is less than $1,000 a year.
>
> I say it is wrong that the ten million men and women over sixty-five years of age in this country . . . are being forced to live in what ought to be their golden years on an average family income of less than $1,500 a year.
>
> I say it is wrong that the American farmer is getting this year only three dollars of income for every four dollars he was making in 1952 while his costs have increased.

In Harlem he decried slums, low minimum wages, low Social Security benefits. In Milwaukee he laid out in detail the deplorable condition of the schools. He made substantive proposals in all these areas. His healthcare proposals led to the passage of Medicare in 1965. But Eisenhower seemed somehow above the fray; no criticisms stuck to him. When revolutions broke out in Europe just before the voting, arguably as a direct result of the Dulles-Eisenhower talk about "liberating" Eastern Europe, it only seemed to enhance Eisenhower's status as a "man of peace" to turn to in times of trouble.

The result of the 1956 campaign was an even greater defeat than in 1952. Stevenson carried only seven Southern states and lost by almost ten million votes. Some said the campaign was at fault; others thought it was better organized and more substantive. One obvious difference was that he had been forced to fight through a long primary campaign that brought him tired to the campaign instead of fresh. Stevenson, moreover, was facing a popular incumbent the second time around and needing to attack instead of defend. "What unites us," said Stevenson in conceding the election, "is deeper than what divides us, love of freedom, love of justice, love of peace."[78]

IX

Stevenson traveled abroad when the election was over, visiting England, where he was given an honorary degree by Oxford, and Ghana, South Africa, and the Congo. Two weeks after his return and ten months after the election, Eisenhower offered to suspend testing nuclear weapons as Stevenson had suggested, and the administration began trying to co-opt him in a variety of roles. He turned down a request that he serve on a presidential Commission on Civil Rights and an "anguished plea" from Secretary of State Dulles that he help formulate American policy for a critically important NATO meeting. He had a reasonable fear that the administration was hoping to give a bipartisan look to their work in controversial areas so as to fend off Democratic criticism and be able to blame him if their "bipartisan" efforts failed. He did, however, agree to serve as a "special consultant," and his recommendations led to the creation of the Organization for Economic Cooperation and Development.[79]

In 1958, he traveled for the first time to Russia. Tensions were rising in the Middle East, and American marines had just landed in Lebanon to support its embattled president, but Stevenson was welcomed warmly everywhere. Official banners in Moscow and Uzbekistan and Siberia announced that the people of each place were "Wrathfully Protesting Imperialist Aggression," but the people under the banners smiled and clapped as Stevenson waved to them.[80]

Interviews with Khrushchev, Gromyko, and others were cordial but demanding. Stevenson came away surprised by the eagerness of the Russian people for contact, despite their ignorance of America and the constant barrage of hostile propaganda. He returned by way of Warsaw, Prague, Zurich, Bern, Florence, and Paris.[81]

Opportunities to speak continued to come, and one of them, a lecture honoring A. Powell Davies, the former pastor of All Souls Unitarian Church in Washington, gave Stevenson an opportunity in January 1959 to look at the moral philosophy that undergirded so much of his life. Americans, he suggested, had forgotten the principles that had made the country great and were reacting only defensively, in self-protection, rather than working to promote the principles of freedom and democracy. He said:

> There is no more urgent duty than to discover why we have failed and to get back into the arena, aspiring, striving, fighting once more for what we believe. An examination of our collective conscience is to my mind far more important than particular projects or programs.

He went on to make a striking statement concerning the difficulty of maintaining freedom:

> We have confused the free with the free and easy. If freedom had been the happy, simple, relaxed state of ordinary humanity, man would have everywhere been free, whereas through most of time and space he has been in chains. Do not let us make any mistake about this. The natural government of man is servitude. Tyranny is the normal pattern of government. It is only by intense thought, by great effort, by burning idealism and unlimited sacrifice that freedom has prevailed as a system of government.

"Most of the major problems of our day," he told his audience, "present themselves in moral terms." Issues of poverty, race, and wealth, he said, were moral issues but must be confronted in the realm of politics. He expected that he would be told that moral issues were remote from politics, and yet, he said, "I wonder. . . ."

> It has been the view of great philosophers and statesmen that our system of free government depends in the first instance on the virtue of its citizens. For no democratic system can survive without at least a large and active leaven of citizens in whom dedication and selflessness are not confined to private life but are the fundamental principles of their activity in the public sphere.

Those who shape the public mind, he went on, from psychiatrists to ad men, have spoken too much about "what we owe ourselves," so that we have forgotten the day when "what man owes to God and his neighbor was a common theme of public discourse." As a result, "this is a dangerous time for our politics and for government by the consent of the governed. For at no time have so many of the great issues of the day demanded clear moral vision to bring them into focus."[82]

He took the same message directly to business leaders at the Harvard Business School in June of the same year, telling them that "you bear a heavy responsibility for the Republic's well-being and democracy's survival":

> What we need, and better have a good deal more of, quickly, is a concern for the *national* interest, and not the selfish interest of business, labor, farmers or any single economic, religious, or racial group. . . . Evolve a vision of the America you would like to see that must take account of considerations above and beyond the success of any business.

More significant still may have been an article in *Foreign Affairs* magazine. He intended it as a manifesto for the 1960 campaign, to draw the lines with the Eisenhower administration and Richard Nixon, the heir apparent. It was, in fact, used by both the Humphrey and Kennedy campaigns and underlay a good deal of the Kennedy-Rusk foreign policy. Why, he asked, had American foreign policy not centered on peace? Failure to do so had enabled the communist bloc to claim it as their own.

First in importance, Stevenson argued, was the income gap between the United States and the poorest third of the world: an average of over $2,000 per person in the United States and less than $100 in the poorest third. Economic development must be a priority. Next in importance was arms control, which seemed to be more of a possibility now that Russia was expressing a new interest in the subject. He wrote about reducing tensions with China, a nuclear-free zone in the Middle East, and the reunification of Germany. But his closing summary was a direct attack on the Eisenhower administration's failures:

> The truth is that nations cannot demonstrate a sense of purpose abroad when they have lost it at home. There is an intimate connection between the temper of our domestic leadership and the effectiveness of American influence in the world at large. . . . If we cannot recover an aspiring, forward-looking, creative attitude to the problems of our own community, there is little hope of recovering a dynamic leadership in the world at large. . . . I view the United States as ready for a new awakening and the achievement of greater goals. Within it are the moral and material elements of new purpose and new policy. It is the task of leadership to marshall our will and point the way. We had better start soon for time is wasting.[83]

Speeches and articles such as these kept Stevenson in the public eye, and questions about his willingness to run a third time continued to be raised. But Stevenson had disliked the primary process intensely and was unwilling to subject himself to it again. On the other hand, though he knew and said that a draft was extremely unlikely, he would not close the door to the possibility, and "draft Stevenson" groups continued to form and do what they could to keep his name in circulation. This did little to slow John F. Kennedy's progress toward the nomination but did much to annoy him. He asked for Stevenson's support but was turned down. He asked Stevenson to nominate him and was turned down. The result was that Stevenson was not made Secretary of State in the new Kennedy administration, the position he had hoped for, but had to be satisfied to become the Ambassador to the United Nations. Whether Stevenson as Secretary of State could have worked with Kennedy and Johnson to shape Vietnam policy differently than Dean Rusk makes an interesting speculation; what we know is that as Ambassador to the United Nations, it gave him a central role in the Cuban missile crisis and probably the most visible moment of his career.

If the UN post was, as Stevenson described it, a splendid exile for "a retired politician," it came with a good many comforts, not least an eighteen-room suite furnished with American, French, and English antiques on the forty-second floor of the Waldorf with a dining room adequate for forty guests. It also kept him rushing from one diplomatic or social engagement to another—especially social engagements—from breakfast to late evening. On the other hand, the rich food, abundant alcohol, and long hours inevitably took their toll.[84]

The first major crisis for the new Ambassador centered on the Bay of Pigs operation in April 1961. Kennedy representatives had briefed Stevenson on the plans, which Kennedy had inherited from the Eisenhower administration, and Stevenson had expressed his complete disapproval. He had, however, promised to make the best case for it that he could. Stevenson, however, had never had a complete understanding of the project and was therefore left providing the Security Council with a less than truthful report. Briefly, he considered resigning, but the UN reaction was surprisingly mild. Such was the respect in which Stevenson was held internationally that the blame was centered not on him but on Washington. It was Stevenson who Kennedy sent off to Latin America afterwards to repair strained relationships.[85]

Tension with Cuba continued. The United States would not recognize the Castro government and orchestrated its expulsion from the Organization of American States, while the CIA worked with the Mafia on bizarre plots to assassinate the Cuban leader. Russian weapons and technicians, not surprisingly, began arriving on the island in July quite openly, but Cuban officials promised to disarm their country if the United States would pledge to respect its territorial integrity. Stevenson's reply was that the United States "could not place the seal of approval on the existence of a communist regime in the Western Hemisphere. The maintenance of communism in the Western Hemisphere," he said, "is not negotiable."

It was in context of that continuing and escalating tension that an American U-2 spy plane came back with photographs showing a newly constructed missile base with at least one ballistic missile on the ground. President Kennedy was shown the pictures two days later and shared them with Stevenson. Stevenson had time only for a brief memo to Kennedy before returning to New York, but he urged the president to make it clear that "the existence of nuclear missile bases anywhere is NEGOTIABLE before we start anything." At the end of the week, Stevenson was back in Washington with a specific proposal: that the United States offer to guarantee the territorial integrity of Cuba and withdraw its bases, weapons, and personnel in Guantanamo, Turkey, and Italy in return for the Russian dismantling and elimination of its missile sites and personnel in Cuba.

By the time Stevenson had returned to Washington, however, positions were hardening and there was no inclination to make such concessions. Earlier, Secretary of Defense Robert McNamara had suggested withdrawing from Guantanamo in exchange for the Russian withdrawal and eventually, of course, the administration did withdraw missiles from Turkey. While strategy was being debated, Stevenson returned to New York for a meeting of the Security Council, at which he demanded an immediate dismantling and withdrawal of Russian missiles and weapons. At that point, Soviet Ambassador Valerian Zorin was denying the existence of any missiles in Cuba; but two days later, he began to waffle a bit, claiming simply that there was no evidence of such weapons. That led to one of the most memorable exchanges in United Nations history and a televised moment that was replayed endlessly on American television. Stevenson, in a speech not prepared and carefully edited by a team of speechwriters, replied to Zorin:

> I want to say to you, Mr. Zorin, that I do not have your talent for obfuscation, for distortion, for confusing language, and for doubletalk. And I must confess to you that I am glad that I do not!
>
> But if I understood what you said, you said that my position had changed, that today I was defensive because we did not have the evidence to prove our assertions that your Government had installed long-range missiles in Cuba.
>
> Well, let me say something to you, Mr. Ambassador—we do have the evidence. We have it, and it is clear and it is incontrovertible. And let me say something else—those weapons must be taken out of Cuba. . . .
>
> But let me also say to you, sir, that there has been a change. You—the Soviet Union has sent these weapons to Cuba. You—the Soviet Union has upset the balance of power in the world. You—the Soviet Union has created this new danger, not the United States.
>
> And you ask with a fine show of indignation why the President did not tell Mr. Gromyko on last Thursday about our evidence,

> at the very time that Mr. Gromyko was blandly denying to the President that the U.S.S.R. was placing such weapons on sites in the New World.
>
> Well, I will tell you why—because we were assembling the evidence, and perhaps it would be instructive to the world to see how a Soviet official—how far he would go in perfidy. Perhaps we wanted to know if this country faced another example of nuclear deceit like that one a year ago, when in stealth the Soviet Union broke the nuclear test moratorium.
>
> And while we are asking questions, let me ask you why your Government—your Foreign Minister—deliberately, cynically deceived us about the nuclear build-up in Cuba. . . .
>
> All right, sir, let me ask you one simple question: Do you, Ambassador Zorin, deny that the U.S.S.R. has placed and is placing medium- and intermediate-range missiles and sites in Cuba? Yes or no—don't wait for the translation—yes or no?
>
> [The Soviet representative refused to answer.]
>
> You can answer yes or no. You have denied they exist. I want to know if I understood you correctly. I am prepared to wait for my answer until hell freezes over, if that's your decision. And I am also prepared to present the evidence in this room.

After a brief exchange with the President of the Security Council, Stevenson announced that he was having an easel set up at the back of the room showing exactly what was going on in Cuba. He would have an aide there to explain the pictures which showed how peaceful fields had been transformed into missile bases. He suggested that a UN team might go to the locations and see for themselves. He concluded by saying:

> And now I hope that we can get down to business, that we can stop this sparring. We know the facts, and so do you, sir, and we are ready to talk about them. Our job here is not to score debating points. Our job, Mr. Zorin, is to save the peace. And if you are ready to try, we are.[86]

Stevenson's aide and biographer John Bartlow Martin calls this speech "by all odds the most popular one Stevenson ever made." That tells us something about the value of a team of speechwriters! Jack Arvey thought it illustrated why Truman won in 1948 and Stevenson lost in 1952. Here was language the farmer and truck driver could understand: "at long last someone had told the communists to go to hell." It didn't matter at all that the phrase they liked best was quite wrong: Stevenson and the United States were not at all prepared to wait "until hell freezes over." They wanted and needed an immediate answer.[87] No wonder Stevenson normally preferred careful phrasing and constant re-editing!

There were still several days of tense negotiations, but finally Khrushchev did offer to withdraw all the missiles in return for an American pledge not to attack Cuba, and then it remained only to carry out the commitments—negotiations dragged on for weeks—and move on. Stevenson received a warm letter of thanks from Kennedy and found himself suddenly the toast of Republican neighbors in Illinois who had previously been indifferent to him. Some of the bloom was taken off the rose by an article in the *Saturday Evening Post* by two reporters, one a known friend of President Kennedy's, that called Stevenson's performance in the crisis "soft" and said he had wanted a "Munich." At first it was treated as the equivalent of a request for Stevenson's resignation, and it required a good deal of work on Kennedy's part to persuade Stevenson that he was not responsible for the article and would regard Stevenson's resignation as a disaster.[88] It was eventually sorted out, but the lingering effect was not good. "After that," said George Ball, a close friend, "he was just going through the motions. . . . History had passed him by. His life had passed him by. He had no place to go."[89]

He had realized in taking the position at the United Nations that he was placing himself in a difficult situation as a spokesman for policies he would have little opportunity to influence. He was quoted as saying that he could not believe in some of the things he had to say.[90] Yet if he resigned, he would be seen as making a statement that might easily be misinterpreted. "How can I honorably and decently leave this United Nations job?" he asked an old friend, Eric Sevareid of CBS News.[91]

There were, nonetheless, important tasks to be carried out. Stevenson traveled several times to Europe and reported to the State Department on what he learned. In August 1963, he went to Moscow for a formal signing of the Limited Nuclear Test Ban Treaty. That had been a risky suggestion when Stevenson first made it in 1956. He wrote to a friend that the signing "brought back poignant memories of the bitter attacks of seven years ago."[92] He went to Dallas to speak at a UN luncheon and found the city flooded with handbills with pictures of President Kennedy and the legend "wanted for treason." When Stevenson left the luncheon, he was surrounded by picketers brandishing signs. One hit him on the head, and two men spat on him. He asked "Are these people or animals?" and thought seriously of warning Kennedy against his planned visit the following month. He told Schlesinger of his concern, but Schlesinger decided not to pass on the concern, since it would have been out of character for Kennedy to fear physical danger. The City Council apologized to Stevenson, and the mayor called on the city to give a better account of itself when the president arrived.

When Stevenson heard that Kennedy had been shot, he said, "I should have *insisted* that he not go there."[93] The polarization of American life was a growing concern. He wrote of the Goldwater candidacy: "Somehow this curious character has raised a standard to which all the fearful, frustrated, suspicious and hateful can repair for mutual support." It worried him especially that "there are so many of them." The disappearance of the liberal consensus that had dominated American society for a generation was a concern he expressed in a speech to the American Bar Association in August 1964:

> I have thought that the strength of the American political system lay precisely in its lack of extreme contrasts, in its rejection of dogma, in the fact that rigid ideology really has no relevance to our great political parties. [Troubled souls] want to repeal the whole thing. They seem to yearn for the old simplicity, for the shorthand analysis, for the black-and-white choice, for the cheap and easy answer, for the child's guide to good and evil.[94]

His sudden death in the summer of 1965 came before the Vietnam war had grown out of control and an increasing number of Americans had come to see it as a "black-and-white choice." He had spent the best years of his life as an advocate for freedom in a rapidly changing America and a world in conflict through the most difficult years of the Cold War. His last speech, made to the Economic and Social Council of the United Nations, Geneva, Switzerland, on July 9, 1965, expanded Lincoln's analysis of a nation divided to look at a divided world, "this little space ship," as he called it, which he said, cannot continue . . .

> half fortunate, half miserable, half confident, half despairing, half slave—to the ancient enemies of man—half free in a liberation of resources undreamed of until this day. No craft, no crew can travel safely with such vast contradictions. On their resolution depends the survival of us all.[95]

That resolution requires, of course, not the efforts of one man but of a multitude who share a common vision. The most enduring difference Adlai Stevenson made was undoubtedly through inspiring others to share that vision and to join in the effort themselves to work out the meaning of freedom.

NINE

Ronald Reagan
1911–2004

MAN IS NOT FREE UNLESS GOVERNMENT IS LIMITED

I

The iconic moment in the life of Ronald Reagan came very early in his career. In 1932, he was working as a sports announcer in Des Moines, Iowa, broadcasting accounts of baseball games being played by the Chicago Cubs. Details of the games came in by teletype, and Reagan's job was to transform the simple statistical report ("Out 4 to 3") into a colorful account that would create the impression of seeing the live action: "Jones hits a ground ball down to the second baseman. Smith picks it up and fires it to first, just in time. One away." Reagan was good at it. "You just couldn't believe you were not actually there," said WHO's program director. When technology later made it possible for WHO to bring in a live broadcast from Chicago, there were listeners who said they preferred Reagan's account.

The day came, however, when the teletype failed at a critical moment, and Reagan, rather than tell the listeners his predicament and ask their forbearance, simply carried on as if nothing were wrong, describing what might or might not actually be happening in Wrigley Field. As Reagan told the story, the batter fouled off one pitch after another, down the left field line, down the right field line, and so on until the teletype resumed. It turned out that the batter had hit a pop fly on the next pitch. Reagan told the story about himself with a chuckle as a "charming and mildly self-deprecating joke."

Biographers find it illuminating—but of what? On that, as on many aspects of Reagan's life, they disagree. Does it show us a man cool in an emergency, or someone who "simply lied" and who was "comfortable . . . with illusion"?[1] James David Barber, author of a best-selling book, *The Presidential Character,* wrote that "Reagan has a propensity to be more interested in theatrical truth than in empirical truth." A biographer, Richard Reeves, wrote that "Reagan was not a man of vision, he was a man of imagination—and he believed in the past he imagined."[2]

Ronald Reagan was never easily typecast. As an actor, he played many parts; sometimes he was a journalist, sometimes a cowboy, sometimes a soldier, sometimes a romantic lead. Sometimes he seemed to lose track of the line between himself and the parts he played. He served in the army during World War II, but poor eyesight limited him to the home front, where he made films supporting the American war effort. Afterwards, however, he told of liberating a Nazi death camp, though he had not been in Europe. When journalists asked questions, they were told that Reagan only meant to say that he had been deeply moved by films he had seen of the death camps. He liked to tell a story of the heroism of two soldiers whose plane had crashed in the Pacific Ocean, leaving no one to tell what had happened. But Reagan told the story he had constructed from scenes in wartime movies as if it were true.[3]

An actor is required to enter deeply into characters other than his or her own. When Reagan's first wife, Jane Wyman, played a deaf-mute, she refused to speak to anyone, even family and friends, for six months. As nearly as possible, she would be Johnny Belinda. So, too, Reagan entered intensely into a number of roles, and surely lines memorized and spoken over and again might well come to seem more real than the unrehearsed and casual moments of "real" life. No wonder it was often hard for him to keep track of the reality of a history in which he had played many parts.

What Reagan had that brought him success in one career after another was a voice and manner that conveyed warmth and sincerity. Roger Rosenblatt wrote for *Time* magazine that Reagan's voice "recedes at the right moments, turning mellow at points of intensity. When it wishes to be most persuasive, it hovers barely above a whisper so as to win you over by intimacy, if not by substance. . . . He likes his voice, treats it like a guest. He makes you part of that hospitality. It was that voice that carried him out of Dixon and away from the Depression. . . ."[4] Ann Edwards, author of a book on Reagan's early life, suggests that Reagan's "distinctive, mellow voice, tinged with a hopeful cadence—a voice that impressed people with the honesty of the words he spoke," was inherited or learned from his mother, who taught him how to lower his voice to "win a confidential intimacy." His voice, Edwards wrote, "had the humility and passion of a true believer, a manly, ingratiating voice made for promises."[5] Reagan had also heard the voice of President Franklin Roosevelt in his Fireside Chats and copied that approach many years later in his Saturday radio broadcasts.[6]

One part Ronald Reagan played with some authenticity was that of the average, small-town American. He was born in Tampico, Illinois, but his family moved frequently when he was small, coming finally to rest in Dixon, Illinois when Ronald was nine.* Reagan spoke of those days as an ideal childhood, but his father was an alcoholic and had trouble holding a job. Whatever security Reagan knew was earned by his mother's hard work and the support of neighbors. With that support, Reagan was able to lead a fairly normal childhood. He was captain of the football team, class president, and an actor in school plays.

One central rock of his life in Dixon was his mother's church, a congregation of the Disciples of Christ, a quintessentially American denomination that was formed in the early nineteenth century by three liberal Presbyterian pastors, Barton Stone and Thomas and Alexander Campbell. Hoping to end the divisions among Christians by requiring no creed and returning to what they imagined as the church's original, inclusive nature, they succeeded only in creating one more division, one marked by an American optimism that saw the United States as playing a special role in carrying out God's purpose. Reagan's pastor liked to quote the words of John Winthrop, who had said that the first New England settlement would be "as a city upon a hill." But Winthrop's "city upon a hill" would not automatically be blessed. Winthrop trusted that God would be with them in their experiment, but he used the word "if" to point out that if they failed to keep God's commands, they would be in trouble:

> . . . if we shall neglect the observation of these articles which are the ends we have propounded, and, dissembling with our God, shall fall to embrace this present world and prosecute our carnal intentions, seeking great things for ourselves and our posterity, the Lord will surely break out in wrath against us, and be revenged of such a people, and make us know the price of the breach of such a covenant.

---

* Four of the eight major figures in this book had deep roots in Illinois, although two were not born there. Lincoln was born in Kentucky but began his adult life in Springfield. Stevenson was born in California but grew up in Bloomington. Bryan was born in Salem and grew up there. Reagan was born in Tampico but called Dixon his hometown.

A city on a hill is visible, Winthrop pointed out, for good or for ill. In such a city, God's chosen would be very visible, and therefore they should watch their step:

> The eyes of all people are upon us. So that if we shall deal falsely with our God in this work we have undertaken, and so cause him to withdraw his present help from us, we shall be made a story and a by-word through the world. We shall open the mouths of enemies to speak evil of the ways of God.

Winthrop warned his followers that if they should fail to obey God's will, they would "be consumed out of the good land whither we are going."[7]

Alexander Campbell, however, read Winthrop's sermon as saying simply that God had a special purpose for America and had raised the country up to bring light to the dark world of Europe. "The light which shines from our political institutions," Campbell wrote, "will penetrate even the dungeons of European despots for the genius of our government is the genius of universal emancipation."[8] Reagan's pastor also spoke of the "city on a hill" in those terms and preached an optimistic theology that saw America as specially chosen to serve God's purpose. The Disciples were opposed to slavery, supporters of the temperance movement, and confident that if they worked hard, they would prosper. That was the message Reagan heard as a child and, having made no special study of American history himself, he had no reason to question it.[9] In his speeches, the "city on a hill" would become a "shining city" and an enemy would become, almost inevitably, an "evil empire."

From this history and his upbringing, Reagan went on to an identification of America with the kingdom of God, and Americans as citizens of that kingdom. It was an identification made most explicit, perhaps, in remarks he made on returning from a "Summit" meeting in Moscow in June 1988. "Let us remember," he said, "that being an American means remembering another loyalty, a loyalty as, the hymn puts it, 'to another country I have heard of, a place whose King is never seen and whose armies cannot be counted.'"* [10] Speaking to a group of exchange students, Reagan specifically linked American history with a divine plan:

> And we are kind of a miracle. I have always said—you may call it mysticism if you will—but there had to be some divine plan that

* The first line, which Reagan misquoted, is "I vow to thee my country." Ironically, the hymn was written by an Englishman in America and expressed his sense of exile first from England and secondly from the kingdom of heaven. It was used at the wedding and funeral of Princess Diana and at the funeral of Margaret Thatcher. One wonders whether Reagan learned it from Thatcher! One English bishop called it heretical for putting love of country ahead of love of God's kingdom and requested that it not be used in the Church of England.

> placed these great continents here between the two great oceans to be found by that kind of people. And that, maybe, is our purpose in life.[11]

When Reagan went away to college, it wasn't far away either geographically or psychologically. Eureka College was a very small institution with fewer than two hundred students, less than a hundred miles away, sponsored by the Disciples' church. There, as in high school, he acted and played football. But there he discovered his voice as a political weapon when financial pressures created a crisis in the college community. Reagan entered college in 1928, the year prior to the Wall Street crash that led to the Great Depression. As the Depression affected the farming communities, enrollment at the college and alumni contributions dropped, and the college president drew up a plan to consolidate departments and eliminate some programs. The college board approved the plan, but the faculty felt threatened and drew the students into opposition. Reagan was the freshman representative on the student strike committee. A meeting was called and a resolution presented, calling for the president's resignation. Reagan spoke at the meeting and the resolution was adopted.

The "rebellion" didn't last long. The president resigned so that the board could work out a solution apart from questions of personality, a few faculty members were fired, a new president was appointed, and life returned to normal. Ronald Reagan, however, always remembered the incident as the time when he found his voice as a leader. "I discovered that night," he wrote later, "that an audience has a feel to it, and, in the parlance of the theater, the audience and I were together. . . . It was heady wine."[12]

Reagan never excelled in academics, but he did have a remarkable memory. Friends said he never studied until the night before an exam, and then he would simply memorize everything. That technique got him a comfortable B average but did nothing to develop his powers of critical thinking.

Reagan graduated from college in 1932, in the depths of the Depression, and went up to Chicago to look for work in the rapidly growing broadcasting industry. There was no work available, but a woman in one of the Chicago stations advised him to go "out into the sticks" and find a job with a small station as a way to begin a career and gain experience. Reagan borrowed his father's car and drove from town to town until he found a beginning position at station WOC in Davenport, Iowa. Five years later, the owner of the Davenport station bought WHO in Des Moines and took Reagan with him to one of the strongest radio signals in the country. Reagan supplemented his income by writing newspaper columns and speaking at banquets. In a few short years, he had become a local celebrity and a solid financial success in the midst of the Depression.[13]

II

Sportscasting was never Ronald Reagan's idea of a career. He had wanted to be an actor as long as he could remember. But what road led from Dixon or Des Moines to Hollywood? Reagan found an answer to that question when the Chicago Cubs went west for spring training on Catalina Island near Los Angeles, and Reagan convinced the radio station that fans would like to hear reports on their team. Once in Los Angeles, Reagan got in touch with a former WHO employee who had already reached the West Coast and could introduce Reagan to her agent. The agent called the Warner Brothers casting director, and the casting director gave Reagan a screen test, liked the result, and passed word on to Jack Warner. Reagan had just arrived back in Iowa when a telegram came from the agent with an offer from Warner Brothers of a seven-year contract at two hundred dollars a week, or $10,100 a year. The average income in the United States that year was $1,788.[14] "How can we not believe in the greatness of America?" asked Ronald Reagan in his State of the Union Address in 1984.[15]

Hollywood, as it turned out, was not altogether the fulfillment of dreams that Reagan might first have imagined. He did well with what he was asked to do, which was to take a variety of roles in a series of "B" films. He appeared in eight movies in less than a year and was offered a new contract with an increased salary. He had just begun to make some "A" films and *King's Row*, made in 1942, had given him a starring role with Claude Rains and Charles Coburn, when World War II interrupted his career. Reagan was assigned to a unit making war propaganda films and stationed in Culver City, where he was ten miles from home and free to spend weekends with his family. After the war, Reagan's career in film never quite picked up where it had left off. He was hospitalized with a life-threatening illness that lingered for months, his wife left him, and Humphrey Bogart and Lauren Bacall backed out of a movie that would have co-starred him with them. He was making the modern equivalent of a million dollars a year and was among the highest-paid stars, but the top level of stardom was still just out of reach.[16]

At the end of the war, Reagan also found himself spending more and more time in organizational activities peripheral to his career as an actor. He had been required to join the Screen Actors Guild as a condition of his employment and had resented it until he was told that it had been formed to protect the ordinary actors against the producers' efforts to keep wages low and increase their control. Eventually Reagan became president of the SAG, and it became a central part of his life. The politics of the actor's life became increasingly complicated as two unions representing stagehands with a variety of skills battled for supremacy, amid charges of corruption on one side and communist infiltration on the other. Reagan kept the SAG out of the fighting but did believe that communists were attempting to infiltrate the industry and use Hollywood to subvert the American way of life. He had been a staunch supporter of Roosevelt and the New Deal and had introduced President Truman at a Los Angeles rally during the 1948 campaign; but he was beginning to move to the right, and by 1952 he was supporting Richard Nixon in his campaign for the presidency.

More important than the fact that his allegiances were shifting was the fact that Reagan was beginning to take a leadership role on political issues. In the early days of the Cold War, there were many ideas as to the best way to respond to the communist threat to human freedom in Eastern Europe. One approach that appealed to Reagan was the use of radio to make broadcasts to the countries that had become Russian satellites. General Lucius Clay was heading up an organization called "Crusade for Freedom" that was launched with government initiative and with a speech by General Eisenhower. The organization was intended to be privately funded and independently operated, but much of the funding came secretly from the CIA. They used the Liberty Bell as a symbol and an adaptation of Lincoln's words "that this world under God shall have a new birth of freedom" as a slogan. Reagan made speeches at fund-raising rallies for the group and taped a short film that was shown to civic groups around the country.[17] He said:

> The battleground of peace today is that strip of strategically located countries stretching from the Baltic to the Black Sea. They are not big countries geographically, but they contain several million freedom-loving people, our kind of people, who share our culture and who have sent millions of their sons and daughters to become part of these United States. . . . My name is Ronald Reagan. Last year the contributions of 16 million Americans to the Crusade for Freedom made possible the World Freedom Bell—symbol of hope and freedom to the communist-dominated people of Eastern Europe.

In a 1952 speech at Fulton, Missouri, where Winston Churchill had spoken six years earlier about the Iron Curtain, Reagan spoke about what America stood for in the Cold War with communism:

> It is simply the idea, the basis of this country and of our religion, the idea of the dignity of man, the idea that deep within the heart of each one of us is something so godlike and precious that no individual or group can decide for the people what is good for the people so well as they can decide for themselves.

America, he said, needed to "strive for freedom" for the sake of all mankind.[18]

1954 was a critical year for Ronald Reagan. His deeper involvement in political issues drew him away from Hollywood; and when General Electric offered him a chance both to host and sometimes act in a weekly program called *General Electric Theater*, Reagan was ready to move. Over the next eight years, Reagan not only hosted the program and acted in it but served also as a spokesman for GE, visiting well over a hundred GE research and manufacturing facilities in forty states and meeting, by his estimate, over a quarter of a million people.[19] He spoke also at other forums such as Rotary clubs and Moose lodges, presenting his views on economic progress that in form and content were often similar to what he said in the introductions and closing comments on the television show. In those factory visits, Reagan met with, and took questions from, blue-collar workers and mid-level managers alike. He often credited these engagements with helping him to develop his public speaking abilities.

"GE was invaluable to Reagan," wrote Lou Cannon, one of his biographers. "It gave him an opportunity to practice speeches and answer questions to sympathetic, but demanding, audiences. He learned how to polish his speeches and incorporate the events of the day into every talk he gave." As Reagan himself explained it afterwards, "When I went on those tours and shook hands with all of those people, I began to see that they were very different than the people Hollywood was talking about. I was seeing the same people that I grew up with in Dixon, Illinois. I realized I was living in a tinsel factory. And this exposure brought me back."[20]

Freedom and the threat of government to freedom was a central theme in Reagan's speeches from the very beginning. In 1957, he addressed the graduating class at Eureka College on the twenty-fifth anniversary of his own graduation and warned the graduates and audience to be careful:

> Remember that every government service, every offer of government financed security, is paid for in the loss of personal freedom. I am not castigating government and business for those many areas of normal cooperation, for those services that we know we must have and that we do willingly support. . . . But in the days to come whenever a voice is raised telling you to let the government do it, analyze very carefully to see whether the suggested service is worth the personal freedom which you must forgo in return for such service.[21]

General Electric prided itself on leaving Reagan free to speak as he wished, but they provided him with all their company publications, and on the long train trips between locations (Reagan avoided flying) he had ample time for reading. Ralph Cordiner, who was president of GE from 1950 to 1958 and chairman and CEO from 1958 to 1963, was a great believer in education and lectured on business principles at Columbia University's Graduate School of Business. Cordiner emphasized what he called "four . . . roadblocks to economic and social progress . . . (1) excessively high taxes, (2) growing, unchecked union power . . . (3) a fantastically growing federal government . . . and (4) the latent suspicion of 'big business'."[22] All this would have been part of Reagan's reading, and Reagan had not learned to be a critical reader.

As the years went by, the speeches Reagan made, whether for GE or other organizations, took on an increasingly partisan cast. In March 1961, for example, he spoke to the Phoenix, Arizona, Chamber of Commerce on "Encroaching Control: The Peril of Ever Expanding Government." The progressive income tax, he told them, came "direct from Karl Marx" and had "no moral justification." He told them that the next major step, playing on the American urge to help the less fortunate, would be government financed medical care.[23] There was peril from foreign enemies as well; he identified "the ideological struggle with Russia" as the "number one problem in the world":

> Many men in high places in government and many who mold public opinion in the press and on the airwaves subscribe to a theory that we are at peace, and we must make no overt move which might endanger that peace. . . . The inescapable truth is that we are at war, and we are losing that war simply because we don't, or won't realize that we are in it.

He went on to say that there could be only one end to the war, both foreign and domestic:

> One of the foremost authorities on communism in the world today has said we have ten years. Not ten years to make up our minds, but ten years to win or lose—by 1970 the world will be all slave or all free.[24]

The relationship with GE ended in 1962, perhaps because of falling ratings,* but perhaps because Reagan's rhetoric had turned increasingly harsh and GE was becoming uncomfortable with its star spokesman. From time to time, communities and organizations asked GE not to send Reagan in their direc-

---

* Some biographers think GE cancelled the program because of negative remarks Reagan made about the TVA, which was a major customer for GE generators. Edmund Morris says Reagan cancelled those remarks when he heard GE was concerned (Morris, 314). Another source claims that GE dropped Reagan because Attorney General Robert Kennedy told GE that he would authorize no federal contracts for GE while Reagan represented them (http://news. investors.com/ibd-editorials-viewpoint/020411-562237-ronald-reagans-son-remembers-the-day-when-ge-fired-his-dad.htm?p=2).

tion. But Reagan saw only a greater challenge to be confronted. 1961 had been a bad year for the new Kennedy administration. The Russians had put a man in space, Castro had made his government openly communist after the Bay of Pigs disaster, the Berlin wall had gone up in August, and Khrushchev had exploded a fifty-eight-megaton hydrogen bomb, still the most powerful bomb ever exploded. In a speech to the Los Angeles County Young Republicans on January 2, 1962, titled "What Price Freedom?" Reagan accused the new administration of policies that could lead to "social slavery." The administration, as Reagan saw it, was not standing up to the communists in Vietnam and was supporting "welfare statism" at home.[25]

California was electing a governor in 1962, and Reagan gave his support to Richard Nixon's doomed campaign. On the eve of the election, Reagan made a half-hour speech that was much more about his fears for America than about Nixon's qualifications

> I'd like to talk to you about what's at stake. . . . We've come to one of those infrequent moments in history when there is a change; when we're choosing between two party philosophies, and a wide ideological gulf separates the policies of the two parties.[26]

One-world socialism, government growth, subsidized agriculture, and welfare abuse were among the topics Reagan dealt with. Nixon lost overwhelmingly, but Reagan began to be talked about as a candidate for governor himself.

Devastated by the loss of his GE role, Reagan pointed his speeches more and more toward political themes. In 1964, the Republican Party decided to make a last desperate attempt to save the Goldwater candidacy by paying for a half hour of prime time for Reagan in the week before the election. Forever afterward, Reagan's address to the nation that night was remembered as "The Speech." Although it enthralled a broad swath of the electorate, it was far from enough to stem the tide that would sweep Lyndon Johnson into office with over 61% of the vote, the highest percentage in a hundred and forty-four years. Yet The Speech drew an amazing response. Millions of dollars poured into Republican coffers, and suddenly Reagan's was the voice that his party wanted most to hear.

Rereading The Speech out of the context of its time is a strange experience. Reagan has gone down in history as the "Great Communicator" with an optimistic message about "morning in America," but The Speech seems now strangely dark and depressing. One typical passage warns of apocalyptic dangers facing America:

> As for the peace that we would preserve, I wonder who among us would like to approach the wife or mother whose husband or son

> has died in South Vietnam and ask them if they think this is a peace that should be maintained indefinitely. Do they mean peace, or do they mean we just want to be left in peace? There can be no real peace while one American is dying some place in the world for the rest of us. We're at war with the most dangerous enemy that has ever faced mankind in his long climb from the swamp to the stars, and it's been said if we lose that war, and in so doing lose this way of freedom of ours, history will record with the greatest astonishment that those who had the most to lose did the least to prevent its happening. Well, I think it's time we ask ourselves if we still know the freedoms that were intended for us by the Founding Fathers.

The closing passage, borrowing phrases from Franklin Roosevelt and Abraham Lincoln, is darkest of all:

> You and I have a rendezvous with destiny. We can preserve for our children this, the last best hope of man on earth, or we can sentence them to take the first step into a thousand years of darkness.

The Speech is strangely "off key" when compared to speeches Reagan made when he was campaigning for his own election, or to his State of the Union messages. Those speeches have variety and changes of pace. The Speech *as given* is largely a recital of statistics about government spending and the dangers of bureaucracy with a few small stories to illustrate his points. Oddly, however, there is a text version of The Speech provided online by the Ronald Reagan Presidential Foundation that is radically different from The Speech as given and that is relied on by some books about Reagan as accurate. That text, most oddly, makes no reference to Goldwater. It also eliminates most of the statistics and centers more strongly on the dangers of the Cold War.* The transcript of the speech as given also reveals some of the misspoken words or phrases that would continue to be characteristic of Reagan's speeches. Intending to say "man's age-old dream," for example, he said "man's old—old-aged dream." The speech as edited has added one further sentence at the end:

> If we fail, at least let our children and our children's children say of us we justified our brief moment here. We did all that could be done.[27]

---

* The text as given can be found in a YouTube version at: http://reagan2020.us/speeches/A_Time_for_Choosing.asp. The speech as edited can be found at: http://reagan2020.us/speeches/The Ronald Reagan Presidential Foundation

It seems like a terribly negative ending for a campaign speech, but the speech as given ends:

> Barry Goldwater has faith in us that we have the ability and the right to make our own decision and determine our own destiny.[28]

The dark spirit of The Speech reflects, of course, the spirit of the Cold War, now an increasingly distant memory, and the fear of Russian and Chinese communism. But it was very much the spirit of the times and was reflected, after Kennedy's victory over Goldwater, in Kennedy's inaugural address two months later, pledging

> . . . that we shall pay any price, bear any burden, meet any hardship, support any friend, oppose any foe, in order to assure the survival and the success of liberty.

That speech went on to contemplate the same apocalyptic struggle depicted by Reagan:

> . . . both sides overburdened by the cost of modern weapons, both rightly alarmed by the steady spread of the deadly atom, yet both racing to alter that uncertain balance of terror that stays the hand of mankind's final war.[29]

Americans were accustomed to such language in the Cold War, but, looking back, it is striking to hear it almost equally from both parties. Striking also is the fact that in Reagan's great, final appeal for Goldwater, Goldwater is mentioned not at all in the edited version and not as a central element even in the speech as given. As in Reagan's final appeal for Richard Nixon in the gubernatorial race two years earlier, what we are given is essentially a paid commercial for Ronald Reagan; it is his views, his rhetoric, his leadership ability that we are given.

No final judgment of The Speech can be made, of course, without actually downloading it and watching it (which was impossible to do at the time). What is striking in watching it now is that the language and the delivery are also dark: Reagan speaks rapidly without any evidence of his trademark smile.[30] He comes on instead like a prosecuting attorney and, even when he makes a jibe at the opposition that brings smiles or laughter from the audience, he simply pauses briefly and moves on. He was not yet the relaxed and confident public speaker he would become.

The speech as given also has a density about it that seems ill suited to an audience. The rapid-fire statistics would be difficult to take in and understand unless the purpose is simply to create an impression of a speaker who has done his homework and knows much more than the audience can hope to understand. Reagan had this to say, for example, about "government's involvement in the farm economy over the last thirty years":

> Since 1955, the cost of this program has nearly doubled. One-fourth of farming in America is responsible for 85 percent of the farm surplus. Three-fourths of farming is out on the free market and has known a 21 percent increase in the per capita consumption of all its produce. You see, that one-fourth of farming—that's regulated and controlled by the federal government. In the last three years we've spent 43 dollars in the feed grain program for every dollar bushel of corn we don't grow.[31]

The Speech is simply too packed with information for anything except a lecture on economics, where a specialized audience would be familiar with the larger picture.

At some point in his past, Reagan began assembling speech material on three-by-five index cards. (College debaters often use the method, and one wonders whether he acquired the habit when he took part in debates in college.*) He made his notes in his own particular shorthand and then put the cards in small piles held together by rubber bands. His son Michael remembered looking in the second drawer of his father's desk and finding piles and piles of those rubber-banded cards.[32] Such a system enabled him to build a speech quickly by simply sorting through the cards to find facts and quotations and pieces of previous speeches that could be quickly assembled into a new speech for a new occasion. The difficulty with the system, of course, was that it could easily become simply a recitation of facts and quotations, rather than true communication with his audience.

A typical paragraph from The Speech, for example, made ten statements of fact in 141 words. No one could absorb that much material that quickly, but it would create an impression of an economic situation in dire straits and a speaker with a profound knowledge of the subject:

> No nation in history has ever survived a tax burden that reached a third of its national income.
>
> Today, 37 cents out of every dollar earned in this country is the tax collector's share, and yet our government continues to spend 17 million dollars a day more than the government takes in.

---

* Thomas Evans's *The Education of Ronald Reagan*, page 9, lists debating among Reagan's college activities.

> We haven't balanced our budget 28 out of the last 34 years.
>
> We've raised our debt limit three times in the last twelve months, and now our national debt is one and a half times bigger than all the combined debts of all the nations of the world.
>
> We have 15 billion dollars in gold in our treasury; we don't own an ounce.
>
> Foreign dollar claims are 27.3 billion dollars.
>
> And we've just had announced that the dollar of 1939 will now purchase 45 cents in its total value.

The difficulty with these facts is that they are taken completely out of context. The last line, for example, states that the dollar has declined in value by more than half in twenty-five years. What Reagan did not say was that the average income in that time had more than tripled, from $1,368 in 1939 to $4,576 in 1964. So the average American was able to buy half again as much with those depreciated dollars.[33]

Reagan's training was as an actor reading lines written by someone else, not speaking his own mind. He would become known as "The Great Communicator" when he learned to use the cards not so much to create a speech as to embellish it.

The Speech did also contain one other element that would become a Reagan trademark: the personal story. There were several of them: one, for example, about a Cuban refugee, and another about a pregnant woman. In the first story, two friends of Reagan's, hearing the Cuban's stories of life in Cuba, say to each other "We don't know how lucky we are." The Cuban responds: "How lucky you are? I had someplace to escape to." That one sentence, Reagan said, is the whole story, because "If we lose freedom here, there's no place to escape to. This is the last stand on earth."

In a second story, a woman pregnant with her seventh child comes to a judge, asking for a divorce. Questioning her, the judge learns that her husband is a laborer earning $250 a month but the woman, if divorced, would be eligible for $330 a month in the Aid to Dependent Children Program. Two women in her neighborhood had given her the idea by doing the same thing themselves.

That story, as told, creates an impression of a system rife with abuse, although the fact that the judge was said to have called Reagan with the story would tend to indicate that it was not usual at all. It would also seem unlikely that a judge, so alarmed, would grant such a divorce. Such a tale, of course, could not be traced or disputed but, in the words of one analyst, could "offer potent confirmation to a listener already convinced of its message."[34]

The fact remains that The Speech, with its stories and tightly packed information, created a strong impression and changed Reagan's life. David Broder of the *Washington Post* compared it with Bryan's "Cross of Gold" speech.[35] On the day after the election, a group of Republicans in Michigan formed a "Reagan for President" club, and some of Goldwater's backers began re-organizing to make Reagan their candidate in 1964.[36]

It would be eighteen years before Reagan was elected president, but meanwhile he would establish himself in politics by serving as Governor of California.

III

The decade of the 1960s was a time of turmoil and dramatic change in American life. The Civil Rights revolution was moving to extend and consolidate the gains made by black Americans, but hidden tensions in American society were coming to light and forcing major realignments. The war in Vietnam was a central factor in this realignment. Liberals increasingly opposed the war while conservatives, seeing it as a critical stand against communist aggression, supported it. In that division, many previously liberal blue-collar workers began to feel that opposition to the war was a failure to support their sons who were risking—and losing—their lives for their country. They had supported the social programs of the New Deal but were also beginning to feel that open housing threatened the value of their hard-earned property.

Ronald Reagan's self-portrait as an ordinary American outraged by the expansion of government control of American life fit well into this changing dynamic. Abortion, gay rights, environmental issues, and gender roles were all part of the changing social setting in which Reagan became a candidate for Governor of California, the state at the center of much of the tension. Pat Brown had served two terms as Governor of California, beating Richard Nixon to win a second term, and no one expected him to have much trouble beating a neophyte like Ronald Reagan to win a third term.

Reagan was a newcomer to campaigning but not to acting, and he found advisers who knew how to make good use of his skills. He would campaign as much as possible on television, and he would prove a master of the rhetorical skills required by a television age. It was no longer necessary for a campaigner to speak with a booming voice to crowds of thousands; on the television screen, a campaigner needed to speak to the two or three people sitting six feet away in the comfort of their living room. What was needed was a low-key, highly personal, friendly manner, illustrated with simple stories. Effective speaking in the television age is radically different from what it had always been in the past. Ronald Reagan pioneered and mastered those skills.

In the gubernatorial campaign of 1964, Ronald Reagan projected a sincerity and sense of humor that blunted Brown's efforts to portray him as either a fool or a dangerous extremist. Most voters saw him as a friendly man who understood their problems and shared their sense of outrage at high taxes, student protesters, and a rapidly changing world. In November, they swept him into office by a margin of nearly a million votes.

In taking the oath of office, Reagan spoke, as always, about the importance of freedom. He wrote the speech himself, and it held no surprises except, perhaps, toward the beginning, for those who had never heard him speak before.

> Freedom is a fragile thing and is never more than one generation away from extinction. It is not ours by inheritance; it must be fought for and defended constantly by each generation, for it comes only once to a people. Those who have known freedom and then lost it have never known it again.

He had said it before, but still it seems curious, coming as it does fewer than twenty years after the end of World War II, in which period a good many people in Western Europe had regained their lost freedom. But for Reagan, the socialist governments of Western Europe were equivalent to communism in creating strong central governments providing security against illness and unemployment. For Reagan, the defense of freedom was centered on the role of government and, in particular, on taxes:

> Those of us here today who have been elected to constitutional office or legislative position are . . . of the people, chosen by them to see that no permanent structure of government ever encroaches on freedom or assumes a power beyond that freely granted by the people. We stand between the taxpayer and the tax spender.

The speech ended with what would become another trademark of Reagan speeches, a "show and tell" type of story with a specific connection, in this case between California and the war in Vietnam.

> If, in glancing aloft, some of you were puzzled by the small size of our state flag . . . there is an explanation. That flag was carried into battle in Vietnam by young men of California. Many will not be coming home. One did, Sergeant Robert Howell, grievously wounded. He brought that flag back. I thought we would be proud to have it fly over the Capitol today. It might even serve to put our problems in better perspective. It might remind us of the need to give our sons and daughters a cause to believe in and banners to follow.[37]

That battle flag was indicative of the way Reagan concerned himself with national and international problems beyond the state, both in the campaign and as governor. He began consulting about the war with World War II generals and, within his first year as governor, urged the governors' association to withdraw support for President Johnson's Vietnam policy. When Johnson planned to mine Haiphong Harbor, Governor Reagan suggested an amphibious invasion of the North. In areas more relevant to his role as a state governor, on the other hand, Reagan's record showed at least an occasional willingness to avoid confrontation. Inheriting a deficit, he approved the largest tax increase in the state's history and, when the legislature acted to remove most barriers to abortion by veto-proof margins, Reagan reluctantly signed the bill rather than register his disapproval with a futile veto.[38]

Reagan was not willing, however, to avoid confrontation in one highly visible area. Although he had first found his voice as a student protester, he began his career in office by confronting student protesters at the Berkeley campus of the University of California. Students were on strike in protest against Navy recruitment efforts on the campus. University president Clark Kerr was looking for ways to avoid confrontation, but Reagan was in no mood to compromise. "In all the sound and fury at Berkeley," he said, "one voice is missing. And since it is the voice of those who built the university and pay the entire cost of its operation, I think it's time that voice was heard."[39]

He had spoken of it also in his inaugural address:

> On the subject of education . . . hundreds of thousands of young men and women will receive an education in our state colleges and universities. We are proud of our ability to provide this opportunity for our youth and we believe it is no denial of academic freedom to provide this education within a framework of reasonable rules and regulations. Nor is it a violation of individual rights to require obedience to these rules and regulations or to insist that those unwilling to abide by them should get their education elsewhere.
>
> It does not constitute political interference with intellectual freedom for the taxpaying citizens—who support the college and university systems—to ask that, in addition to teaching, they build character on accepted moral and ethical standards.[40]

Freedom always requires rules or guidelines or laws that prevent one person's freedom from intruding on another's. Reagan believed that student demonstrators were using their freedom improperly—to interfere with the freedom of other students to come and go without interference. Student unrest increased with the escalation of the Vietnam war and eventually reached such a level that Reagan called in the National Guard at the University of California in Berkeley. Democrats and Republicans alike believed he had acted properly to prevent further violence. Similar strong action was required at the University of California in Santa Barbara the following year. Reagan could be intemperate in his remarks about student demonstrators, but his actions were generally seen as firm but fair.

Reagan had campaigned with three incompatible promises: to cut taxes, to reduce deficits, and to balance the budget. He pledged it again in his inaugural address, saying "The cost of California's government is too high. It adversely affects our business climate. We are going to squeeze and cut and trim until we reduce the cost of government."[41]

Once inaugurated, however, it became necessary to find ways to carry out the pledge. It didn't help that he had no administrative experience. Cut as he might—and did—the budget could not be balanced without a tax increase. It turned out that balancing the budget was his first priority; so when he had cut as much as he could, taxes went up. The required tax increase was the largest ever asked for by any governor, but freedom to visit recreation areas, send children to schools and colleges, and provide care for patients with mental illnesses limits freedom from taxes. Reagan put an end to the tradition of tuition-free education at the state colleges and universities, but those schools still required an enormous commitment of state funds.

Looking back just after completing his two terms, Reagan felt that what he had done in California demonstrated the truth of his theories:

> The "lab test" of my theory—California—was pretty messed up after eight years of a road show version of the Great Society. . . . California state government was increasing by about 5,000 new employees a year. We were the welfare capital of the world with 16 percent of the nation's caseload. Soon, California's caseload was increasing by 40,000 a month.
>
> We instituted a policy of "cut, squeeze and trim" and froze the hiring of employees as replacements for retiring employees or others leaving state service.
>
> . . . That was four years ago. Today, the needy have had an average increase of 43 percent in welfare grants in California, but the taxpayers have saved $2 billion by the caseload not increasing that 40,000 a month. Instead, there are some 400,000 fewer on welfare today than then. . . .
>
> That $750-million deficit turned into an $850-million surplus which we returned to the people in a one-time tax rebate. That

> wasn't easy. One state senator described that rebate as "an unnecessary expenditure of public funds."
>
> . . . We have just turned over to a new administration in Sacramento a government virtually the same size it was eight years ago. With the state's growth rate, this means that government absorbed a workload increase, in some departments as much as 66 percent.
>
> We also turned over—for the first time in almost a quarter of a century—a balanced budget and a surplus of $500 million. In these eight years just passed, we returned to the people in rebates, tax reductions and bridge toll reductions $5.7 billion. All of this is contrary to the will of those who deplore conservatism and profess to be liberals, yet all of it is pleasing to its citizenry.[42]

In 1977, two years after completing his two terms as governor, he summed up his philosophy in a speech defining a "New Republican Party":

> We believe that liberty can be measured by how much freedom Americans have to make their own decisions, even their own mistakes. Government must step in when one's liberties impinge on one's neighbor's. Government must protect constitutional rights, deal with other governments, protect citizens from aggressors, assure equal opportunity, and be compassionate in caring for those citizens who are unable to care for themselves.

Reagan was attempting to define a "New Republican Party" because he was hoping to be that party's candidate in 1978, for the upcoming 1980 election. The problem he faced was an incumbent Republican president, Gerald Ford, and a party reluctant to turn away from the decent but uninspiring man who had had to put the pieces back together after the Watergate disaster and Nixon's resignation. Ford had won the nomination but had lost a close election to Jimmy Carter in 1976.

Four years later, Reagan announced his candidacy once again, this time with a more optimistic, almost visionary speech that called for developing a close relationship with Mexico and Canada and moving to develop less dependence on foreign sources of energy. "Freedom," as Reagan now defined it, included less dependence on foreign suppliers of energy:

> We need more energy and that means diversifying our sources of supply away from the OPEC countries. Yes, it means more efficient automobiles. But it also means more exploration and development of oil and natural gas here in our own country. The only way to

> free ourselves from the monopoly pricing power of OPEC is to be less dependent on outside sources of fuel.
>
> The answer obvious to anyone except those in the administration, it seems, is more domestic production of oil and gas. We must also have wider use of nuclear power within strict safety rules, of course. There must be more spending by the energy industries on research and development of substitutes for fossil fuels.

Early in his speech, he provided an emotional story, one that helped create a contingent of "Reagan Democrats," as he recalled the day during the Depression when his father got notice that he no longer had a job.

> I have lived through one depression. I carry with me the memory of a Christmas Eve when my brother and I and our parents exchanged modest gifts—there was no lighted tree as there had been on Christmases past. I remember watching my father open what he thought was a greeting from his employer. We all watched and yes, we were hoping for a bonus check. It was notice that he no longer had a job. And in those days the government ran radio announcements telling workers not to leave home looking for jobs—there were no jobs. I'll carry with me always the memory of my father sitting there holding that envelope, unable to look at us. I cannot and will not stand by while inflation and joblessness destroy the dignity of our people.

As so often in Reagan's speeches, there was an over-reliance on facts and statistics, but this time he came back at the end to his enduring vision of the "shining city" and his continuing and repeated use of that Rooseveltian phrase about a "rendezvous with destiny":

> . . . there remains the greatness of our people, our capacity for dreaming up fantastic deeds and bringing them off to the surprise of an unbelieving world. When Washington's men were freezing at Valley Forge, Tom Paine told his fellow Americans: "We have it in our power to begin the world over again." We still have that power.
>
> We—today's living Americans—have in our lifetime fought harder, paid a higher price for freedom and done more to advance the dignity of man than any people who ever lived on this earth. The citizens of this great nation want leadership—yes—but not a "man on a white horse" demanding obedience to his commands. They want someone who believes they can "begin the world over

> again." A leader who will unleash their great strength and remove the roadblocks government has put in their way. I want to do that more than anything I've ever wanted. And it's something that I believe with God's help I can do. . . .
>
> We who are privileged to be Americans have had a rendezvous with destiny since the moment in 1630 when John Winthrop, standing on the deck of the tiny *Arabella* off the coast of Massachusetts, told the little band of pilgrims, "We shall be as a city upon a hill. The eyes of all people are upon us so that if we shall deal falsely with our God in this work we have undertaken and so cause Him to withdraw His present help from us, we shall be made a story and a byword throughout the world."
>
> A troubled and afflicted mankind looks to us, pleading for us to keep our rendezvous with destiny; that we will uphold the principles of self-reliance, self-discipline, morality, and—above all—responsible liberty for every individual that we will become that shining city on a hill.
>
> I believe that you and I together can keep this rendezvous with destiny.[43]

Local campaigning, however, brought out a different side of Ronald Reagan. Some were horrified when he announced his intention to open his formal campaign in Neshoba, Mississippi, where three civil rights workers had been murdered fourteen years earlier. Against advice from some of his advisers, Reagan went ahead with the speech—which, like many local campaign speeches, had little to say about any substantive issues. In a twenty-minute speech, Reagan used a tenth of his time to talk about a football game involving Tennessee and Mississippi. A quarter of the speech was devoted to a visit Reagan had made to the Olympic swimming team. Less than half of the speech made any reference to the campaign, and most of that was "zingers" directed at the Democratic Party and President Carter. The "meat of the speech," what he went to Mississippi to say, was practically hidden away in the midst of the jibes. It was almost unnoticed at the time; but when Reagan said, almost in passing, "I believe in states' rights," he was heard throughout the South, and the continuing reorientation of the "Solid South" from the Republican to the Democratic column continued.

IV

Rampant inflation and the continuing hostage crisis in Iran undercut Jimmy Carter's bid for reelection, and Ronald Reagan became the first former Hollywood actor to be elected President of the United States. Although he had always prided himself on writing his own speeches, Reagan had used occasional assistance as Governor of California, and he employed a former Nixon speechwriter, Ken Khachigian, during the campaign. The two had worked well together, and Khachigian wrote a draft for an inaugural address. Reagan was uncomfortable with the draft and wrote a new speech, using some of Khachigian's ideas but incorporating much material of his own on economic issues. He wanted to begin his administration by making clear his philosophy of government, and he did that in short order:

> In this present crisis, government is not the solution to our problem; government is the problem. . . . It is my intention to curb the size and influence of the Federal establishment and to demand recognition of the distinction between the powers granted to the Federal Government and those reserved to the States or to the people.

Then he spelled out his understanding of American government on an issue that went back to Patrick Henry:

> All of us need to be reminded that the Federal Government did not create the States; the States created the Federal Government.

Lincoln, for one, would have disagreed completely with the second half of the statement. Indeed, Reagan himself had often stressed the fact that the Constitution begins "We, the people of the United States. . . ."

Reagan understood freedom in terms of a conflict between the individual and the government, especially the federal government:

> If we look to the answer as to why for so many years we achieved so much, prospered as no other people on Earth, it was because here in this land we unleashed the energy and individual genius of man to a greater extent than has ever been done before. . . . It is no coincidence that our present troubles parallel and are proportionate to the intervention and intrusion in our lives that result from unnecessary and excessive growth of government.

Having made that as clear as he could, Reagan moved on, as he always wanted to do, to evoke patriotic emotions. In doing so, he began with a perspective provided by Khachigian that he liked because, as an actor, Reagan was always conscious not only of the speech but of its setting. When he was asked to make The Speech for Goldwater in a television studio, he arranged that it be given instead to a live audience. For his inauguration as governor, he arranged for a battle flag from Vietnam to be installed above the state Capitol building in Sacramento. For his inauguration as president, Reagan was given a radical revision of the previous arrangements, with the oath administered for the first time on the west front of the Capitol building rather than the east.* The result was that the president, as he spoke, looked down the Mall to the Washington and Lincoln memorials and to Arlington Cemetery in the distance. Khachigian incorporated the revised scene into a dramatic ending for the speech:

> This is the first time in history that this ceremony has been held, as you have been told, on this West Front of the Capitol. Standing here, one faces a magnificent vista, opening up on this city's special beauty and history. At the end of this open mall are those shrines to the giants on whose shoulders we stand.

Some of the lines describing the Washington, Jefferson, and Lincoln memorials sound more like a professional writer than Reagan:

> Directly in front of me, the monument to a monumental man: George Washington, father of our country. . . . Off to one side, the stately memorial to Thomas Jefferson. The Declaration of Independence flames with his eloquence.
>
> And then beyond the Reflecting Pool the dignified columns of the Lincoln Memorial. Whoever would understand in his heart the meaning of America will find it in the life of Abraham Lincoln.
>
> Beyond those monuments to heroism is the Potomac River, and on the far shore the sloping hills of Arlington National Cemetery with its row on row of simple white markers bearing crosses or Stars of David. They add up to only a tiny fraction of the price that has been paid for our freedom.
>
> Each one of those markers is a monument to the kinds of hero I spoke of earlier. Their lives ended in places called Belleau Wood, The Argonne, Omaha Beach, Salerno and halfway around the world on Guadalcanal, Tarawa, Pork Chop Hill, the Chosin

* Although the decision to move the inauguration is often attributed to Reagan, the Joint Committee on the Inauguration announced its decision to move the inauguration from the east to the west side of the Capitol in June 1980, more than a month before Reagan was nominated. The congressional committee calculated that the move would save money since they could use the West Front terraces as an inaugural platform rather than build one from scratch, and that the Mall side of the Capitol would provide more space for spectators. Construction of the inaugural platform began in September 1980, when Reagan and Jimmy Carter were running even in the polls and the election's outcome remained uncertain.

> Reservoir, and in a hundred rice paddies and jungles of a place called Vietnam.

Thus Reagan invited those listening to picture American history as it is summed up at the Mall; and for those watching on television, the cameras obligingly followed the president's words and showed the scenes he was describing. The final scene, over which Reagan and Khachigian struggled, zeroed in on those "markers" in Arlington National Cemetery. A friend had sent Reagan the story of a soldier killed in France in World War I who had left behind a diary with the words "My Pledge" written on the flyleaf. Under that title, the soldier, Martin Treptow, had written "America must win this war. Therefore I will work, I will save, I will sacrifice, I will endure, I will fight cheerfully and do my utmost as if the issue of the whole struggle depended on me alone."

The story brought tears to Reagan's eyes, and he wanted to bring tears as well to the eyes of everyone listening. The difficulty that Khachigian foresaw lay in the fact that Reagan planned to say that Martin Treptow was lying under one of the markers in Arlington. Khachigian knew the Washington press corps and was certain they would go looking for the marker and make enormous trouble if they failed to find it. Khachigian went looking himself and found that Treptow was, in fact, buried not in Arlington but in Wisconsin. Reagan, however, was determined to tell the story and at last they agreed on language that was acceptable to both: "under one such marker lies Martin Treptow."

The Washington press corps did, indeed, check out the story and learned within hours where Treptow was buried. Reagan's aides, Khachigian among them, admitted the error and took the blame. They did not point out that the error had been spotted in advance and that Reagan had insisted on using it nonetheless because it was "too theatrically imposing" to be sullied with accuracy. It was the first time, but not the last, that Reagan would encounter such problems.[44]

Once past the inauguration, Reagan was faced with the task of governing. He had governed California by finding skilled administrators to carry out the functions of government. Some of them came to Washington with him, and he would find others to share the necessary administrative tasks. Congress and the Washington press corps would spend the next eight years marveling at a style of administration they had never before encountered because, more than anyone else who had ever served as President of the United States, Reagan was not an administrator. He was a salesman for certain ideas but had no idea how to carry out those ideas, nor did he have any great interest in learning the details of programs to attain his goals.

Some of the professionals Reagan dealt with were appalled at his ignorance of legislative and administrative matters, even of the names of key people in

Congress and his own administration. Conservative columnist George Will wondered out loud how anyone so uninformed could have found his way to the Oval Office, and Clark Clifford, a consummate Washington insider, dismissed Reagan in a widely quoted remark as an "amiable dunce."[45] What some of those around him came to realize with time was that his was a different type of intellect than that of most people in the political world. He was not interested in the details of policy, but he was very interested in goals and was able to concentrate on them to the exclusion of almost everything else.*

On February 5, 1981, two weeks after his inauguration, Reagan spoke to the nation for the first time from the Oval Office and centered attention on the economy. Washington professionals may have been shocked by Reagan's ignorance of the detailed information that was their livelihood, but Reagan knew what the voters needed to know, and he knew how to tell them in plain language:

> I regret to say that we're in the worst economic mess since the Great Depression.
>
> A few days ago I was presented with a report I'd asked for, a comprehensive audit, if you will, of our economic condition. You won't like it. I didn't like it. But we have to face the truth and then go to work to turn things around. And make no mistake about it, we can turn them around.

He would not, he told his audience, "subject you to the jumble of charts, figures, and economic jargon of that audit." Reagan had obviously reacted to the "jumble" of that report like any other citizen in the presence of economic experts. His eyes had glazed over, but he had experts available to tell him what he needed to know. He would perform the same service for the nation and give them first what he called "a few 'attention getters' from the audit":

> The Federal budget is out of control, and we face runaway deficits of almost $80 billion for this budget year that ends September 30th. That deficit is larger than the entire Federal budget in 1957, and so is the almost $80 billion we will pay in interest this year on the national debt.

---

* David Gergen, an aide to several presidents, relied on a book by Harvard psychologist Howard Gardner that speaks of the variety of personality types. Gergen concluded that Reagan was high in "emotional intelligence," as distinct from the "logical-mathematical intelligence" that is more common in lawyers and politicians. "Emotional intelligence," however, is said to be a critical component of effective leadership. Evans, 11.

> Twenty years ago, in 1960, our Federal Government payroll was less than $13 billion. Today it is $75 billion. During these 20 years our population has only increased by 23.3 percent.* The Federal budget has gone up 528 percent.**
>
> . . . In 1960 mortgage interest rates averaged about 6 percent. They're 2½ times as high now, 15.4 percent.
>
> The percentage of your earnings the Federal Government took in taxes in 1960 has almost doubled.
>
> And finally there are 7 million Americans caught up in the personal indignity and human tragedy of unemployment. If they stood in a line, allowing 3 feet for each person, the line would reach from the coast of Maine to California.***
>
> Well, so much for the audit itself. Let me try to put this in personal terms.

It was vintage Reagan: a blizzard of facts and then some stories and simple illustrations to make it personal. He told them what it meant in terms of a dollar "such as you earned, spent, or saved in 1960," and he had charts to display to help make it clearer still. And he could provide a simple analogy:

> Well, you know, we can lecture our children about extravagance until we run out of voice and breath. Or we can cure their extravagance by simply reducing their allowance.

The cost of government must be reduced, he told them, because it was "out of control," and he intended to reduce taxes by ten per cent in each of the next three years. It was a tough lesson on economics, but it ended with an upbeat affirmation of faith that all would be well.

> We can leave our children with an unrepayable massive debt and a shattered economy, or we can leave them liberty in a land where every individual has the opportunity to be whatever God intended us to be. All it takes is a little common sense and recognition of our own ability. Together we can forge a new beginning for America.[46]

---

* In the first two years of Reagan's administration, the Federal payroll declined slightly, but it grew by over 10% in the remaining six years.

** Federal budgets in the Reagan era increased by over 50%, and the deficits were the largest of any post-war president.

*** Reagan underestimated: actually, the imaginary line would have reached halfway to Hawaii.

Reagan had always admired Franklin D. Roosevelt; and in his frequent Oval Office talks on television and Saturday radio broadcasts, he would attempt to do what Roosevelt had done in his Fireside Chats: keep the public informed and supportive of his program.

Two months later, Reagan presented his program to Congress. In the meantime, there had been an attempted assassination, which Reagan survived in style, winning additional support for whatever he might propose. Ronald Reagan had only a few ideas, but they were strongly held and frequently repeated. He said once:

> You have to keep pounding away with your message, year after year, because that's the only way it will sink into the collective consciousness. . . . I'm a big believer in stump speeches—speeches you can give over and over again with slight variations. Because if you have something you believe in deeply, it's worth repeating time and again until you achieve it.[47]

Thus, when he presented his program to Congress, it was a program designed to do what he had always talked about: first of all cut taxes, secondly increase defense spending, and thirdly plan for a balanced budget by 1984, the end of his first term. He tied it in with a recent space shuttle voyage to add emotional impact:

> With the space shuttle we tested our ingenuity once again, moving beyond the accomplishments of the past into the promise and uncertainty of the future. Thus, we not only planned to send up a 122-foot aircraft 170 miles into space, but we also intended to make it maneuverable and return it to earth, landing 98 tons of exotic metals delicately on a remote, dry lake bed. The space shuttle did more than prove our technological abilities. It raised our expectations once more. It started us dreaming again.
>
> The poet Carl Sandburg wrote, "The republic is a dream. Nothing happens unless first a dream." And that's what makes us, as Americans, different. We've always reached for a new spirit and aimed at a higher goal. We've been courageous and determined, unafraid and bold. Who among us wants to be first to say we no longer have those qualities, that we must limp along, doing the same things that have brought us our present misery? I believe that the people you and I represent are ready to chart a new course. They look to us to meet the great challenge, to reach beyond the commonplace and not fall short for lack of creativity or courage.

> Someone, you know, has said that he who would have nothing to do with thorns must never attempt to gather flowers. Well, we have much greatness before us. We can restore our economic strength and build opportunities like none we've ever had before. As Carl Sandburg said, all we need to begin with is a dream that we can do better than before. All we need to have is faith, and that dream will come true. All we need to do is act, and the time for action is now.[48]

He made it sound easy; but the hard economic numbers that he recited, and that his advisers had run by him, would not go away so easily. A major part of the difficulty was that Reagan was also determined to enact a major increase in defense spending. An existing deficit, enhanced by greatly increased defense spending and further increased by cutting taxes, would not disappear in the face of even fairly radical cuts in the budget—and neither Reagan nor his advisers were prepared for drastic cuts in Social Security or other social programs.

V

Unlike any other president before or after, Ronald Reagan's greatest talent was his ability to communicate with the American people. Lincoln, both Roosevelts, and Kennedy were remarkably effective communicators, but they were also effective administrators with specific, measurable, and attainable goals. Reagan's goals, while clear and specific—cut taxes, build up the military, reduce the size of government—were not easy to measure and harder still to attain; there will, after all, always be taxes and a budget to balance; government of some size will always be necessary; and if a military buildup was to be measured against an imagined Russian military strength, it was difficult to say when it would be accomplished.

Reagan, moreover, was not an administrator. Biographer Lou Cannon wrote of him:

> He loved being president and respected the traditions of the office, but he was neither awed by his new role nor bowed by the burdens of office. He wanted to do what he had always done—make speeches, delight his aides with anecdotes, write letters, work out every day in the small gym adjacent to his living quarters, and, in general, take more time for himself than most presidents would have considered possible.[49]

Gradually, his staff learned to live with the president they had rather than the one they might have wished they had. The president they had was one who could speak effectively to the country, so that even while taxes and the size of government continued to rise, he could persuade them that they were moving in the right direction, that America was a great country and they were lucky to be Americans. Deliberately or not, he conserved his energy for what he did best.

For Reagan to be an effective leader, there had to be speechwriters. Reagan had learned years ago, as Governor of California, that he needed speechwriters. There were simply too many public occasions for any one speechwriter to provide for. More than ever, he needed them in Washington; his effective use of them would shape his presidency. The six Reagan speechwriters were a diverse and frequently shifting group, but all of them quickly learned to adapt themselves to Reagan's particular style.

Ken Khachigian, whose work on the First Inaugural Address has already been discussed, had worked for the Nixon election campaign in 1967 and 1968, and then had gone to Washington almost immediately after graduating from law school, to do research and eventually to become a speechwriter, first for President Nixon and then for President Ford. Returning to California to help Nixon with his memoirs, he was recruited for the Reagan campaign and became Reagan's chief speechwriter. He was succeeded in 1984 by Bentley Elliott, who had come to Washington by way of CBS News, and whose four-year tenure as Reagan's chief writer was the longest anyone served in that capacity. Elliott prepared himself for his role with Reagan by spending three weeks reading all his speeches and making copious notes about Reagan's stated positions on a wide variety of issues. Commenting on Reagan's style, he said:

> He uses hard words. He concentrates and speaks with great conciseness. There is very little dead language in his style. . . . His stuff is very concisely written. We overwrite for him, whereas he is prone to economize in language. He has a tremendous austerity in style. And little known to others, he loves facts. I think he's that way because he projects so much emotion and gets emotional quite readily. He will break down, as he did when in the Vietnam Memorial Speech we put something in like, "Dear Son, we put you in God's loving arms." But the president has a sense of himself, and he sees himself talking in a matter of fact way to the man in the street. He is very aware when he is talking out of character.[50*]

Peggy Noonan, like Elliott, came to Washington from CBS, where she had been chief writer for Dan Rather's CBS Evening News. One of the most

* If these remarks seem not carefully crafted, it is because they come from an interview rather than a published paper.

important speeches she wrote for Reagan was the one he gave at Pointe du Hoc, one of the D-Day beaches in Normandy, where Rangers had been assigned to scale a cliff on top of which were German gun emplacements. In the face of enemy fire, the Rangers took the position and held it against German counterattacks. Noonan later said:

> I wanted it to be a knockout. . . . I wanted people to have pictures in their mind of what the past had been like. I wanted the president vividly to describe what these men did forty years ago.

As background for that assignment, she read a number of books about the Normandy invasion, found pictures of the area and of the graves and cemetery where the president would be speaking, and imagined the scene—the weather and time of day and audience—so as to be able to imagine exactly what Reagan would be seeing as he spoke. She worked through fifteen drafts before she was satisfied, and then had to defend it against the various criticisms and suggestions of the fifty-some members of staff and agencies who had the right to review it. She won some of those battles and lost others, but somehow the result was one of Reagan's most memorable and emotional speeches:[51]

> We stand on a lonely, windswept point on the northern shore of France. The air is soft, but forty years ago at this moment, the air was dense with smoke and the cries of men, and the air was filled with the crack of rifle fire and the roar of cannon. At dawn, on the morning of the 6th of June, 1944, 225 Rangers jumped off the British landing craft and ran to the bottom of these cliffs. Their mission was one of the most difficult and daring of the invasion: to climb these sheer and desolate cliffs and take out the enemy guns. The Allies had been told that some of the mightiest of these guns were here, and they would be trained on the beaches to stop the Allied advance.
>
> The Rangers looked up and saw the enemy soldiers—at the edge of the cliffs shooting down at them with machine guns and throwing grenades. And the American Rangers began to climb. They shot rope ladders over the face of these cliffs and began to pull themselves up. When one Ranger fell, another would take his place. When one rope was cut, a Ranger would grab another and begin his climb again. They climbed, shot back, and held their footing. Soon, one by one, the Rangers pulled themselves over the top, and in seizing the firm land at the top of these cliffs, they began to seize back the continent of Europe. Two hundred and

> twenty-five came here. After two days of fighting, only 90 could still bear arms.

Noonan had seen the Brooklyn Dodgers of 1955 described as "the boys of summer," and the phrase seemed to her an apt way to refer to the young soldiers who had scaled the cliffs.[52]

> Behind me is a memorial that symbolizes the Ranger daggers that were thrust into the top of these cliffs. And before me are the men who put them there. These are the boys of Pointe du Hoc. These are the men who took the cliffs. These are the champions who helped free a continent. These are the heroes who helped end a war.
>
> Gentlemen, I look at you and I think of the words of Stephen Spender's poem. You are men who in your "lives fought for life . . . and left the vivid air signed with your honor. . . ."
>
> Forty summers have passed since the battle that you fought here. You were young the day you took these cliffs; some of you were hardly more than boys, with the deepest joys of life before you. Yet you risked everything here. Why? Why did you do it? What impelled you to put aside the instinct for self-preservation and risk your lives to take these cliffs? What inspired all the men of the armies that met here? We look at you, and somehow we know the answer. It was faith, and belief; it was loyalty and love. . . .
>
> You all knew that some things are worth dying for. One's country is worth dying for, and democracy is worth dying for, because it's the most deeply honorable form of government ever devised by man. All of you loved liberty. All of you were willing to fight tyranny, and you knew the people of your countries were behind you.[53]

Six weeks later, Noonan met Reagan for the first time and was struck by his frailty and confusion. He had to be told who she was, but he responded, "That was wonderful! It was like Flanders Field."[54]

Noonan also wrote the brief speech Reagan made following the *Challenger* disaster. She remembered how, when she was still a child, she had seen John Glenn make the first American space flight. She remembered reading a poem by an airman who was killed during World War I and who had written the words Reagan quoted toward the end of his speech. As it turned out, Reagan also knew the poem because Hollywood star Tyrone Power, a friend of Reagan's, had carried it with him when he flew missions during World War II, and Reagan had read it at Power's funeral.[55]

> The crew of the Space Shuttle *Challenger* honored us by the manner in which they lived their lives. We will never forget them, nor the last time we saw them, this morning, as they prepared for their journey and waved goodbye and "slipped the surly bonds of earth" to "touch the face of God."[56*]

Those two speeches were ranked among the top one hundred political speeches of the twentieth century in a list compiled by professors at the University of Wisconsin-Madison and Texas A&M University and based on the opinions of "137 leading scholars of American public address."[57] Noonan recalled later how she had loved to sit in her speechwriter's office and read through the speeches of Franklin D. Roosevelt. "I'd think," she said, "this is how Reagan should sound." She had, after all, grown up in a blue-collar family on Long Island and was—as Reagan himself was—a "Reagan Democrat, remembering still the great days of the New Deal and the impact of the speeches of FDR."[58]

Others of the speechwriting team had come from a background of newspaper work and political involvement. None had the kind of literary or intellectual credentials of some of those who had served Franklin D. Roosevelt and Adlai Stevenson, but Reagan was looking for language that would appeal to the ordinary American, and a background in radio, television, and print was a better fit for that purpose. Increasingly in the second term, Reagan relied on his speechwriters; after all, he had admitted even in his first term that he had nothing new to say: "Now some of you may be thinking, 'Well, he hasn't said a thing that's new.' I guess that's true. Some values shouldn't change." He said that he never thought of himself as a great man, but as a man committed to great ideas. He was "The Great Communicator," not an original thinker.[59]

VI

The speech Reagan made when he was renominated in 1984 was quintessential Reagan. He began with a cute story:

> Four years ago, I didn't know precisely every duty of this office, and not too long ago, I learned about some new ones from the first graders of Corpus Christi School in Chambersburg, Pennsylvania. Little Leah Kline was asked by her teacher to describe my duties. She said: "The President goes to meetings. He helps the animals.

---

* The lines are engraved on the tombstone of an American, John Gillespie Magee, Jr., who served in the Canadian air force and wrote the poem before his death in a mid-air collision over England. They are the first and last lines of the poem that students at the Air Force Academy are still required to memorize.

> The President gets frustrated. He talks to other Presidents." How does wisdom begin at such an early age?

He spent the bulk of the speech talking about his concerns for lower taxes and smaller government, and his hope for progress toward arms control. And he ended with a soaring invocation of the Olympic torch that had passed across the country a few weeks earlier on its way to the Los Angeles Olympics:

> All through the spring and summer, we marveled at the journey of the Olympic torch as it made its passage east to west. Over 9,000 miles, by some 4,000 runners, that flame crossed a portrait of our nation.
>
> From our Gotham City, New York, to the Cradle of Liberty, Boston, across the Appalachian springtime, to the City of the Big Shoulders, Chicago. Moving south toward Atlanta, over to St. Louis, past its Gateway Arch, across wheat fields into the stark beauty of the Southwest and then up into the still, snowcapped Rockies. And, after circling the greening Northwest, it came down to California, across the Golden Gate and finally into Los Angeles. And all along the way, that torch became a celebration of America. And we all became participants in the celebration.
>
> Each new story was typical of this land of ours. There was Ansel Stubbs, a youngster of 99, who passed the torch in Kansas to four-year-old Katie Johnson. In Pineville, Kentucky, it came at 1 A.M., so hundreds of people lined the streets with candles. At Tupelo, Mississippi, at 7 A.M. on a Sunday morning, a robed church choir sang "God Bless America" as the torch went by.
>
> That torch went through the Cumberland Gap, past the Martin Luther King, Jr., Memorial, down the Santa Fe Trail, and alongside Billy the Kid's grave.
>
> In Richardson, Texas, it was carried by a 14-year-old boy in a special wheelchair. In West Virginia, the runner came across a line of deaf children and let each one pass the torch for a few feet, and at the end these youngsters' hands talked excitedly in their sign language. Crowds spontaneously began singing "America the Beautiful" or "The Battle Hymn of the Republic."
>
> And then, in San Francisco, a Vietnamese immigrant, his little son held on his shoulders, dodged photographers and policemen to cheer a 19-year-old black man pushing an 88-year-old white woman in a wheelchair as she carried the torch.
>
> My friends, that's America.

Reagan was often criticized for his ignorance of statistics and policy; but his mind worked by stories and analogies, and those stories brought people together in support of the policies and programs that others would administer in his name. It was, in a way, a new kind of leadership; but it worked for him, and it changed the terms of the political debate. Eight years later, when William Clinton became the next Democrat to be elected president, he made a speech that echoed Reagan's themes:

> We must do what America does best: offer more opportunity to all and demand more responsibility from all. It is time to break the bad habit of expecting something for nothing from our Government or from each other. Let us all take more responsibility not only for ourselves and our families but for our communities and our country.[60]

Even four years later, in his State of the Union message of 1996, Clinton was channeling Reagan in saying:

> We know big Government does not have all the answers. We know there's not a program for every problem. We know, and we have worked to give the American people a smaller, less bureaucratic Government in Washington. And we have to give the American people one that lives within its means. The era of big Government is over.[61]

Barack Obama, thirty years after Reagan, though the government had continued to grow, still felt a need to tell Congress that "our government is leaner, quicker, and more responsive to the needs of the American people."[62]

Reagan's impact on his successors can be traced in large matters and small. They adopted his anti-government rhetoric, and they also adopted his penchant for personalizing the message. He had always told stories; but with his first inaugural, he went one step further and told stories about people who were actually there and sitting in the gallery of the House of Representatives chamber of the United States Capitol. He introduced Jeremiah Denton, a former prisoner of war in Vietnam and "one of our young government employees, Lenny Skutnik," who had dived into the icy waters of the Potomac to rescue a woman who had fallen from a helicopter rescue line after an airplane crash in the river. These, he said, were just two . . .

> of the countless quiet, everyday heroes of American life, parents who sacrifice long and hard so their children will know a better life than they've known; church and civic volunteers who help to

> feed, clothe, nurse and teach the needy; millions who've made our nation, and our nation's destiny, so very special; unsung heroes who may not have realized their own dreams themselves but then who reinvest those dreams in their children.[63]

He came back to this pattern two years later when he spoke about the need to create jobs and cited "people like Barbara Proctor, who rose from a ghetto to build a multimillion-dollar advertising agency in Chicago; [and] Carlos Perez, a Cuban refugee, who turned $27 and a dream into a successful importing business in Coral Gables, Florida." Toward the end of the speech he cited "Sergeant Stephen Trujillo, a medic in the 2nd Ranger Battalion, 75th Infantry, who was involved in the action in Grenada" and "ran across 25 yards of open terrain through enemy fire to rescue wounded soldiers. He directed two other medics, administered first aid, and returned again and again to the crash site to carry his wounded friends to safety." Cited also were "Father Ritter [whose] Covenant House programs in New York and Houston provide shelter and help to thousands of frightened and abused children each year," and "Dr. Charles Carson. Paralyzed in a plane crash, he still believed nothing is impossible. Today in Minnesota, he works 80 hours a week without pay, helping pioneer the field of computer-controlled walking. He has given hope to 500,000 paralyzed Americans that some day they may walk again." These individuals, seated in the gallery, were examples, Reagan said:

> . . . of the unsung heroes: single parents, couples, church and civic volunteers. Their hearts carry without complaint the pains of family and community problems. They soothe our sorrow, heal our wounds, calm our fears, and share our joy.*

All this led into the triumphant summation:

> How can we not believe in the greatness of America? How can we not do what is right and needed to preserve this last best hope of man on Earth? After all our struggles to restore America, to revive confidence in our country, hope for our future, after all our hard-won victories earned through the patience and courage of every citizen, we cannot, must not, and will not turn back. We will finish our job. How could we do less? We're Americans.[64]

---

* This line would seem to be built on a memory of G. K. Heber's hymn: "How sweet the Name of Jesus sounds In a believer's ear! It soothes his sorrows, heals his wounds, And drives away his fear."

Reagan's successor, George H. W. Bush, adopted Reagan's pattern of personalizing his points by quoting a letter from "Kathy Blackwell of Massachusetts" who had written to express her concern about the economy and to tell him "I think that you should know—your people out here are hurting badly." As preparations for the First Gulf War continued, Bush also introduced the wives of two military commanders, "Mrs. Norman Schwarzkopf," whose husband was Commander-in-Chief of the United States Central Command, and "Alma Powell, the wife of the distinguished Chairman of the Joint Chiefs."* Reagan would probably have introduced wives of rank-and-file soldiers, but Bush did continue the tradition of guests in the gallery in his own way.[65] So, too, did Bill Clinton in 1993 by introducing Jim Brady when he talked about gun control and a "young detective, Kevin Jett," when he spoke about community policemen.[66]

Over twenty years later, President Barack Obama was still following the pattern of introducing people in the gallery to Congress and the nation: "Jackie Bray . . . a single mom from North Carolina who was laid off from her job as a mechanic," and "Bryan Ritterby [who] was laid off from his job making furniture [and] worried that at 55, no one would give him a second chance." Both had now found work and illustrated Obama's point, that new jobs were being created.[67] Reagan's proclivity for using stories to convey his points had become a standard part of the politician's rhetoric. The difficulty, of course, with stories is that they may be one example, perhaps typical of thousands or millions, or maybe the only such story in the whole country. It is heartwarming to know that Bryan Ritterby found a job, but more useful to have some information from the Bureau of Labor Statistics. Statistics and rhetoric were, in fact, somewhat at odds in the Reagan era. The size of the federal government, which had declined slightly under President Carter, resumed its steady growth under President Reagan and was almost 10% larger when he left than when he arrived.**

Reporters who looked into the origin of Reagan's stories were often unable to verify them and sometimes discovered that they had been drastically changed in the telling. Reagan told a story, for example, of how he and Nancy had entertained former prisoners of war and how, after their departure, he had turned to her and asked: "Where did we find them, where did we find such

---

* Oddly, Bush seemed not to know Mrs. Schwarzkopf's first name.

** The Office of Personnel Management Federal Employment Reports show a total of 2,840,000 Executive branch civilian employees in 1977, 2,806,000 in 1981, and 3,064,000 in 1989. Totals including the military, legislative, and judicial follow the same pattern with the military, oddly, showing the least growth. http://www.opm.gov/policy-data-oversight/data-analysis-documentation/federal-employment-reports/historical-tables/total-government-employment-since-1962/

men?" On another occasion, speaking to the crew of the U.S.S. *Constellation* off the coast of Korea, Reagan cited a book by James Michener, *The Bridges at Toko-Ri*, in which an admiral, watching for the return of pilots who had taken part in a daring raid, wondered aloud, "Where did we get such men?" So did he say it to Nancy, or did he read it in a book? The difficulty with many of Reagan's stories was that they were given without specifics that would enable verification.

VII

Inflation was down and a different tone had been established in Washington after Reagan's first term, and he was reelected overwhelmingly in 1984. The second term produced two important pieces of domestic legislation: a significant tax-reform bill that modified the effect of the 1981 tax cuts by shifting some of the tax burden back to the wealthy, and an immigration law that upset conservatives by offering amnesty to millions of undocumented aliens.[68] As often happens to a second-term president, the opposition party had control of the House of Representatives and the president found it easier to accomplish his objectives in foreign affairs. Reagan made headlines in Berlin but scored perhaps his most important accomplishment in signing an arms-control agreement with the Russians. He also suffered his most embarrassing defeat in the so-called "Iran-Contra Affair" as a result of his lack of engagement with the details of administration.

The primary focus of Reagan's foreign policy was set in early 1982 when he told the British Parliament that he was thinking in terms of "a plan and a hope for the long term—the march of freedom and democracy which will leave Marxism-Leninism on the ash-heap of history* as it has left other tyrannies which stifle the freedom and muzzle the self-expression of the people." Reagan was interested in assisting that development with a foreign policy that did not simply resist communism but actively worked to increase the area of freedom and democracy. He told the Parliament that "We must be staunch in our conviction that freedom is not the sole prerogative of a lucky few but the inalienable and universal right of all human beings."[69]

Looking at the issue in a negative vein, he spoke to the National Association of Evangelicals and referred to the Soviet Union as an "evil empire."[70] In speaking to the United Nations, he accused the Soviet Union of "tyranny," "ruthless repression," and "atrocities." In a more positive direction, he ended his UN address by saying "We must serve mankind through genuine disarmament."[71] Arms-control treaties with the Soviet Union in his second term would become perhaps his most important achievement.

---

* The "ash-heap" phrase came from speechwriter Tony Dolan.

In view of that, it may seem odd that the most significant measurable change accomplished in Reagan's two terms was the largest peacetime military buildup in American history, with expenditures nearly doubling, from about $157 billion in 1981 to $304 billion in 1989. That buildup is often credited with creating the Soviet willingness to negotiate, but others argue that Russia had already run out of resources to continue an arms race and had no realistic alternative.

The results of this expenditure and an activist foreign policy often involved in clandestine actions, whatever the long-term accomplishments, created some enormous problems in the short term. To counter Soviet efforts to control Afghanistan, for example, the government shipped arms to Afghan guerrillas, who used them later to install an Islamic regime that provided a base for al Qaeda and Osama bin Laden. America also supported Iraq's Saddam Hussein in his war with Iran, only to become involved in two wars to remove the same Iraqi dictator under the two Presidents Bush.[72]

Far more complicated—ultimately so complicated that the administration's left hand and right hand lost track of each other—was what became known as the "Iran-Contra" affair, in which the Executive Branch of the government became involved in operations both in Iran and Central America that violated specific actions of the Congress.

Although President Reagan had spoken before about his view of events in Central America, he had not made a central issue of it until he did so in a speech to the nation from the Oval Office in March 1986. The issue was the nature of a newly elected government in Nicaragua, which Reagan believed was irredeemably dedicated to spreading communism through Central America.

> My fellow Americans, you know where I stand. The Soviets and the Sandinistas must not be permitted to crush freedom in Central America and threaten our own security on our own doorstep. Now the Congress must decide where it stands. . . .
>
> So, tonight I ask you to do what you've done so often in the past. Get in touch with your Representative and Senators and urge them to vote yes; tell them to help the freedom fighters. Help us prevent a Communist takeover of Central America.
>
> I have only 3 years left to serve my country; 3 years to carry out the responsibilities you entrusted to me; 3 years to work for peace. Could there be any greater tragedy than for us to sit back and permit this cancer to spread, leaving my successor to face far more agonizing decisions in the years ahead? . . .
>
> We still have time to do what must be done so history will say of us: We had the vision, the courage, and good sense to come

> together and act—Republicans and Democrats—when the price was not high and the risks were not great. We left America safe, we left America secure, we left America free—still a beacon of hope to mankind, still a light unto the nations.[73]

Three months later, the president again pleaded for support for the Contras, setting it in the largest context of the American commitment to human freedom:

> President Kennedy wrote on the day of his death that history had called this generation of Americans to be "watchmen on the walls of world freedom." A Republican President, Abraham Lincoln, said much the same thing on the way to his inauguration in 1861. Stopping in Philadelphia, Lincoln spoke in Independence Hall, where our Declaration of Independence had been signed. He said far more had been achieved in that hall than just American independence from Britain. Something permanent, something unalterable, had happened. He called it "Hope to the world for all future time."
>
> Hope to the world for all future time. In some way, every man, woman, and child in our world is tied to those events at Independence Hall, to the universal claim to dignity, to the belief that all human beings are created equal, that all people have a right to be free. We Americans have not forgotten our revolutionary heritage, but sometimes it takes others to remind us of what we ourselves believe.[74]

Unfortunately for the president, the Congress saw things differently and voted to block any aid to the so-called "Contras." This led to the president turning to the CIA and his national security adviser to find ways to channel assistance to the Contras in spite of Congress. Further complicating matters was an attempt to communicate with "moderate" elements in Iran and sell them missiles through an international arms merchant, using profits from the deal to support the Contras. It was hoped that the Iranians, in exchange for weapons, would use their influence to free American hostages being held in Lebanon. All this would have been problematic enough if it had been done legally, but to have it done illegally and against the opposition within the administration of the Secretaries of State and Defense made it a train wreck waiting to happen.*

Eventually, of course, the train left the rails and Congress conducted an investigation that revealed an administration at cross purposes with itself and

* Among the more helpful accounts of all this are Schaller, 73–80, and Pemberton, 172–196.

a president, who was compelled to admit publicly that he had not told the nation the truth. First, however, he denied the truth, speaking to the nation from the Oval Office:

> Good evening. I know you've been reading, seeing, and hearing a lot of stories the past several days attributed to Danish sailors, unnamed observers at Italian ports and Spanish harbors, and especially unnamed government officials of my administration. Well, now you're going to hear the facts from a White House source, and you know my name.
>
> I wanted this time to talk with you about an extremely sensitive and profoundly important matter of foreign policy. For 18 months now we have had underway a secret diplomatic initiative to Iran. That initiative was undertaken for the simplest and best of reasons: to renew a relationship with the nation of Iran, to bring an honorable end to the bloody 6-year war between Iran and Iraq, to eliminate state-sponsored terrorism and subversion, and to effect the safe return of all hostages. Without Iran's cooperation, we cannot bring an end to the Persian Gulf war; without Iran's concurrence, there can be no enduring peace in the Middle East. For 10 days now, the American and world press have been full of reports and rumors about this initiative and these objectives. Now, my fellow Americans, there's an old saying that nothing spreads so quickly as a rumor. So, I thought it was time to speak with you directly, to tell you firsthand about our dealings with Iran. As Will Rogers once said, "Rumor travels faster, but it don't stay put as long as truth." So, let's get to the facts.
>
> The charge has been made that the United States has shipped weapons to Iran as ransom payment for the release of American hostages in Lebanon, that the United States undercut its allies and secretly violated American policy against trafficking with terrorists. Those charges are utterly false. The United States has not made concessions to those who hold our people captive in Lebanon. And we will not. The United States has not swapped boatloads or planeloads of American weapons for the return of American hostages. And we will not. Other reports have surfaced alleging U.S. involvement: reports of a sealift to Iran using Danish ships to carry American arms; of vessels in Spanish ports being employed in secret U.S. arms shipments; of Italian ports being used; of the U.S. sending spare parts and weapons for combat aircraft. All these reports are quite exciting, but as far as we're concerned, not one of them is true.[75]

Unfortunately, however, the reports *were* true, and less than three weeks later, in December 1986, Reagan spoke to the nation again to tell them that an independent review board had been created to determine the truth, and in March of the next year he spoke again to tell the country that his head and his heart had been on different tracks:

> A few months ago I told the American people I did not trade arms for hostages. My heart and my best intentions still tell me that's true, but the facts and the evidence tell me it is not. As the Tower board reported, what began as a strategic opening to Iran deteriorated, in its implementation, into trading arms for hostages. This runs counter to my own beliefs, to administration policy, and to the original strategy we had in mind. There are reasons why it happened, but no excuses. It was a mistake. I undertook the original Iran initiative in order to develop relations with those who might assume leadership in a post-Khomeini government.
>
> It's clear from the Board's report, however, that I let my personal concern for the hostages spill over into the geopolitical strategy of reaching out to Iran. I asked so many questions about the hostages' welfare that I didn't ask enough about the specifics of the total Iran plan. . . .[76]

This was worse than embarrassing but, fortunately, was not the largest foreign initiative of Reagan's administration. Far more important in the larger scheme of things were the negotiations going on between President Reagan and Russian General Secretary Gorbachev to reduce the weapons that threatened world peace and human freedom. As so often before, Reagan used an iconic moment to symbolize the changes taking place in the world when he went to the Brandenburg Gate in Berlin and challenged Gorbachev to tear down the Berlin Wall. Almost twenty-five years earlier, President John F. Kennedy had made the fate of Berlin a matter of mutual German and American concern by going to the wall and saying "Ich bin ein Berliner." In 1987, Reagan outdid him with a dazzling display of linguistic skills—presumably the result of careful collaboration with his speechwriters—when he lapsed three times into German:*

> You see, like so many Presidents before me, I come here today because wherever I go, whatever I do: *Ich hab noch einen koffer in Berlin.* [I still have a suitcase in Berlin.]

* Handwritten above the German phrases are phonetic equivalents for Reagan's benefit (Vilade, 231).

> For I join you, as I join your fellow countrymen in the West, in this firm, this unalterable belief: *Es gibt nur ein Berlin.* [There is only one Berlin.]
>
> But, my friends, there were a few things the Soviets didn't count on—*Berliner herz, Berliner humor, ja, und Berliner schnauze.* [Berliner heart, Berliner humor, yes, and a Berliner schnauze.] [Laughter.]

More important and memorable, of course, was the challenge that Peter Robinson, the speechwriter, had drafted with the famous challenge—which made West German officials and State Department advisers nervous. Robinson had picked up the phrase in discussion with a family in Berlin, who told him that if Gorbachev was serious about peace, he would tear down that wall.[77] It had been struck more than once from drafts of the speech, but Reagan finally put the question to the revisers:

> Now, I'm the President aren't I?
> Yes, sir!
> So I get to decide?
> Yes, sir!
> Well, then the line stays in.[78]

And it was, of course, the line that would always be remembered:

> There is one sign the Soviets can make that would be unmistakable, that would advance dramatically the cause of freedom and peace. General Secretary Gorbachev, if you seek peace, if you seek prosperity for the Soviet Union and Eastern Europe, if you seek liberalization: Come here to this gate! Mr. Gorbachev, open this gate! Mr. Gorbachev, tear down this wall![79]

The Wall was, perhaps, "only a symbol," but Reagan knew well the importance of symbols. It would be two and a half years before the Wall was torn down; by that time, Reagan was no longer president; but the initiatives he and Gorbachev took had, in effect, brought the Cold War to an end and brought not only greater political freedom to the people of Eastern Europe but freedom from fear of nuclear catastrophe to the whole world. It was not something many had expected from a hardline anti-communist like Reagan, but the president's anti-communism was not as deeply held a position as his abhorrence of nuclear weapons. Reagan may have been as surprised as anyone else when he found that he could, in fact, negotiate with a communist leader, even respect him and find friendship where he might least have expected to find it.

A critical turning point in that development came, not surprisingly, when Ronald Reagan at Geneva created an opportunity to use the skills that had brought him there. He was a speaker, it was suggested earlier, ideally suited to the television age, most effective in personal conversation. The time came in Geneva when the two sides were facing each other across a table and becoming more and more angry. Reagan then suggested that they take a break and that he and Gorbachev go outside for a walk. They needed to get away from their advisers and talk to each other without other voices. Reagan's speechwriters, Pat Buchanan and Peggy Noonan, for example, wanted to avoid words like "compromise" and "cooperation." Speaking with Gorbachev without speechwriters, Reagan discovered a man who was not the visible embodiment of an "evil empire" but a politician looking for a way to move his country away from a focus on military spending and toward a better life for the ordinary Russian.

The notion of deterrence had led to a nuclear stalemate in which both nations depended on mechanical systems that had proven to be fallible. When the American *Challenger* rocket in January 1986, and the Russian nuclear facility at Chernobyl in April 1986, both exploded, the fallibility of mechanical systems was made evident. Reagan and Gorbachev met at Reykjavik in October of that year knowing that systems were unreliable. They failed to reach new agreements there, but Gorbachev made proposals that would lead to historic agreements over the course of Reagan's final two years in office. He was able to sum that progress up in his final address to the United Nations:

> In Geneva at this very hour, there are numerous negotiations underway—multilateral negotiations at the Conference on Disarmament as well as bilateral negotiations on a range of issues between the Soviets and ourselves. And these negotiations, some of them under U.N. auspices, involve a broad arms control agenda—strategic offensive weapons and space, nuclear testing and chemical warfare—whose urgency we have witnessed anew in recent days. And, Mr. Secretary-General, the negotiators are busy. And over the last few years, they've been engaged in more than an academic exercise. There is movement. The logjam is broken. Only recently, when the United States and the Soviet Union signed the INF agreement, an entire class of U.S. and Soviet nuclear missiles was eliminated for the first time in history. Progress continues on negotiations to reduce, in massive number, strategic weapons with effective verification. And talks will begin soon on conventional reductions in Europe.
>
> Much of the reason for all of this goes back, I believe, to Geneva itself, to the small chateau along the lake where I and the General Secretary of the Soviet Union had the first of several fireside chats,

exchanges characterized by frankness, but friendliness, too. I said at the first meeting in Geneva that this was a unique encounter between two people who had the power to start World War III or to begin a new age of peace among nations. And I also said peace conferences, arms negotiations, proposals for treaties could make sense only if they were part of a wider context, a context that sought to explore and resolve the deeper, underlying differences between us. I said to Mr. Gorbachev then, as I've said to you before: Nations do not mistrust each other because they're armed; they're armed because they mistrust each other.

And in that place, by that peaceful lake in neutral Switzerland, Mr. Gorbachev and I did begin a new relationship based not just on engagement over the single issue of arms control but on a broader agenda about our deeper differences—an agenda of human rights, regional conflicts, and bilateral exchanges between our peoples. Even on the arms control issue itself, we agreed to go beyond the past, to seek not just treaties that permit building weapons to higher levels but revolutionary agreements that actually reduced and even eliminated a whole class of nuclear weapons.

What was begun that morning in Geneva has shown results—in the INF treaty; in my recent visit to Moscow; in my opportunity to meet there with Soviet citizens and dissidents and speak of human rights, and to speak, too, in the Lenin Hills of Moscow to the young people of the Soviet Union about the wonder and splendor of human freedom.[80]

VIII

The average tenure among those in the Office of Public Liaison was about eighteen months. Peggy Noonan had been there for over two years when the chief speechwriter was fired and she was turned down for the position. She resigned as a result and got a form letter from the president thanking her "for her contribution to the administration" and signed with the automatic pen.[81] She had admired Reagan but also was clear-sighted enough to see his deficiencies. She wrote:

He was to popular politics what Henry James was to American literature. He was the master. No one could do what he did, move people that way, talk to them so that they understood. . . . He was probably the sweetest, most innocent man ever to serve in the Oval Office. . . . "No great men are good men," said Lord Acton, who was right, until Reagan. . . . He gleams; he's a mystery. He is for

> everyone there, for everyone who worked for him. None of them understood him. In private they admit it. You say to them, Who was that masked man?, and they shrug and hypothesize.[82]

When he let her go without a personal word, she went off and worked for George H. W. Bush to succeed him and was amazed when word came that Reagan wanted her to write his "Farewell Address," that he had asked for her personally. Newly elected President George H. W. Bush insisted that she must write his Inaugural Address, and she found herself working on both at the same time: hail and farewell. She was given five meetings with Reagan and was not sure at the first meeting whether he really remembered her or not. She tried to draw him out, with limited success. He talked about Gorbachev; but when he was asked what the most difficult day had been, he could think of nothing. He was asked about the day the Marines died in the explosion in Lebanon, about the *Challenger* disaster, but there was not much response. When she asked him about policy, about the great events, the answers seemed rote. Attempts to draw him out on personal matters were equally frustrating. "He will not reflect," she wrote; "I want to shake him, I want the long tape of triumph. Where is the anguish that usually comes with greatness?"[83]

After many drafts, however, the president had the speech he wanted. She tried to get him to talk about things he had hoped to do, but he refused. In saying "Farewell," Ronald Reagan said nothing he hadn't said many times before: it was all about the shining city and morning in America. Typically, he tried to sum things up in stories:

> I've been reflecting on what the past 8 years have meant and mean. And the image that comes to mind like a refrain is a nautical one—a small story about a big ship, and a refugee, and a sailor. It was back in the early eighties, at the height of the boat people. And the sailor was hard at work on the carrier *Midway*, which was patrolling the South China Sea. The sailor, like most American servicemen, was young, smart, and fiercely observant. The crew spied on the horizon a leaky little boat. And crammed inside were refugees from Indochina hoping to get to America. The *Midway* sent a small launch to bring them to the ship and safety. As the refugees made their way through the choppy seas, one spied the sailor on deck, and stood up, and called out to him. He yelled, "Hello, American sailor. Hello, freedom man!"
>
> A small moment with a big meaning, a moment the sailor, who wrote it in a letter, couldn't get out of his mind. And, when I saw it, neither could I. Because that's what it was to be an American

> in the 1980s. We stood, again, for freedom. I know we always have, but in the past few years the world again—and in a way, we ourselves—rediscovered it.

He did, at last, express one regret: that the deficit had not been dealt with. He recalled a letter from Lisa Zanatta Henn, whose father had served in Normandy, and spoke of the need to remember. And he closed, inevitably, with his central image:

> I've spoken of the shining city all my political life, but I don't know if I ever quite communicated what I saw when I said it. But in my mind it was a tall, proud city built on rocks stronger than oceans, wind-swept, God-blessed, and teeming with people of all kinds living in harmony and peace; a city with free ports that hummed with commerce and creativity. And if there had to be city walls, the walls had doors and the doors were open to anyone with the will and the heart to get here. That's how I saw it, and see it still.
>
> And how stands the city on this winter night? More prosperous, more secure, and happier than it was 8 years ago. But more than that: After 200 years, two centuries, she still stands strong and true on the granite ridge, and her glow has held steady no matter what storm. And she's still a beacon, still a magnet for all who must have freedom, for all the pilgrims from all the lost places who are hurtling through the darkness, toward home.
>
> We've done our part. And as I walk off into the city streets, a final word to the men and women of the Reagan revolution, the men and women across America who for 8 years did the work that brought America back. My friends: We did it. We weren't just marking time. We made a difference. We made the city stronger, we made the city freer, and we left her in good hands. All in all, not bad, not bad at all.[84]

Americans, by and large, agreed: not bad—but not all that wonderful either. Reagan's average job approval rating while in office was 53%, which ranks sixth among the eleven presidents from Eisenhower to Obama. In a poll taken in November 2013, however, when Americans were asked how they thought those same presidents would go down in history, Americans ranked Reagan second only to John F. Kennedy with a 61% approval rating.[85] Ratings are highly subjective and change over the years; but Ronald Reagan's advocacy for freedom—defined in terms of the size of government, taxes, and deficit—continues to shape the American political agenda a full generation later.

TEN

Martin Luther King, Jr.

1929–1968

I HAVE A DREAM

I

His father was a Baptist preacher; his grandfather was a Baptist preacher; his great-grandfather was a Baptist preacher. Growing up in Atlanta, Georgia, Martin Luther King, Jr. had two career choices: to be a Baptist preacher—or something else. Most of the time, he felt inclined to the second alternative. He had an accelerated education, skipping first grade and being advanced to tenth grade at age thirteen when his private school closed and he was found to be well ahead of his public-school peers.

Encouraged to think for himself, he found doubts rising about the fundamentalist faith of his father. At age thirteen, he became a skeptic and denied the bodily resurrection of Jesus; his doubts only increased as he moved on to college. Having skipped ninth grade, he skipped twelfth grade also and entered Morehouse College at age fifteen without formally graduating from high school.[1] It was at Morehouse that King encountered the writings of Henry David Thoreau, the New England philosopher and poet who had written about the relationship between a citizen and a government that the citizen cannot support. Thoreau had written an essay on "Civil Disobedience" and had gone to jail when he refused to pay his taxes. King was convinced by Thoreau that non-cooperation with evil is as much an obligation as cooperation with good.[2]

King entered college with the idea of becoming a doctor; but biological sciences were too cold and mathematical for his taste, so he decided to become a lawyer. Nevertheless, when he graduated from Morehouse with a B.A. degree in sociology, he enrolled in Crozer Theological Seminary in Chester, Pennsylvania. Crozer exposed King to Northern liberal Christianity as well as, in his final year, the writing of Reinhold Niebuhr. Niebuhr was a Protestant theologian whose books had been widely influential before and after the Second World War. He disagreed with the liberal Christian belief that human beings could make the world a better place and stressed the abiding influence of sin. Love remains the central Christian message; but love in human society must be expressed by insistence on justice, and justice can be obtained only by nonviolence.

Later in life, King would travel to India and see firsthand what Gandhi had achieved there through nonviolence, but King learned nonviolence from Niebuhr first. Most important was Niebuhr's challenge to think through the relationship between Christian faith and an immoral society, a matter of little concern to the fundamentalist faith of King's father. King would continue to work at his own synthesis of ideas gathered from Niebuhr and others, but he had come to see the challenge of applying his faith to a sinful world in a way that might establish justice. He seems never to have encountered the strong tradition of social criticism in Roman and Anglican Catholicism.[3]

Given a Bachelor of Divinity (BDiv) degree in 1951 but not yet committed to parish ministry (although he had taken nine courses in preaching), King went on to Boston University in search of a doctoral degree that would qualify him to teach. Completing the residential requirements for a PhD in 1954, he was offered teaching positions but decided instead to be a candidate for the position of pastor of the Dexter Avenue Baptist Church, one of the two oldest and most prestigious churches in Montgomery, Alabama. He discussed the decision with his wife and, in spite of the difficulties of going back into a segregated society, they agreed that they would accept the challenge.

In early January 1954, King therefore drove from his home in Atlanta to Montgomery and preached a sermon he had preached several times before in other churches—and which he would continue to preach in still other churches for the rest of his life.* In presenting the sermon, titled "The Three Dimensions of a Complete Life," King began by outlining his three main points:

* He is known, for example, to have preached this sermon at the New Covenant Baptist Church, Chicago, Illinois, on April 9, 1967. The basic sermon is the same that he preached thirteen years earlier in Montgomery but includes several references to the Montgomery Bus Boycott, among other changes. Clergy of all denominations frequently reuse sermons, as politicians ordinarily reuse speeches.

> There are three dimensions of any complete life to which we can fitly give the words of this text: length, breadth, and height. Now the length of life as we shall use it here is the inward concern for one's own welfare. In other words, it is that inward concern that causes one to push forward, to achieve his own goals and ambitions. The breadth of life as we shall use it here is the outward concern for the welfare of others. And the height of life is the upward reach for God. Now you got to have all three of these to have a complete life.*

King did not point out that his analysis was based on the epistemological theories of a seventeenth-century philosopher named Baruch Spinoza, who held that there are three levels to knowledge that can be related to three levels of moral life. Later in the sermon, there's a paragraph that provides evidence, however, not only of King's scholarly accomplishments but also of his roots in the African American homiletic tradition. That paragraph combines the two elements perfectly:

> You may not be able to define God in philosophical terms. Men through the ages have tried to talk about him. Plato said that he was the Architectonic Good. Aristotle called him the Unmoved Mover. Hegel called him the Absolute Whole. Then there was a man named Paul Tillich who called him Being-Itself. We don't need to know all of these high-sounding terms. Maybe we have to know him and discover him another way. One day you ought to rise up and say, "I know him because he's a lily of the valley." He's a bright and morning star. He's a rose of Sharon. He's a battle-axe in the time of Babylon. And then somewhere you ought to just reach out and say, "He's my everything. He's my mother and my father. He's my sister and my brother. He's a friend to the friendless." This is the God of the universe. And if you believe in him and worship him, something will happen in your life. You will smile when others around you are crying. This is the power of God.

The academic references to Plato, Aristotle, Hegel, and Tillich are there for those who want to be impressed, but they are immediately played down with the statement that "We don't need to know all of these high-sounding terms,"

---

* Notice the ungrammatical phrase "you got to have," which is also characteristic of King's preaching. He deliberately allowed himself to use more colloquial phrasing from time to time. Other contemporary preachers and politicians have the same tendency to use colloquial language so as not to seem too sophisticated (cf. Stevenson and the "egghead" label discussed in Chapter 8).

followed by a series of references to phrases from evangelical hymns that would be familiar to the least educated members of the congregation.

The sermon also includes a traditional pattern of black preaching that can be traced back to West Africa and would become familiar to white Americans in King's "I have a dream" speech. The pattern is sometimes called a "cadence," in which a phrase is repeated again and again, but with a changing conclusion. Referring to the three relationships at the center of the sermon, King said:

> And when you get all three of these together, you can walk and never get weary. You can look up and see the morning stars singing together, and the sons of God shouting for joy.
>
> When you get all of these working together in your very life, judgement will roll down like waters, and righteousness like a mighty stream.
>
> When you get all three of these together, the lamb will lie down with the lion.
>
> When you get all three of these together, you look up and every valley will be exalted, and every hill and mountain will be made low; the rough places will be made plain, and the crooked places straight; and the glory of the Lord shall be revealed and all flesh will see it together.
>
> When you get all three of these working together, you will do unto others as you'd have them do unto you.
>
> When you get all three of these together, you will recognize that out of one blood God made all men to dwell upon the face of the earth.

This "cadence" pattern is typical of the African American tradition in preaching and can be traced back to African roots. One authority on the subject tells us:

> One of the very noticeable skills of the Black preacher is the use of cadence. This characteristic is probably as prevalent among highly trained Black ministers as it is among the storefront clergy. It is effective and adds a degree of credibility to the speaker. Dr. Martin Luther King's cadences were essentially Black. Despite his formal training and language, his national status and reputation, he was heard as a soul brother, as a down-home Baptist preacher.[4]

Tracing it further back, we find that:

> The Black folk preacher in the United States emerged during the period of slavery as a panegyric or praise poet, in the tradition of his cultural predecessor, the West African griot. Like African praise poems, the content of black sermons often praises heroic exploits, but of Biblical personalities and events instead of fearless hunters. Likewise, both West African and Afro-American boys begin to learn the formulaic expressions necessary to construct their verses by listening to accomplished adults who either chant at festive occasions or speak in church. . . . While griot and preacher both monopolize verbal functions in their communities, the former's reliance on a rhythmic delivery, manipulation of formulaic expression to construct his genealogies, call-and-response from an audience, and chanted speech are preserved in the latter's delivery. . . .[5]

King may have used the cadence pattern in all his preaching, but at the Dexter Avenue Church he did not experience another familiar aspect of the African American sermon: the call-and-response dialogue between preacher and congregation consisting of shouts of approval such as "A-men" and "That's right" and "Preach it." Such interjections were common in the Lincoln-Douglas debates (mentioned in chapter 5) but were not part of the life of the Dexter Avenue Church or of its sister church, First Baptist, that together served the elite of Montgomery's black community. When King arrived in Montgomery the day before his "trial sermon," he had dinner with First Baptist's pastor, Ralph Abernathy, and was told "you will be the only one preaching. The congregation is not going to help you out . . . the preacher preaches and the congregation listens."[6] The call and response was a part of the African heritage but not considered quite respectable by congregations like those at Dexter Avenue and First Baptist.*

One month after that first visit, a special delivery letter arrived calling Martin Luther King, Jr., to the Dexter Avenue pulpit. He thought about it some more, talked about it with his wife and his colleagues and advisers in Boston, and accepted the position. He asked for and was given time to make a beginning on his doctoral thesis and then to begin his new ministry on September 4, 1954.

At the age of twenty-five, Martin Luther King, Jr., was the pastor of a large and distinguished congregation; but he had been assistant pastor at his father's church for four years, doing most of the preaching in the summer and paying close attention to the way his father carried out his ministry. He knew now

---

* Respectable or not, the author can testify from very limited experience to the stimulating power of a congregation that provides vocal response.

exactly what he wanted to do, and he put a whole new structure in place in a matter of weeks. In his first sermon as pastor, he told the congregation that he had thirty-four specific suggestions for a reorganization of the church's life. Copies were distributed to all members at the end of the service. Specific goals ranged from the installation of a new carpet to the creation of a whole new education building within five years. He called for a political action committee to promote membership in the NAACP and to organize forums and mass meetings. Only five percent of the black residents of Alabama were registered voters, but every member of the Dexter Avenue church, King told them, must be registered to vote. Finally, there would be careful, centralized control of the finances. Each organization within the church would turn its fund over to the church treasurer by November 1.

While making an impact on his new church, King was also completing his doctoral dissertation and typically was up at 5:30 A.M. to put in three hours on the dissertation before going to the church to deal with whatever the day might bring, whether a funeral or consultation with staff or meeting with other clergy or counseling with church members. The dissertation was completed in due course, and the degree was awarded in June 1955. King also had married Coretta Scott in the previous year, and their first child was born in November of their first year in Montgomery.

With the dissertation completed, King could begin to think about the larger community. The increasing affluence of the Montgomery black community had led to the establishment of a black-owned radio station that was happy to broadcast some of King's sermons. That summer of 1955, he made clear his attitude toward the segregation that confronted him on every side:

> It scars the soul and degrades the personality. It inflicts the segregated with a false sense of inferiority, while confirming the segregator in a false estimate of his own superiority. It destroys community and makes brotherhood impossible. The underlying philosophy of Christianity is diametrically opposed to the underlying philosophy of racial segregation.[7]

In August 1955, King met with a woman named Rosa Parks, representing the NAACP, who wanted to tell him that he had been elected to the executive committee of the Montgomery chapter. On December 1 of that same year, Rosa Parks was arrested for refusing to yield her seat on the bus to a white man. It was not the first time such an arrest had been made. James Pennington had been arrested for sitting in a New York City trolley a hundred years earlier, and other protests had been made over the years in other cities. A high school student had been arrested in March in Birmingham, and another woman in

October, for refusing to yield seats to white people; but both times, lawyers agreed that they lacked a strong case and paid the fine. Rosa Parks, on the other hand, was an ideal subject for a challenge to the segregation laws and customs. In fact, she had been making her quiet protest for years, refusing to use "Colored" drinking fountains and walking up rather than use the segregated elevators. She was "humble enough to be claimed by the common folk, and yet dignified enough in manner, speech, and dress to command the respect of the leading classes."[8] Sparks fly off from a source of heat but seldom land where there is tinder enough to start a fire. This time, conditions were right.

Rosa Parks's attorney, Fred Gray, telephoned Jo Ann Robinson, an English professor at the all-black Alabama State College and president of the black Women's Political Council. She had written to the mayor months earlier, calling for an end to the humiliating system that made black passengers stand while white seats were empty. She already had a plan and suggested to Gray that they should call a one-day boycott of the buses on Monday, December 5, the day Parks was to appear in court. Robinson stayed up all night printing thousands of handbills to be distributed around the city and telling people to stay off the buses on Monday. "Take a cab, share a ride, or walk," they were told, and come to a meeting that night at the Holt Street Baptist Church for further instructions.

Parks was fined ten dollars plus four dollars for "court costs" but appealed the verdict to enable the boycott to continue. The buses that day were almost completely empty. Seventy black clergy met together in the afternoon but came to no agreement. They did agree to Ralph Abernathy's suggestion that they form a Montgomery Improvement Association to coordinate any plans they made. They also unanimously agreed to make Martin Luther King, Jr., the president of the MIA. He was still too new in town to have made enemies or joined factions, too new also for them to have learned much about his leadership skills or oratorical abilities. He had twenty minutes to plan a speech to the mass meeting called for that evening at the Holt Street Church in a working-class neighborhood.

King thought carefully about what kinds of things he ought to say to balance the need for militancy with the need to avoid stirring up hatred. The church was packed by the time he arrived, and so was the basement. Loudspeakers had been rigged for the benefit of those who were outside and unable to get in. As he arrived, hymns were being sung and appeals made for financial support for the new organization. Few had heard Martin Luther King, Jr., speak before that night, and he began slowly and carefully outlining what had happened. It might not have been the custom at Dexter Avenue to "help the preacher out," but this was a congregation drawn from all the black churches in Montgomery, and most of them were quite accustomed to providing support to the preacher.

> We are here this evening for serious business. [Audience: Yes!] We are here in a general sense because first and foremost we are American citizens [That's right] and we are determined to apply our citizenship to the fullness of its meaning. [Yeah, that's right.] But we are here in a specific sense, because of the bus situation in Montgomery. [Yes.] We are here because we are determined to get the situation corrected.

He told them about Rosa Parks: "one of the finest citizens in Montgomery [Amen]—not one of the finest Negro citizens [That's right], but one of the finest citizens in Montgomery" who had been "taken from a bus [Yes] and carried to jail and arrested [Yes] because she refused to get up to give her seat to a white person."

After describing the situation carefully and methodically, he picked up the pace and spoke from the heart with the cadences of "there comes a time" to drive the message home:

> And you know, my friends, there comes a time when people get tired of being trampled over by the iron feet of oppression. [Thundering applause.] There comes a time, my friends, when people get tired of being plunged across the abyss of humiliation, where they experience the bleakness of nagging despair. [Keep talking.] There comes a time when people get tired of being pushed out of the glittering sunlight of life's July and left standing amid the piercing chill of an alpine November. [That's right.] [Applause.] There comes a time. [Yes sir, Teach.] [Applause continues.]

He had a way of building phrases into speech pictures that allowed time for the meaning to sink in. It was not just "oppression" he inveighed against, but "the iron feet of oppression," not just "despair" but "the bleakness of nagging despair." That was the reason for what they were doing. He told them also about the method they would use. The protest being called, he emphasized, was to be non-violent; there would be no use of violence:

> We are here, we are here this evening because we're tired now. [Yes.] [Applause.] And I want to say that we are not here advocating violence. [No.] We have never done that. [Repeat that, Repeat that.] [Applause.] I want it to be known throughout Montgomery and throughout this nation [Well.] that we are Christian people. [Yes.] [Applause.] We believe in the Christian religion. We believe in the teachings of Jesus. [Well.] The only weapon that

> we have in our hands this evening is the weapon of protest. [Yes.] [Applause.] That's all.

Throughout the talk and throughout his ministry, those varied word pictures continued to punctuate his speech:

> the paralysis of crippling fear
> the thick fog of oblivion
> the boundless outreach of her integrity
> the glittering sunlight of life's July
> the piercing chill of an alpine November
> the height of her character
> the abyss of humiliation
> the glory of our democracy
> the long night of captivity
> the daybreak of freedom and justice and equality
> a grim and bold determination
> the veins of history and of civilization.*

From beginning to end of his ministry, King used language, as he does here, both to impress his audience with elaborate phrases and, at the same time, to connect with them by using colloquial words like "gonna."

King ended his appeal by emphasizing the historic importance of the moment:

> . . . let us go out with a grim and bold determination that we are going to stick together. [Applause.] We are going to work together. [Applause.] Right here in Montgomery, when the history books are written in the future [Yes], somebody will have to say, "There lived a race of people [Well], a black people [Yes sir], 'fleecy locks and black complexion' [Yes], a people who had the moral courage to stand up for their rights. [Applause.] And thereby they injected a new meaning into the veins of history and of civilization." And

---

* It may not be irrelevant to study the research done in the Balkans before World War II by Milman Parry and Albert Lord. They found there a living tradition that they believed could be traced back to the Homeric epics of ancient Greece, in which stock phrases such as "rosy-fingered dawn" and "the milk-white steed" were used by the bards to facilitate composition and memorization of their sagas. In a similar way, King presumably did not coin these phrases in the short time he had to prepare that evening but drew them from previous talks and sermons. See: Lord, Albert. *The Singer of Tales*. Cambridge: Harvard University Press, 1960.

> we're gonna do that. God grant that we will do it before it is too late. [Oh yeah.] As we proceed with our program let us think of these things.* [Yes.] [Applause.]

As the boycott went on, King began to think of Henry David Thoreau, who had just over a century earlier articulated a philosophy of civil disobedience in response to what he saw as American aggression in the war with Mexico. Taking his guidance from Thoreau, King referred to the Montgomery action ordinarily as "an act of massive non-cooperation" rather than as a boycott.[9]

King had begun with the notion that reasonable people would act reasonably. The issue, however, was not reason but power, and those with power were not willing to yield it easily. Most difficult for King was the continual attempt to make him the problem. Leaders in the white community went to older clergy and tried to persuade them to put aside younger leadership and assert their own seniority. The same approach was made to other members of the MIA leadership. King did offer his resignation, but it was rejected. He was not the problem. Segregation was the problem, and the purpose of segregation was to perpetuate injustice and inequality.[10]

"Massive non-cooperation" was the best description of a heroic saga that stretched over a full year. It meant that ordinary black citizens had to find a way to get to work every day while the established authorities constantly sought new ways to impede their efforts. At first black-owned taxis agreed to take the former bus riders for the bus fee of ten cents. That worked until the police noted that law forbade the taxis from taking anything but the set minimum fare of forty-five cents.

Individual car owners, like King, could pick up people walking to work, but the police could harass such drivers at every turn. When they arrested King for going thirty miles an hour in a twenty-five-mile-per-hour zone, there was no evidence except the word of the arresting policeman, but the word of the white policeman trumped that of the black preacher. A white citizen would have been given a warning or perhaps a ticket, but King was searched and taken off to the city jail, finger-printed, and thrown into a crowded cell with a teacher arrested in the same way, as well as vagrants and drunks and more serious offenders. He was released before the evening was over, but the harassment—and worse—continued. Sitting alone at his kitchen table late one night, he turned to prayer and heard a voice saying "Stand up for righteousness.

---

* Is there an echo here of Archbishop Thomas á Becket's last sermon in T. S. Eliot's play *Murder in the Cathedral*, which ends "I would have you keep in your hearts these words that I say, and think of them at another time"?

Stand up for justice. . . . And lo, I am with you always." The voice promised "never to leave me, never to leave me alone. No never alone."[11]

It was four nights later, at the end of January 1956, while one of the evening mass meetings was in progress, that a bomb exploded in front of King's home. His wife and baby were there, as well as a friend who had come to be with Coretta while her husband was at the meeting. No one was injured, but a crowd gathered and some were ready for violence. The mayor and city commissioners reached the scene before King. When the mayor expressed regret that "this unfortunate incident has taken place in our city," a church trustee responded that it was the mayor's words and actions that had "created the atmosphere for this bombing." When King arrived and assured himself that Coretta and the baby were uninjured, he went out and spoke to the crowd. He told them that he and his family were uninjured, and went on:

> We believe in law and order. Don't get panicky. Don't do anything panicky at all. Don't get your weapons. He who lives by the sword will perish by the sword. Remember that is what God said. We are not advocating violence. We want to love our enemies. I want you to love our enemies. Be good to them. Love them and let them know you love them.
>
> I did not start this boycott. I was asked by you to serve as your spokesman. I want it known the length and breadth of this land that if I am stopped this movement will not stop. For what we are doing is right. What we are doing is just. And God is with us.[12] Go home with this glowing faith and this radiant assurance. With love in our hearts, with faith and with God in front, we cannot lose.[13]

Two nights later, another bomb went off at the home of another boycott leader. Once again a crowd gathered, and once again violence was avoided. Urged to get a gun and a bodyguard, King discussed it with his wife and decided to get rid of the one weapon they had. Weapons would not resolve the problem.

The next Sunday, King preached at Dexter Avenue and told his congregation of the voice he had heard. He went on to use language he would use again at the end of his life. Since that night, he told them,

> I can stand up without fear. So I'm not afraid of anybody this morning. Tell Montgomery they can keep shooting and I'm going to stand up to them. Tell Montgomery they can keep bombing and I'm going to stand up to them. If I have to die tomorrow morning I would die happy because I've been to the mountaintop and I've seen the promised land and it's going to be here in Montgomery.[14]

Nobody thought the protest would last so long. The original goal was one day, then two, then as long as the support was there. And the support continued. Negotiations between the two sides took place from time to time. At first the MIA demands were modest, not ending segregation but asking for better treatment: that black passengers be treated courteously, that passengers be seated on a first-come, first-served basis but with black riders still starting to fill from the back, and that black drivers be hired for the predominantly black routes. White leadership, however, resisted any solution and, indeed, brought the MIA leadership to court for violating the state's anti-boycott law. The MIA leaders were found guilty; but the case was appealed and finally, in November, reached the U.S. Supreme Court. Without bothering to hear arguments, the Supreme Court simply affirmed the decision of the District Court that bus segregation was unconstitutional. When that order reached Montgomery, King told the overflow crowd: "We must now move from protest to reconciliation. . . . With this dedication we will be able to emerge from the bleak and desolate midnight of man's inhumanity to man to the bright and glittering daybreak of freedom and justice."[15]

Montgomery, King said, "marked the psychological turning point for the American Negro in his struggle against segregation. . . . He had a new determination to achieve freedom and human dignity no matter what the cost."[16] The American Revolution had won freedom in name for every American, but many were still slaves. The Civil War had won freedom for the slaves as well, but the bondage of restrictive laws and customs remained. In the Montgomery bus boycott, a mass movement of those not yet free shook off one of those restrictive laws and showed that freedom could be won without violence.

II

The Montgomery bus campaign had made Martin Luther King a nationally known figure, and the national publicity given to Montgomery raised questions in many other places: If they can do that, why can't we? As a result, King found himself traveling constantly from one place to another, soliciting funds and hoping to spark a national movement.

To coordinate such a movement, King and other leaders came together in Atlanta in January 1957 to ponder ways of implementing the Supreme Court's decision banning bus segregation, and to agree on other measures. The meeting had barely begun when word came of new bombings in Montgomery. Ralph Abernathy's home and church had been bombed, as well as two other churches in the city. Two and a half weeks later, there were more bombs, including one on King's front porch that failed to explode. Finally the city responded by announcing rewards for information leading to the arrest of the bombers, and seven men were actually arrested and brought to trial. The accused had signed confessions, but the jury found them innocent. Nevertheless, it seemed as if the poison had been drained out of the system. The buses continued to run smoothly, and people of both races rode together without incident.[17]

The Atlanta meeting had continued in spite of the bombings. King and Abernathy hurried back to Montgomery but returned as soon as possible. Having returned, they agreed to create a new organization called the Southern Christian Leadership Conference. Martin Luther King was chosen to be president of the new organization, and telegrams were sent to President Eisenhower, Vice President Nixon, and Attorney General Herbert Brownell, asking them to come south and speak in support of the Supreme Court's school-integration decision. The president's assistant replied that it would not be possible, and the Attorney General replied that enforcement of the laws was the responsibility of the states. Nixon didn't respond.

The years of Martin Luther King's ministry were a strange transition time in national politics. At the beginning of that era, there were strong supporters of civil rights within both parties but timid leadership at the top. The Republican Party as the party of Lincoln had been the historic party of black Americans, and there were still Republican leaders like Nelson Rockefeller who attempted to provide leadership in the civil-rights struggle. King and Abernathy both voted for Eisenhower in 1956. President Eisenhower (1953–1961) had no patience with those violating the law, and sent troops to Little Rock in September 1957 to protect black students integrating the Central High School; but Eisenhower's interest was in the law more than in civil rights for black Americans. Roosevelt and Truman had begun to draw black voters into the Democratic Party, but John F. Kennedy (1961–1963) was cautious about civil rights since his election depended on the "Solid South" that voted for the national Democratic ticket but opposed any weakening of the segregation system. Lyndon Johnson (1963–1969) seized the moment in the aftermath of King's assassination to call for and sign the most significant civil rights legislation since the years after the Civil War. The consequence of that action was, as Johnson had foreseen, that the Solid South became solidly Republican and civil rights became an increasingly partisan issue. As Martin Luther King put it:

> Both political parties have betrayed the cause of justice. The Democrats have betrayed it by capitulating to the prejudices and undemocratic practices of the southern Dixiecrats. The Republicans have betrayed it by capitulating to the blatant hypocrisy of right wing, reactionary northerners.

In February 1957, Eisenhower attended a service in Newport, Rhode Island, where a Navy chaplain preached about civil rights. Leaving church, Eisenhower shook his hand and said "You can't legislate morality." King would tell that story many times to point out that the president, like many others, misunderstood the purpose of law. All laws govern behavior, not attitudes, but it is behavior that needs to be kept within certain limits for human society to function. "A law may not make a man love me," King said, "but it can stop him from lynching me."[18] Governments can provide freedom by outlawing behavior that limits freedom.

Lacking a positive response from Washington, the SCLC decided to lead a prayer pilgrimage to Washington to urge national leaders to act. Timed to celebrate the third anniversary of the Supreme Court's decision outlawing school segregation, the pilgrimage drew some thirty thousand to the Lincoln Memorial on May 17, 1957, for a three-hour program featuring preachers and celebrities like Harry Belafonte, Mahalia Jackson, Sammy Davis, and Ruby Dee. King spoke last and put his stress on the need for blacks to vote. It was all very well that the Supreme Court had broken down the old idea of separate but equal, but Southern states were erecting new barriers to equality. In the final analysis, King told those listening, there was one simple solution: break down the barriers to voting and black people could take it from there.

> Give us the ballot, and we will no longer have to worry the federal government about our basic rights.
>
> Give us the ballot [Yes], and we will no longer plead to the federal government for passage of an anti-lynching law; we will by the power of our vote write the law on the statute books of the South [All right] and bring an end to the dastardly acts of the hooded perpetrators of violence.
>
> Give us the ballot [Give us the ballot], and we will transform the salient misdeeds of bloodthirsty mobs [Yeah] into the calculated good deeds of orderly citizens.
>
> Give us the ballot [Give us the ballot], and we will fill our legislative halls with men of goodwill [All right now] and send to the sacred halls of Congress men who will not sign a "Southern Manifesto" because of their devotion to the manifesto of justice. [Tell 'em about it.]
>
> Give us the ballot [Yeah], and we will place judges on the benches of the South who will do justly and love mercy [Yeah], and we will place at the head of the southern states governors who will, who have felt not only the tang of the human, but the glow of the Divine.
>
> Give us the ballot [Yes], and we will quietly and nonviolently, without rancor or bitterness, implement the Supreme Court's decision of May seventeenth, 1954. [That's right.]

The last part of the speech emphasized the method of passive resistance and love. There must be no triumphalism and no hatred, and the goal must never be narrowed down to particular issues and moments. The goal is freedom for everyone:

> Our aim must never be to defeat or humiliate the white man. We must not become victimized with a philosophy of black supremacy. God is not interested merely in freeing black men and brown men and yellow men, but God is interested in freeing the whole human race. [Yes, All right.] We must work with determination to create a society [Yes], not where black men are superior and other men are inferior and vice versa, but a society in which all men will live together as brothers [Yes] and respect the dignity and worth of human personality. [Yes.]

All this had been set in a broader perspective when King was invited to a celebration of independence in Ghana, a British colony on the west coast of Africa, that was being given its freedom. Walking the streets of Accra in March 1957, he heard little children and old men and women chanting "Freedom! Freedom!" and he thought of the old Negro spiritual that he would cite again at the end of the March on Washington six years later: "Free at last! Free at last! Great God Almighty, I'm free at last!"[19] Lincoln and others had often set American freedom in a worldwide context, and here, most vividly, King was reminded that freedom is a human cause not limited by political boundaries.

In meeting President Kwame Nkrumah of Ghana, King not only met a head of state for the first time, but he also met for the first time the American Vice President, Richard Nixon, who had not responded to King's telegram to Washington but, on meeting him in Ghana, invited him to Washington for private talks on civil rights.[20] King and Abernathy did, therefore, meet with Nixon for two hours in June 1957. The vice president tried to paint a picture of himself as an ally of the two preachers, confronting the difficult dynamics of a Congress where Southern Democrats wanted no progress and Northern Democrats tended to "grandstand" while Republicans were often indifferent since they lacked a constituency interested in civil rights. King and Abernathy should work with him, Nixon implied, in the fight against a common enemy.

King never spoke publicly about the discussion with Nixon, but reported privately that the vice president had been a mixture of enthusiasm and pragmatism, willing to work for civil rights if he could do so without political cost. A year later, King wrote a public letter stating that Nixon "has a genius for convincing one that he is sincere. . . . And so I would conclude by saying that if Richard Nixon is not sincere he is the most dangerous man in America."[21]

Congress did pass a civil-rights bill that summer, the first such legislation in eighty-two years, in spite of the efforts of Southern senators. Senator Strom Thurmond of South Carolina filibustered against it for a record-breaking twenty-four hours, but Republicans in both Houses of Congress supported the bill overwhelmingly while Democrats gave it a bare majority. President Eisenhower signed the bill in September. The legislation was intended primarily to enable more black citizens to vote, but was greatly weakened in its passage through Congress. It was significant more because it broke the ice in creating new civil rights legislation and was followed by further legislation in 1960 and 1963 extending the procedures put in place to expand voting rights.

Perhaps because of the initiative provided by the Montgomery bus boycott and the new national legislation, but probably as much or more because of changes in American society, a variety of civil-rights initiatives focused American attention on various places over the next few years. Little Rock, Arkansas; Greensboro, North Carolina; Selma and Birmingham, Alabama; and Neshoba County, Mississippi were some of the names that appeared in newspaper headlines. Sometimes it was a school-integration issue, sometimes a sit-in demonstration, sometimes a voter-education project or freedom march, sometimes the imprisonment or death of those working to expand civil rights. After World War II, there had been a significant increase in black migration from the rural South to the urban North, and even those who stayed in the South heard stories that came back of greater freedom and opportunity elsewhere. Then, too, the American military, disproportionately drawn from and based in the Southern states, increasingly modeled a fully integrated society in which rank depended primarily on ability. That, too, made a difference. In that larger picture, King continued to be the most conspicuous figure and leading voice, sometimes closely involved in events and at other times not directly involved at all.

These were also years, however, in which resistance to the movement for civil rights grew stronger and more organized. The Ku Klux Klan grew in numbers and visibility, White Citizens Councils were organized, and increasingly militant segregationist politicians came into office. Many African Americans meanwhile stepped back from confrontation and white moderates stayed "above the battle." Even more damaging was the reluctance of the Kennedys, President John and Attorney General Robert, to become involved in a fight that was costing them support in a key area of the country for the Democratic Party. Within the government, also, a loud voice in their ears was that of J. Edgar Hoover, heading an all-white Federal Bureau of Investigation, who continued to charge that King and his allies were infiltrated and influenced by communists.

King, meanwhile, was having difficulty finding a way to refocus the energy that had been brought to bear in Montgomery. At the end of 1959, he made the decision to leave Montgomery and move to Atlanta as co-pastor of his father's congregation. It wasn't really possible to be pastor of a large congregation and yet travel constantly to speak in cities across the country and at the same time give leadership to the SCLC. His father's congregation gave him a significant pulpit but more freedom to respond to requests for his presence elsewhere. Atlanta also was a city with a liberal reputation and an airport hub to make travel easier.

1960, nonetheless, was a difficult year for Martin Luther King. In mid-February, he found himself facing imprisonment on income-tax charges that would never have put a white citizen behind bars. The State of Alabama charged that he had committed perjury in his state income-tax returns, a charge the state had never before brought against anyone. A white judge and white prosecutor tried the case before an all-white jury in a segregated courtroom. As it turned out, however, King had kept a meticulous record of his expenses in a travel diary and, after a three-day trial, an all-white jury needed only a few hours to find him not guilty.[22]

Not long after that, however, Georgia police pulled him over when they saw him driving with a white woman in the car and noticed that he had not transferred his driver's license from Alabama to Georgia in the required ninety days. He was fined and given a year's probation.

Meanwhile, in April, students in Greensboro, North Carolina, began sitting in at a Woolworth's lunch counter and demanding to be served. It was, King commented, "an electrifying moment that shattered the placid surface of campuses and communities across the South." Immediately, similar demonstrations broke out all over the South as hundreds of students sat down at dozens of lunch counters and endured taunts and abuse by white citizens as well as police guns, tear gas, arrests, and jail.[23] By the end of the year, over seventy thousand students had taken part in such sit-ins, and King had gladly responded to their requests for advice and praised their efforts as "one of the most significant developments in the civil rights struggle" and "a glowing example of disciplined, dignified non-violent action against the system of segregation." The students, however, wanted King to be with them physically as well as spiritually, and finally, in October, he joined them in a sit-in at the Magnolia Room, a restaurant in Atlanta's largest department store. King, as agreed, went to jail with fifty others and refused to seek bail or pay the fines. The mayor, however, struck a deal with the black "old guard" so that the students were released on their own recognizance. King, on the other hand, was found to have violated the terms of his one-year probation on the earlier traffic charge and was sentenced to four months at hard labor and transferred to Georgia's maximum-security Reidsville State Penitentiary.

With two toddlers underfoot and a third child about to be born, Coretta Scott King telephoned Harris Wofford, an old friend and presidential candidate John F. Kennedy's civil-rights adviser. "They're going to kill him," she told Wofford. "I know they are going to kill him." Wofford spoke to Sargent Shriver, Kennedy's brother-in-law, who persuaded the candidate to call Coretta King and express his concern and to call the Governor of Georgia and gain King's release. Hints of patronage in a future Democratic administration helped persuade the governor to release King on bail, and the Kennedy campaign flooded black communities with over a million pieces of literature publicizing what had happened. Nixon, the pamphlets noted, had had "no comment," while Kennedy was "the candidate with a heart." Kennedy scored a major breakthrough with black voters in that November's election that may have made the difference in such key states as Illinois.[24]

In spite of his debt to black voters, Kennedy was reluctant to alienate the remaining core of the Democratic Solid South, and King was only able to harass the new administration from the outside by charging, for example, that while "The President has proposed a ten-year plan for putting a man on the moon[,] We do not yet have a plan to put a Negro in the state legislature of Alabama."[25]

The sit-ins that began in April were followed quickly by Freedom Riders, six white and seven black, who set out in May to test compliance with a recent Supreme Court decision outlawing segregation in interstate transportation facilities. Setting out from Washington, they reached Atlanta with only a minor scuffle and were met and praised by Martin Luther King. Then they traveled westward toward Alabama. They crossed the state line outside Anniston, Alabama, and were met by a mob armed with iron bars, clubs, knives, and chains that smashed the windows of the first bus, punctured the tires, and set it ablaze.* The second bus was attacked even more savagely.**

When the bus drivers refused to go any farther, the frightened passengers, beaten and bloodied, decided to fly on to New Orleans. Other students decided that they could not allow the mob to win, so they hired new buses, intending to ride from Birmingham to New Orleans. Even before they reached the bus terminal, however, a new mob of men, women, and children appeared to attack them. One man hit a student over the head with his suitcase and then held his

---

* Accounts of this event differ. Branch (417–418) tells of nine Freedom Riders and five regular passengers and places the initial assault in the terminal at Anniston, while Sitkoff (73–74) says that there were thirteen Freedom Riders, six white and seven black, and places the attack on the highway outside Anniston.

** Again, accounts differ. Branch says the Riders were attacked both in the Anniston terminal and in Birmingham, while Sitkoff says the second bus bypassed Anniston and was attacked before reaching Birmingham.

head between his knees while a woman scratched his face with her fingernails and another man kicked out his teeth. Another Rider was beaten over the head with a baseball bat so that his skull was fractured and permanent damage was done that shortened his life.

Next day, a rally was held at a Montgomery church and a white mob gathered outside, ready for more violence. When King called the Attorney General and told him that a thousand black citizens were being threatened, Robert Kennedy blasted him for providing "good propaganda for America's enemies." Telling him that federal intervention would only make things worse, Kennedy called for a "cooling off" period. James Farmer, of the Congress of Racial Equality, a sponsoring group for the Freedom Riders, responded that black Americans had been "cooling off for a hundred years" and the ride would go on.[26]

Throughout that summer, state and federal authorities struggled to maintain order while new demonstrators continued to appear, white mobs formed, and Southern jails filled with students. Finally, in September, the Interstate Commerce Commission (ICC) put new guidelines in place for interstate travel that moved the Supreme Court ruling from theory to practice. To draw more poison out of the system, the federal government offered new support for voter-registration work. After the new ICC rule took effect, there would be no more segregated seating on interstate buses and trains; racially segregated drinking fountains, toilets, and waiting rooms serving interstate customers were consolidated; and the lunch counters began serving all customers, regardless of race.[27]

Martin Luther King had only tangential involvement in the Freedom Rides but became deeply involved in events that began that same summer in Albany, Georgia, where students from the Student Nonviolent Coordinating Committee (SNCC) had begun work on a voter-registration drive. That work expanded into the "Albany Movement" as a variety of groups came together to work on desegregating transportation and medical facilities, libraries and parks, as well as ending police brutality and ending the exclusion of black citizens from juries and elections. In a city where forty percent of the population was black, there was not a single African American official. There had been massive arrests and hundreds were in jail, but no real progress had been made and the Movement was beginning to falter. Over the objections of SNCC volunteers who feared transforming a people's movement into a "leadership event," King was invited to bring what assistance he could, even just "to speak to us one night."

On December 15, with fifteen hundred black citizens crammed into two churches, King went to the pulpit to do what he could to build their morale. He told them what he had seen in Africa and what he had learned in India, but before long he had moved into one of his standard cadences. It began with

King asking rhetorically, "How long?" and answering himself, "Not long." But soon it was a call and response with the congregation:

> How long will we have to suffer injustice? How long?
> Response: Not long!
> Not long, because the moral arc of the universe bends toward justice!*
> How long will justice be crucified and truth buried? How long?
> Response: Not long!
> How long?!
> Response: Not long!

He ended with another series of familiar phrases: "Don't stop now. Keep moving. Get on your walking shoes. Walk together, children. Dontcha get weary. There's a great camp meeting coming. . . ." As he stopped, the strains of "We Shall Overcome" came up spontaneously from the congregation.[28] That was why they wanted him to come. He could say things in a way that gave them renewed energy for the battle.

But the Albany campaign was a failure. Montgomery had been a success:

> Like no other, he convinced black Montgomery of its proud destiny, raised its morale, and inspired self-sacrifice. He made oratory a handmaid of social revolution.[29]

In Albany, however, the necessary pieces were not in place. King, in the first place, was not a resident of Albany and had not been there through the first months of the campaign. In the second place, the black community was not united in support. Many black professionals were comfortable with the life they had and feared that protest would make their lives harder, not better. Thirdly, the NAACP was unwilling to support the SCLC, and the SNCC resented the way King had been brought in after their months of hard work. In the fourth place, there was never a clear focus for the Movement. The attempt to end segregation in every aspect of Albany life was asking too much at one

---

* This phrase in various forms was based on a favorite quotation of King's from Theodore Parker, a nineteenth-century abolitionist, who said "I do not pretend to understand the moral universe; the arc is a long one, my eye reaches but a little ways; I cannot calculate the curve and complete the figure by the experience of sight; I can divine it by conscience. And from what I see I am sure it bends towards justice."—Theodore Parker, *The Present Aspect of Slavery in America and the Immediate Duty of the North: A Speech Delivered in the Hall of the State House, Before the Massachusetts Anti-Slavery Convention, on Friday Night, January 29, 1858*. Boston: B. Marsh, 1858.

time. Perhaps most important of all, Albany Police Chief Laurie Pritchett had learned from Montgomery and had instructed his troops to avoid violence and provocation.

When King and the Albany Movement leaders set out the next morning to march to City Hall, the police blocked their path and Chief Pritchett asked whether they had a written permit to march or demonstrate. King responded that they were only planning to pray and saw no need for a permit. The police politely loaded them into vans and took them to the jail, where they refused to post bond. Two days later, a separate group of Albany blacks met separately with Pritchett and agreed to post bond in return for desegregation of the bus and train terminals and the creation of a biracial committee to work out further desegregation arrangements. The City Commission, however, denied that any such arrangements had been made and refused to discuss the "demands" made by Albany Movement leaders. King wrote later that "we got nothing, and the people were left very depressed and in despair." The best he could say about it was that they had learned some lessons that were useful in future campaigns.[30] The national papers reported it as a "devastating" defeat for King. When an Albany court, months later, ordered King to pay $178 or spend forty-five days in jail, King opted for jail, only to find himself bailed out a few days later by an unidentified, well-dressed black citizen. Pritchett had won again by refusing to allow King to gain national publicity.[31]

It was a very different story, however, in Birmingham. Needing a dramatic victory in the centennial year of the Emancipation Proclamation, the SCLC decided to focus attention on Birmingham in a campaign that they would organize and carry out without having to negotiate with other organizations. Birmingham was "the most segregated city in America," with even elevators segregated by race and not a single black clerk in a white-owned store or any black police or firefighters. The Ku Klux Klan and White Citizens Councils were powerfully present, and the police chief, Eugene "Bull" Connor, prided himself on "keeping the niggers in their place." The *New York Times* described the city as a "racist tyranny."

To lead a Birmingham campaign, the SCLC had a corps of new and talented assistants to work with King, and a staff that had grown from five to sixty in the last three years.[32] Local support in Birmingham was not strong, but the SCLC leadership hoped Connor would "help them out" by overreacting and getting the sort of national publicity that would draw federal intervention.[33]

The campaign began with a series of mass meetings and sit-ins at lunch counters, but there was still not much support from the local black community. Finally, however, Connor did what the SCLC had hoped for when he blocked some fifty African Americans marching on City Hall and let loose a police dog to attack a black man with a knife. The national media printed the picture of the man on his back with the dog pinning him to the ground, and Birmingham officials responded by obtaining a state court order barring further demonstrations.

Two days later, Martin Luther King led fifty hymn-singing protesters through streets lined with black residents chanting "Freedom." Connor, true to type, came with his police dogs, arrested King, and threw him into jail. There, two days later, a jailer slipped him a copy of the Birmingham newspaper with the story of a statement issued by eight leading white clergy. Led by Episcopal Bishop C. C. J. Carpenter, the letter was co-signed by Carpenter's coadjutor, as well as Methodist and Roman Catholic bishops, a Presbyterian stated clerk, a senior Baptist pastor, and a rabbi. Regretting the presence of "outsiders," the letter commended the authorities for "the calm manner in which these demonstrations have been handled," and urged "restraint" on all sides. The clergy called on "law enforcement officials to remain calm and continue to protect our city from violence." Any issues, they said, "should be pressed in the courts and in negotiations among local leaders, and not in the streets."[34]

A few months earlier, the same clergy had responded to Governor George Wallace's 1963 inaugural address (often known as the "Segregation Forever" speech) by issuing an "Appeal for Law and Order and Common Sense," in which they affirmed basic principles of equality, justice, and free speech, but also the need to obey current law.[35] They were playing the classic role of well-intentioned moderates.

With no other paper available, King began to write around the margins of the newspaper. A trusty of the jail then began to provide him with scraps of paper; and finally his attorney, Clarence Jones, brought him a pad of paper. Eventually Jones smuggled twenty sheets of paper out of the jail, and King's colleagues began to edit the material into what became "Letter from a Birmingham Jail." Over a million copies were eventually distributed in churches across the country, and it remains one of the most important of all King's statements on America's racial divisions.

"My Dear Fellow Clergymen," King began, "While confined here in the Birmingham city jail, I came across your recent statement calling my present activities 'unwise and untimely' . . . [S]ince I feel that you are men of genuine good will and that your criticisms are sincerely set forth, I want to try to answer your statements in what I hope will be patient and reasonable terms."

Carefully, King explained to his white clergy brethren that he was part of an organization operating in all the Southern states and that he had been specifically invited to Birmingham by local clergy. "But more basically," he wrote, "I am in Birmingham because injustice is here. . . . Injustice anywhere is a threat to justice everywhere."

In responding to the letter's request for patience, King's writing began to match the eloquence of his speeches:

> For years now I have heard the word "Wait." It rings in the ear of every Negro with piercing familiarity. This "Wait" has almost always meant "Never." We must come to see, with one of our distinguished jurists, that "justice too long delayed is justice denied." We have waited for more than 340 years for our constitutional and God-given rights. The nations of Asia and Africa are moving with jetlike speed toward gaining political independence, but we still creep at horse-and-buggy pace toward gaining a cup of coffee at a lunch counter.
>
> Perhaps it is easy for those who have never felt the stinging darts of segregation to say, "Wait." But when you have seen vicious mobs lynch your mothers and fathers at will and drown your sisters and brothers at whim;
>
> when you have seen hate-filled policemen curse, kick and even kill your black brothers and sisters;
>
> when you see the vast majority of your twenty million Negro brothers smothering in an airtight cage of poverty in the midst of an affluent society;
>
> when you suddenly find your tongue twisted and your speech stammering as you seek to explain to your six-year-old daughter why she can't go to the public amusement park that has just been advertised on television, and see tears welling up in her eyes when she is told that Funtown is closed to colored children, and see ominous clouds of inferiority beginning to form in her little mental sky, and see her beginning to distort her personality by developing an unconscious bitterness toward white people;
>
> when you have to concoct an answer for a five-year-old son who is asking: "Daddy, why do white people treat colored people so mean?";
>
> when you take a cross-county drive and find it necessary to sleep night after night in the uncomfortable corners of your automobile because no motel will accept you;
>
> when you are humiliated day in and day out by nagging signs reading "white" and "colored"; when your first name becomes "nigger," your middle name becomes "boy" (however old you are) and your last name becomes "John," and your wife and mother are never given the respected title "Mrs.";
>
> when you are harried by day and haunted by night by the fact that you are a Negro, living constantly at tiptoe stance, never quite

> knowing what to expect next, and are plagued with inner fears and outer resentments;
>
> when you are forever fighting a degenerating sense of "nobodiness"—then you will understand why we find it difficult to wait.
>
> There comes a time when the cup of endurance runs over, and men are no longer willing to be plunged into the abyss of despair.

King explained to his colleagues why it was that he felt it necessary to break unjust laws. He quoted the Bible, he quoted Paul Tillich, Thomas Aquinas, Martin Buber, and T. S. Eliot. He told them that he had come to the "regrettable conclusion that the Negro's great stumbling block in his stride toward freedom is not the White Citizen's Counciler or the Ku Klux Klanner, but the white moderate, who is more devoted to 'order' than to justice. . . ." And he ended with a prayer:

> that the dark clouds of racial prejudice will soon pass away and the deep fog of misunderstanding will be lifted from our fear-drenched communities, and in some not too distant tomorrow the radiant stars of love and brotherhood will shine over our great nation with all their scintillating beauty.
>
> Yours for the cause of Peace and Brotherhood,
> Martin Luther King, Jr.

Bishop Carpenter read the letter through to the end and turned to his bishop coadjutor with a sigh of resignation, saying "This is what you get when you try to do something. You get it from both sides, George; you just have to live with it."[36]

King agreed to be released on bail after nine days in early April and the campaign lost focus, until early in May the decision was made to use students and even children to fill the jails and push Chief Connor to respond. Unable to hold back when provoked, Connor responded as King and his allies had hoped. He turned loose the police dogs, turned on water cannons, sent his troops against the demonstrators with clubs, and provided the network news with images that horrified the country. President Kennedy was still reluctant to respond publicly but did everything he could through Justice Department mediators to persuade business leaders in Birmingham that the time had come to find a peaceful solution. Fred Shuttlesworth, a local pastor and black leader, was no more eager to compromise than the businessmen, but he finally agreed with King that they had gained as much as they could. By phases, fitting rooms, lunch counters, water fountains, and restrooms would be integrated, black sales clerks would be hired, and a biracial committee would be created to work on improving employment opportunities for African Americans. King called it "the most magnificent victory for justice we've ever seen in the Deep South."[37]

The agreement was followed by new violence, not only in Birmingham but across the South that summer. Nonviolence had led to violence, but Wyatt Walker, King's administrative assistant, saw it as evidence of a transformed mentality in black America. "The most important thing that happened," in Wyatt's opinion, "was that people decided they weren't going to be afraid of white folks anymore. Dr. King's most lasting contribution is that he emancipated black folk's psyche. We threw off the slave mentality."[38] In June, President Kennedy finally addressed the nation on civil rights, calling it a moral issue as old as the Bible and as clear as the Constitution. A week later, he proposed civil-rights legislation based on "the proposition that race has no place in American life or law." By the end of the year, some three hundred cities had accepted various forms of desegregation.[39]

III

The idea of a March on Washington for civil rights seems to have originated with A. Philip Randolph, the head of the Brotherhood of Sleeping Car Porters, the first predominantly black labor union. Randolph proposed such a march in 1941 to force the country to give African Americans their proper place in the war effort, but President Roosevelt forestalled the march by moving to give black citizens equal opportunity in defense industries. Randolph used the same technique in 1948 to get President Truman to desegregate the armed forces. In 1957, of course, the SCLC had actually brought off a march on the capital, but in the form of a "prayer pilgrimage." The purpose, in fact, was to bring pressure to bear on the administration for civil-rights legislation, but it provided some background and experience for a larger and more specifically directed action. Such a proposal was made in the winter of 1962–1963 by Randolph, again, who now suggested a "descent on Washington" to demand more job opportunities for black citizens.

Months of negotiations followed. The NAACP and the Urban League were opposed. President Kennedy and Vice President Johnson met with King and Randolph—as well as the leaders of the NAACP, SNCC, Urban League, and CORE—and tried to persuade them that a march would be counterproductive, that it would give conservatives an excuse for opposing an attempt to coerce the Congress. Finally, however, the supporters of the March won support from the administration by agreeing to march to the Lincoln Memorial instead of the Capitol, to avoid any protest actions such as sit-ins, and to limit placards to five agreed slogans. Kennedy then saluted the March as being in "the great tradition" of peaceful assembly for "redress of grievances" and began to worry whether they would reach their goal of a hundred thousand participants.

The event itself exceeded all expectations when at least a quarter of a million people, almost a third of them white, flooded the Mall on August 28, 1963 for a day of joyful celebration. Joan Baez began the singing at ten A.M., and Peter, Paul, and Mary, Bob Dylan, Odetta, Mahalia Jackson, Josh White, and Marian Anderson were among those who sang. Church and synagogue representatives offered prayers, and leaders of the various black organizations spoke. Last on the program was Martin Luther King, Jr.; Randolph introduced him as "the moral leader of our nation."

King began by reminding the crowd of the Emancipation Proclamation issued "five score years ago," but told them that

> one hundred years later, the Negro still is not free.
>
> One hundred years later, the life of the Negro is still sadly crippled by the manacles of segregation and the chains of discrimination.
>
> One hundred years later, the Negro lives on a lonely island of poverty in the midst of a vast ocean of material prosperity.
>
> One hundred years later, the Negro is still languished in the corners of American society and finds himself an exile in his own land. And so we've come here today to dramatize a shameful condition. . . .

He told the crowd that there was work to be done to redeem the promises of the Constitution and Declaration of Independence. He spoke, in one of his most memorable phrases, of "the fierce urgency of Now" and told those listening:

> This is no time to engage in the luxury of cooling off or to take the tranquilizing drug of gradualism.
>
> Now is the time to make real the promises of democracy.
>
> Now is the time to rise from the dark and desolate valley of segregation to the sunlit path of racial justice.
>
> Now is the time to lift our nation from the quicksands of racial injustice to the solid rock of brotherhood.
>
> Now is the time to make justice a reality for all of God's children.

In working for justice and freedom, however, he reminded the crowd that they must avoid violence and work together. He took notice of those who had come there "out of great trials and tribulations . . . from narrow jail cells . . . battered by the storms of persecution and staggered by the winds of police brutality." His prepared text urged those who had suffered to go back to their communities "as members of the international association for the advancement of creative dis-satisfaction." That night have been an amusing line for an audience of twenty-five, but not for a quarter of a million. King knew instinctively that he would lose his audience with a phrase like that. Instead he began to improvise and urged them instead:

> Go back to Mississippi, go back to Alabama, go back to South Carolina, go back to Georgia, go back to Louisiana, go back to the slums and ghettos of our northern cities, knowing that somehow this situation can and will be changed.

Once free of his text, he continued to improvise, drawing on other speeches made in other places. "Tell them about the dream," urged Mahalia Jackson, and King launched into a new, revised version of speeches he had made in Birmingham and Detroit and St. Louis and other places as well.[40] To point this out is not to denigrate perhaps the greatest orator America has produced, because preachers and politicians have been recycling material as long as speakers have addressed audiences. William Jennings Bryan had given his "Cross of Gold" speech to many audiences before he astounded the Democratic National Convention with it in 1896. Abraham Lincoln repeated himself often in his debates with Stephen A. Douglas. Ronald Reagan had a set of index cards with material he used again and again. King had an excellent memory. He would often take a folder containing his sermon into the pulpit with him and ostentatiously close it before beginning to preach, to let the congregation know that he was not relying on a text.[41] He also used material from other preachers—as other preachers also do. His first sermon in his father's church at age eighteen was largely based on a sermon by Harry Emerson Fosdick.[42]

None of that is remarkable. It is, however, interesting to be able to see the orator at work by noticing the way Martin Luther King, in his most famous and important speech, improvised, as an organist does also, by reworking material and themes used before, modifying them to the occasion as he did so. It was a masterful performance by a master orator at his best. Some forty percent of the delivered speech was not given as planned but improvised there and then for the occasion.

Michael Eric Dyson comments on this aspect of King's style from the point of view of a black preacher when he says:

> King spoke much the way a jazz musician plays, improvising from minimally or maximally sketched chords or fingering changes that derive from hours of practice and performance. The same song is never the same song, and for King, the same speech was certainly

> never the same speech. He constantly added and subtracted . . . to suit the situation. He could blend ideas and slide memorized passages through his trumpet of a voice with remarkable sensitivity to his audience's makeup. King endlessly reworked themes, reshaped stories, and repackaged ideas to uplift his audience or drive them even further into a state of being—whether it was compassion or anger, rage or reconciliation—to reach for justice and liberation. King had a batch of rhetorical ballads, long, blue, slow-building meditations on the state of race, and an arsenal of simmering mid-tempo reflections on the high cost of failing to fix what fundamentally ails us—violence, hatred, and narrow worship of tribe and custom. King knew how to play as part of a rhetorical ensemble that stretched back in time to include Lincoln and Jefferson and stretched across waters to embrace Gandhi and Du Bois in Ghana. But he played piercing solos as well, imaginatively riffing off themes eloquently voiced by black preachers Prathia Hall and Archibald Carey. In the end, King brilliantly managed a repertoire of rhetorical resources that permitted him to play an unforgettable, haunting melody of radical social change.[43]

Another biographer, Marshall Frady, sums it up:

> He brought now for the first time, to millions across the nation watching the live telecast on all three networks, those pulpit grandeurs of the revival services of his origins, the oratorical raptures of countless mass meetings in black sanctuaries over the south. . . . It had suddenly become a pentecostal moment. A huge shiver of exhilaration moved through the expanses of the throng, shouts, bursts of clapping. . . . A running surf of cries and applause was now gathering after the baritone amplitudes of his voice.[44]

In Detroit, two months earlier in the year, he had also spoken of "going back," though in Detroit it was King who was going back to the South while in Washington he was urging others to go back. In both cases, they were to go back with a dream. In Detroit, he had said:

> And so I go back to the South not in despair. I go back to the South not with a feeling that we are caught in a dark dungeon that will never lead to a way out. I go back believing that the new day is coming. And so this afternoon, I have a dream. It is a dream deeply rooted in the American dream.

In Washington, those phrases were only slightly changed:

> Let us not wallow in the valley of despair, I say to you today, my friends. And so even though we face the difficulties of today and tomorrow, I still have a dream. It is a dream deeply rooted in the American dream.
>
> I have a dream that one day this nation will rise up and live out the true meaning of its creed: "We hold these truths to be self-evident, that all men are created equal."
>
> I have a dream that one day on the red hills of Georgia, the sons of former slaves and the sons of former slave owners will be able to sit down together at the table of brotherhood.

The Detroit version had been:

> *I have a dream that one day, right down in Georgia and Mississippi and Alabama, the sons of former slaves and the sons of former slave owners will be able to live together as brothers.*

In Washington, he said:

> I have a dream that one day even the state of Mississippi, a state sweltering with the heat of injustice, sweltering with the heat of oppression, will be transformed into an oasis of freedom and justice.
>
> I have a dream that my four little children will one day live in a nation where they will not be judged by the color of their skin but by the content of their character.

In Detroit, he had said:

> *I have a dream this afternoon that my four little children, that my four little children will not come up in the same young days that I came up within, but they will be judged on the basis of the content of their character, not the color of their skin.*

In Washington, he said:

> I have a dream today!
>
> I have a dream that one day, down in Alabama, with its vicious racists, with its governor having his lips dripping with the words of "interposition" and "nullification"—one day right there in Alabama

> little black boys and black girls will be able to join hands with little white boys and white girls as sisters and brothers.

In Detroit, he had said:

> *I have a dream this afternoon that one day, one day little white children and little Negro children will be able to join hands as brothers and sisters.*

In Detroit, however, he had spent more time developing the dream:

> *I have a dream this afternoon that one day, that one day men will no longer burn down houses and the church of God simply because people want to be free.*
>
> *I have a dream this afternoon that there will be a day that we will no longer face the atrocities that Emmett Till had to face or Medgar Evers had to face, that all men can live with dignity.*
>
> *I have a dream this afternoon that one day right here in Detroit, Negroes will be able to buy a house or rent a house anywhere that their money will carry them and they will be able to get a job.*
>
> *Yes, I have a dream this afternoon that one day in this land the words of Amos will become real and "justice will roll down like waters, and righteousness like a mighty stream."*
>
> *I have a dream this evening that one day we will recognize the words of Jefferson that "all men are created equal, that they are endowed by their Creator with certain unalienable Rights, that among these are Life, Liberty and the pursuit of Happiness." I have a dream this afternoon.*

In Washington, he said:

> I have a dream today!
>
> I have a dream that one day every valley shall be exalted, and every hill and mountain shall be made low, the rough places will be made plain, and the crooked places will be made straight; "and the glory of the Lord shall be revealed and all flesh shall see it together."

In Detroit, he had said:

> *I have a dream that one day every valley shall be exalted, and "every valley shall be exalted, and every hill shall be made low; the crooked places shall be made straight, and the rough places plain; and the glory of the Lord shall be revealed, and all flesh shall see it together."*

> *I have a dream this afternoon that the brotherhood of man will become a reality in this day.*

In Detroit, King had spoken of dealing with the mountain of despair by carving a tunnel of hope through it. This led to a new day when "all God's children" would be able to sing the old spiritual about freedom.

> *And with this faith I will go out and carve a tunnel of hope through the mountain of despair. With this faith, I will go out with you and transform dark yesterdays into bright tomorrows. With this faith, we will be able to achieve this new day when all of God's children, black men and white men, Jews and Gentiles, Protestants and Catholics, will be able to join hands and sing with the Negroes in the spiritual of old:*
> *Free at last! Free at last!*
> *Thank God almighty, we are free at last!*

In Washington, less logically, he spoke of hewing a "stone of hope" out of the "mountain of despair" and moved on from that to the first verse of "America." That, in turn, led to a passage borrowed from a far older speech in St. Louis and, at last, to the spiritual.

> With this faith, we will be able to hew out of the mountain of despair a stone of hope. With this faith, we will be able to transform the jangling discords of our nation into a beautiful symphony of brotherhood. With this faith, we will be able to work together, to pray together, to struggle together, to go to jail together, to stand up for freedom together, knowing that we will be free one day.
>
> And this will be the day—this will be the day when all of God's children will be able to sing with new meaning:
>
> My country 'tis of thee, sweet land of liberty, of thee I sing.
> Land where my fathers died, land of the Pilgrim's pride,
> From every mountainside, let freedom ring!
>
> And if America is to be a great nation, this must become true.
>
> And so let freedom ring from the prodigious hilltops of New Hampshire.
>
> Let freedom ring from the mighty mountains of New York.
>
> Let freedom ring from the heightening Alleghenies of Pennsylvania.
>
> Let freedom ring from the snow-capped Rockies of Colorado.
>
> Let freedom ring from the curvaceous slopes of California.
>
> But not only that:

Let freedom ring from Stone Mountain of Georgia.
Let freedom ring from Lookout Mountain of Tennessee.
Let freedom ring from every hill and molehill of Mississippi.
From every mountainside, let freedom ring.

And when this happens, and when we allow freedom to ring, when we let it ring from every village and every hamlet, from every state and every city, we will be able to speed up that day when all of God's children, black men and white men, Jews and Gentiles, Protestants and Catholics, will be able to join hands and sing in the words of the old Negro spiritual:

Free at last! Free at last!
Thank God Almighty, we are free at last!

Six years earlier, at a rally in St. Louis, King had also moved from a recitation of a verse of "America" to an invocation of the mountains and mountain ranges of America:

Freedom must ring from every mountain side. Let us go out this evening with that determination. Yes, let it ring from the snow-capped Rockies of Colorado.

Let it ring from the prodigious hill tops of New Hampshire.
Let it ring from the mighty Alleghenies of Pennsylvania.
Let it ring from the curvaceous slopes of California.
But not only that. From every mountain side, let freedom ring.

Yes, let us go out and be determined that freedom will ring from every mole hill in Mississippi.

Let it ring from Stone Mountain of Georgia.
Let it ring from Lookout Mountain of Tennessee.
Let it ring from every mountain and hill of Alabama.
From every mountain side, let freedom ring.

And when that happens we will be able to go out and sing a new song "Free at last, free at last, great God almighty, I'm free at last."[45]

Late that afternoon, King and other leaders met with President Kennedy in the White House. Kennedy admired King's speech but was doubtful about the prospects for passage of the pending civil-rights legislation. No clear strategy emerged from the conference, nor did King himself have a clear vision for his own next steps.

IV

Less than three weeks after that shimmering day in Washington, a bomb tore through the Sixteenth Avenue Baptist Church in Birmingham, killing four little girls who were attending Sunday school. Another child was shot outside by the police, and a sixth child later in the day by white young people. King told the parents, "[Y]ou do not walk alone. You gave to this world wonderful children. They didn't live long lives, but they lived meaningful lives." He told the congregation what that meaning was:

> They are the martyred heroines of a holy crusade for freedom and human dignity. And so this afternoon in a real sense they have something to say to each of us in their death. They have something to say to every minister of the gospel who has remained silent behind the safe security of stained-glass windows. They have something to say to every politician who has fed his constituents with the stale bread of hatred and the spoiled meat of racism. They have something to say to a federal government that has compromised with the undemocratic practices of southern Dixiecrats and the blatant hypocrisy of right-wing northern Republicans. They have something to say to every Negro who has passively accepted the evil system of segregation and who has stood on the sidelines in a mighty struggle for justice. They say to each of us, black and white alike, that we must substitute courage for caution. They say to us that we must be concerned not merely about who murdered them, but about the system, the way of life, the philosophy which produced the murderers. Their death says to us that we must work passionately and unrelentingly for the realization of the American dream.[46]

The question, however, was not so much what needed to be done as it was how to do it. A few white clergy attended the funeral, but no city officials. Once again, black leaders conferred with the president, and King told Kennedy: "The Negro community is about to reach the breaking point . . . there is a feeling of being alone and not protected." Even in church, he pointed out, you are no longer safe, and the commitment to nonviolence was becoming ever harder to sustain.[47] White leaders also conferred with Kennedy but had no answer to his repeated pleas for some constructive, positive response to so dangerous a situation. The failure of any efforts to come together in a common cause was most evident in the lack of an invitation to King to attend the funeral after Kennedy was assassinated. King flew to Washington and stood unrecognized in the street as the president's coffin passed by.[48]

King was invited to the White House in July 1964 to see President Lyndon Johnson sign the most sweeping civil-rights legislation yet, but he went there from a campaign in St. Augustine, Florida, which, in spite of more jail time for King, had produced no significant results. The Democratic Convention that summer produced further discouragement, as Johnson tried to avert a final break with Southern Democrats. While Johnson tried to conciliate intransigent Southerners, King faced an increasingly militant SNCC. James Forman, Stokely Carmichael, John Lewis, and others insisted that the time had come to "wreak havoc."

King went off to Europe with Coretta to rest and recharge spent batteries, but returned with a viral infection and high blood pressure that put him in a hospital bed. There he received the phone call telling him that he had become, at age thirty-five, the youngest person ever to receive the Nobel Peace Prize.[49] In December, King went to Oslo to accept the prize on behalf of all those who had worked to change America nonviolently. He said:

> I accept this award today with an abiding faith in America and an audacious faith in the future of mankind.
>
> I refuse to accept despair as the final response to the ambiguities of history.
>
> I refuse to accept the idea that the "isness" of man's present nature makes him morally incapable of reaching up for the eternal "oughtness" that forever confronts him.
>
> I refuse to accept the idea that man is mere flotsam and jetsam in the river of life, unable to influence the unfolding events which surround him.
>
> I refuse to accept the view that mankind is so tragically bound to the starless midnight of racism and war that the bright daybreak of peace and brotherhood can never become a reality.
>
> I have the audacity to believe that peoples everywhere can have three meals a day for their bodies, education and culture for their minds, and dignity, equality and freedom for their spirits. I believe that what self-centered men have torn down men other-centered can build up. I still believe that one day mankind will bow before the altars of God and be crowned triumphant over war and bloodshed, and nonviolent redemptive good will proclaim the rule of the land. "And the lion and the lamb shall lie down together and every man shall sit under his own vine and fig tree and none shall be afraid." I still believe that We *Shall* overcome![50]

Elsewhere on the same trip, King set the Nobel Prize in a broader perspective, identifying the American struggle with "the far more deadly struggle for freedom in South Africa," where Nelson Mandela and others remained in prison. American investments, he pointed out, were guilty of supporting South

African tyranny. In Oslo, he spoke of the need for a worldwide war against poverty. "Ultimately," he said, "a great nation is a compassionate nation. No individual or nation can be great if it does not have concern for 'the least of these'."

Back in America, King found his focus shifting to a campaign for voting rights in Selma, Alabama. President Johnson told King he was unwilling to push for voting rights until other "Great Society" legislation had been adopted, but King and his colleagues were impatient.[51] In Selma and the surrounding Dallas County, only 350 black citizens were registered to vote out of 15,000 who were eligible. Governor Wallace was working in every way he could to maintain segregation and keep African Americans from the polls. When the suggestion was made that a march from Birmingham to Selma might dramatize the situation, Wallace obliged by vowing to prevent such a march from taking place.

King was not present for the march on that March 7, 1965. He had Sunday obligations in Atlanta, and his colleagues had urged him not to take part because of threats to his life. No one had expected the level of violence that occurred on that day. When the marchers met a solid line of troopers and refused to disperse, the troopers charged in a flying wedge, trampling and beating those they encountered. Mounted troopers followed, swinging bullwhips and rubber tubing wrapped in barbed wire; tear gas was used as well. The sheriff could be heard yelling "Get those goddamn niggers," and the marchers were driven back into the church from which they had started. The parsonage was used as a makeshift emergency room to treat the injured.

Before there was television, it had been possible to do things that would have horrified the nation had they been seen. Gruesome lynchings had taken place in those days because no one saw them except those who were there. But when Sheriff Clark now sent his troopers to ride down old women and children, the television cameras were there and the whole world saw what was done and was appalled. All that was needed then was to let those who had seen it express their feelings by joining hands with those who had been there.

King therefore announced that there would be a second march on Tuesday, just two days later, and invited clergy from across the nation to join him in a nonviolent march for freedom. Nuns, priests, ministers, and rabbis poured in from across the nation, and a complicated series of events involving President Johnson, Governor Wallace, Attorney General Nicholas Katzenbach, and the district judge followed. The proposed march was enjoined by the federal judge, but King arranged with the authorities to march up to the troopers and then turn back so long as there was no violence. Over the objections of many, King did lead the marchers, who faced the troopers, knelt to pray, and then turned around and walked back to the chapel from which they had started.

Meanwhile, other protests broke out across the country. Six hundred pickets at the White House demanded federal intervention, ten thousand marched in Detroit, fifteen thousand in Harlem, and thousands more in Washington. Meanwhile, lawyers in the Justice Department and White House rushed to prepare a voting-rights bill for Congress. Eight days after "Bloody Sunday," President Johnson addressed a joint session of Congress and told them that the time had come to pass voting-rights legislation.

In his address, Johnson confronted the problem of racism and racial discrimination head-on. He declared that "every American citizen must have an equal right to vote. There is no reason which can excuse the denial of that right." Johnson reminded the nation that the Fifteenth Amendment, which was passed just five years after the Civil War, gives all citizens the right to vote regardless of "race, color, or previous condition of servitude," yet many states had defied the Constitution and erected barriers based on those forbidden grounds. In Johnson's view, no constitutional or moral issue was at stake: Congress simply needed to enforce the amendment with strict penalties.

> I speak tonight for the dignity of man and the destiny of democracy.
>
> I urge every member of both parties—Americans of all religions and of all colors—from every section of this country—to join me in that cause.
>
> At times history and fate meet at a single time in a single place to shape a turning point in man's unending search for freedom. So it was at Lexington and Concord. So it was a century ago at Appomattox. So it was last week in Selma, Alabama.
>
> There is no Negro problem. There is no southern problem. There is no northern problem. There is only an American problem. And we are met here tonight as Americans—not as Democrats or Republicans—we are met here as Americans to solve that problem.

It was not a long speech, but Johnson made clear that there must be action and that voting rights were only one part of a larger struggle for human rights:

> But even if we pass this bill, the battle will not be over. What happened in Selma is part of a far larger movement which reaches into every section and State of America. It is the effort of American Negroes to secure for themselves the full blessings of American life.
>
> Their cause must be our cause too, because it is not just Negroes but really it is all of us, who must overcome the crippling legacy of bigotry and injustice. And we shall overcome. . . .

> This great, rich, restless country can offer opportunity and education and hope to all—all black and white, all North and South, sharecropper and city dweller. These are the enemies—poverty, ignorance, disease—they are our enemies, not our fellow man, not our neighbor. And these enemies too—poverty, disease, and ignorance—we shall overcome.

The following Sunday, King led the way on the first stage of a five-day march along the Jefferson Davis Highway from Selma to Birmingham. Now the marchers were no longer only African American but all Americans, black and white, Jews and Christians, and others of no clear ethnicity or religious affiliation. Now also they were protected by helicopters overhead and a federalized National Guard along the highway. On the fifth day, thirty thousand marchers walked the last few miles into Birmingham to gather in front of the State Capitol and hear Martin Luther King make what some considered his finest speech. He said:

> They told us we wouldn't get here. And there were those who said that we would get here only over their dead bodies, but all the world today knows that we are here and we are standing before the forces of power in the state of Alabama saying, "We ain't goin' let nobody turn us around."

Knowing that the nation and the world were listening, King gave them a lesson in American history. He told how segregation came to be, as a strategy to keep not only black people from power, but poor whites as well.

> If it may be said of the slavery era that the white man took the world and gave the Negro Jesus, then it may be said of the Reconstruction era that the southern aristocracy took the world and gave the poor white man Jim Crow. . . .
>
> They segregated southern money from the poor whites; they segregated southern mores from the rich whites; they segregated southern churches from Christianity; they segregated southern minds from honest thinking; and they segregated the Negro from everything.

Like President Johnson, King also refused to settle for the limited agenda of voting rights. There was more still to be done:

> Let us therefore continue our triumphant march to the realization of the American dream.

> Let us march on segregated housing until every ghetto or social and economic depression dissolves, and Negroes and whites live side by side in decent, safe, and sanitary housing.
>
> Let us march on segregated schools [Let us march] until every vestige of segregated and inferior education becomes a thing of the past, and Negroes and whites study side-by-side in the socially-healing context of the classroom.
>
> Let us march on poverty until no American parent has to skip a meal so that their children may eat.
>
> March on poverty until no starved man walks the streets of our cities and towns in search of jobs that do not exist.
>
> Let us march on poverty until wrinkled stomachs in Mississippi are filled, and the idle industries of Appalachia are realized and revitalized, and broken lives in sweltering ghettos are mended and remolded.

The ballot would be the means to all these ends, and King chanted out cadence after cadence of "Let us march on the ballot boxes" until it led him into Joshua's march around Jericho that brought down the walls of that fortified city. He recited the old spiritual and ended it with the words "'Cause the battle is in my hands." Half mocking, half admiring, African Americans sometimes referred to King as "De Lawd," but he sounded like that on that day as he said "My people, my people, listen. The battle is in our hands." There would be no return to "normalcy," he told them, until they had arrived at "the normalcy of brotherhood, the normalcy of true peace, the normalcy of justice." How long would that take? He concluded with that question and the answer chanted back by the crowd:

> I know you are asking today, "How long will it take?"
>
> Somebody's asking, "How long will prejudice blind the visions of men, darken their understanding, and drive bright-eyed wisdom from her sacred throne?" Somebody's asking, "When will wounded justice, lying prostrate on the streets of Selma and Birmingham and communities all over the South, be lifted from this dust of shame to reign supreme among the children of men?"
>
> Somebody's asking, "When will the radiant star of hope be plunged against the nocturnal bosom of this lonely night, plucked from weary souls with chains of fear and the manacles of death? How long will justice be crucified, and truth bear it?"
>
> I come to say to you this afternoon, however difficult the moment, however frustrating the hour, it will not be long, because "truth crushed to earth will rise again."

> How long? Not long, because "no lie can live forever."
> How long? Not long, because "you shall reap what you sow."
> How long? Not long:
> How long? Not long, because the arc of the moral universe is long, but it bends toward justice.
> How long? Not long, because:
> Mine eyes have seen the glory of the coming of the Lord;
> He is trampling out the vintage where the grapes of wrath are stored;
> He has loosed the fateful lightning of his terrible swift sword;
> His truth is marching on.
> He has sounded forth the trumpet that shall never call retreat;
> He is sifting out the hearts of men before His judgment seat.
> O, be swift, my soul, to answer Him! Be jubilant, my feet!
> Our God is marching on.
> Glory, hallelujah! Glory, hallelujah!
> Glory, hallelujah! Glory, hallelujah!
> His truth is marching on.[52]

Some printed and online versions of this speech show responses of "All right" and "Yes" and "Not long," but no such text can include the varied responses of "Amen" and "That's right" and "Tell it" and many others that made so many of King's speeches corporate events. He not only used his voice for himself but gave voice to millions of others who had no voice.

V

King and Johnson both had spoken of a wider issue than that of race and the ballot box; injustice was older than segregation and deeper than race. It manifested itself that same summer of 1965, as riots broke out in the Watts section of Los Angeles and in Chicago. In Watts, thirty-four people died, all but two of them black. King described it as a "temper tantrum" such as a child indulges in when no one pays attention, and said the riots were "massive temper tantrums from a neglected and voiceless people." When rioting broke out in Chicago, King felt that he must respond by turning the attention of the SCLC north to confront *de facto* school segregation, police brutality, substandard housing, and racially divisive real estate customs.

Some of King's closest advisers saw only trouble ahead in confronting behavior patterns far less easily addressed than the stark evil of legal segregation. Northern leaders like Mayor Richard J. Daley of Chicago would not use police dogs and water cannons, but they would resist and they would have the support of the great majority of contented white citizens. Increasingly also,

King was hearing demands from black leaders for an end to nonviolence and the use instead of "Black power." King now saw the need for "basic structural changes in the architecture of American society," but he would not yield to demands that he forsake his basic principles. As if the endemic injustices of Northern cities were not enough, King found himself also increasingly drawn to denounce America's growing involvement in the war in Vietnam.

In January 1966, King announced a campaign to reshape Chicago, "one of the most segregated cities in the nation."[53] Marches that summer in blue-collar white neighborhoods like the Chicago suburb of Cicero demonstrated the depth of white resistance to breaking down the racial divisions in their communities. He and Coretta moved into a slum apartment and experienced for themselves the entry-level dirt floors, the smell of stale beer and rotting rubbish, the drugs and prostitutes available on the street corner.[54] Lacking the deep church roots of Southern communities as a base, King spent endless hours talking nonviolence to gang leaders. Meanwhile, the mayor killed off King's initiatives with kindness: he called on the clergy to join him in working to end the slums, announced new urban housing initiatives in press releases, and predicted the end of slums in Chicago within four years. King said it was like fighting a pillow.[55]

Freedom, King insisted, was more than the right to vote, and it involved not only American freedom but freedom of other nations from American power. Early in 1967, he attacked the war in Vietnam at a rally in Los Angeles. Other black leaders told him to focus on jobs; if he failed to stand by Johnson on the war, why should Johnson stand with African Americans on their daily concern for jobs? King countered that he was concerned for truth and for Vietnamese children burned with napalm. In March 1967, he led his first antiwar march in Chicago with Dr. Benjamin Spock, and in April he went into the pulpit of the Riverside Church in New York to attack the war in Vietnam directly. The war in Vietnam, he told the congregation, "was being waged on behalf of the wealthy and secure while we create a hell for the poor." Acknowledging that he had been urged to stay out of the movement against the war, he listed his reasons for opposing it. First among these reasons was the way it undercut the effort to end poverty in America. That program, he said, had been

> broken and eviscerated as if it were some idle political plaything in a society gone mad on war. And I knew that America would never invest the necessary funds or energies in rehabilitation of its poor so long as adventures like Vietnam continued to draw men and skills and money like some demonic, destructive suction tube. So I was increasingly compelled to see the war as an enemy of the poor and to attack it as such.

He also opposed the war, he said, because it took young men whose lives had been crippled by poverty and sent them off to die in Asia. He opposed it because it made nonsense of his struggle to advocate nonviolence. He opposed it because he felt the Nobel Prize compelled him to look beyond national boundaries and local concerns. He ended his sermon, as he had so often ended his speeches before, by quoting the familiar lines of James Russell Lowell and the words of the prophet Amos:

> Once to every man and nation comes a moment to decide,
> In the strife of truth and falsehood, for the good or evil side;
> . . . If we will make the right choice, we will be able to transform the jangling discords of our world into a beautiful symphony of brotherhood. If we will but make the right choice, we will be able to speed up the day, all over America and all over the world, when justice will roll down like waters, and righteousness like a mighty stream.[56]

Criticism rolled down on King from every side: his own staff opposed him; major newspapers attacked him; J. Edgar Hoover of the FBI, always opposed to King, saw it as the final proof that King was an instrument in the hands of the communists. King, nonetheless, continued to insist that "Injustice anywhere is a threat to justice everywhere."

> Cowardice asks the question, is it safe?
> Expediency ask the question, is it politic?
> Vanity asks the question, is it popular?
> But conscience ask the question, is it right?
> And there comes a time when we must take a position that is neither safe, nor politic, nor popular, but he must do it because Conscience tells him it is right.[57]

Eventually, of course, the vast majority of Americans would come to agree with King, but not until he was dead.

The summer of 1967 saw an unprecedented wave of urban violence. In Newark twenty-five were killed, and in Detroit the death toll was forty-three as an untrained and nervous National Guard tried to cope with looting and fires. King saw it as the natural result of the governmental indifference to the poverty and lack of jobs that afflicted the predominantly black inner cities.

In mid-August, at a tenth-anniversary meeting of the SCLC, he told his colleagues that the time had come to disrupt business as usual in "earthquake proportions." "Let us be dissatisfied," he exhorted them,

> until the tragic walls that separate the outer city of wealth and comfort from the inner city of poverty and despair shall be crushed by the battering rams of the forces of justice.
>
> Let us be dissatisfied until those who live on the outskirts of hope are brought into the metropolis of daily security.
>
> Let us be dissatisfied until slums are cast into the junk heaps of history, and every family will live in a decent, sanitary home.
>
> Let us be dissatisfied until the dark yesterdays of segregated schools will be transformed into bright tomorrows of quality integrated education.
>
> Let us be dissatisfied until integration is not seen as a problem but as an opportunity to participate in the beauty of diversity.
>
> Let us be dissatisfied until men and women . . . will be judged on the basis of the content of their character, not on the basis of the color of their skin.
>
> Let us be dissatisfied until from every city hall, justice will roll down like waters, and righteousness like a mighty stream.
>
> Let us be dissatisfied until that day when nobody will shout, "White Power!" when nobody will shout, "Black Power!" but everybody will talk about God's power and human power.[58]

King began to speak that fall about an idea that came to him from Marian Wright,* a lawyer for the NAACP's Legal Defense Fund, who suggested bringing the destitute to Washington to stage sit-ins. King adapted the idea and proposed a "Poor People's Crusade" to march on Washington and demand jobs and real measures to counteract endemic poverty. Like the Bonus Army of 1932, he envisioned poor people descending on Washington in waves, camping in the Mall, and staging protests until the government made dealing with poverty one of its top priorities. If that meant imprisonment, they would accept it easily, since "the millions of poor are already imprisoned by exploitation and discrimination." As he spoke about the idea, his terminology shifted away from simple "nonviolence" to become "aggressive nonviolence" and "nonviolent sabotage." He spoke about "civil disobedience," which would block access to government offices, disrupt traffic, and boycott schools.[59] Few SCLC board members, however, supported their leader's obsession with an issue that seemed to them a distraction unlikely to gain widespread support.

---

* Marian Wright may be better known now as Marian Wright Edelman, the founder, leader, and principal spokesperson for the Children's Defense Fund, a voice for poor, minority, and disabled children.

With the new year, King became deeply discouraged by the lack of support from friends and colleagues and the increasing opposition from others. He became obsessed with the failures of the movement to deal with poverty in Mississippi, and the deaths of children in Vietnam kept him awake at night. Death threats, fifty recorded by the FBI, came more often. Two supporters of George Wallace's Independent Party posted a reward of $100,000 for King's death. In February, he preached about it at his Ebenezer Church in Atlanta:

> [E]very now and then I think about my own death and I think about my own funeral. And I don't think about it in a morbid sense. And every now and then I ask myself what it is that I would want said and I leave the word to you this morning.
>
> If any of you are around when I have to meet my day, I don't want a long funeral. And if you get somebody to deliver the eulogy tell him not to talk too long. . . .
>
> I'd like somebody to mention that day that Martin Luther King Jr. tried to give his life serving others. I'd like for somebody to say that day that Martin Luther King Jr. tried to love somebody.
>
> I want you to say that day that I tried to be right and to walk with them. I want you to be able to say that day that I did try to feed the hungry. I want you to be able to say that day that I did try in my life to clothe the naked. I want you to say on that day that I did try in my life to visit those who were in prison. And I want you to say that I tried to love and serve humanity.
>
> Yes, if you want to, say that I was a drum major. Say that I was a drum major for justice. Say that I was a drum major for peace. I was a drum major for righteousness. And all of the other shallow things will not matter.[60]

Two months later, those words would be played at his funeral at his wife's request.

In spite of the opposition, the Poor People's Crusade did begin to gain traction and aggravate the fears of the FBI. Once again, however, he ignored the advice of colleagues when a former associate begged him to come to Memphis to support a strike by garbage workers demanding recognition for their union. In January, heavy rain in Memphis had made it impossible to work, so black workers had been sent home with two hours' pay, while white workers received a full day's compensation. Two black workers had been crushed when they took shelter in the back of a garbage compacter while white co-workers sat in the cab. The newly elected segregationist mayor had given the workers an ultimatum: return to work, or be fired. King saw it as an opportunity to dramatize exactly the issues he would highlight in the Poor People's Crusade.

So it was that King went to Memphis on April 3, only to learn that a court judge had issued a restraining order against the planned march the next day. Determined to march anyway, King agreed at the last minute to speak to a small gathering the evening before. As rain beat down outside, he told them what Patrick Henry had told the Virginia Assembly: that the issue was freedom.

> If I lived in China or even Russia, or any totalitarian country, maybe I could understand some of these illegal injunctions. Maybe I could understand the denial of certain basic First Amendment privileges, because they hadn't committed themselves to that over there.
>
> But somewhere I read of the freedom of assembly.
>
> Somewhere I read of the freedom of speech.
>
> Somewhere I read of the freedom of press.
>
> Somewhere I read that the greatness of America is the right to protest for rights. And so just as I said, we aren't going to let dogs or water hoses turn us around. We aren't going to let any injunction turn us around.
>
> The issue is injustice. The issue is the refusal of Memphis to be fair and honest in its dealings with its public servants, who happen to be sanitation workers. Now, we've got to keep attention on that. That's always the problem with a little violence. You know what happened the other day, and the press dealt only with the window-breaking. I read the articles. They very seldom got around to mentioning the fact that one thousand three hundred sanitation workers are on strike, and that Memphis is not being fair to them.

But King had his mind on more than those immediate issues. He told them how his plane from Atlanta had been delayed that morning for an extra security check because of his presence.

> And then I got to Memphis. And some began to say the threats, or talk about the threats that were out. What would happen to me from some of our sick white brothers? . . .
>
> Well, I don't know what will happen now. We've got some difficult days ahead. But it doesn't matter with me now. Because I've been to the mountaintop. And I don't mind. Like anybody, I would like to live a long life. Longevity has its place. But I'm not concerned about that now. I just want to do God's will. And He's allowed me to go up to the mountain. And I've looked over. And

> I've se-e-e-e-e-en the Promised Land.* I may not get there with you. But I want you to know tonight that we as a people will get to the Promised Land. And I'm happy, tonight. I'm not worried about anything. I do not fear any man. Mine eyes have seen the glory of the coming of the Lord.[61]

Late in the next afternoon, word came that the judge had decided to allow a restricted march the next Monday, when they had planned to march anyway. Relaxed and happy, King and his friends got ready to go to a friend's house for a soul-food dinner. With time to spare, King stepped out onto the balcony overlooking the motel parking lot. James Earl Ray, a small-time criminal and campaign worker for George Wallace, killed King with a single rifle shot fired from a rooming house near King's motel.

On the balcony of the motel in Memphis there is a simple plaque with two verses inscribed from the Biblical story of Joseph. Before selling him into slavery, his brothers had first thought to kill him, and one of them said

> Here comes the dreamer. Come now, let us kill him . . . and we shall see what will become of his dreams. [Genesis 37:19–20]

* It should be noted that King always placed the stress on the first syllable of the phrase "pro´mised land."

EPILOGUE

Speeches are not significant because we have the technological ability to make them heard by every member of our huge nation simultaneously. Speeches are important because they are one of the great constants of our political history. For two hundred years, from "Give me liberty or give me death," to "Ask not what your country can do for you," they have been not only the way we measure public man, they have been how we tell each other who we are. For two hundred years they have been changing—making, forcing—history: Lincoln, Bryan and the cross of gold, FDR's first inaugural, Kennedy's, Martin Luther King in '63, Reagan and the Speech in '64. They count. They more than count, they shape what happens.

—*Peggy Noonan*[1]

I

Consider this:

Daniel Webster gave his great speech on "Liberty and Union" from twelve pages of notes.

Abraham Lincoln sometimes went through seven or eight drafts of a speech before he was ready to give it.

Franklin Roosevelt sat down with a team of speechwriters every week to spend an evening planning upcoming addresses.

Adlai Stevenson had four Pulitzer Prize winners on his speechwriting team.

William Jennings Bryan's "Cross of Gold Speech" and Ronald Reagan's speech in support of the Goldwater campaign had been given many times before and polished again and again.

Isn't it remarkable, then, that Patrick Henry, so far as we know, had no notes, no speech writers, and had never given the speech that set the American Revolution in motion until that day in March 1775 when he stood up at a meeting of the House of Burgesses in Saint John's Church in Richmond, Virginia, to demand "liberty or death"?

Isn't it also remarkable that the demand for freedom has remained a central issue in American life for well over two hundred years, although its meaning has been continually debated and reinterpreted?

One thing is certain: when the various speakers included in this book spoke of freedom, they had many different things in mind, and some had very limited agendas. For all of them, however, it was a goal beyond themselves, a gift for others also. For Patrick Henry it was independence from British rule; for Daniel Webster it was the basis of unity between the states; for James Pennington, Wendell Phillips, and Frederick Douglass it was an end of human slavery; for Angelina Grimké, Abby Foster, and Elizabeth Stanton it was a woman's right to be recognized as a full citizen; for William Jennings Bryan it included economic freedom; for Franklin Roosevelt it meant freedom from fear of unemployment and of German and Japanese domination; for Adlai Stevenson it mean the right to dissent even when dissent was most unpopular; for Ronald Reagan it meant freedom from an over-reaching government and from the fear of nuclear war; for Martin Luther King, Jr., it meant the freedom to participate fully and freely in every aspect of American life.

Human freedom is constantly threatened in numerous ways and worn away by the "death of a thousand cuts" unless those who possess it are vigilant. But freedom also expands as human understanding of it expands and new generations commit themselves to the risk of a wider and more inclusive vision.

II

William Jennings Bryan was the first of these speakers to focus attention on the economic aspect of the struggle for freedom, but economic factors are always involved. Patrick Henry's demand for political freedom was supported by powerful people in Virginia because the value of their tobacco crop was controlled by English merchants. Human slavery lasted as long as it did because planters, ship owners, and Northern industrialists benefited from it. Women's suffrage took as long as it did to achieve because women were leaders in the temperance and prohibition movement, and the liquor interests, ranging from the owners of breweries and distilleries to the proprietors of the neighborhood pubs, feared giving them more power. Only after the prohibition amendment was adopted did women gain the right to vote. Martin Luther King, Jr.'s last campaign was centered on poverty, and Ronald Reagan's campaign for smaller government focused on taxes, corporate and individual.

Franklin Roosevelt was probably the speaker who was clearest about the economic basis of freedom. Freedom, he said, "is no half-and-half affair. If the average citizen is guaranteed equal opportunity in the polling place, he must have equal opportunity in the market place." His State of the Union message in 1944 called for a Second Bill of Rights "providing a new basis of security and prosperity . . . for all—regardless of station, race, or creed."[2] "True individual freedom," Roosevelt said more than once, "cannot exist without economic security and independence. 'Necessitous men are not freemen.' People who are hungry and out of a job are the stuff of which dictatorships are made."[3]

III

Reagan might well have disagreed with Roosevelt's economics, but he quoted Roosevelt and imitated his methods, using a weekly radio address modeled after Roosevelt's Fireside Chats. That weekly address—with a response from the opposition—has become a standard part of American life. Reagan also initiated the continuing pattern of presenting living witnesses in the gallery during the State of the Union Address.

What qualities make for a great speaker? A strong and resonant voice is invaluable. Henry, Webster, Roosevelt,* and King are remembered for the rich baritone voices with which they commanded attention; but Lincoln, perhaps the greatest of them all, spoke in what was described by a Chicago reporter at the Lincoln-Douglas debates as "a thin, high-pitched falsetto voice of much carrying power that could be heard a long distance in spite of the bustle and tumult of a crowd."[4] Herndon wrote in 1887 that Lincoln's voice could be shrill at first but became "harmonious, melodious—musical, if you please." Roosevelt's voice was strong but could also be remarkably intimate in, for example, the Fireside Chats. Ronald Reagan and Adlai Stevenson had voices that were resonant but perhaps not as strong and clear and deep as those of Henry, Webster, Roosevelt, and King. Columnist Richard Reeves said Reagan had "a wonderful voice, husky and honeyed," and speechwriter Ken Khachigian described it as "a fine Merlot being poured gently into a crystal goblet."[5] Reagan's was a voice for the age of television, intimate and personal.

The quality of a speaker's voice, however, is not simply a matter of timbre, of richness. Stevenson's voice in those respects was not remarkable, yet it was his voice that people remembered and cited when he died. President Johnson called him "one of [America's] finest voices for peace" and spoke of his "thoughtful eloquence." Stevenson's old friend Carl McGowan, in his eulogy for him, spoke again and again of his "voice" whose echoes, he said, "are likely to be sounding down the corridors of history for a long time." The *New York Times* editorialized about his "incisive eloquence." A voice expresses ideas, but the quality of that voice and the words it uses are made more or less effective by the speaker's ability to project convictions in a way that is not only heard but

---

* Halford R. Ryan *(Franklin D. Roosevelt's Rhetorical Presidency)* calls Roosevelt a tenor and says that his speaking voice was consistently from E-flat to F below middle C, but most studies speak of Roosevelt as a baritone and only of Lincoln as a tenor.

that produces a response. That quality is spoken of as "personality," but that is a word often used too cheaply. "Character" is better, and "conviction" perhaps better still. It remains, nevertheless, mysteriously indefinable, yet essential.

IV

The challenges to the preservation of freedom are constantly new, but those whose lives and words are remembered in this book drew from a great variety of sources, past and present, to make their points. It is striking how often they learned from each other. Lincoln and Bryan memorized the great orations of Patrick Henry and Daniel Webster, and all those who came after quoted Lincoln. Franklin Roosevelt not only quoted English case law, but he also quoted Lincoln, of course, and his cousin-predecessor Theodore. The first President Roosevelt said "Much has been given us, and much will rightfully be expected from us,"[6] and the second President Roosevelt said "To some generations much is given. Of other generations much is expected."[7] Both were drawing on Jesus' words in the Gospel according to Saint Luke.[*]

Lincoln had copy books, Reagan had file cards, and Roosevelt had file folders of things that struck them as interesting and useful in their reading and stories told them by friends. Some, like Lincoln, wrote their own speeches; some, like Roosevelt, worked closely with their speechwriters. Some, like Reagan, delegated the writing but still edited closely and carefully the texts they were given. Lincoln may not have had designated speechwriters to work with him, but even he took advice frequently from friends. He made significant use of Seward's suggestions for his first inaugural and perhaps at Gettysburg.

Material came to them from a wide variety of sources. There have been prodigious readers among the presidents: Theodore Roosevelt and John F. Kennedy, who could read 2,500 words a minute, inhaled books at the rate of two or three a day. Reagan also read constantly but very slowly, wanting to memorize what he read. FDR and Stevenson, on the other hand, read little and preferred to learn from people, but Roosevelt apparently picked up a copy of Thoreau in the days before his inauguration and found the phrase about "nothing to fear except fear itself."

V

Speeches are composed of words, and great speakers tend to choose words with great care. Lincoln, above all, wanted to be clear and to be understood. He remembered how, as a child, he had been frustrated when people used words he didn't understand and how he worked to put what had been said "in language

* Luke 12:48—"For unto whomsoever much is given, of him shall be much required: and to whom men have committed much, of him they will ask the more" [King James Version].

plain enough . . . for any boy I knew to comprehend."[8] Roosevelt worked to find "simple and understandable language."[9] Reagan's chief speechwriter in his first term, Bentley Elliott, remarked that Reagan "uses hard words. He concentrates and speaks with great conciseness." But Reagan was always ready to include some of Peggy Noonan's softer language and poetic quotations. Martin Luther King, on the other hand, loved to use elaborate words and preferred elaboration to concision. Adjectives and adjectival phrases abounded: "the stale bread of hatred and the spoiled meat of racism."

Lincoln cared about the sound of words. He had written some fairly decent poetry as a young man and had a "strong sense of cadence and sophisticated ear for rhythmic patterns." King's ear for rhythm was powerfully shaped by an African American tradition that can be traced back to Africa. The influence of the King James Version of the Bible can be noticed in such phrases as Lincoln's "Four score and seven years," in Theodore and Franklin Roosevelt's indirect quotations from the Gospel, and in direct quotations used by William Jennings Bryan, Adlai Stevenson, Ronald Reagan, and Martin Luther King, Jr.

To quote or refer to the Bible has been a constant aspect of American speeches, but perhaps only toward the end of the twentieth century did it begin to be used as a weapon, to be claimed by one party against the other. The subject deserves careful study, but a quick analysis suggests that the problem begins with the McCarthy era's search for communists in government and Republican charges that the Democratic Party was the party of "war, crisis, subversion, and treason."

VI

All these tools and techniques, of course, are employed to communicate with an audience, the American people. Stories have always been used to keep the hearer's attention. Reagan liked to use stories—it is surprising that Lincoln, a great storyteller in private, almost never told stories in his speeches—and liked to illustrate his stories and objectives with the living presence of people whose stories would "connect" with listeners and viewers. Martin Luther King, Jr., on the other hand, was able (though not at the Dexter Avenue Church) to employ the ancient African call and response—"Amen," "That's right, Brother," "Tell it!"—to establish a relationship with his audience, to make his speeches corporate events, and to use his voice to give voice to millions of others who had no voice.

Patrick Henry may be an exception, but all the others worked hard at their craft. Reagan and King had unusually strong memories, but they also worked hard at preparing themselves to speak. Whether they had speechwriters or not, those whose speeches are remembered—Patrick Henry again may be the exception that proves the rule—worked hard over their texts, ceaselessly revising and polishing to get exactly the phrasing they wanted. Lincoln's speeches may be the best remembered, simply because he was most aware of the audience beyond the reach of his voice who would not hear his words but would read them. Webster and Reagan may have had better voices for their time, but succeeding generations have only the words. Even now, though we have the ability to record and play back the speaker and the speech, it is finally the text, the written word, that will commend itself or not when the immediate moment has passed.

Speeches are, of course, intended to persuade, but an effective speech must always to some degree reflect what an audience already understands and believes. The effective speaker must speak *for* people as well as *to* them. Perhaps the ultimate test of a speaker's effectiveness is the extent to which his or her words are reused and quoted by others. Again and again, the American speakers whose words are remembered have been those who most effectively expressed the continuing American search for a fuller expression of freedom.

BIBLIOGRAPHY

PATRICK HENRY

Côté, Richard N. *Strength and Honor: The Life of Dolley Madison*. Mt. Pleasant, SC: Corinthian Books, 2004.

Elliot, Jonathan (ed.). *The Debates in the Several State Conventions on the Adoption of the Federal Constitution*. Philadelphia: J. B. Lippincott.

Kidd, Thomas S. *Patrick Henry: First Among Patriots*. New York: Basic Books, 2011.

Meade, Robert Douthat. *Patrick Henry*. Philadelphia: Lippincott, 1957.

Morgan, George. *The True Patrick Henry*. Philadelphia: J. B. Lippincott, 1907.

Unger, Harlow Giles. *Lion of Liberty: Patrick Henry and the Call to a New Nation*. Cambridge, MA: Da Capo, 2010.

Wirt, William. *Life of Patrick Henry*. Philadelphia: J. Webster, 1817.

DANIEL WEBSTER

Adams, Ephraim Douglass. "Lord Ashburton and the Treaty of Washington." *The American Historical Review*, Vol. 17, No. 4, July 1912.

Bartlett, Irving H. *Daniel Webster*. New York: W. W. Norton, 1978.

Benét, Stephen Vincent. *The Devil and Daniel Webster*. New York: Farrar & Rinehart, 1937.

Binkley, Wilfred Ellsworth, and Malcolm Charles Moos. *A Grammar of American Politics: The National Government*. New York: Alfred A. Knopf, 1949.

Current, Richard Nelson. *Daniel Webster and the Rise of National Conservatism*. Boston: Little, Brown, 1955.

Fuess, Claude Moore. *Daniel Webster*. Boston: Little, Brown, 1930.

Lyman, S. P. *The Public and Private Life of Daniel Webster*. Philadelphia: J. E. Potter, 1852.

March, Charles W. *Daniel Webster and his Contemporaries*. New York: C. Scribner, 1852.

Remini, Robert. *Daniel Webster, the Man and his Time*. New York: W. W. Norton, 1997.

Smith, Craig R. *Daniel Webster and the Oratory of Civil Religion*. Columbia: University of Missouri Press, 2005.

Webster, Daniel. "On Conscription." U.S. House of Representatives, December 9, 1814. www.constitution.org/dwebster/conscription.htm

Webster, Daniel. *The Works of Daniel Webster*. Boston: Little, Brown, 1856.

Whipple, Edwin P. (ed.). *The Great Speeches and Orations of Daniel Webster, With an Essay on Daniel Webster as a Master of English Style*, 1923. The Project Gutenberg eBook. http://www.gutenberg.org/ebooks/12606

JAMES W. C. PENNINGTON

Alexander, Leslie. *African or American? Black Identity and Political Activism in New York City, 1784–1861.* Chicago: University of Illinois Press, 2008.

Brawley, Benjamin Griffith. *A Social History of the American Negro.* New York: Macmillan, 1921.

Pennington, J. W. C. *Covenants Involving Moral Wrong Not Obligatory Upon Man: A Sermon Delivered in the Fifth Congregational Church, Hartford, on Thanksgiving Day, November 17th, 1842 by J. W. C. Pennington, Pastor of the Church.* Hartford, CT: John C. Wells, 1842.

Pennington, James W. C. *The Fugitive Blacksmith or, Events in the History of James W. C. Pennington, Pastor of a Presbyterian Church, New York, Formerly a Slave in the State of Maryland, United States.* Second ed. London: Charles Gilpin, 1849.

Pennington, James W. C. *A Text Book of the Origin and History, &c. &c. of the Colored People.* Hartford, CT: L. Skinner, 1841.

Webber, Christopher L. *American to the Backbone: The Life of James W. C. Pennington, the Fugitive Slave Who Became One of the First Black Abolitionists.* New York: Pegasus, 2011.

FREDERICK DOUGLASS

Buccola, Nicholas. *The Political Thought of Frederick Douglass: In Pursuit of American Liberty.* New York: New York University Press, 2012.

Douglass, Frederick. *The Church and Prejudice.* November 4, 1841, Plymouth County, MA. http://www.greatamericandocuments.com/speeches/douglass-church-prejudice.html

Douglass, Frederick. *Life and Times of Frederick Douglass: His Early Life as a Slave, His Escape from Bondage, and His Complete History. Written by Himself.* London: Collier, 1962.

Douglass, Frederick. *Life of an American Slave.* Boston: Anti-Slavery Office, 1845.

Douglass, Frederick. *My Bondage and My Freedom.* New York: Modern Library, 2003.

Douglass, Frederick. *An Oration, at Rochester, July 5, 1852.* http://www.lib.rochester.edu/index.cfm?page=2945

Douglass, Frederick. "A Plea for Free Speech in Boston." 1860.

Douglass, Frederick. Benjamin Quarles, ed. *Narrative of the Life of Frederick Douglass, an American Slave, written by himself.* Cambridge, MA: Belknap, 1960.

Douglass, Frederick. "What the Black Man Wants." Speech at the Annual Meeting of the Massachusetts Anti-Slavery Society in Boston, April 1865.

WENDELL PHILLIPS

Austin, George Lowell. *Life and Times of Wendell Phillips.* Boston: Lee and Shepard, 1901.

Bartlett, Irving H. *Wendell Phillips, Brahmin Radical.* Boston: Beacon, 1961.

Phillips, Wendell. *The Freedom Speech of Wendell Phillips.* Boston: Wendell Phillips Hall Association, 1890.

Sherwin, Oscar. *Prophet of Liberty: The Life and Times of Wendell Phillips.* New York: Bookman, 1958.

ANGELINA GRIMKÉ

Browne, Stephen Howard. *Angelina Grimké: Rhetoric, Identity, and the Radical Imagination.* East Lansing: Michigan State University Press, 1999.

Ceplair, Larry. *The Public Years of Sarah and Angelina Grimké.* New York: Columbia University Press, 1989.

Collins, Gail. *America's Women.* New York: HarperCollins, 2003.

Grimké, Angelina Emily. *An Appeal to the Christian Women of the South.* http://www.gutenberg.org/9/9/1/9915/

Grimké, Angelina. *Letters to Catherine Beecher in Reply to An Essay on Slavery and Abolitionism.* Boston: Isaac Knapp, 1838.

Henry, Katharine. "Angelina Grimké's Rhetoric of Exposure." *American Quarterly* 49:2 (1997), 328–355.

Lumpkin, Katherine Du Pre. *The Emancipation of Angelina Grimké.* Chapel Hill: University of North Carolina Press, 1974.

Weld, Angelina Grimké. "Speech in Pennsylvania Hall, May 17, 1838." http://www.sojust.net/speeches/grimke_weld_pa_hall.html

Weld, Theodore D. *American Slavery As It Is: Testimony of a Thousand Witnesses.* New York: American Anti-Slavery Society Office, 1839.

Weld, Theodore Dwight. *In Memory Angelina Grimké Weld: born in Charleston, South Carolina, Feb. 20, 1805, died in Hyde Park, Massachusetts, October 26, 1879.* Boston: G. H. Ellis, 1880.

Yellin, Jean Fagan, and John C. Van Horne. *The Abolitionist Sisterhood: Women's Political Culture in Antebellum America.* Ithaca, NY: Cornell University Press, 1994.

ABBY KELLEY FOSTER

Bacon, Margaret Hope. *I Speak for My Slave Sister: The Life of Abby Kelley Foster.* New York: Thomas Y. Crowell, 1974.

Sterling, Dorothy. *Ahead of Her Time: Abby Kelley and the Politics of Antislavery.* New York: W. W. Norton, 1991.

ELIZABETH CADY STANTON

Bacon, Margaret Hope. *Valiant Friend: The Life of Lucretia Mott.* New York: Walker, 1980.

Banner, Lois W. *Elizabeth Cady Stanton: A Radical for Women's Rights.* Boston: Little, Brown, 1980.

Griffith, Elisabeth. *In Her Own Right.* New York: Oxford University Press, 1984.

Stanton, Elizabeth Cady. *Eighty Years and More: Reminiscences of Elizabeth Cady Stanton.* New York: European Publishing Company, 1898.

Stanton, Elizabeth Cady, Susan B. Anthony, and Matilda Joslyn Gage. *History of Woman Suffrage, Volume I.* Rochester, NY: Charles Mann, 1881.

Stanton, Theodore, and Harriot Stanton Blatch. *Elizabeth Cady Stanton as Revealed in Her Letters, Diary and Reminiscences.* New York: Harper, 1922.

Waggenspack, Beth M. *The Search for Self-Sovereignty: The Oratory of Elizabeth Cady Stanton.* New York: Greenwood, 1989.

ABRAHAM LINCOLN

Angle, Paul M. (ed.). *Created Equal? The complete Lincoln-Douglas debates of 1858.* Chicago: University of Chicago Press, 1958.

"A Word to the Adopted Citizens of the United States." Middletown, NY: *Banner of Liberty* (newspaper), August 3, 1859.

Basler, Roy P. (ed.). *The Collected Works of Abraham Lincoln, Second Supplement 1848–1865.* Brunswick, NJ: Rutgers University Press, 1990.

Benét, Stephen Vincent. *John Brown's Body.* Garden City, NY: Doubleday, Doran, 1928.

Boritt, Gabor. *The Gettysburg Gospel: The Lincoln Speech that Nobody Knows.* New York: Simon & Schuster, 2006.

Braden, Waldo W. *Abraham Lincoln: Public Speaker.* Baton Rouge: Louisiana State University Press, 1988.

Donald, David Herbert. *Lincoln.* New York: Simon & Schuster, 1995.

Hirsch, David, and Dan Van Haften. *Abraham Lincoln and the Structure of Reason.* New York: Savas Beatie, 2010.

Holzer, Harold. *Lincoln at Cooper Union.* New York: Simon & Schuster, 2004.

Keneally, Thomas. *Abraham Lincoln.* New York: Lipper/Viking, 2003.

Lincoln, Abraham. Address at Cooper Union. http://www.abrahamlincolnonline.org/lincoln/speeches/cooper.htm

Lincoln, Abraham. Reply to Horace Greeley. http://www.nytimes.com/1862/08/24/news/letter-president-lincoln-reply-horace-greeley-slavery-union-restoration-union.html

Lincoln, Abraham. July 4th Message to Congress (July 4, 1861) http://millercenter.org/president/speeches/detail/3508

Sandburg, Carl. *Abraham Lincoln: The War Years.* New York: Harcourt, Brace, 1939.

Strong, George Templeton, ed. Allan Nevins and Milton Halsey Thomas. *Diary.* New York: Macmillan, 1952.

White, Ronald C., Jr. *The Eloquent President: A Portrait of Lincoln through His Words.* New York: Random House, 2005.

Wills, Garry. *Lincoln at Gettysburg: The Words that Remade America.* New York: Simon & Schuster, 1992.

WILLIAM JENNINGS BRYAN

Bryan, William Jennings. *Memoirs of William Jennings Bryan, by himself and his wife Mary Baird Bryan.* Philadelphia: John C. Winston, 1925.

Bryan, William Jennings. *Speeches of William Jennings Bryan.* New York: Funk & Wagnalls, 1913.

Coletta, Paolo E. *William Jennings Bryan.* Lincoln: University of Nebraska Press, 1964–1969.

Glad, Paul W. *McKinley, Bryan, and the People.* Philadelphia: Lippincott, 1964.

Kazin, Michael. *A Godly Hero: The Life of William Jennings Bryan.* New York: Alfred A. Knopf, 2006.

Melder, Keith. *Bryan the Campaigner.* Washington: Smithsonian Institution, 1966.

Bryan at the Scopes Trial: personal.uncc.edu/jmarks/Darrow.htm

Bryan's Acceptance Speech, 1896: http://railroads.unl.edu/documents/view_document.php?id=rail.wjb.18960812.01

Newspapers: *The Sunday Oregonian* (Portland, OR), July 18, 1920. *San Francisco Examiner,* July 6, 1915.

FRANKLIN DELANO ROOSEVELT

Brands, H. W. *Traitor to His Class: The Privileged Life and Radical Presidency of Franklin Delano Roosevelt.* New York: Doubleday, 2009.

Brooks, Phillips. *Lectures on Preaching, Delivered Before the Divinity School of Yale College.* New York: E. P. Dutton, 1877.

Burns, James MacGregor. *Roosevelt: The Lion and the Fox.* New York: Harcourt, Brace, 1956.

Craig, Douglas B. *Fireside Politics: Radio and Political Culture in the United States, 1920–1940.* Baltimore: Johns Hopkins University Press, 2000.

Freidel, Frank. *Franklin D. Roosevelt: A Rendezvous with Destiny.* Boston: Little, Brown, 1990.

Gelderman, Carol W. *All the Presidents' Words: The Bully Pulpit and the Creation of the Virtual Presidency.* New York: Walker, 1997.

Hand, Samuel B. "Rosenman, Thucydides, and the New Deal." *The Journal of American History,* Vol. 55, No. 2 (Sept. 1968).

Houck, Davis W. *Rhetoric as Currency: Hoover, Roosevelt, and the Great Depression.* College Station: Texas A&M University Press, 2001.

Kennedy, David M. *Freedom from Fear: The American People in Depression and War, 1929–1945.* New York: Oxford University Press, 1999.

Lindley, Ernest K. *Franklin D. Roosevelt: A Career in Progressive Democracy.* Indianapolis: Bobbs-Merrill, 1931.

Pederson, William D. *The FDR Years.* New York: Facts on File, 2006.

Ryan, Halford Ross. *Franklin D. Roosevelt's Rhetorical Presidency.* New York: Greenwood Press, 1988.

Ryan, Halford Ross. "Roosevelt's First Inaugural: A Study of Technique." *Quarterly Journal of Speech* (65), April 1979.

Schlaes, Amity. *The Forgotten Man: A New History of the Great Depression*. New York: HarperCollins, 2007.

Sharon, John. "Roosevelt and Truman: The Fireside Technique." *Daily Princetonian*, March 22, 1950.

Ward, Geoffrey C. *A First Class Temperament: The Emergence of Franklin Roosevelt*. New York: Harper & Row, 1989.

ADLAI E. STEVENSON

Broadwater, Jeff. *Adlai Stevenson: The Odyssey of a Cold War Liberal*. New York: Twayne, 1994.

Liebling, Alvin (ed.). *Adlai Stevenson's Lasting Legacy*. New York: Palgrave Macmillan, 2007.

Martin, John Bartlow. *Adlai Stevenson of Illinois: The Life of Adlai E. Stevenson*. Garden City, NY: Doubleday, 1976.

Martin, John Bartlow. *Adlai Stevenson and the World: The Life of Adlai E. Stevenson*. Garden City, NY: Doubleday, 1977.

McKeever, Porter. *Adlai Stevenson: His Life and Legacy*. New York: William Morrow, 1989.

Muller, Herbert J. *Adlai Stevenson: A Study in Values*. New York: Harper and Row, 1967.

Sievers, Rodney M. *The Last Puritan?: Adlai Stevenson in American Politics*. Port Washington, NY: Associated Faculty Press, 1983.

Stevenson, Adlai. *Call to Greatness: A Survey of a Troubled World*. New York: Harper, 1954.

Stevenson, Adlai E. *Major Campaign Speeches of Adlai E. Stevenson, 1952*. New York: Random House, 1953.

Whitman, Alden. *Portrait: Adlai E. Stevenson: Politician, Diplomat, Friend*. New York: Harper, 1965.

RONALD REAGAN

Bates, Toby Glenn. *The Reagan Rhetoric: History and Memory in 1980s America*. DeKalb: Northern Illinois University Press, 2011.

Cannon, Lou. *Reagan*. New York: Perigee, 1982.

Cannon, Lou. *President Reagan: The Role of a Lifetime*. New York: Public Affairs, 1991.

Cannon, Lou. *Governor Reagan: His Rise to Power*. New York: Public Affairs, 2003.

Erickson, Paul D. *Reagan Speaks: The Making of an American Myth*. New York: New York University Press, 1985.

Evans, Thomas W. *The Education of Ronald Reagan: The General Electric Years and the Untold Story of His Conversion to Conservatism*. New York: Columbia University Press, 2006.

Hanska, Jan. *Reagan's Mythical America: Storytelling as Political Leadership*. New York: Palgrave Macmillan, 2012.

Morris, Edmund. *Dutch: A Memoir of Ronald Reagan*. New York: Random House, 1999.

Noonan, Peggy. *What I Saw at the Revolution: A Political Life in the Reagan Era*. New York: Random House, 1990.

Pemberton, William E. *Exit with Honor: The Life and Presidency of Ronald Reagan*. Armonk, NY: M. E. Sharpe, 1997.

Reeves, Richard. *President Reagan: The Triumph of Imagination*. New York: Simon & Schuster, 2005.

Schaller, Michael. *Ronald Reagan*. New York: Oxford University Press, 2011.

MARTIN LUTHER KING, JR.

Branch, Taylor. *Parting the Waters*. New York: Simon & Schuster, 1988.

Carson, Clayborne. *The Autobiography of Martin Luther King, Jr.* New York: IPM in association with Warner Books, 1998. New York: Grand Central Publishing, 1998.
Dyson, Michael Eric. *I May Not Get There With You.* New York: Free Press, 2000.
Niles, Lyndrey A. "Rhetorical Characteristics of Traditional Black Preaching." *Journal of Black Studies*, Vol. 15, No. 1 (Sept. 1984), pp. 41–52.
Pitts, Walter. "West African Poetics in the Black Preaching Style." *American Speech*, Vol. 64, No. 2 (Summer 1989), pp. 137–149.
Sitkoff, Harvard. *Pilgrimage to the Mountaintop.* New York: Hill and Wang, 2008.

USE THESE LINKS TO SEE AND HEAR SOME GREAT AMERICAN SPEECHES

A recreation of Patrick Henry's "Liberty or Death" speech by David Baldwin.
http://www.youtube.com/watch?v=iEOets_L7vg
A recreation of Daniel Webster's reply to Hayne by Orson Welles
http://www.youtube.com/watch?v=k5oZwHfpPVI
A recreation of Lincoln's Cooper Union speech by Sam Waterston
http://www.youtube.com/watch?v=aQ2De8VcSLw
A recreation of Bryan's Cross of Gold Speech by Don Fielder
http://www.c-span.org/video/?74624-1/william-jennings-bryan-cross-gold-speech
A later recoding made by Bryan himself twenty-seven years later.
http://www.youtube.com/watch?v=HeTkT5-w5RA
Roosevelt's First Inaugural Address
http://www.presidency.ucsb.edu/youtubeclip.php?clipid=14473&admin=32
Adlai Stevenson's convention speech accepting nomination 1952
http://www.youtube.com/watch?v=yDORrpgvZog
Ronald Reagan's Inaugural Address
http://www.presidency.ucsb.edu/youtubeclip.php?clipid=43130&admin=40
Martin Luther King Jr.'s "I Have a Dream" speech
http://www.youtube.com/watch?v=smEqnnklfYs

ENDNOTES

ONE: PATRICK HENRY (PAGES 1–27)

1. Morgan, George. *The True Patrick Henry*. Philadelphia: J. B. Lippincott, 1907, 71.
2. Kidd, Thomas S. *Patrick Henry: First Among Patriots*. New York: Basic Books, 2011, 251–252.
3. Kidd, 233–234.
4. Meade, Robert Douthat. *Patrick Henry*. Philadelphia: Lippincott, 1957, Vol. I, 70–71.
5. Kidd, 167.
6. Wirt, William. *Life of Patrick Henry*. Philadelphia: J. Webster, 1817, 6.
7. Unger, Harlow Giles. *Lion of Liberty: Patrick Henry and the Call to a New Nation*. Cambridge, MA: Da Capo, 2010, 11.
8. Morgan, 33.
9. Morgan, 440.
10. Morgan, 33.
11. Unger, 13.
12. Unger, 13.
13. Meade, Vol. I, 133.
14. Meade, Vol. I, 134.
15. Meade, Vol. I, 165.
16. Meade, Vol. I, 171.
17. Wirt, 61.
18. Meade, Vol. I, 173.
19. Wirt, 106.
20. Kidd, 83.
21. Côté, Richard N. *Strength and Honor: The Life of Dolley Madison*. Mt. Pleasant, SC: Corinthian Books, 2004, 47–48.
22. Meade, Vol. I, 37.
23. Meade, Vol. I, 256–257.
24. Meade, Vol. I, 306.
25. Meade, Vol. I, 268.
26. Meade, Vol. II, 31.
27. Wirt, 38.
28. Meade, Vol. II, 322.
29. Wirt, 73–75.
30. Meade, Vol. II, 344.
31. Meade, Vol. II, 39.
32. Meade, Vol. II, 43.
33. Kidd, 99.
34. Wirt, 232.
35. Elliot, Jonathan (ed.). *The Debates in the Several State Conventions on the Adoption of the Federal Constitution*, 2nd ed. Philadelphia: J. B. Lippincott, 1836–1859, 56.
36. Elliot, 59–60.
37. Elliot, 59–60.
38. Elliot, 66.
39. Elliot, 140.

40. Elliot, 590–591.
41. Elliot, 142.
42. Unger, 216–217.
43. Morgan, 352.
44. Elliot, 626.
45. Elliot, 626.
46. Elliot, 653.
47. Meade, Vol. II, 436.

TWO
DANIEL WEBSTER (PAGES 28–56)

1. Benét, Stephen Vincent. *The Devil and Daniel Webster.* New York: Farrar and Rinehart, 1937, 1.
2. Lyman, S.P. *The Public and Private Life of Daniel Webster.* Philadelphia: J. E. Potter, 1852. Vol. 17, 95.
3. Bartlett, Irving H. *Daniel Webster.* New York: W.W. Norton, 1978.
4. Remini, Robert. *Daniel Webster: The Man and His Time.* New York: W.W. Norton, 1997, 28.
5. Remini, 125.
6. March, Charles W. *Daniel Webster and His Contemporaries.* New York: C. Scribner, 1852.
7. Fuess, Claude Moore. *Daniel Webster.* Boston: Little, Brown, 1930. Vol. 1, 23.
8. *Writings*, Vol. 18, 228. Daniel Webster to R. M. Blatchford, May 3, 1846.
9. *Writings*, Vol. 17, 9.
10. Bartlett, 21.
11. Bartlett, 26–27.
12. Whipple, Edwin P. (ed.). *The Great Speeches and Orations of Daniel Webster, With an Essay on Daniel Webster as a Master of English Style.* The Project Gutenberg eBook, 1923. http://www.gutenberg.org/cache/epub/12606/pg12606.html
13. Smith, Craig R. *Daniel Webster and the Oratory of Civil Religion.* Columbia: University of Missouri Press, 2005, 30.
14. Webster, Daniel. "On Conscription," U.S. House of Representatives, December 9, 1814. www.constitution.org/dwebster/conscription.htm
15. Webster, "On Conscription."
16. Webster, Peroration, The Dartmouth College Case, March 10, 1818. http://books.google.com/books/about/The_Great_Speeches_and_Orations_of_Danie.html?id=otJBAAAAIAAJ
17. Smith, 47.
18. Smith, 40.
19. Bartlett, 279–280.
20. Whipple, Edwin P. (ed.). *The Great Speeches and Orations of Daniel Webster*, "First Settlement of New England, A Discourse delivered at Plymouth, on the 22d of December, 1820." http://www.gutenberg.org/files/12606/12606-8.txt
21. Whipple, "First Settlement."
22. Whipple, Edwin P. (ed.). *The Great Speeches and Orations of Daniel Webster*, "The Bunker Hill Monument, An Address delivered at the Laying of the Corner-Stone of the Bunker Hill Monument at Charlestown, Massachusetts, on the 17th of June, 1825." http://www.gutenberg.org/files/12606/12606-8.txt
23. Smith, 85–96.
24. Current, Richard Nelson. *Daniel Webster and the Rise of National Conservatism.* Boston: Little, Brown, 1955, 36.
25. Current, 27.
26. *Writings*, Vol. 6, 75.
27. Smith, 118.
28. Whipple, Edwin P. (ed.). *The Great Speeches and Orations of Daniel Webster*, "The Presidential Veto of the United States Bank Bill. A Speech Delivered in the Senate of the United States, on the 11th of July, 1832, on the President's Veto of the Bank Bill." http://www.gutenberg.org/files/12606/12606-8.txt
29. Smith, 166.
30. Bartlett, 152.
31. Binkley, Wilfred Ellsworth, and Malcolm Charles Moos. *A Grammar of American Politics: The National Government.* New York: Alfred A. Knopf, 1949, 265.
32. Baumgartner, Jody C., and Peter L. Francia. *Conventional Wisdom and American Elections: Exploding Myths, Exploring Misconceptions.* Lanham, MD: Rowman & Littlefield, 2008.

33. Smith, 173–174.
34. Bartlett, 174.
35. Smith, 185.
36. Adams, Ephraim Douglass. "Lord Ashburton and the Treaty of Washington." *The American Historical Review*, Vol. 17, No. 4, July 1912.
37. Adams, 780.
38. Adams, 778.
39. Smith, 180.
40. Bartlett, 188.
41. Webster, Daniel. *The Works of Daniel Webster.* Boston: Little, Brown, 1856, Vol. 5, 299–300.
42. Webster, *Works*, Vol. 5, 299–300.
43. Bartlett, 234.
44. Remini, 659.
45. Remini, 663.
46. Remini, 665.
47. Whipple, Edwin P. (ed.). *The Great Speeches and Orations of Daniel Webster*, "The Constitution and the Union, A Speech delivered in the Senate of the United States, on the 7th of March, 1850." http://www.gutenberg.org/cache/epub/12606/pg12606.html
48. George, A. J. (ed.). *Select Speeches of Daniel Webster, 1817–1845.* Boston: D. C. Heath, 1905, 1.
49. Bartlett, 252.
50. Smith, 250.
51. Lounsbury, Thomas R. (ed.). *Yale Book of American Verse.* New Haven: Yale University Press, 1912, 75.
52. Smith, 239.
53. Smith, 252.
54. Bartlett, 292.
55. Daniel Webster, July 17, 1850, Address to the Senate.

THREE: THE ABOLITIONISTS

JAMES W. C. PENNINGTON (PAGES 57–65)

1. *Torch Light and Public Advertiser*, Hagerstown, Maryland, November 1, 1827.
2. Pennington, James W. C. *The Fugitive Blacksmith or, Events in the History of James W. C. Pennington, Pastor of a Presbyterian Church, New York, Formerly a Slave in the State of Maryland, United States.* Second ed. London: Charles Gilpin, 1849, 50–51.
3. "From Our Brooklyn Correspondent," *Frederick Douglass' Paper* (hereafter *FDP*), July 30, 1852.
4. Pennington, *Fugitive Blacksmith*, 38.
5. "Slavery in the United States," *Gloucester Journal*, November 2, 1850. *BAP* 6:0662.
6. *Liberator*, July 2, 1831.
7. "The Pembroke Family," *New York Tribune*, June 15, 1854.
8. *FDP*, August 14, 1851. This article gives Pennington's own account of his status at Yale and is cited in Warner, Robert A., *New Haven Negroes: A Social History.* New Haven: Yale University Press, 1940. Other reports of Pennington's status at Yale usually cite Warner, often inaccurately.
9. Pennington, James W. C., *A Text Book of the Origin and History, &c. &c. of the Colored People.* Hartford, CT: L. Skinner, 1841.
10. Pennington, J. W. C. *Covenants Involving Moral Wrong Not Obligatory Upon Man: A Sermon Delivered in the Fifth Congregational Church*, Hartford, on Thanksgiving Day, November 17th, 1842 by J. W. C. Pennington, Pastor of the Church. Hartford, CT: John C. Wells, 1842.
11. *Anti-Slavery Reporter*, June 28, 1843. (*BAP*, Doc. No. 06951)
12. "Wholesome Verdict," *New York Times*, February 23, 1855.
13. Alexander, Leslie. *African or American? Black Identity and Political Activism in New York City, 1784–1861.* Chicago: University of Illinois Press, 2008, 129.
14. Brawley, Benjamin Griffith. *A Social History of the American Negro.* New York: Macmillan, 1921, 239.
15. Brawley, 397.
16. Brawley, 397.

WENDELL PHILLIPS (PAGES 66–78)

17. Austin, George Lowell. *The Life and Times of Wendell Phillips.* Boston: Lee and Shepard, 1888, 86.
18. Sherwin, Oscar. *Prophet of Liberty: The Life and Times of Wendell Phillips.* New York: Bookman, 1958, 56.

19. Sherwin, 30.
20. Bartlett, Irving H. *Wendell Phillips: Brahmin Radical.* Boston: Beacon, 1961, 34–36.
21. Bartlett, 46.
22. Douglass, *My Life and Times*, 446.
23. Phillips, Wendell. *The Freedom Speech of Wendell Phillips.* Boston: Wendell Phillips Hall Association, 1890, 8.
24. Morris, Charles. *The World's Great Orators and their Orations.* Philadelphia: John C. Winston, 1917, 149.
25. An 1884 memorial oration by Henry Ward Beecher for famed abolitionist Wendell Phillips. http://antislavery.eserver.org/tracts/beecherphillips
26. Sherwin, 112–113.
27. Sherwin, 117.
28. *The Liberator*, Vol. 1, No. 1, January 1, 1831.
29. Sherwin, 138.
30. Sherwin, 141.
31. Sherwin, 140.
32. Ruchames, Louis. *The Abolitionists: A Collection of Their Writings.* New York: G.P. Putnam, 1963.
33. Sherwin, 153.
34. Sherwin, 154.
35. Austin, 209.
36. Pease, Theodore C. *Speeches, Lectures and Letters of Wendell Phillips.* Boston: Lee and Shepard, 1905. Volume 1.
37. Lowell, James Russell. *Complete Poetical Works of James Russell Lowell.* Boston: Houghton, Mifflin, 1896. (First published 1848.)
38. Pease, 449.
39. Sherwin, 513.
40. Sherwin, 534.
41. Sherwin, 537.
42. Pease, Theodore C. *Speeches, Lectures and Letters of Wendell Phillips.* Boston: Lee and Shepard, 1905, Volume 1, 236.
43. Austin, 318.
44. Pease, 497.
45. Austin, 381.
46. Austin, 311–312.
47. Pease, 101.
48. Pease, 97–98.
49. Bartlett, 88.
50. Pease, 139.
51. Austin, 168–169.
52. Pease, 114–116.

FREDERICK DOUGLASS (PAGES 78–90)

53. Douglass, Frederick, ed. Benjamin Quarles. *Narrative of the Life of Frederick Douglass, an American Slave, written by himself.* Cambridge, MA: Belknap Press, 1960, Preface, 1.
54. Douglass, Frederick. *The Church and Prejudice*, November 4, 1841, Plymouth County, Massachusetts. http://www.greatamericandocuments.com/speeches/douglass-church-prejudice.html
55. Douglass, Frederick. *My Bondage and My Freedom.* New York: Modern Library, 2003.
56. Douglass, *Bondage*, 80.
57. Douglass, *Bondage*, 81–82.
58. Douglass, *Bondage*, 123–124.
59. Douglass, *Narrative*, 143–144.
60. Douglass, Frederick, *Life and times of Frederick Douglass: his early life as a slave, his escape from bondage, and his complete history. Written by himself.* London: Collier, 1962, 205.
61. Douglass, *Narrative*, 2.
62. Douglass, *Bondage*, 46–47.
63. Douglass, *Narrative*, Ch. 5, 1.
64. Douglass, Frederick. *Life of an American Slave.* Boston: Anti-Slavery Office, 1845, xii.
65. Douglass, *Bondage*, 222.
66. Douglass, *Bondage*, 238.
67. Douglass, Frederick. *An Oration, at Rochester, July 5, 1852.* http://www.lib.rochester.edu/index.cfm?page=2945

68. Douglass, Frederick. *Life and Times of Frederick Douglass*, 453–454.
69. Douglass, Frederick. *What the Black Man Wants*, Speech at the Annual Meeting of the Massachusetts Anti-Slavery Society in Boston, April 1865. http://www.lib.rochester.edu/index.cfm?PAGE=2946
70. Buccola, Nicholas. *The Political Thought of Frederick Douglass: In Pursuit of American Liberty.* New York: New York University Press, 2012.
71. Douglass, *Life and Times of Frederick Douglass*, 609–611.
72. Douglass, Frederick. *What the Black Man Wants.* Speech at the Annual Meeting of the Massachusetts Anti-Slavery Society in Boston, April 1865.

FOUR: THE SUFFRAGISTS

ANGELINA GRIMKÉ (PAGES 91–101)

1. Weld, Angelina Grimké. "Speech in Pennsylvania Hall, May 17, 1838." http://www.sojust.net/speeches/grimke_weld_pa_hall.html
2. Weld, Theodore D. *American Slavery As It Is: Testimony of a Thousand Witnesses.* New York: American Anti-Slavery Society Office, 1839, 53.
3. Lumpkin, Katherine DuPre. *The Emancipation of Angelina Grimké.* Chapel Hill: University of North Carolina Press, 1974, 9.
4. Lumpkin, 15ff.
5. Weld, Theodore Dwight. *In Memory Angelina Grimké Weld: born in Charleston, South Carolina, Feb. 20, 1805, died in Hyde Park, Massachusetts, October 26, 1879.* Boston: G. H. Ellis, 1880, 19.
6. Lumpkin, 12, 15.
7. Lumpkin, 36–37.
8. Browne, Stephen Howard. *Angelina Grimké: Rhetoric, Identity, and the Radical Imagination.* East Lansing: Michigan State University Press, 1999, 59.
9. Lumpkin, 94.
10. Grimké, Angelina Emily. *Appeal to Christian Women of the South.* New York: American Anti-Slavery Society, 1836, 12.
11. Grimké, *Appeal*, 20.
12. Lumpkin, 91–92.
13. Birney, Catherine. *The Grimké Sisters, Sarah and Angelina Grimke: The First American Women Advocates of Abolition and Woman's Rights.* Boston: Lee and Shepard, 1885, 163.
14. Yellin and Van Horne, 52–53.
15. Collins, Gail. *America's Women.* New York: HarperCollins, 2003, 167.
16. Lumpkin, 109.
17. Henry, Katharine. "Angelina Grimké's Rhetoric of Exposure." *American Quarterly* 49:2 (1997), 328–355.
18. Birney, 190.
19. Lumpkin, 109.
20. Browne, 94.
21. Letter to Jane Smith, August 10, 1837. Lumpkin, 120.
22. Grimké, Angelina. *Letters to Catherine Beecher in Reply to An Essay on Slavery and Abolitionism.* Boston: Isaac Knapp, 1838, 119.
23. Collins, 167.
24. Ceplair, Larry. *The Public Years of Sarah and Angelina Grimké.* New York: Columbia University Press, 1989, 303.
25. Project Gutenberg EBook of *An Appeal to the Christian Women of the South,* by Angelina Emily Grimké. http://www.gutenberg.org/9/9/1/9915/
26. Weld, Theodore Dwight. *American Slavery as it is: Testimony of a Thousand Witnesses.* New York: Arno Press, 1968.
27. Lumpkin, 169.
28. Lumpkin, 219.
29. Weld, Theodore. *In Memory Angelina Grimke Weld: born in Charleston, South Carolina, Feb. 20, 1805, died in Hyde Park, Massachusetts, October 26, 1879.* Boston: G. H. Ellis, 1880, 28–29.

ABBY KELLEY FOSTER (PAGES 102–114)

30. Sterling, Dorothy. *Ahead of Her Time: Abby Kelley and the Politics of Anti-Slavery.* New York: W.W. Norton, 1991, 44.
31. Sterling, 108.
32. Sterling, 21–23.

33. Melder, Keith. "Abby Kelley Foster and the Process of Liberation," *in* Jean Fagan Yellin and John C. Van Horne, *The Abolitionist Sisterhood*. Ithaca, NY: Cornell University Press, 1994, 234.
34. Chandler, Elizabeth Margaret. *The Poetical Works of Elizabeth Margaret Chandler: With a Memoir of Her Life and Character.* Philadelphia: Lemuel Howell, 1836.
35. Melder, 234.
36. Annual Report of the Boston Female Anti-slavery Society. Boston: Isaac Knapp, 1837, 33-34.
37. Melder, 235–236.
38. Sterling, 64–65.
39. Sterling, 68–69.
40. Sterling, 72–73.
41. Bacon, Margaret Hope. *I Speak for My Slave Sister.* New York: Thomas Y. Crowell, 1974, 45.
42. Sterling, 84.
43. Sterling, 104–105.
44. *The Liberator*, October 23, 1840. This speech actually was made in Boston but is typical of speeches she made at this time.
45. Bacon, 62–66.
46. *Bay State Democrat*, quoted in the *Liberator*, February 18, 1842.
47. Sterling, 154.
48. Foster, Stephen S. *Brotherhood of Thieves, or, a True Picture of the American Church and Clergy.* Boston: Anti-Slavery Office, 1843.
49. Bacon, 123.
50. Bacon, 136–138.
51. Bacon, 141.
52. Sterling, 221.
53. Worcester Women's History Project. http://www.wwhp.org/Resources/WomansRights/akfoster_1851.html
54. Worcester Women's History Project, Abby Kelley Foster's speech. http://www.wwhp.org/Resources/WomansRights/akfoster_1851.html
55. Bacon, 184–188.
56. Bacon, 195.
57. Sterling, 333–334.
58. Sterling, 366.
59. Bacon, 212–213.
60. Sterling, 387.

ELIZABETH CADY STANTON (PAGES 114–125)

61. Banner, Lois W. *Elizabeth Cady Stanton: A Radical for Women's Rights.* Boston: Little, Brown, 1980, 18.
62. Griffith, Elisabeth. *In Her Own Right*. New York: Oxford University Press, 1984, 24.
63. Griffith, 25–26.
64. Griffith, 37.
65. Griffith, 38.
66. Griffith, 39.
67. Banner, 29.
68. Banner, 30.
69. Stanton, Elizabeth Cady, Susan B. Anthony, and Matilda Joslyn Gage. *History of Woman Suffrage*. Rochester, NY: Charles Mann, 1881, I:69.
70. Stanton, Elizabeth Cady. "Address by Elizabeth Cady Stanton on Woman's Rights," September 1848. http://ecssba.rutgers.edu/docs/ecswoman3.html
71. Stanton, Anthony, and Gage, *History of Woman Suffrage*, 1:70–71.
72. Banner, 53.
73. Stanton, Elizabeth Cady. *Eighty Years and More: Reminiscences of Elizabeth Cady Stanton*. New York: European Publishing Company, 1898, 165.
74. Banner, 62–63.
75. Stanton, Theodore, and Harriot Stanton Blatch. *Elizabeth Cady Stanton as Revealed in Her Letters, Diary and Reminiscences.* New York: Harper & Brothers, 1922, 41–52.
76. Griffith, 91.
77. http://www.nps.gov/wori/historyculture/address-to-the-new-york-legislature-1854
78. "Early Letters," 1189.
79. Griffith, 95.
80. Banner, 69.
81. Griffith, 104.

82. Griffith, 106.
83. Griffith, 127.
84. *Republican Party Platform of 1872*. http://www.presidency.ucsb.edu/ws/?pid=29623
85. Griffith, 135–136.
86. Stanton, *Eighty Years and More*, 279.
87. Stanton, 317.
88. Stanton, 336.
89. Griffith, 191.
90. Griffith, 193.
91. Stanton, 453.
92. Stanton, v.

FIVE
ABRAHAM LINCOLN (PAGES 126–167)

1. Holzer, Harold. *Lincoln at Cooper Union*. New York: Simon & Schuster, 2004, 50.
2. Braden, Waldo W. *Abraham Lincoln: Public Speaker.* Baton Rouge: Louisiana State University Press, 1988, 50.
3. Holzer, 34; Wilson, Douglas L. *Lincoln's Sword.* New York: Vintage, 2006, 44–45.
4. Wilson, 8.
5. Holzer, 60–61, 63.
6. Holzer, 78.
7. Holzer, 105–110.
8. Holzer, 51.
9. Holzer. The text used here is provided in the Appendix, 284.
10. http://www.abrahamlincolnonline.org/lincoln/speeches/cooper.htm
11. Holzer, 190.
12. Donald, David Herbert. *Lincoln*. New York: Simon & Schuster, 1995, 14.
13. Basler, Roy P. (ed.). *The Collected Works of Abraham Lincoln, Second Supplement 1848–1865*. Brunswick, NJ: Rutgers University Press, 1990, 4:62.
14. Hirsch, David, and Dan Van Haften. *Abraham Lincoln and the Structure of Reason*. New York: Savas Beatie, 2010.
15. Wills, Garry. *Lincoln at Gettysburg: The Words that Remade America*. New York: Simon & Schuster, 1992, 162–163.
16. Wilson, 234.
17. Hirsch and Van Haften, 47.
18. Hirsch and Van Haften, 37–38.
19. Wilson, 201.
20. Wilson, 71.
21. Wilson, 280.
22. Wilson, 280.
23. Wilson, 180–181.
24. Wilson, 166.
25. Wilson, 25.
26. Donald, 156–157.
27. Holzer, 20.
28. http://www.abrahamlincolnonline.org/lincoln/speeches/house.htm
29. Braden, 51–52.
30. Donald, 112.
31. Angle, Paul M. (ed.). *Created Equal? The Complete Lincoln-Douglas debates of 1858*. Chicago: University of Chicago Press, 1958.
32. Angle, 68.
33. Angle, 111.
34. Angle, 117.
35. White, 79–80.
36. Angle, 387.
37. Angle, 390–393.
38. Angle, 402.
39. Braden, 27.
40. Donald, 233.
41. "A Word to the Adopted Citizens of the United States." Middletown, NY: *Banner of Liberty* (newspaper), August 3, 1859.

42. "Speech at Cincinnati, Ohio," *Collected Works*, 3:453–454.
43. "Speech at Cincinnati, Ohio," *Collected Works*, 3:460–462.
44. Lincoln to Samuel Galloway, March 24, 1860, *Collected Works*, 4:34.
45. Holzer, 209.
46. Holzer, 210.
47. Donald, 248.
48. Donald, 251.
49. http://www.presidency.ucsb.edu/showelection.php?year=1860#axzz2g9Xv7XAq
50. Braden, 56–57.
51. Wilson, 46–54.
52. White, 20.
53. Donald, 273.
54. White, 33.
55. White, Ronald C., Jr. *The Eloquent President: A Portrait of Lincoln Through His Words*. New York: Random House, 2005, 90.
56. Strong, George Templeton, ed. Allan Nevins and Milton Halsey Thomas. *Diary*. New York: Macmillan, 1952. Entry for March 4, 1861.
57. White, 174.
58. White, 195–196.
59. White, 221.
60. White, 252.
61. http://www.nytimes.com/1862/08/24/news/letter-president-lincoln-reply-horace-greeley-slavery-union-restoration-union.html
62. Benét, Stephen Vincent. *John Brown's Body*. Garden City, NY: Doubleday, Doran, 1928.
63. Wills, Garry. *Lincoln at Gettysburg*. New York: Simon & Schuster, 1992, 25.
64. White, 229.
65. Wilson, 216.
66. Wilson, 219.
67. Wilson, 229.
68. Wilson, 235.
69. Donald, 515.
70. White, 303.
71. Lincoln, Abraham. *Second Inaugural Address of Abraham Lincoln*, Saturday, March 4, 1865. http://avalon.law.yale.edu/19th_century/lincoln2.asp

SIX
WILLIAM JENNINGS BRYAN (PAGES 168–205)

1. Kazin, Michael. *A Godly Hero: The Life of William Jennings Bryan*. New York: Alfred A. Knopf, 2006, 24.
2. Kazin, 33.
3. Bryan, William Jennings. *Speeches of William Jennings Bryan*. New York: Funk & Wagnalls, 1913, 3–77.
4. Kazin, 34.
5. Melder, Keith. *Bryan the Campaigner*. Washington: Smithsonian Institution, 1966, 70–71.
6. Bryan, William Jennings. *Memoirs of William Jennings Bryan, by himself and his wife Mary Baird Bryan*. Philadelphia: John C. Winston, 1925, 104.
7. Bryan, *Memoirs*, 115.
8. Coletta, Paolo E. *William Jennings Bryan* (three volumes). Lincoln: University of Nebraska Press, 1964–1969, 142.
9. Bryan, *Memoirs*, 116.
10. Coletta, Vol. I, 168, 180.
11. http://railroads.unl.edu/documents/view_document.php?id=rail.wjb.18960812.01
12. Glad, Paul W. *McKinley, Bryan, and the People*. Philadelphia: Lippincott, 1964, 200–201.
13. Coletta, 190.
14. Coletta, 213.
15. Kazin, 100–101.
16. Kazin, 118.
17. Bryan, *Speeches*, Vol. II, 63.
18. Ibid., Vol. II, 64.
19. Ibid., Vol. II, 68.
20. Ibid., Vol. II, 72.

21. Ibid., Vol. II, 74.
22. Ibid., Vol. II, 75–76.
23. Ibid., Vol. II, 80.
24. Coletta, 378.
25. Coletta, 385.
26. Bryan, *Speeches*, Vol. II, 115.
27. Coletta, 430.
28. http://www.youtube.com/watch?v=HeTkT5-w5RA
29. Bryan, *Speeches*, Vol. II, 261.
30. Kazin, 126.
31. Kazin, 217.
32. Kazin, 218.
33. Coletta, Vol. II, 92.
34. Coletta, Vol. II, 93–94.
35. Coletta, Vol. II, 244–245.
36. Coletta, Vol. II, 252–259.
37. Coletta, Vol. II, 265–267.
38. Kazin, 140.
39. *San Francisco Examiner*, July 6, 1915.
40. Kazin, 247.
41. Coletta, Vol. II, 38–39.
42. Coletta, Vol. III, 40.
43. *The Sunday Oregonian* (Portland, OR), July 18, 1920.
44. Kazin, 274–275.
45. William Jennings Bryan at the Scopes Trial: personal.uncc.edu/jmarks/Darrow.htm
46. Bryan, *Memoirs*, 550.
47. Ibid., 550–551.
48. Ibid., 487.

SEVEN
FRANKLIN D. ROOSEVELT (PAGES 206–249)

1. Ward, Geoffrey C. *A First Class Temperament: The Emergence of Franklin Roosevelt*. New York: Harper & Row, 1989, 122.
2. Ward, 35.
3. Brands, H. W. *Traitor to His Class: The Privileged Life and Radical Presidency of Franklin Delano Roosevelt*. New York: Doubleday, 2008, 43.
4. Brands, 50.
5. Ward, 120.
6. Ward, 122.
7. http://pastdaily.com/2012/09/05/fdr-1920-vice-presidential-acceptance-speech-past-daily-reference-room/
8. Brands, 163.
9. Brands, 180.
10. Brands, 250.
11. Ward, 695–696.
12. http://fdrlibrary.wordpress.com/tag/1924/
13. Lindley, Ernest K. *Franklin D. Roosevelt: A Career in Progressive Democracy*. Indianapolis: Bobbs-Merrill, 1931, 223.
14. Ward, 692–693.
15. The *New York Times*, July 10, 1924.
16. Brands, 197.
17. Ward, 784.
18. Brands, 215.
19. Brands, 215.
20. Brands, 221.
21. http://www.presidency.ucsb.edu/ws/?pid=75174#ixzz2jPqODmAs
22. Freidel, Frank. *Franklin D. Roosevelt: A Rendezvous with Destiny*. Boston: Little, Brown, 1990, 74.
23. Franklin D. Roosevelt: "Campaign Address in Portland, Oregon on Public Utilities and Development of Hydro-Electric Power," September 21, 1932. The American Presidency Project. http://www.presidency.ucsb.edu/ws/?pid=88390

24. Houck, Davis W. *Rhetoric as Currency: Hoover, Roosevelt, and the Great Depression*. College Station: Texas A&M University Press, 2001, 55.
25. Brands, 263.
26. Houck, 56.
27. Kennedy, David M. *Freedom from Fear: The American People in Depression and War, 1929–1945*. New York: Oxford University Press, 1999, 90–91.
28. Hand, Samuel B. "Rosenman, Thucydides, and the New Deal," *The Journal of American History*, Vol. 55, No. 2 (Sept. 1968), 338.
29. http://www.bartleby.com/124/pres48.html
30. Houck, 31.
31. Houck, 32.
32. Brands, 128.
33. Gelderman, Carol W. *All the Presidents' Words: The Bully Pulpit and the Creation of the Virtual Presidency*. New York: Walker, 1997.
34. Gelderman, 338.
35. Vilade, C. Edwin. *The President's Speech: The Stories Behind the Most Memorable Presidential Addresses*. Guilford, CT: Lyons Press, 2012.
36. Ward, 534.
37. Craig, Douglas B. *Fireside Politics: Radio and Political Culture in the United States, 1920–1940*. Baltimore: Johns Hopkins University Press, 2000, 155.
38. Ryan, Halford Ross, "Roosevelt's First Inaugural: A Study of Technique," *Quarterly Journal of Speech* (65), April 1979, 21.
39. Ryan, 24.
40. Gelderman, 338.
41. Ryan, 137–149.
42. Brooks, Phillips. *Lectures on Preaching, Delivered Before the Divinity School of Yale College*. New York: E. P. Dutton, 1877, 5.
43. http://www.austincc.edu/lpatrick/his2341/fdr36acceptancespeech.htm
44. http://www.infoplease.com/ipa/A0104719.html#ixzz2jbTv17Fr
45. Roosevelt, Franklin D., Inaugural Address, January 20, 1937. http://historymatters.gmu.edu/d/5105/
46. http://millercenter.org/president/speeches/detail/3310
47. Roosevelt, Franklin D., Address at University of North Carolina, Chapel Hill, North Carolina, December 5, 1938. www.presidency.ucsb.edu/ws/?pid=15578?
48. Roosevelt, Franklin D., State of the Union, January 3, 1939. http://www.infoplease.com/t/hist/state-of-the-union/150.html
49. Roosevelt, Franklin D., "Fireside Chat," September 3, 1939. http://www.presidency.ucsb.edu/ws/?pid=15801
50. Roosevelt, Franklin D., "Stab in the Back" Speech, June 10, 1940. http://millercenter.org/president/speeches/detail/3317
51. Roosevelt, Franklin D., Radio Address to the Democratic National Convention Accepting the Nomination. http://www.presidency.ucsb.edu/ws/?pid=15980#ixzz2joaKPiPe
52. Roosevelt, Franklin D., Fireside Chat, December 29, 1940. https://www.mtholyoke.edu/acad/intrel/WorldWar2/arsenal.htm
53. Roosevelt, Franklin D., State of the Union (Four Freedoms Speech), January 6, 1941. http://www.americanrhetoric.com/speeches/fdrthefourfreedoms.htm
54. Brands, 631.
55. Vilade, 130.
56. http://historymatters.gmu.edu/d/5166/
57. Roosevelt, Franklin D., "State of the Union Address," January 6, 1942. The American Presidency Project. http://www.presidency.ucsb.edu/ws/?pid=16253
58. Brands, 663–664.
59. Freidel, 443.
60. Roosevelt, Franklin D., "Fireside Chat.," October 12, 1942. The American Presidency Project. http://www.presidency.ucsb.edu/ws/?pid=16178
61. Brands, 694.
62. Brands, 708.
63. Roosevelt, Franklin D., "Fireside Chat.," July 28, 1943. The American Presidency Project. http://www.presidency.ucsb.edu/ws/?pid=16437
64. Brands, 439.

65. Roosevelt, Franklin D., "Fireside Chat.," December 24, 1943. The American Presidency Project. http://www.presidency.ucsb.edu/ws/?pid=16356
66. Roosevelt, Franklin D., State of the Union Address, 1944. http://teachingamericanhistory.org/library/document/state-of-the-union-address-3/
67. Roosevelt, Franklin D., "Prayer on D-Day," June 6, 1944. The American Presidency Project. http://www.presidency.ucsb.edu/ws/?pid=16515
68. Roosevelt, Franklin D. "Address to the Democratic National Convention in Chicago," July 20, 1944. The American Presidency Project. http://www.presidency.ucsb.edu/ws/?pid=16537
69. Roosevelt, Franklin D., "Campaign Address to the International Brotherhood of Teamsters," September 23, 1944, Washington, D.C. http://www.wyzant.com/resources/lessons/history/hpol/fdr/fala
70. Ryan, 97–104.
71. Roosevelt, Franklin D., Inaugural Address, January 20, 1945. http://www.bartleby.com/124/pres52.html
72. Brands, 802–804.
73. Brands, 807.
74. Freidel, 601.
75. Freidel, 607.
76. Freidel, 607.

EIGHT
ADLAI STEVENSON (PAGES 250–293)

1. Broadwater, Jeff. *Adlai Stevenson: The Odyssey of a Cold War Liberal*. New York: Twayne, 1994, 1.
2. Martin, John Bartlow. *Adlai Stevenson of Illinois: The Life of Adlai E. Stevenson*. Garden City, NY: Doubleday, 1976, 58. [Hereafter Martin I.]
3. Broadwater, 7–8.
4. Broadwater, 11.
5. McKeever, Porter. *Adlai Stevenson: His Life and Legacy*. New York: William Morrow, 1989.
6. Martin, 73.
7. McKeever, 53–54.
8. Broadwater, 33–34.
9. Martin, 157.
10. Broadwater, 39.
11. Martin, 168–169.
12. McKeever, 74.
13. Broadwater, 44.
14. Martin, 169.
15. McKeever, 76.
16. McKeever, 85.
17. McKeever, 87.
18. McKeever, 87.
19. McKeever, 88.
20. McKeever, 88–89.
21. Broadwater, 55.
22. Martin, 245.
23. Broadwater, 64–65.
24. Martin, 247.
25. Martin, 250.
26. Martin, 251.
27. Mckeever, 102. Martin, 262–263.
28. Martin, 260.
29. McKeever, 115.
30. McKeever, 121.
31. McKeever, 121.
32. Martin, 311.
33. McKeever, 122.
34. Martin, 315.
35. Martin, 339.
36. Broadwater, 84–87.

37. Broadwater, 90–91.
38. Martin, 403.
39. Martin, 419.
40. Martin, 430.
41. Martin, 431.
42. Martin, 444.
43. Martin, 445–446.
44. Martin, 470.
45. Broadwater, 113.
46. Stevenson, Adlai E. *Major Campaign Speeches of Adlai E. Stevenson*. New York: Random House, 1953, 3–6.
47. McKeever, 196.
48. McKeever, 198.
49. Stevenson, 7–10.
50. McKeever, 203.
51. McKeever, 208.
52. Stevenson, 17–22.
53. Stevenson, 21.
54. Martin, 655.
55. McKeever, 212–213.
56. Stevenson, 127.
57. Stevenson, 29.
58. McKeever, 222–223.
59. Martin, 637.
60. Muller, Herbert J. *Adlai Stevenson: A Study in Values*. New York: Harper & Row, 1967, 251.
61. Stevenson, 311.
62. Whitman, Alden. *Portrait: Adlai E. Stevenson: Politician, Diplomat, Friend*. New York: Harper & Row, 1965, 4.
63. McKeever, 264.
64. McKeever, 281.
65. McKeever, 297.
66. Broadwater, 137.
67. Windes, Russell. "Adlai E. Stevenson's Speech Staff in the 1956 Campaign." *Quarterly Journal of Speech*, Vol. 46, No. 1, 1960, 33–34.
68. Martin, John Bartlow. *Adlai Stevenson and the World*. Garden City, NY: Doubleday, 1977, 87–89. (Hereafter Martin II).
69. McKeever, 322–323.
70. McKeever, 322–325.
71. Stevenson, Adlai. *The American Vision Speech*, June 5, 1954. http://www.fofweb.com/History/MainPrintPage.asp?iPin=E14471&DataType=AmericanHistory&WinType=Free
72. McKeever, 351.
73. McKeever, 356.
74. Martin I, 312.
75. Stevenson, Adlai E. *A New America*. http://voicesofdemocracy.umd.edu/deliberative-topics/war-peace/adlai-e-stevenson-a-new-america-acceptance-address-at-the-democratic-national-convention-17-august-1956/
76. Windes, 36.
77. Slaybaugh, Douglas. "Adlai Stevenson, Television, and the Presidential Campaign of 1956." *Illinois Historical Journal*, Vol. 89, No. 1 (Spring 1996), 3.
78. Martin I, 391.
79. McKeever, 404–405.
80. McKeever, 409.
81. McKeever, 413.
82. McKeever, 420–421.
83. McKeever, 434.
84. Broadwater, 197.
85. Broadwater, 206–207.
86. Stevenson, Adlai. *Statement by Ambassador Stevenson to U.N. Security Council*, October 25, 1962. https://www.mtholyoke.edu/acad/intrel/adlai.htm
87. Martin I, 735.

88. Martin I, 742–746.
89. Martin I, 747–748.
90. Whitman, 269.
91. Whitman, 270.
92. Martin I, 769.
93. Martin I, 774.
94. Broadwater, 219.
95. Roland, Albert, Richard Wilson, and Michael Rahill, eds. *Adlai Stevenson of the United Nations*, 1965, 224.

NINE
RONALD REAGAN (PAGES 294–339)

1. Cannon, Lou. *President Reagan: The Role of a Lifetime*. New York: Perigee, 1982, 46. Erickson, Paul D. *Reagan Speaks: The Making of an American Myth*. New York: New York University Press, 1985, 14–15. Schaller, Michael. *Ronald Reagan*. New York: Oxford University Press, 2011, 3–4. Pemberton, William E. *Exit with Honor: The Life and Presidency of Ronald Reagan*. Armonk, NY: M. E. Sharpe, 1997, 15. Morris, Edmund. *Dutch: A Memoir of Ronald Reagan*. New York: Random House, 1999, 127.
2. Reeves, Richard. *President Reagan: The Triumph of Imagination*. New York: Simon & Schuster, 2005, 8.
3. Schaller, 6–7.
4. Erickson, 14.
5. Evans, Thomas W. *The Education of Ronald Reagan: The General Electric Years and the Untold Story of his Conversion to Conservatism*. New York: Columbia University Press, 2006, 10.
6. Evans, 10.
7. https://www.mtholyoke.edu/acad/intrel/winthrop.htm
8. Hanska, Jan. *Reagan's Mythical America*. New York: Palgrave Macmillan, 2012, 163.
9. Pemberton, 9.
10. Hanska, 162.
11. Reagan, Ronald. *Remarks to Participants in the People to People International Youth Exchange Program*. June 24, 1987. http://www.reagan.utexas.edu/archives/speeches/1987/062487b.htm
12. Pemberton, 11–12.
13. Pemberton, 14–15.
14. Pemberton, 21.
15. Reagan, Ronald. *Address Before a Joint Session of the Congress on the State of the Union*, January 25, 1984. http://www.presidency.ucsb.edu/ws/?pid=40205
16. Pemberton, 26–27.
17. Schweizer, Peter. *Reagan's War: The Epic Story of His Forty-year Struggle and Final Triumph over Communism*. New York: Doubleday, 2002, 25–26.
18. Schweizer, 27.
19. Evans, 3.
20. Lewis, Matt. "GE and Ronald Reagan: The Mutual Gift That Keeps On Giving." *Politics Daily*, March 17, 2010. http://www.politicsdaily.com/2010/03/17/ge-and-ronald-reagan-the-mutual-gift-that-keeps-on-giving/
21. Reagan, Ronald. *Your America to be Free: 1957 Commencement Address at Eureka College*. http://reagan2020.us/speeches/Your_America_to_be_Free.asp
22. Evans, 72–73.
23. Pemberton, 50.
24. Erickson, 22–23.
25. Morris, 320.
26. Morris, 327.
27. Reagan, Ronald. *A Time for Choosing*. http://reagan2020.us/speeches/A_Time_for_Choosing.asp
28. Reagan, *A Time for Choosing*. http://www.reagan.utexas.edu/archives/reference/timechoosing.html
29. Kennedy, John F. *Inaugural Address*. http://www.americanrhetoric.com/speeches/jfkinaugural.htm
30. http://www.reaganfoundation.org/tgcdetail.aspx?p=TG0923RRS&h1=0&h2=0&lm=reagan&args_a=cms&args_b=1&argsb=N&tx=1736
31. Reagan, *A Time for Choosing*. http://www.reagan.utexas.edu/archives/reference/timechoosing.html
32. Schweizer, 33–34.

33. Official Social Security Website, National Average Wage Index. http://www.ssa.gov/oact/cola/AWI.html
34. Erickson, 26–7.
35. Schweizer, 44.
36. Pemberton, 54.
37. Reagan, Ronald. *California and the Problem of Government Growth*, January 5, 1967. http://reagan2020.us/speeches/California_and_Gov_Growth.asp
38. Schaller, 21.
39. Schweizer, 49.
40. Reagan, Ronald. *Inaugural Address*. January 5, 1967. http://www.reagan.utexas.edu/archives/speeches/govspeech/01051967a.htm
41. Reagan, Ronald. *California and the Problem of Government Growth*, January 5, 1967. http://reagan2020.us/speeches/California_and_Gov_Growth.asp
42. Reagan, Ronald, *Let Them Go Their Way*, March 1, 1975, 2nd Annual CPAC Convention. http://reagan2020.us/speeches/Let_Them_Go_Their_Way.asp
43. Reagan, Ronald. *Announcement of Candidacy*, November 13, 1979. http://www.reagan.utexas.edu/archives/reference/11.13.79.html
44. Cannon, 76–77.
45. Cannon, 105–106.
46. Reagan, Ronald. *Address to the Nation on the Economy*, February 5, 1981. http://www.reagan.utexas.edu/archives/speeches/1981/20581c.htm
47. Cannon, 73.
48. Reagan, Ronald. *Economic Recovery Program*, April 28, 1981. http://reagan2020.us/speeches/Economic_Recovery_Program.asp
49. Cannon, 116.
50. Muir, William Ker, Jr. *The Bully Pulpit: The Presidential Leadership of Ronald Reagan*. San Francisco: ICS Press, 1992.
51. Vilade, 210–211.
52. Vilade, 211.
53. Reagan, Ronald. *Remarks at a Ceremony Commemorating the 40th Anniversary of the Normandy Invasion*, D-Day, June 6, 1984, Pointe du Hoc. http://reagan2020.us/speeches/40th_anniversary_of_d-day.asp
54. Vilade, 211.
55. Vilade, 222.
56. Reagan, Ronald. *Address to the Nation on the Explosion of the Space Shuttle Challenger*, January 28, 1986. http://reagan2020.us/speeches/challenger_explosion.asp
57. *American Rhetoric: Top 100 Speeches*. http://ww.americanrhetoric.com/top100speechesall.html
58. Noonan, 52.
59. Hanska, 43.
60. Clinton, William J. *First Inaugural*, January 20, 1993. http://millercenter.org/scripps/archive/speeches/detail/3434
61. Clinton, William J. *Address Before a Joint Session of the Congress on the State of the Union*, January 23, 1996. http://www.presidency.ucsb.edu/ws/?pid=53091
62. Obama, Barack. *Remarks by the President in State of the Union Address*, January 24, 2012. http://www.whitehouse.gov/the-press-office/2012/01/24/remarks-president-state-union-address
63. Reagan, Ronald. *First State of the Union Address*, January 26, 1982. http://reagan2020.us/speeches/First_State_of_the_Union.asp
64. Reagan, Ronald. *Address Before a Joint Session of the Congress Reporting on the State of the Union*, January 25, 1984. http://reagan2020.us/speeches/state_of_the_union_1984.asp
65. Bush, George H. W. *State of the Union Address, Envisioning One Thousand Points of Light*, January 29, 1991. Infoplease.com http://www.infoplease.com/ipa/A0900156.html#ixzz2pRigz4dN
66. Clinton, William J. *Address Before a Joint Session of the Congress on the State of the Union*, January 25, 1994. http://www.presidency.ucsb.edu/ws/?pid=50409
67. Obama, Barack. *Remarks by the President in State of the Union Address*, January 24, 2012. http://www.whitehouse.gov/the-press-office/2012/01/24/remarks-president-state-union-address
68. Schaller, 57–58.
69. Reagan, Ronald. *Federalism and the New Conservatives—Address to Members of the British Parliament*, June 8, 1982. http://reagan2020.us/speeches/westminster_address.asp
70. Reagan, Ronald. *Remarks at the Annual Convention of the National Association of Evangelicals in Orlando Florida*, March 8, 1983. http://reagan2020.us/speeches/The_Evil_Empire.asp

71. Reagan, Ronald. *Remarks in New York, New York, Before the United Nations General Assembly Special Session Devoted to Disarmament*, June 17, 1982. http://www.reagan.utexas.edu/archives/speeches/1982/61782a.htm
72. Schaller, 62.
73. Reagan, Ronald. *Address to the Nation on the Situation in Nicaragua*, March 16, 1986. http://www.reagan.utexas.edu/archives/speeches/1986/31686a.htm
74. Reagan, Ronald. *Address to the Nation on United States Assistance for the Nicaraguan Democratic Resistance*, June 24, 1986. http://www.reagan.utexas.edu/archives/speeches/1986/62486b.htm
75. Reagan, Ronald. *Address to the Nation on the Iran Arms and Contra Aid Controversy*, November 13, 1986. http://www.reagan.utexas.edu/archives/speeches/1986/111386c.htm
76. Reagan, Ronald. *Address to the Nation on the Iran Arms and Contra Aid Controversy,* March 4, 1987. http://www.reagan.utexas.edu/archives/speeches/1987/030487h.htm
77. Vilade, 229.
78. Reeves, 401.
79. Reagan, Ronald. *Remarks on East-West Relations at the Brandenburg Gate in West Berlin*, June 12, 1987. http://www.reagan.utexas.edu/archives/speeches/1987/061287d.htm
80. Reagan, Ronald. *Address to the 43d Session of the United Nations General Assembly in New York, New York*, September 26, 1988. http://www.reagan.utexas.edu/archives/speeches/1988/092688b.htm
81. Noonan, 290–293.
82. Noonan, 149–150.
83. Noonan, 330.
84. Reagan, Ronald. *President Reagan's Farewell Speech*, January 11, 1989. http://reagan2020.us/speeches/Farewell.asp
85. Dugan, Andrew, and Frank Newport. *Americans Rate JFK as Top Modern President.* Gallup Politics, November 15, 2013. http://www.gallup.com/poll/165902/americans-rate-jfk-top-modern-president.aspx

TEN
MARTIN LUTHER KING (PAGES 340–384)

1. Branch, Taylor. *Parting the Waters*. New York: Simon & Schuster, 1988, 59.
2. Carson, Clayborne. *The Autobiography of Martin Luther King, Jr.* New York: IPM in association with Warner Books, 1998. New York: Grand Central Publishing, 1998, 14.
3. Carson, 23–26.
4. Niles, Lyndrey A. "Rhetorical Characteristics of Traditional Black Preaching," *Journal of Black Studies*, Vol. 15, No. 1, Communication and the Afro-American (Sept. 1984), 41–52.
5. Pitts, Walter, "West African Poetics in the Black Preaching Style," *American Speech*, Vol. 64, No. 2 (Summer 1989), 137–149.
6. Branch, 107.
7. Sitkoff, Harvard. *Pilgrimage to the Mountaintop*. New York: Hill and Wang, 2008, 23.
8. Branch, 130.
9. Carson, 54.
10. Carson, 70–71.
11. Sitkoff, 38.
12. Carson, 80.
13. Sitkoff, 39.
14. Sitkoff, 40.
15. Carson, 96–97.
16. Carson, 98.
17. Carson, 103–104.
18. Branch, 213.
19. Carson, 113.
20. Branch, 214.
21. Branch, 219.
22. Sitkoff, 70.
23. Carson, 137.
24. Sitkoff, 72.
25. Sitkoff, 73.
26. Sitkoff, 76.
27. Carson, 153.
28. Sitkoff, 79.

29. Sitkoff, 55.
30. Carson, 168.
31. Sitkoff, 84.
32. Sitkoff, 90.
33. Sitkoff, 91.
34. http://www.stanford.edu/group/King//frequentdocs/clergy.pdf
35. http://en.wikipedia.org/wiki/A_Call_for_Unity
36. Branch, 745.
37. Sitkoff, 107.
38. Sitkoff, 109.
39. Sitkoff, 109.
40. Sitkoff, 123.
41. Branch, 66.
42. Branch, 66.
43. Dyson, Michael Eric. *I May Not Get There with You*. New York: Free Press, 2000, 143.
44. Frady, Marshall. *Martin Luther King, Jr.* New York: Penguin Group, 2002, 123.
45. "A Realistic Look at the Question of Progress in the Area of Race Relations," address delivered at St. Louis Freedom Rally, April 10, 1957. http://mlk-kpp01.stanford.edu/primary-documents/Vol4/10-Apr-1957_ARealisticLook.pdf
46. "Eulogy for the Martyred Children," Birmingham, Alabama, September 18, 1963. http://mlk-kpp01.stanford.edu/index.php/kingpapers/article/eulogy_for_the_martyred_children/
47. Carson, 233.
48. Sitkoff, 129.
49. Sitkoff, 141.
50. Martin Luther King, Jr. "Acceptance Speech." November 14, 2013. http://www.nobelprize.org/nobel_prizes/peace/laureates/1964/king-acceptance_en.html
51. Carson, 270–271.
52. Martin Luther King, Jr. "Our God is Marching On!" March 25, 1965. http://mlk-kpp01.stanford.edu/index.php/kingpapers/article/our_god_is_marching_on/
53. Carson, 299.
54. Sitkoff, 178.
55. Sitkoff, 183.
56. Martin Luther King, Jr. "Beyond Vietnam," April 4, 1967. http://mlk-kpp01.stanford.edu/index.php/encyclopedia/documentsentry/doc_beyond_vietnam/
57. Sitkoff, 218.
58. Martin Luther King, Jr. "Where Do We Go from Here?" The Southern Christian Leadership Conference Presidential Address, August 16, 1967. http://www.blackshearolprice.com/category/famous-speeches/
59. Sitkoff, 223–224.
60. Martin Luther King, Jr. "His Own Eulogy," September 3, 2001. http://www.awakin.org/read/view.php?tid=193
61. Martin Luther King, Jr. "I've Been to the Mountaintop," April 3, 1968. http://library.thinkquest.org/C004391F/promis_land_speech.htm

EPILOGUE (PAGES 385–390)

1. Noonan, Peggy. *What I Saw at the Revolution: A Political Life in the Reagan Era*. New York: Random House, 1990, 68–69.
2. Roosevelt, Franklin Delano. *Fireside Chat 28: On the State of the Union* (January 11, 1944). http://millercenter.org/president/speeches/detail/3955
3. Roosevelt, Franklin Delano. *Democratic National Convention* (June 27, 1936). http://millercenter.org/president/speeches/detail/3305
4. Braden, 17.
5. Khachigian, Ken. "What made Reagan the Great Communicator." *The Orange County Register*, August 21, 2013. http://www.ocregister.com/articles/reagan-287119-great-dollar.html
6. Roosevelt, Theodore. *Inaugural Address*, March 1905. http://www.pbs.org/wgbh/americanexperience/features/primary-resources/tr-inaugural05/
7. Roosevelt, Franklin Delano. *Speech before the 1936 Democratic National Convention*, June 27, 1936. http://www.austincc.edu/lpatrick/his2341/fdr36acceptancespeech.htm
8. Wilson, 22.
9. Ryan, 29.

INDEX

ACKNOWLEDGMENTS

I sometimes think about Anthony Trollope dipping his quill pen in his inkwell and scratching out his daily thousand words before going off to work, or Karl Marx lifting heavy tomes from the shelves of the British Museum, and wonder that they produced so much against such odds. Skipping lightly past the typewriter and the ballpoint pen, a modern writer's acknowledgment should surely begin with those who invented the computer, the Internet, and microfilm. In spite of all that, I set my daily goal where Trollope did and feel that I have done well when I have a thousand words mysteriously stored somewhere in my laptop computer. Electronics or not, however, even today no writer is an island, entire of itself, and I am grateful to Caroline Grant for orienting me to San Francisco and providing more sorts of assistance than I can begin to acknowledge, to Elisabeth Gruner, Robert Picken, Fred Martin, Jr., and W. Mark Richardson for invaluable assistance with my research, to Velma Doherty for such editorial assistance as no one could ask for or ever pay for, and to Tony Grant for critical technical support.